Strategic Intervention Teacher Guide

Kindergarten

Harcourt School Publishers

www.harcourtschool.com

Copyright © by Harcourt, Inc.

All rights reserved. No part of this publication may be reproduced or transmitted in any form or by any means, electronic or mechanical, including photocopy, recording, or any information storage and retrieval system, without permission in writing from the publisher.

Requests for permission to make copies of any part of the work should be addressed to School Permissions and Copyrights, Harcourt, Inc., 6277 Sea Harbor Drive, Orlando, Florida 32887-6777. Fax: 407-345-2418.

STORYTOWN is a trademark of Harcourt, Inc. HARCOURT and the Harcourt Logo are trademarks of Harcourt, Inc., registered in the United States of America and/or other jurisdictions.

Printed in the United States of America

ISBN 10: 0-15-365496-1
ISBN 13: 978-0-15-365496-1

2 3 4 5 6 7 8 9 10 059 16 15 14 13 12 11 10 09 08 07

If you have received these materials as examination copies free of charge, Harcourt School Publishers retains title to the materials and they may not be resold. Resale of examination copies is strictly prohibited and is illegal.

Possession of this publication in print format does not entitle users to convert this publication, or any portion of it, into electronic format.

CONTENTS

Introduction v
Components vi
Suggested Lesson Planners viii

- LESSON 1 2
- LESSON 2 14
- LESSON 3 26
- LESSON 4 38
- LESSON 5 50
- LESSON 6 62
- LESSON 7 74
- LESSON 8 86
- LESSON 9 98
- LESSON 10 110
- LESSON 11 122
- LESSON 12 134
- LESSON 13 146
- LESSON 14 158
- LESSON 15 170

LESSON 16	182
LESSON 17	194
LESSON 18	206
LESSON 19	218
LESSON 20	230
LESSON 21	242
LESSON 22	254
LESSON 23	266
LESSON 24	278
LESSON 25	290
LESSON 26	302
LESSON 27	314
LESSON 28	326
LESSON 29	338
LESSON 30	350

INTRODUCTION

Research has shown the importance of building a strong foundation early in the process of learning to read. Most children will acquire the foundational skills needed for success in learning to read in kindergarten and grade 1. These requisite skills, which include academic language, concepts of print, phonemic awareness, letter names and sounds, letter-sound associations, and recognition of high-frequency words, all contribute to success in learning to read.

However, research also shows us that children enter school with a wide range of previous experiences with forms and functions of print. In addition, there are enormous individual differences in learning rates and learning needs that will affect children's progression in learning to read. Many children will have difficulty learning to read unless extensive additional instruction and practice is provided.

Intervention that addresses the learning needs of these children is paramount to effective prevention of reading difficulties. Intervention offered early and targeted to children who need it most will facilitate success. Intervention requires additional engaged academic time and support through strategic and systematic instruction in the foundational and requisite reading skills.

The *Strategic Intervention Resource Kit* provides additional intensive systematic teaching and practice to help children learn the skills and strategies important for proficient reading. Aligned with and correlated to the instructional goals and objectives of *StoryTown* Kindergarten program, the *Strategic Intervention Resource Kit* optimizes the learning opportunities and outcomes for children at risk. The additional targeted teaching and practice will help children build a strong foundation in the fundamental skills for successfully learning to read.

Components of the Strategic Intervention Resource Kit

The goal of this *Strategic Intervention Resource Kit* is to provide the scaffolding, extra support, and extra reading practice that struggling readers need to succeed. Each kit includes the following components:

Teacher Guide with lessons directly aligned with and correlated to the lessons in the *StoryTown* Teacher Edition.

- *Practice Book* with a write-in, consumable text to provide direct application and practice of phonic elements, high-frequency words, and comprehension skills.
- *Teacher Resource Book* with Copying Masters that include activities providing additional reinforcement of phonics and decoding skills and concepts of print.
- *Assessment Book* to monitor progress and ensure success.
- *Photo Cards* with four-color illustrations to support instruction.
- *Sound/Spelling Cards* to support recognition of letter names and letter forms.
- *Sounds of Letters CD* containing the sounds of 44 phonic elements.
- *Phoneme Phone* for children to practice and apply the sounds in phonemic awareness lessons. The phone comes with a mirror for a child to look at the position of the mouth when he or she says a sound. Disks provide children the opportunity to count the sounds.
- *Word Builder and Word Builder Card*s to demonstrate blending and word building. Children practice with these to develop blending and word building skills.
- *Write-On/Wipe-Off Board with Phonemic Awareness Disks* help make the abstract concept of the phonemes more concrete. One side of the board has Elkonin boxes so children can track phonemes in two- and three-phoneme words or syllables in two- and three-syllable words. The other side provides a model of the uppercase and lowercase alphabet, space for writing or drawing with dry-erase markers, and write-on lines to practice letter formation and handwriting.

Using the Strategic Intervention Teacher Guide

The *Strategic Intervention Teacher Guide* gives support for struggling readers in key instructional strands, plus prerequisite phonics skills and oral-reading fluency. Each five-day lesson plan includes the following resources:

- *Phonemic Awareness* instruction with activities to teach phonemic awareness skills.
- *Phonics* lessons to systematically preteach and reteach basic phonics skills and connect spelling and phonics.
- *High-Frequency Words* lessons to preteach and reteach, and provide cumulative review and reinforcement of the high-frequency words taught, increasing the exposure to and experiences with words children should be learning.
- *Robust Vocabulary* lessons and Student-Friendly Explanations to enrich children's listening and speaking vocabularies and help children master the language of school.
- *Comprehension* lessons to ensure that children get the in-depth instruction they need to reach grade-level standards.
- *Writing* lessons to practice various writing forms and writing traits.
- *Reading* activities to practice the lesson's phonics skills and High-Frequency Words in the context of a story.

Depending on your individual classroom and school schedules, you can tailor the instruction to suit your needs. The following pages show two options for pacing the instruction in this guide.

SUGGESTED LESSON PLANNERS

Grade K OPTION 1
(for use with *StoryTown*)

DAY 1

BEFORE beginning Day 2 of the *StoryTown* lesson

PHONEMIC AWARENESS
- Reteach the skill that was introduced on Day 1 in *StoryTown*.

PHONICS
- Preteach the aspect of the phonics skill that will be introduced on Day 2 in *StoryTown*.

HIGH-FREQUENCY WORDS
- Reteach High-Frequency Words that were introduced on Day 1 in *StoryTown*.

COMPREHENSION
 Preteach the Focus skill that will be introduced on Day 2 in *StoryTown*.

ROBUST VOCABULARY
- Reteach the Robust Vocabulary words that were introduced on Day 1 in *StoryTown*.

DAY 5

BEFORE beginning next week's *StoryTown* lesson

PHONEMIC AWARENESS
- Preteach the skill that will be introduced on Day 1 next week in *StoryTown*.

PHONICS
- Preteach the skill that will be introduced on Day 1 next week in *StoryTown*.

HIGH-FREQUENCY WORDS
- Preteach the High-Frequency Words that will be introduced next week in *StoryTown*.

ROBUST VOCABULARY
- Preteach the Robust Vocabulary that will be introduced on Day 1 next week in *StoryTown*.

Grade K OPTION 2
(for use as a stand-alone program)

DAY 1

PHONEMIC AWARENESS
- Reteach the Phonemic Awareness skill.

PHONICS
- Teach another aspect of the week's Phonics skill.

HIGH-FREQUENCY WORDS
- Reteach the High-Frequency Words.

COMPREHENSION
 Teach the Comprehension Focus Skill.

ROBUST VOCABULARY
- Reteach the Robust Vocabulary words.

DAY 5

PHONEMIC AWARENESS
- Teach the Phonemic Awareness skill.

PHONICS
- Teach one aspect of the week's Phonics skill.

HIGH-FREQUENCY WORDS
- Teach High-Frequency Words.

ROBUST VOCABULARY
- Teach the Robust Vocabulary for this week.

Strategic Intervention Teacher Guide

DAY 2

BEFORE beginning Day 3 of the *StoryTown* lesson

PHONEMIC AWARENESS
- Continue practicing the Phonemic Awareness skill.

PHONICS
- Preteach a Day 3 Phonics Skill.

HIGH-FREQUENCY WORDS
- Continue practicing the High-Frequency Words for the week.

COMPREHENSION
- Preteach the Focus Strategy for Day 3 in *StoryTown*.

BUILD ROBUST VOCABULARY
- Preteach Robust Vocabulary words that will be introduced on Day 3 in *StoryTown*.

DAY 3

BEFORE beginning Day 4 of the *StoryTown* lesson

PHONEMIC AWARENESS
- Continue practicing the Phonemic Awareness skill.

PHONICS
- Preteach a Day 4 Phonics Skill.

HIGH-FREQUENCY WORDS
- Continue practicing the High-Frequency Words for the week.

COMPREHENSION
- Reteach the Focus Skill that will be reviewed on Day 4 in *StoryTown*.

BUILD ROBUST VOCABULARY
- Reteach Robust Vocabulary words that will be reviewed on Day 4 in *StoryTown*.

WRITING
- Reteach the week's writing trait.

DAY 4

BEFORE beginning Day 5 of the *StoryTown* lesson

PHONEMIC AWARENESS
- Continue practicing the Phonemic Awareness skill.

PHONICS
- Reteach the week's Phonics skill.

READING
- Review the week's Phonics skill and High-Frequency Words.
- Read the Practice Reader.

BUILD ROBUST VOCABULARY
- Reteach Robust Vocabulary words that will be reviewed on Day 5 in *StoryTown*.

WRITING
- Reteach the week's writing form that will be reviewed on Day 5 in *StoryTown*.

DAY 2

PHONEMIC AWARENESS
- Continue practicing the Phonemic Awareness skill.

PHONICS
- Teach an aspect of the Phonics skill.

HIGH-FREQUENCY WORDS
- Continue practicing the High-Frequency Words for the week.

COMPREHENSION
- Teach the Focus Strategy.

BUILD ROBUST VOCABULARY
- Teach additional Robust Vocabulary words for the week.

DAY 3

PHONEMIC AWARENESS
- Continue practicing the Phonemic Awareness skill.

PHONICS
- Teach an aspect of the Phonics Skill.

HIGH-FREQUENCY WORDS
- Continue practicing the High-Frequency Words for the week.

COMPREHENSION
- Practice the week's Focus Skill.

BUILD ROBUST VOCABULARY
- Review Robust Vocabulary words.

WRITING
- Teach the writing trait.

DAY 4

PHONEMIC AWARENESS
- Continue practicing the Phonemic Awareness skill.

PHONICS
- Review the week's Phonics skills.

READING
- Review the week's Phonics skills and High-Frequency Words.
- Read the *Practice Reader*.

BUILD ROBUST VOCABULARY
- Review the week's Robust Vocabulary.

WRITING
- Teach the week's writing form.

LESSON 1

PHONEMIC AWARENESS
Words in a Sentence

PHONICS
Preteach Consonant *Mm*

HIGH-FREQUENCY WORDS
Preteach *I*

COMPREHENSION
Preteach Make Predictions

BUILD ROBUST VOCABULARY
Preteach ability, confident, reverse

Materials Needed:

Sound/Spelling Card *Mm* | Write-On/Wipe-Off Boards | Sounds of Letters CD

Word Builder and Word Builder Cards | Copying Master | Practice Book

Phonemic Awareness

Words in a Sentence Explain to children that sentences are groups of words that tell about something. Say: ***I can read.* That is a sentence. Now I will say the sentence again and clap for each word in it.** Clap once for each word as you say the sentence again. Have children repeat the following sentences after you, clapping for each word in the sentence.

The dog runs.   **We play.**   **I like juice.**

PRETEACH

Phonics

 Consonant *Mm* Display *Sound/Spelling Card Mm*. Say: **The name of this letter is *m*. Say the name with me.** (*m*) Point to the uppercase *M*. Say: **This is uppercase *M*.** Point to the lowercase *m*. Say: **This is lowercase *m*.**

 Writing *M* and *m* Write *M* and *m* on the board and have children identify the letters. Say: **Watch as I write the letter *M*.** As you give the Letter Talk, trace the uppercase *M*. Do the same for lowercase *m*.

Letter Talk for *M*	Letter Talk for *m*
1. Straight line down.	1. Straight line down.
2. Go to the top of this line.	2. Go to the top of the line and
3. Slanted line down.	3. curve down.
4. Slanted line up.	4. Go up again and curve down.
5. Straight line down again.	

Tell children to finger-write the uppercase *M* and lowercase *m* in the air as you repeat the Letter Talk. Distribute *Write-on/Wipe-off Boards* to children. Ask them to write uppercase *M* and lowercase *m* on their *Write-on/Wipe-off Boards*.

 Relate *m* to /m/ Have children listen as you introduce the /m/ sound, using the *Sounds of Letters CD*. Then say: **The letter *m* stands for the /m/ sound.** Say: **/m/.** Have children repeat several times.

2   Lesson 1

Day 1

  Discriminate /m/ Give each child *Word Builder Card m*. Say: **I am going to say some words. If a word begins with /m/, hold up the *m* card. If the word does not begin with /m/, hold your card behind your back.** Say the words *mop, rod, mat, cut, mole,* and *mist*.

Distribute *Copying Master 1*. Have children trace the letter *M* or *m*. Have them look at each picture and circle the letter for the beginning sound. (Children circle letter *m* in each box: *monkey, mouse, motorcycle, mop, mitt*.)

PRETEACH
High-Frequency Words

High-Frequency Word

I

Distribute index cards with the word *I* to children. Say the word aloud: **I**. Use it in a sentence: **I like flowers.** Have children point to the word on their cards and read it with you. Ask them to complete the sentence frame *I like_____*. Have children hold up their index card each time they hear the word *I*.

PRETEACH
Comprehension

  Make Predictions Tell children that they can make a prediction, or guess, about what might happen next in a story. Then read this story aloud to them.

One hot summer day, Karen and her mother walked to the park. Near the gate they saw a clown. The clown was juggling water balloons. "He is so silly," said Mother. The clown dropped the balloons and water splashed everywhere. Uh-oh! Karen's pants were soaking wet. Karen and her mother just laughed and laughed!

Guide children to turn to page 2 in their *Practice Books*. Have them identify the pairs of pictures on the page and circle the picture that helps them make predictions about the story.

PRETEACH
Build Robust Vocabulary

Tell children the Student-Friendly Explanations for *ability, confident,* and *reverse*. Then discuss each word, using the following examples.

ability
Do you have the *ability* to brush your teeth? Explain.

confident
Are you *confident* that it is sunny outside? Why or why not?

reverse
Is it safer to walk forward or in *reverse* down the stairs? Why?

VOCABULARY
Student-Friendly Explanations

ability If you can do something, you have the ability to do it.

confident When you are confident about something, you feel very sure about it.

reverse If you do something in reverse, you do it in the opposite way, or backwards.

Grade K 3

LESSON 1

DAY AT A GLANCE — Day 2

PHONEMIC AWARENESS
Words in a Sentence

PHONICS
Preteach Consonant *Ss*

HIGH-FREQUENCY WORDS
Reteach *I*

COMPREHENSION
Preteach Summarize

BUILD ROBUST VOCABULARY
Preteach *complained, talent, encourage*

Materials Needed:

Sound/Spelling Card *Ss*   Write-On/Wipe-Off Boards

Copying Master   Practice Book

Phonemic Awareness

Words in a Sentence   Remind children they have been learning about words and sentences. Tell them that sentences are made of words. Say: **I will say a sentence and clap for each word:** *The cat plays.* **I hear these words in this sentence:** *the, cat, plays.* **I count three words. There are three words in this sentence.** Continue a similar procedure with the sentences below. Allow children an opportunity to clap for each word. Ask them to share how many words that they hear in each sentence.

We will swim. (3)

Jan can run. (3)

They climb. (2)

The dog is small. (4)

PRETEACH
Phonics

Consonant *Ss*   Display *Sound/Spelling Card Ss*. Say: **This is the letter *s*. Say the name with me.** Point to uppercase *S* and say: **This is uppercase *S*.** Point to lowercase *s* and say: **This is lowercase *s*.** Have children identify the letters. (*S, s*)

Writing *S* and *s*   Write *S* and *s* on the board and have children identify the letters. Say: **Watch as I write the letter *S* so that everyone can read it.** As you give the Letter Talk, trace the uppercase *S*. Do the same for lowercase *s*.

Letter Talk for *S*	Letter Talk for *s*
1. Curve left and down to the dotted line; then curve right.	1. Curve left and down to the middle of the space; then curve right.

Tell children to finger-write the uppercase *S* in the air as you repeat the Letter Talk. Have them do the same for lowercase *s*. Distribute *Write-on/Wipe-off Boards* to children. Ask them to write uppercase *S* and then lowercase *s* several times on their *Write-on/Wipe-off Boards*.

Then distribute *Copying Master 2*. Have children circle each uppercase *S* and underline each lowercase *s*. Then have them trace each letter and practice writing it on the line.

4 Lesson 1

Day 2

RETEACH

High-Frequency Word

Practice Book 3

Distribute *I* index cards to each child. Have children point to the word and read it. Say: **I am happy.** Say the word *I*, and have children say it with you. Tell children that you are going to say another sentence with the word *I*. Explain to children that like the first letter of a name, the word *I* is an uppercase letter. Point to the word *I* as you say the sentence: **I jump.** Call on volunteers to say sentences that begin with *I*. Have them hold up their cards as they say the word *I*.

Have children turn to *Practice Book* page 3 to review and practice the newly-learned word. Complete the page together.

High-Frequency Word

I

PRETEACH

Comprehension

 Summarize Tell children that when you read, it helps to stop and think about what has happened so far in a story to help understand what is happening. Tell children to recall the story about Karen. Say: **I can use a story map as I read the story about Karen and her mother. I can pay attention to the important things that happen in a story and record them on my story map. When I finish reading, I can tell someone else about the story.** Summarize the story using a story map like the one below.

Karen
Karen and her mother see a clown at the park.
They see a clown juggling water balloons.
Karen gets wet.

PRETEACH

Build Robust Vocabulary

Tell children the Student-Friendly Explanations for *complained*, *talent*, and *encourage*. Then discuss each word, using the following examples.

complained
If you *complained* about the weather, did you like it or not like it?

talent
Which shows *talent*, scoring a goal in a soccer game or eating a sandwich?

encourage
How can a crowd *encourage* a team during a game? Show your answer.

VOCABULARY
Student-Friendly Explanations

complained If you complained about something, you told how it made you unhappy.

talent If you are very good at doing something, you have a talent for it.

encourage When you encourage someone, you help them feel good about trying something.

Grade K 5

LESSON 1

PHONEMIC AWARENESS
Words in a Sentence

PHONICS
Preteach Relate *Ss* to /s/

HIGH-FREQUENCY WORDS
Reteach *I*

COMPREHENSION
Reteach Make Predictions

BUILD ROBUST VOCABULARY
Reteach *complained, talent, encourage*

WRITING
Reteach Writing Trait: Conventions

Materials Needed:

Sound/Spelling Card *Ss*   Sounds of Letters CD   Word Builder and Word Builder Cards

Phoneme Phone   Photo Cards   Practice Book

Phonemic Awareness

Words in a Sentence Remind children that a sentence is a group of words that tells about something. Ask children to listen as you say a sentence. Model the process of holding up fingers to count words. Say this sentence: ***Throw the ball.*** Then say the first word *throw* and hold up one finger. Say the second word *the* and hold up a second finger. Say the third word *ball* and hold up a third finger. Count the fingers.

Ask children to count the words in another sentence. Say: **Listen to the sentence. Say it with me and hold up a finger for each word:** ***Stand up.*** **What are the words in the sentence? How many words are in that sentence?** (2)

Continue the same procedure with the sentences below.

Go home. (2)	We dance. (2)
Feed the fish. (3)	Liam hops. (2)

PRETEACH

Phonics

  Relate *Ss* to /s/ Display *Sound/Spelling Card Ss*. Ask: **What is the name of this letter?** (s) **The letter *s* stands for the /s/ sound.** Have children listen as you introduce the sound of *s*, using the *Sounds of Letters CD*. Have children repeat the sound that they hear on the CD. Then say: **The letter *s* stands for the /s/ sound. Say /s/.**

Distribute *Word Builder Card s*. Tell children to listen for the /s/ sound as you say some words, and to show their *s* card if they hear the /s/ sound. Model by saying the word *sit* and holding up *Word Builder Card s*. Have children listen for the /s/ sound in these words:

song   sun   sing   sad   sip

Discriminate /s/ Give each child the *Word Builder Card s*. Say: **I am going to say some words. If a word begins with the /s/ sound, trace the *s* on your card with a finger and say /s/. If the word does not begin with /s/, hold your card behind your back.** Use the following words:

set   rug   sell   pot   sap

---

6 Lesson 1

Identify Sound Position Tell children that /s/ can also come at the end of words, such as *yes, bus, dress,* and *this.* Model how to use the *Phoneme Phone* as they say words that begin and end with /s/. Show children how to elongate the sound and look at their mouth position to help them determine the sound position. Then say: **Listen to the words that I will say. In each word you will hear the /s/ sound. It will come at the beginning or at the end of each word.** Use the following words and have children identify whether the /s/ sound is at the beginning or at the end of these words:

| sew | sip | less | toss | bus |

RETEACH
High-Frequency Words

On the board, write the word *I.* Say: *I.* Point to the word. Say: *I* **is always spelled with an uppercase letter.**

Distribute index cards with the word *I.* Have children match the card with the word *I* on the board. Then tell children that they are going to play a game called "I Spy." Model how to play the game. Say: **I'm going to find something in our class. You have to figure it out by listening to my clues. You begin by saying "I spy ." Here's my turn: I spy something red.** Hold up your index card with the word *I* as you say "I spy." Tell children that they must hold up their card when they hear the word *I* as well. Explain that the person who figures out the secret object gets to go next. Continue until several children have gotten a chance.

Day 3

High-Frequency Word

I

Day 3

RETEACH

Comprehension

 Make Predictions Remind children that they can make predictions, or use what they know and clues in the story to guess what might happen next. Tell them that they are going to listen to a story. Remind them to listen carefully as you read. Ask children to think about what might happen next.

> One warm spring day, Sam walked to the store with his dad. Sam felt a cool breeze. He looked in the sky and saw gray clouds. Oh, no! Sam wondered if it was going to rain. Sam and his dad began to walk more quickly, heading toward their house. They still had six blocks to go. Suddenly, a large boom shook the sky and Sam felt water on his head. Rain! Just then, Sam noticed his mom's car coming around the corner. Sam was so happy to see her! The car pulled up and Sam and his dad got inside. "Thanks for finding us, Mom," Sam said. "Let's go home to dry off!"

Guide children to *Practice Book* page 4. Have children use the pictures to make predictions about the story. Ask: **What did Sam see in the sky that made you think it was going to rain?** (dark clouds) **What happened after Sam heard the loud boom?** (Raindrops began to fall.) **Where did Sam and his dad go after they got in the car?** (They went home to dry off.) Then ask children to name additional details about the story.

RETEACH

Build Robust Vocabulary

Remind children of the Student-Friendly Explanations for *complained*, *talent*, and *encourage*. Then discuss each word by using the following examples.

complained
If your friend *complained* about her weekend, do you think she liked it or didn't like it?

talent
If you have a *talent* for doing somersaults, are you good at it or are you just learning? Explain.

encourage
What is something to say to *encourage* someone: "Keep trying, I know you can do it!" or "It's time to go home now!" Tell why.

VOCABULARY

Student-Friendly Explanations

complained If you complained about something, you told how it made you unhappy.

talent If you are very good at doing something, you have a talent for it.

encourage When you encourage someone, you help them feel good about trying something.

8 Lesson 1

Day 3

RETEACH

Writing

Writing Trait: Conventions Remind children that names should begin with an uppercase letter and that the other letters in the name should be lowercase. Write children's names on the board. Read them aloud and have children identify their names. Ask: **Does your name begin with an uppercase letter?**

Write children's names in yellow marker or dotted-line letters that children can trace. Help children name each letter of their names as they write them.

Then write the name *Sam* on the board. Read it aloud. Remind children that it is the name of the boy in the story. Ask a child to circle the uppercase *S*. Elicit from children that his name begins with an uppercase letter, too.

Kamryn
Cody
Brady
Lin
Grace Ann

LESSON 1

DAY AT A GLANCE
Day 4

PHONEMIC AWARENESS
Words in a Sentence

PHONICS
Reteach /m/m, /s/s

READING
Review /m/m, /s/s
Review High-Frequency Words

BUILD ROBUST VOCABULARY
Review ability, confident, reverse, complained, talent, encourage

WRITING
Reteach Writing Form: Names

Materials Needed:

Sound/Spelling Cards *Mm*, *Ss*

Word Builder and Word Builder Cards

Photo Cards

Practice Book

Phonemic Awareness

Words in a Sentence   Tell children that a sentence is a group of words that tells something. Remind them that they have learned how to divide sentences into words. Say: **Listen to this sentence.** *I like apples.* **For each word I hear, I will hold up a finger. Now say the sentence with me:** *I like apples.* **I am holding up three fingers because there are three words in the sentence.**

Ask children to count the words in another sentence. Say: **Listen to this sentence:** *Jerome swims.* **Say the sentence with me and hold up one finger for each word:** *Jerome . . . swims.* **How many words are in that sentence?** (2)

Use the same procedure with the following sentences.

Kate ran. (?)	**I drive.** (2)	**We play house.** (3)
Kwong smiled. (2)	**Roy ate.** (2)	**The mouse hid.** (3)

RETEACH

Phonics

/m/m, /s/s   Display *Sound/Spelling Card Mm*. Ask: **What sound do you hear at the beginning of** *mat*? **What letter stands for the /m/ sound at the beginning of** *mat*? Repeat the process with *Sound Spelling Card Ss* and the word *sand*.

Discriminate /m/m and /s/s   Distribute *Word Builder Cards m* and *s* to children. Display *Photo Cards milk, sandwich,* and *sun.* Have children name each picture with you. Hold the cards in random order. Ask children to hold up *Word Builder Card m* if the sound they hear at the beginning of the word is /m/. Have them hold up the *s* card if the sound they hear at the beginning is /s/.

Continue a similar process, saying the following words aloud and having children hold up *Word Builder Card m* or *s*.

    mug   sit   man   soap   most   sick   mud

Then have children listen for words ending with the sounds /m/ and /s/. Have them hold up the correct *Word Builder Card* for the following words:

    drum   bus   ram   us   rim   gas

Day 4

REVIEW
Reading

/m/m, /s/s Review the /m/ and /s/ sounds. Say the words *mud* and *sip*, and help children name the letter that stands for the sound at the beginning of each word. Repeat with the words *moon, sing, many,* and *sat.*

High-Frequency Words Distribute index cards with the word *I* to children. Say: **I see [child's name].** Have that child hold up the card, point to *I,* and say: **I see [another child's name].** Continue until each child has had a chance to participate.

Have children turn to *Practice Book* pages 5 and 6. Help children cut and fold the book. Encourage them to read it with their families to practice newly-learned sounds and words.

High-Frequency Word

I

REVIEW
Robust Vocabulary

Remind children of the Student-Friendly Explanations for *ability, confident, reverse, complained, talent,* and *encourage.* Then determine their understanding of the words by asking the following questions.

- Do you have a *talent* for singing? Show us.
- What does an owl have the *ability* to do?
- Would you *complain* if you liked your lunch or didn't like your lunch?
- What would you say to *encourage* a friend who needs help with a puzzle?
- Show how a truck would move if it were in *reverse.*
- Are you *confident* that it is daytime right now? Why or why not?

VOCABULARY
Student-Friendly Explanations

ability If you can do something, you have the ability to do it.

confident When you are confident about something, you feel very sure about it.

reverse If you do something in reverse, you do it in the opposite way, or backwards.

complained If you complained about something, you told how it made you unhappy.

talent If you are very good at doing something, you have a talent for it.

encourage When you encourage someone, you help them feel good about trying something.

RETEACH
Writing

Writing Form: Names Remind children that names begin with an uppercase letter and are followed by lowercase letters. Tell children that together you will write some children's names on the board. Invite them to assist you in writing letters that they know. Remind children that each name will start with an uppercase letter.

> Mary
> Juan
> Lin

Read each name to children. Ask a volunteer to circle the uppercase letters in each name.

Grade K 11

LESSON 1

PHONEMIC AWARENESS
Syllable Blending

PHONICS
Preteach Consonant *Rr*

HIGH-FREQUENCY WORDS
Preteach *a*

BUILD ROBUST VOCABULARY
Preteach *differ, stalking, mellow*

Materials Needed:

Sound/Spelling Card *Rr*   Write-On/Wipe-Off Boards   Practice Book

Phonemic Awareness

Blend Syllables Tell children that words are like puzzles. They are made of parts that can be taken apart and put back together again. Tell children that they will be listening to parts of words and putting the parts together to make a word. Say: **Listen as I say a word:** *bathroom*. **Bathroom has two parts:** *bath-room*. Clap as you say each word part. **Now I will put the two word parts together and say the word again:** *bathroom*. Say: **Let's try one together. Repeat the word after me:** *pigpen*. **Listen to the word parts and clap for each word part you hear:** *pig pen*. **Say each word part after me:** *pig-pen*. **Now say the word with me:** *pigpen*.

Follow the same procedure, using the words below. Ask children to repeat the words parts and then say the word.

dog-house (doghouse)   **sun-shine** (sunshine)   **back-yard** (backyard)
rose-bud (rosebud)   **sky-light** (skylight)

PRETEACH

Phonics

 Consonant *Rr* Display *Sound/Spelling Card Rr*. Say: **The name of this letter is** *r*. **Say the name with me.** (*r*) Point to the uppercase *R* on the *Sound/Spelling Card*. Say: **This is the uppercase *R*.** Point to the lowercase *r*. Say: **This is the lowercase *r*.**

 Writing *R* and *r* Model how to write the letter *R*. As you write *R* on the board, say: **Watch as I write the letter *R* so that everyone can read it.** As you give the Letter Talk, trace the uppercase *R*. Do the same for the lowercase *r*.

Letter Talk for *R*	Letter Talk for *r*
1. Straight line down.	1. Straight line down.
2. Go to the top of this line. Curved line out and around.	2. Curved line up and over.
3. Slanted line down.	

Have children finger-write the uppercase *R* in the air as you repeat the Letter Talk. Have them do the same for lowercase *r*. Have children practice writing upper and lowercase *R* on their *Write-on/Wipe-off Boards* several times. Then have children turn to page 7 in their *Practice Book* to write and identify *Rr*.

12   Lesson 1

Day 5

PRETEACH

High-Frequency Words

Write the word *a* on the board. Point to and read *a*. Say: **a pen** Then display an index card with the word *a* written on it. Say: *a*. Remind children that like the word *I*, this word only has one letter. Match the index card *a* with the word on the board. Say *a* and have children repeat several times.

Distribute index cards with these words written on them: *a* and *I*. Have children point to each word and read it. Tell the children that you will show them two words, and when they see *a*, they should say the word and point to it on their card. Randomly hold up *High-Frequency Word Cards a* and *I,* until children consistently identify the word *a*.

PRETEACH

Build Robust Vocabulary

Read aloud to the children the Student-Friendly Explanations for *differ, stalking,* and *mellow*. Then discuss each word, using the following examples.

differ
Ask two volunteers to stand next to each other. Ask, "How do these two children *differ*?"

stalking
When a large animal is *stalking* a small animal, is the large animal more likely to move fast or slow? Why?

mellow
When I lay on the sofa I feel *mellow*. Would you be more likely to feel *mellow* playing a soccer game or watching a movie?

High-Frequency Words

a   I

VOCABULARY

Student-Friendly Explanations

differ When things differ from one another, they are not the same.

stalking When an animal is stalking another animal, it sneaks up on it to try to catch it.

mellow When you are mellow, you feel gentle and relaxed.

LESSON 2

DAY 1

PHONEMIC AWARENESS
Syllable Blending

PHONICS
Preteach Relate *Rr* to /r/

HIGH-FREQUENCY WORDS
Reteach *a*

COMPREHENSION
Reteach Make Predictions

BUILD ROBUST VOCABULARY
Reteach *differ, stalking, mellow*

Materials Needed:

Sound/Spelling Card *Rr* Sounds of Letters CD Word Builder and Word Builder Cards

Phoneme Phone Copying Master Photo Cards

Practice Book

Phonemic Awareness

Blend Syllables Remind children that the sounds in words can be taken apart and put back together again. Tell children that today they will be putting word parts together to make words. Say: **Listen to the parts of this word: sis-ter. Now I am going to put the words together: sister. Say the word parts after me: sis-ter. Now say the word: sister.**

Continue by asking children to putting the following word parts together to say words: *mo-ther, bas-ket, cher-ry,* and *le-mon*.

PRETEACH

Phonics

   Relate R*r* to /r/ Display *Sound/Spelling Card Rr*. Ask: **What is the name of this letter?** (*r*) **The letter *r* stands for the /r/ sound.** Have children listen as you introduce the /r/ sound, using the *Sounds of Letters CD*. Then say: **The letter *r* stands for the /r/ sound.** Say: **/r/.** Have children repeat several times.

    Discriminate /r/ Give each child a *Word Builder Card r*. Say: **I am going to say some words. If a word begins with /r/, hold up the card and say /r/. If the word does not begin with /r/, hold your card behind your back.** Say the words *ring, pig, do, rat, rip,* and *roll*.

Continue by having children repeat the following words after you: *red, rug, row, rib, rig, ram, run,* and *rub*. Children can pass the *Phoneme Phone* around the group as you say each word. Ask children to look at the closed position of their mouths in the mirror to help them recognize the /r/ sound in each word.

Distribute *Copying Master 3*. Have children trace each letter. Then have them look at each picture and circle the letter that stands for the beginning sound of each picture name. (Children should circle letter *r* for *rabbit, rose, run;* circle letter *m* for *mitt, mask*.)

14 Lesson 2

Day 1

RETEACH

High-Frequency Words

Make index cards with the words *I*, *am*, and *a*. Show each card and read the word. Have children repeat after you.

Copy the following sentence frame on the board. Ask volunteers to read sentence, pointing to the *Photo Card boy* or the *Photo Card girl* to complete the frame.

High-Frequency Words
a   I

RETEACH

Comprehension

  Make Predictions Remind children that they can make a prediction, or guess, about what might happen next in a story. Read the beginning, then have children make predictions. Then read the remainder of the story.

One cold winter day, Mary went to the pond and began to skate. Mary was so excited! She felt the chilly air blow on her face as she circled the pond. Just as Mary was imagining that she was a bird, flying in the sky, ahhh - boom! Oh, no! Mary had taken a fall. She lay there for a moment. Then Mary stood up and a big smile came across her face. She remembered what her Dad had told her, "You have to take a few falls to become a great skater!" Mary knew her Dad was right. With that, she pushed forward and began to skate quickly across the pond.

Then guide children to turn to page 8 in their *Practice Books*. Have them identify the pairs of pictures on the page and circle the correct picture.

RETEACH

Build Robust Vocabulary

Remind children of the Student-Friendly Explanations for *differ*, *stalking*, and *mellow*. Then discuss each word, using the following examples.

differ
Have a child stand next to you. Ask: how does our size *differ*?

stalking
Would a fox be more likely to *stalk* a rabbit or a whale? Explain your answer.

mellow
What activities make you feel *mellow*?

VOCABULARY

Student-Friendly Explanations

differ When things differ from one another, they are not the same.

stalking When an animal is stalking another animal, it sneaks up on it to try to catch it.

mellow When you are mellow, you feel gentle and relaxed.

Grade K 15

LESSON 2

DAY AT A GLANCE — Day 2

PHONEMIC AWARENESS
Syllable Blending

PHONICS
Reteach Review /r/r, /s/s

HIGH-FREQUENCY WORDS
Reteach *a*

MONITOR COMPREHENSION
Preteach Monitor Comprehension: Reread

BUILD ROBUST VOCABULARY
Preteach *automatic, perfectly, resemblance*

Materials Needed:

Sound/Spelling Cards *Rr, Ss* Word Builder and Word Builder Cards Photo Cards

Copying Master Practice Book

Phonemic Awareness

Blend Syllables Remind children that words can be broken up into parts that can be put back together. Model an example for children. Say: **I am going to say two parts of a word. Say each word part after me. Then we will say the word together. Here is the first word part: *pan*. Say it with me: *pan*. Here is the next part: *cake*. Say it with me: *cake*. Now let's say the word: *pancake*.** Have children blend the following syllables into words: **pig-tail** (pigtail), **thumb-tack** (thumbtack), **tea-pot** (teapot), **sand-box** (sandbox), and **car-toon** (cartoon).

Then have children blend the syllables to say the following words and tell how many word parts each word contains.

pig-pen (pigpen, 2)   **thumb-print** (thumbprint, 2)

eye-lid (eyelid, 2)   **pres-i-dent** (president, 3)

PRETEACH
Phonics

 Review /r/r, /s/s Display *Sound/Spelling Card Rr*. Ask: **What letter is this? What sound do you hear at the beginning of *rat*? What letter stands for /r/ in the word *rat*?** (*r*) Then display the *Sound/Spelling Card Ss*. Ask: **What letter is this? What sound do you hear at the beginning of *sad*? What letter stands for the /s/ at the beginning of *sad*?** Tell the children you are going to point to *Sound/Spelling Cards Ss* and *Rr* many times. Ask the children to say the name of each letter as you point to it. Then ask children to say the sound that the letter makes. Continue until children confidently recognize each letter and sound.

   Discriminate /r/ and /s/ Display *Word Builder Cards r* and *s*. Then display *Photo Cards rabbit, ring, sandwich,* and *sun* in random order. Tell children that they are going to sort the cards by their beginning sound. Begin by having children say the name of each picture. Invite volunteers to place the card beneath the letter that stands for the sound at the beginning of the picture name. Then ask children to read each letter and name of the pictures below it.

Distribute *Copy Master 4*, and help children to identify and write the letter that stands for the beginning sound of each picture. (Children should write letter *r* for *rug, rip, rose;* letter *s* for *sun;* letter *m* for *mop*.)

Day 2

RETEACH
High-Frequency Words

 Practice Book 9 Distribute an index card with the word *a* to each child. Have children point to the word and read it. Say: **This is a pencil.** Say the word *a* and have children say it with you. Then prepare index cards with either the word *a* or the word *I*. Have children sit in a circle. Give each child one index card. At your signal, have them pass their cards around the circle until you tell them to stop. Ask: **Which of you has the word *a*?** The children with the word *a* should stand and read the word together. Repeat with the word *I*.

Have children turn to *Practice Book* page 9 to practice newly-learned word *a*. Complete the page together.

High-Frequency Words

a   I

PRETEACH
Comprehension

Monitor Comprehension: Reread Remind children that stories contain many details. Explain to children that sometimes it helps to go back and reread parts of the story that are confusing. Recall the story about Mary from Day 1. Reread the first few sentences and model how seeing these sentences a second time, can be helpful to the reader. Say: **I remember now, Mary was going to the pond to ice skate.** As you continue reading, stop at appropriate points in the story to model how to reread to help remember what is happening in the story. On the board, record information the children remembered because of rereading.

> Mary went ice-skating on the pond.
> Mary pretended she was a bird.

PRETEACH
Build Robust Vocabulary

Read the Student-Friendly Explanations for *automatic, perfectly,* and *resemblance*. Then discuss each word, using the following examples.

automatic
Which is *automatic*, a real car with an engine or a plastic car that you push?

perfectly
If you wash the windows *perfectly*, are they more likely to look clean and neat, or dirty and messy?

resemblance
Many people say that I *resemble* my mother. Who do people say you *resemble*?

VOCABULARY
Student-Friendly Explanations

automatic Something that is automatic runs by itself.

perfectly If you do something perfectly, you do it in just the right way.

resemblance People or things that have a resemblance look alike or are alike in some way.

Grade K 17

LESSON 2

DAY 3

PHONEMIC AWARENESS
Syllable Blending

PHONICS
Reteach Review /r/r, /m/m

HIGH-FREQUENCY WORDS
Reteach *a*

COMPREHENSION
Reteach Make Predictions

BUILD ROBUST VOCABULARY
Reteach automatic, perfectly, resemblance

WRITING
Reteach Writing Trait: Conventions

Materials Needed:

Write-On/Wipe-Off Boards

Sound/Spelling Cards *Rr, Mm*

Word Builder and Word Builder Cards

Practice Book

Phonemic Awareness

 Blend Syllables Remind children that words have parts that can be taken apart and put back together again. Tell children that you are going to say word parts, and they are going to say the word when you call on them. Say: **Listen to these word parts: star-fish. When I blend the two word parts together, the word is *starfish*.**

Distribute *Write-on/Wipe-off Boards* and counters to the children. Make sure that children use the side with the heart in the corner. Tell children that for every word part they hear, they will put a counter into a box. Then they will count the counters and tell how many word parts each word has.

eye-brow (2)	**bed-time** (2)	**vol-can-o** (3)	**hand-shake** (2)
news-pa-per (3)	**ar-tis-tic** (3)	**foot-ball** (2)	

RETEACH

Phonics

 Review: /r/r, /m/m Display *Sound/Spelling Card Rr*. Ask: **What letter is this? What sound do you hear at the beginning of *rat*? What letter stands for /r/ in the word *rat*?** (*r*) Then display the *Sound/Spelling Card Mm*. Ask: **What letter is this? What sound do you hear at the beginning of *mud*?** (*m*) **What letter stands for the /m/ at the beginning of *mud*?** Tell the children you are going to point to *Sound/Spelling Cards Mm* and *Rr* many times. Ask the children to say the name of each letter as you point to it. Then ask children to say the sound that the letter makes. Continue until children confidently recognize each letter and sound.

Discriminate /r/ and /m/ Distribute *Word Builder Cards r* and *m* to the children. Tell the children you are going to say some words. Ask children to listen for the sound at the beginning of each word. If a word begins with the /r/ sound, have children hold up letter card *r*. If the words start with the /m/ sound, have them hold up letter *m*.

rock	**mop**	**mill**	**mom**
rude	**ring**	**mole**	**rip**

18 Lesson 2

Day 3

RETEACH

High-Frequency Words

 Display an index card with the word *a*. Point to the word as you read it. Display *Photo Card drum* and ask children to identify the picture. Write the following phrase on the board. Read the phrase aloud.

Continue by changing the Photo Card to create new phrases. Invite volunteers to read them.

Then have children write the phrase on paper. Have children write the word *a* and complete the phrase with a picture.

High-Frequency Words

a

Grade K 19

Day 3

RETEACH
Comprehension

Practice Book 10 **Make Predictions** Remind children that they can make a prediction, or guess, about what will happen next in a story by using clues in the pictures and words. Read the first two sentences of the following story. Ask children to make predictions about what the story is going to be about. Then read the remainder of the story.

Priscilla walked quickly down her block. She could hardly wait to get home because her Grandfather was going to be there. Grandpa was visiting for one week all the way from Arkansas. When Priscilla arrived home, she gave Grandpa a very big hug. Grandpa told Priscilla that he was very hungry from his long trip. So, Grandpa and Priscilla went to the kitchen to make a snack. Priscilla took out the bread and jelly. Grandpa took out the peanut butter. Together Grandpa and Priscilla made sandwiches. They laughed and told stories. Priscilla loved hearing all about Grandpa's fishing trips in Arkansas. She also loved to hear his stories about his camping adventures. Priscilla loved spending time with Grandpa.

Confirm children's predictions about the story. Then guide children to *Practice Book* page 10. Have children use the pictures to make predictions about the story.

RETEACH
Build Robust Vocabulary

Remind children of the Student-Friendly Explanations for *automatic, perfectly,* and *resemblance*. Then discuss each word by asking children the following questions.

automatic
What items in our classroom are *automatic*?

perfectly
What type of activity would need to be done *perfectly*, a puzzle or a playing with a stuffed animal? Why?

resemblance
In what ways do you show *resemblance* to a family member?

VOCABULARY
Student-Friendly Explanations

automatic Something that is automatic runs by itself.

perfectly If you do something perfectly, you do it in just the right way.

resemblance People or things that have a resemblance look alike or are alike in some way.

Day 3

RETEACH
Writing

Writing Trait: Conventions Tell children that labels convey meaning and provide information. Point out labels in the classroom. Explain to children that labels are written just below or next to the things they tell about. Also, sometimes labels begin with an uppercase letter, but they do not have to.

Write the following labels on sentence strips. Ask volunteers to point to the uppercase and lowercase letters on the labels. Point out that any labels that include someone's name should always use uppercase letters.

| garbage can |

| pencil sharpener |

| Mrs. Jay's desk |

Grade K 21

LESSON 2

DAY AT A GLANCE — Day 4

PHONEMIC AWARENESS
Syllable Blending

PHONICS
Review /r/r, /s/s, /m/m

READING
Review /r/r, /s/s, /m/m
Review High-Frequency Words

BUILD ROBUST VOCABULARY
Review differ, stalking, mellow, automatic, perfectly, resemblance

WRITING
Reteach Writing Form: Labels

Materials Needed:

Sound/Spelling Cards Rr, Ss, Mm

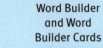
Word Builder and Word Builder Cards

Photo Cards

Practice Book

Phonemic Awareness

Blend Syllables Remind children that they can blend word parts together to say a word. Say: *eye-brow*. **When I put the word parts *eye-brow* together, I make the word *eyebrow*.** Then have children listen to some word parts and blend them together to say the word.

sis-ter   **bro-ther**   **mo-ther**   **fa-ther**   **fam-i-ly**

Have children blend the syllables listed below into words, and count the syllables in each word they say. Suggest that children use their fingers to count syllables as they say each word.

mon-key (monkey, 2)   **but-ter-fly** (butterfly, 3)   **ba-by** (baby, 2)
ze-bra (zebra, 2)   **li-on** (lion, 2)   **dol-phin** (dolphin, 2)
an-i-mal (animal, 3)   **ti-ger** (tiger, 2)   **train-er** (trainer, 2)
cam-el (camel, 2)   **jun-gle** (jungle, 2)   **gor-ril-a** (gorilla, 3)

RETEACH

Phonics

 Review /r/r, /s/s, /m/m Display *Sound/Spelling Card Rr*. Ask: **What letter is this? What sound do you hear at the beginning of *rat*? What letter stands for /r/ in the word *rat*?** (*r*) Then repeat with the *Sound/Spelling Cards Mm* and *Ss*. Tell the children your are going to point to *Sound/Spelling Cards Rr, Ss,* and *Mm* many times. Ask the children to say the name of each letter as you point to it. Then ask children to say the sound the letter makes. Continue until children confidently recognize each letter and sound.

  Discriminate /r/, /s/, and /m/ Display *Word Builder Cards r, m,* and *s*. Then display *Photo Cards rabbit, ring, sandwich, milk,* and *sun* in random order. Tell children that they are going to sort the cards by their beginning sound. Begin by having children say the name of each picture. Invite volunteers to place the card beneath the letter that stands for the sound at the beginning of the picture name. Then ask children to read the each letter and name the pictures below it.

22 Lesson 2

Day 4

REVIEW

Reading

Review /m/, /s/, /r/   Review the /m/, /s/ and /r/ sounds. Write the words *mud, sun,* and *rat* on the board, and read and blend the sounds for the children. Then have children name other words that begin with each sound.

Practice Book 11–12

Review High-Frequency Words   Distribute index cards for *a* and *I* to children. Explain that you will play "Match." As you say and display these words, have children find the corresponding index card, say the word, and display the card back to you. Repeat until each word has been identified correctly many times.

Have children turn to *Practice Book* pages 11–12. Help children cut and fold the book. Encourage them to read it at home.

High-Frequency Words

a

REVIEW

Robust Vocabulary

Remind children of the Student-Friendly Explanations of *differ, stalking, mellow, automatic, perfectly,* and *resemblance*. Then determine children's understanding of the words by asking the following questions.

- Look at a picture of an apple and an orange. Is there any *resemblance*? How do they *differ*?
- How would you open an *automatic* window? Explain.
- If you are relaxing at a pool, are you *mellow* or *stalking*? Explain.
- If you get every answer right on a test, did you do it *perfectly*? Explain.

VOCABULARY

Student-Friendly Explanations

differ When things differ from one another, they are not the same.

stalking When an animal is stalking another animal, it sneaks up on it to try to catch it.

mellow When you are mellow, you feel gentle and relaxed.

automatic Something that is automatic runs by itself.

perfectly If you do something perfectly, you do it in just the right way.

resemblance People or things that have a resemblance look alike or are alike in some way.

RETEACH

Writing

Writing Form: Labels   Review the idea that a label gives information. Show an illustration or a photograph of an activity they have done or a place they have gone. Tell children that they are going to help you write a label for the picture.

Write a label for the picture together. Remind children that the label is usually below the picture or beside it. Then invite children to write letters or words they know. Read the finished label together.

> at the playground

Grade K   23

LESSON 2

PHONEMIC AWARENESS
Syllable Segmentation

PHONICS
Preteach Consonant *Tt*

HIGH-FREQUENCY WORDS
Preteach *my*

BUILD ROBUST VOCABULARY
Reteach *ability, confident, encourage, talent*

Materials Needed:

Photo Cards   Sound/Spelling Card *Tt*   Write-On/Wipe-Off Boards

Practice Book

Phonemic Awareness

 Syllable Segmentation Remind children that words are like puzzles that can be taken apart and put back together again. Display *Photo Card sandwich*. Say: **I am going to say a word: *sandwich*. Listen as I break the word into two parts: *sand-wich*. I will say the word again and clap for each part: *sand-wich*. Now listen as I say the whole word again: *sandwich*.**

Have children practice segmenting their own names into syllables. As you say each name, pause slightly between syllables. Then guide children to identify the syllables in the words below. Say each word. Give a visual clue, such as a slight nod, as you say each syllable. Then have children clap the syllables with you.

ocean (*o-cean*)   **turtle** (*tur-tle*)   **brother** (*broth-er*)

gentle (*gen-tle*)   **slipping** (*slip-ping*)   **pencil** (*pen-cil*)

PRETEACH

Phonics

 Consonant *Tt* Display *Sound/Spelling Card Tt*. Say: **This is the letter *t*. Say the name with me.** Point to uppercase *T* and say: **This is uppercase *T*.** Point to lowercase *t* and say: **This is lowercase *t*.** Have children identify the letters. (T, t)

Writing *T* and *t* Write *T* and *t* on the board and have children identify the letters. Say: **Watch as I write the letter *T* so that everyone can read it.** As you give the Letter Talk, trace the uppercase *T*. Do the same for lowercase *t*.

Letter Talk for *T*	**Letter Talk for *t***
1. Straight line down.	1. Straight line down.
2. Cross at the top.	2. Cross at the line.

Tell children to finger-write the uppercase *T* in the air as you repeat the Letter Talk. Have them do the same for lowercase *t*. Direct them to write uppercase *T* and then lowercase *t* several times on their *Write-on/Wipe-off Boards*.

Have children turn to *Practice Book* page 13. Help children circle each uppercase *T* and underline each lowercase *t*. Have them trace the letters and write them on the lines.

24   Lesson 2

Day 5

PRETEACH

High-Frequency Words

Write the high-frequency word *my* on the board and on an index card. Point to and read the word *my* on the board. Have children say it with you. Say: **This is *my* desk.** Display the index card and say the word. Match the index card to the word on the board, say the word, and have children say it with you.

Write *my* on index cards, one for each child. Hand the cards to children. Say the word, and have children point to the word and read it. Then write the high-frequency words *I* and *a* on index cards for your use. Tell children that you will show them words, and when they see *my,* they should say the word and point to it on their card. Display the index cards for *my, I,* and *a* in random order until children can consistently identify the word *my*. Keep the index cards for use in Lesson 3.

High-Frequency Words	
a	my
I	

RETEACH

Build Robust Vocabulary

Recall the Student-Friendly Explanations for the words *ability, confident, encourage,* and *talent*. Then discuss each word, using the following examples:

ability
What is an *ability* that you would like to have?

confident
Would you feel more *confident* playing a game if you had played it before, or if you had never played it?

encourage
If someone says, "Great job!" to you, did the person *encourage* you or not? How can you tell?

talent
What is a *talent* you can share with your classmates? Can you share it now?

VOCABULARY
Student-Friendly Explanations

ability If you can do something, you have the ability to do it.

confident If you are confident about something, you feel very sure about it.

encourage When you encourage someone, you help that person feel good about trying something.

talent If you are very good at doing something, you have a talent for it.

Grade K

LESSON 3

PHONEMIC AWARENESS
Syllable Segmentation

PHONICS
Preteach Relate *Tt* to /t/

HIGH-FREQUENCY WORDS
Reteach *my*

COMPREHENSION
Reteach Make Predictions

BUILD ROBUST VOCABULARY
Reteach *differ, perfectly, resemblance, reverse*

Materials Needed:

Write-On/Wipe-Off Boards

Sound/Spelling Card *Tt*

Sounds of Letters CD

Word Builder and Word Builder Cards

Photo Cards

Copying Master

Practice Book

Phonemic Awareness

Syllable Segmentation Distribute a button or a marker and a *Write-on/Wipe-off Board* to each child. Guide children to the three boxes next to the heart shape on side B of the *Write-on/Wipe-off Board*. Tell children that they will be putting a button or marker in a box for each word part, or syllable, that they hear in a word. Draw three connected boxes on the board, and model how to break a word into syllables. Say: **Let's try with the word *lemon*. *Lem-on*.** Mark a box on your chart for each syllable you say. Say each syllable again, pointing to each marked box: ***Lemon* has two word parts: *lem-on*.** Continue counting syllables with the following words:

football (*foot-ball*, 2)   **lion** (*li-on*, 2)

PRETEACH

Phonics

Develop Phonemic Awareness of /t/ Say: ***time, tan*. The words *time* and *tan* both begin with the sound /t/.** Have children say /t/ several times.

  Relate *Tt* to /t/ Display *Sound/Spelling Card Tt*. Ask: **What is the name of this letter? The letter *t* stands for /t/, the sound at the beginning of *tickle*. Say /t/.** Then play the /t/ sound on the *Sounds of Letters CD*, and have children repeat the sound.

Discriminate /t/ Give each child *Word Builder Card t*. Say: **I will say some words. If the word begins with /t/, hold up the card and say /t/. If the word does not begin with /t/, put your card face-down.** Say the words *ten, boy, two, tip,* and *win*.

  Identify Sound Position Draw three boxes on chart paper, and display *Photo Cards ant* and *taxi*. Say: **If /t/ is at the beginning of the word, put letter *t* in the beginning box. If /t/ is at the end, put letter *t* in the end box.** Model the activity using the words *ant* and *taxi*. Continue with these words: *cut, tub, cat, sat, tell*.

Distribute *Copying Master 5*. Have children trace the letter *T* and *t*. Then help them to identify each picture and circle the letter for the beginning sound of each picture name. (Children circle letter *t* for *truck, tree, tiger, ten, top*.)

Day 1

RETEACH
High-Frequency Words

Distribute the index cards for *my, I,* and *a,* used on Day 5 of Lesson 2. Say the words, and have children repeat. Tell children that you will show them words, and when they see *my,* they should say the word and point to it on their card. If they don't see the word *my,* they should read the word shown. Hold up the index cards randomly until children can consistently identify *my.*

High-Frequency Words

a	my
I	

RETEACH
Comprehension

  Make Predictions Draw a ball on the roof of a house. Above it, write this title: "*The Ball on the Roof.*" Read the title aloud and discuss the picture. Say: **I can use clues to predict what the story will be about. The title of the story is "The Ball on the Roof." The picture shows a ball on a roof. I think the story will be about this ball.**

Read the story aloud:

Linda was playing catch with her brother, Brian. She threw the ball too high. It landed on the roof. "How will we get it down?" she asked. "Let's throw another ball up on the roof to knock it down," Brian said.

They threw another ball up. It got stuck, too. "Let's tell Mom," Linda said. Mom got out a ladder and climbed up. She brought down three balls. "Hey, there's the ball that got stuck last week!" Brian said.

"Let's play catch again," Linda said.

Discuss the story. Ask children to predict what might happen next, and to explain their response. Then guide them to *Practice Book* page 14. Have them circle the picture that shows what the children might do next, recalling story clues to support their prediction, or guess.

RETEACH
Build Robust Vocabulary

Remind children of the Student-Friendly Explanations for *differ, perfectly, resemblance,* and *reverse.* Then ask the following questions:

differ
How does winter *differ* from summer?

perfectly
If you spell your name correctly, is it spelled *perfectly*?

resemblance
How does a puppy have a *resemblance* to a grownup dog?

reverse
Show what it looks like to walk in *reverse*.

VOCABULARY
Student-Friendly Explanations

differ When things differ from one another, they are not the same.

perfectly If you do something perfectly, you do it in just the right way.

resemblance People or things that have a resemblance look alike or are alike in some way.

reverse If you do something in reverse, you do it in the opposite way, or backward.

LESSON 3

PHONEMIC AWARENESS
Syllable Segmentation and Deletion

PHONICS
Reteach /t/t, /m/m

HIGH-FREQUENCY WORDS
Reteach my

COMPREHENSION
Preteach Make Inferences

BUILD ROBUST VOCABULARY
Reteach automatic, complained, mellow, stalking

Materials Needed:

Phoneme Phone | Sound/Spelling Card Tt, Mm | Photo Cards

Word Builders and Word Builder Cards | Copying Master | Practice Book

---

Phonemic Awareness

Syllable Segmentation and Deletion Review with children how to break a word into syllables, or word parts. Say: **Listen to this word—circle. Say the word with me. Now let's say the parts of the word: cir-cle.**

Syllable Deletion Model for children how to delete syllables. Say: **Listen to this word—anything. Say it with me. I can break this word into its parts: any-thing. I can also say the word without one of its parts. Anything without any is thing. Say it with me: Anything without any is thing.**

Model using the *Phoneme Phone* to look at the position of your mouth as you say the word *anything* without *any*. (*thing*) Tell children they should repeat the word you say and then say the word without one of its parts. Have them use their *Phoneme Phones* to look at their mouth position.

bookshelf (*book-shelf*)   bookshelf without *book-* (*shelf*)
notebook (*note-book*)   notebook without *-book* (*note*)
downstairs (*down-stairs*)   downstairs without *-stairs* (*down*)

RETEACH
Phonics

Connect Letters and Sounds Display *Sound/Spelling Card Tt*. Ask: **What sound do you hear at the beginning of *talk*? What letter stands for /t/ at the beginning of *talk*?** Then display *Sound/Spelling Card Mm*. Repeat with the word *milk* and the beginning sound /m/.

Review /t/t, /m/m Display *Sound/Spelling Cards Tt* and *Mm*. Then randomly distribute *Photo Cards milk, taxi, tiger,* and *truck*. Say the picture names. Guide children to stand next to the letter that stands for the beginning sound of their picture. Shuffle the cards and redistribute until all have had a turn.

Identify initial /t/ and /m/ Give each child *Word Builder Cards* for *t* and *m*. Tell children that you are going to say some words. Ask children to listen for the sound at the beginning of each word. If the word begins with /t/, children should hold up their letter card *t* and say /t/. If the word starts with /m/, children should hold up letter card *m* and say /m/. Use the following words:

      mom   toe   ten   me   two   my

Distribute *Copying Master 6*. Have children trace the letter *Tt*. Then identify the pictures with the children. Have them write the beginning letter of the picture name. (Children write letter *t* for *table, toothbrush, turtle*; children write letter m for *mouse, mop*.)

Day 2

RETEACH
High-Frequency Words

  On the board, write the high-frequency word *my*. Display *Photo Card quarter* next to the word *my* to form the phrase *my ‹quarter›*. Read the phrase and have children repeat it. Replace *Photo Card quarter* with *Photo Card cat*. Repeat the activity.

Have children turn to *Practice Book* page 15 to review high-frequency words and practice newly learned words. Complete the page together.

High-Frequency Words
my

PRETEACH
Comprehension

Make Inferences Ask children what they remember about the story "The Ball on the Roof." Explain that authors and illustrators sometimes give clues about things that are happening in the story without putting the information in the story's words. Begin a three-column chart. Reread the story, and model how to make inferences about it.

Say: **The brother and sister are playing catch.** Record the information in the *Story Clues* column. **Children who play together like each other.** Record the information in the *What I Know* column. **I think the brother and sister are friends.** Record the information in the *Inferences* column.

Story Clues +	What I Know =	Inference
The brother and sister play catch.	Children who play together like each other.	The brother and sister are friends.

Make additional inferences about the story, and add them to the chart.

RETEACH
Build Robust Vocabulary

Remind children of Student-Friendly Explanations for *automatic, complained, mellow,* and *stalking*. Discuss each word, using the following examples.

automatic
Which is *automatic*: a toy car with a battery or a toy car that you push? Why?

complained
If your friend *complained* about a chore, was he happy or unhappy about it?

mellow
Would you be *mellow* if you were lying on a blanket or running a race? Why?

stalking
Show how you might look if you were an animal *stalking* something.

VOCABULARY
Student-Friendly Explanations

automatic Something that is automatic runs by itself.

complained If you complained about something, you told how it makes you unhappy.

mellow When you feel mellow, you feel gentle and relaxed.

stalking When an animal is stalking another animal, it sneaks up on it to try to catch it.

LESSON 3

DAY AT A GLANCE
Day 3

PHONEMIC AWARENESS
Syllable Deletion

PHONICS
Reteach /t/t, /r/r

HIGH-FREQUENCY WORDS
Reteach my

COMPREHENSION
Reteach Make Predictions

BUILD ROBUST VOCABULARY
Reteach confident, differ, resemblance

WRITING
Guided Practice Writing Trait: Ideas

Materials Needed:

Sound/Spelling Card Tt, Rr | Photo Cards | Word Builder and Word Builder Cards

Practice Book

Phonemic Awareness

Syllable Deletion Remind children that they have been learning about breaking words into word parts, or syllables, and saying a word without one of its word parts. Model again for children how to delete a syllable from a word. Say: **Listen to this word—*snowy*. I can break this word into its parts: *snow-y*. Now I am going to say *snowy* without the *-y*. *Snowy* without *-y* is *snow*.**

Have children repeat the following words after you say each one, and then follow your directions to say the word without one of its parts. As you tell children which syllables to delete from words, pronounce them as you say them in the words, rather than the way they may be spelled.

- ***handshake*** without ***hand-*** (*shake*)   ***distant*** without ***dis-*** (*tant*)
- ***donkey*** without ***don-*** (*key*)   ***grandma*** without ***-ma*** (*grand*)
- ***medal*** without ***-al*** (*med*)   ***equal*** without ***-qual*** (*e*)
- ***wagon*** without ***wag-*** (*on*)   ***kangaroo*** without ***-roo*** (*kanga*)

RETEACH

Phonics

 Connect Letters and Sounds Display *Sound/Spelling Card Tt*. Ask: **What sound do you hear at the beginning of *teacher*? What letter stands for the sound /t/ at the beginning of *teacher*?** (*Tt*)

Display *Sound/Spelling Card Rr*. Ask: **What sound do you hear at the beginning of *rabbit*? What letter stands for /r/ at the beginning of *rabbit*?** (*Rr*)

 Review /t/t, /r/r Display *Sound/Spelling Cards Tt* and *Rr* where children can access them. Tell children that you will show them pictures of things that begin with the sounds /t/ and /r/. Show the *Photo Cards taxi, tiger, tree, truck, rabbit,* and *ring,* having children say each picture name. Pass out the *Photo Cards* to children. Ask them to look at their card and place it beside the letter that stands for the sound at the beginning of the picture name. Continue reshuffling and redistributing cards until all have had a turn.

Give each child *Word Builder Cards t* and *r*. Tell children that you are going to say some words. Have children listen for the sound at the beginning of each word. If the word begins with /t/, children should hold up letter card *t* and say /t/. If the word starts with /r/, children should hold up letter card *r* and say /r/.

| red | time | rude | tiger |
| rose | rabbit | table | take |

30 Lesson 3

Day 3

RETEACH
High-Frequency Words

On the board, write the word *my*. Hold *Photo Card umbrella* next to the word *my* to form the phrase *my ‹umbrella›*. Read the phrase aloud. Ask a child to find the word *my* in the phrase. Then read the phrase aloud with children.

Continue making phrases with other *Photo Cards,* such as *Photo Cards truck, dog, yarn,* and *pan*. Work with children to read the phrases aloud.

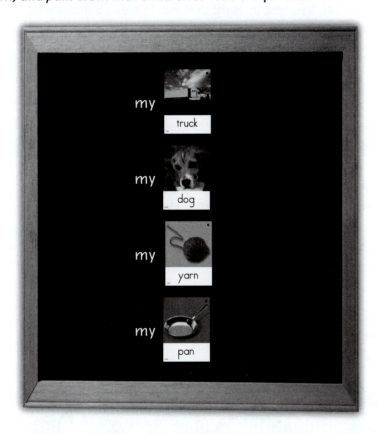

High-Frequency Words

my

Day 3

RETEACH
Comprehension

 Make Predictions Remind children that they can use clues in the words and pictures to make a prediction, or guess, about what might happen next in a story. Have children listen as you read aloud the following story.

> Jenny the hornbill bird wanted to make a nest and lay eggs. She found a hole in an oak tree and thought that would make a nice place. Then a big squirrel came and said, "That's my home. Find another one!"
>
> She flew to another tree to make a nest. Then in the morning she heard a woodpecker knocking on the side of the tree. He was looking for bugs to eat. "This is too loud!" Jenny said.
>
> Finally she found an empty tree. It looked cozy and safe. "This will make a great home for my eggs," she said.

Ask: **What does Jenny want to do?** (She wants to find tree to make a nest.) **What did you think would happen after she left the first tree?** (Possible response: I thought she would look for another tree.) **What clues helped you make that guess?** (Possible response: She needs to find a home to build a nest, and I guessed that she probably wouldn't give up looking until she found one.)

Guide children to *Practice Book* page 16. Have children circle what they think might happen next in the story. Discuss the clues that helped them make their prediction.

RETEACH
Build Robust Vocabulary

Remind children of the Student-Friendly Explanations for the words *confident, differ,* and *resemblance.* Then discuss the words by asking children the following questions.

confident
If you are *confident* when you dance, are you feeling happy and good? Why or why not?

differ
How does the weekend *differ* from a school day? Name three ways.

resemblance
Does a dog have a *resemblance* to a wolf? Why or why not?

VOCABULARY
Student-Friendly Explanations

confident If you are confident about something, you feel very sure about it.

differ When things differ from one another, they are not the same.

resemblance People or things that have a resemblance look alike or are alike in some way.

32 Lesson 3

Day 3

GUIDED PRACTICE

Writing

Writing Trait: Ideas Explain to children that it is important to have good ideas for a story before writing it. Tell them that thinking of ideas before writing helps writers choose the best idea.

Remind children that they heard a story about a bird named Jenny who wanted to find a tree in which to make a nest. You may wish to reread the story. Then invite children to think of what Jenny might do next. Record children's ideas on chart paper. Display any *Photo Cards* that relate to the ideas to help children understand the ideas. Then have them choose one idea to add to the story. Ask: **Why is it helpful to think of a lot of ideas before choosing one? Why does everyone like this idea?**

What does Jenny do next in the story?

After you add the story idea, read aloud the longer version to children.

Grade K 33

LESSON 3

DAY AT A GLANCE — Day 4

PHONEMIC AWARENESS
Syllable Segmentation and Deletion

PHONICS
Review /t/t, /m/m, /r/r

READING
Review /t/t, /m/m, /r/r
Review High-Frequency Words

BUILD ROBUST VOCABULARY
Review ability, confident, talent, encourage, differ, resemblance

WRITING
Reteach Writing Form: Signs

Materials Needed:

Sound/Spelling Card Tt, Mm, Rr

Photo Cards

Practice Book

Phonemic Awareness

Syllable Segmentation and Deletion Remind children that they have been breaking words into their parts, or syllables, and working with word parts. Remind children how to segment a word into syllables. Then model how to delete a syllable from a word. Say: **I'm going to say a word: *sunshine*. Listen as I break the word into two parts: *sun-shine*. Now I will say *sunshine* without *sun*: *shine*. I will do this for another word, *rooftop*. First, I will break *rooftop* into its parts, *roof-top*. Now I will say it without *-top*. Rooftop without *-top* is *roof*.**

Say the following words for children. Have them first break the words into syllables. Then have them delete a syllable from the word as instructed.

finish (*fin-ish*)	**Say *finish* without *fin-*** (*ish*)
camping (*camp-ing*)	**Say *camping* without *-ing*** (*camp*)
igloo (*ig-loo*)	**Say *igloo* without *-loo*** (*ig*)
pony (*po-ny*)	**Say *pony* without *po-*** (*ny*)
scissors (*scis-sors*)	**Say *scissors* without *-sors*** (*scis*)

REVIEW

Phonics

Review /t/t, /m/m /r/r Display *Sound/Spelling Card Tt*. Ask: **What sound do you hear at the beginning of *toothbrush*? What letter stands for /t/ at the beginning of *toothbrush*?**

Repeat the process with *Sound/Spelling Cards Mm* and *Rr*, using the words *marble* and *rooster*.

Discriminate /t/, /m/, and /r/ Place *Sound/Spelling Cards Tt, Mm,* and *Rr,* on the chalk ledge. Distribute *Photo Cards taxi, tiger, tree, truck, milk, rabbit* and *ring* to children. Tell children to name the picture on their card and place the cards beside the letter that stands for the beginning sound in the picture name.

Tt

taxi — tiger — tree — truck

Mm Rr
milk — rabbit — ring

REVIEW

Reading

/t/t, /m/m, /r/r Review the /t/, /m/, and /r/ sounds with children. Have children name the letter that stands for the beginning sound of the following words: *trick, mine,* and *root*.

High-Frequency Words Reuse or create index cards for *I, a,* and *my*. Distribute them to children. Ask children to take turns holding up a card. Read the card as a group, and then have children find the matching card. Continue until all the cards have been read. Repeat as needed.

Have children turn to *Practice Book* pages 17–18. Help children cut and fold the book, and read it together. Have children take it home to read with their families.

REVIEW

Robust Vocabulary

Remind children of the Student-Friendly Explanations of *ability, confident, encourage, talent, differ,* and *resemblance*. Then determine children's understanding of the words by asking the following questions.

- What *ability* would you like to have? Who could teach you?
- What words might a *confident* person say?
- If you have a *talent* for making people laugh, are you good at telling jokes or not? Tell why.
- If you *encourage* someone to toss a ball to you, what do you say?
- How does an orange *differ* from an apple?
- How might two spiders have a *resemblance* to each other?

RETEACH

Writing

Writing Form: Signs Remind children that the pictures and words on signs give us information about what to do, where to go, or where there is danger. Draw a picture of an arrow sign.

Guide children to recognize that print conveys meaning and provides information. Say: **The arrow on an ARROW sign tells us which way to go. The shape of the sign and its color help people know that it is an arrow sign.**

Then tell children that together you will make a cafeteria sign. Ask: **What kind of sign would be helpful in our cafeteria? What words could we put on the sign? What pictures would give more information?**

Record children's ideas on chart paper. Then have them choose one idea to make a sign. Ask: **What words would we put on our sign? Would a picture help people understand the sign better?** Use children's ideas to make a simple sign for the cafeteria.

High-Frequency Words

a	my
I	

VOCABULARY

Student-Friendly Explanations

ability If you can do something, you have the ability to do it.

confident If you are confident about something, you feel very sure about it.

talent If you are very good at doing something, you have a talent for it.

encourage When you encourage someone, you help that person feel good about trying something.

differ When things differ from one another, they are not the same.

resemblance People or things that have a resemblance look alike or are alike in some way.

Grade K 35

LESSON 3

PHONEMIC AWARENESS
Word Segmentation

PHONICS
Preteach Consonant *Nn*

HIGH-FREQUENCY WORDS
Preteach *the*
Reteach *I, a*

BUILD ROBUST VOCABULARY
Reteach *feast, gusto, prepare*

Materials Needed:

Photo Cards | Sound/Spelling Card *Nn* | Write-On/Wipe-Off Boards

Practice Book

Phonemic Awareness

 Word Segmentation Display *Photo Card ring*. Say: **This is a ring. Now I'm going to say the sentence again, but I'm going to clap for each word that I say. This . . . is . . . a . . . ring.** Clap once for each word in the sentence.

Display *Photo Card fish*. Say: **This . . . is . . . a . . . fish.** As you say the sentence, have children track the spoken words by clapping once for each word. Write a check mark on the board for each word you say. Then say the line again, and point to the check marks to help children track the words. Repeat with *Photo Cards zebra, frog,* and *fox*.

PRETEACH
Phonics

 Consonant *Nn* Display *Sound/Spelling Card Nn*. Say: **This is the letter *n*. Say the name with me.** Point to uppercase *N* and say: **This is uppercase *N*.** Point to lowercase *n* and say: **This is lowercase *n*.** Have children identify the letters. (N, n)

Writing *N* and *n* Write *N* and *n* on the board and have children identify the letters. Say: **I will write the letter *N* so that everyone can read it.** As you give the Letter Talk, trace the uppercase *N*. Do the same for lowercase *n*.

Letter Talk for *N*	**Letter Talk for *n***
1. Straight line down.	1. Straight line down.
2. Go to the top of this line.	2. Up, curve, and down.
3. Slanted line down.	
4. Straight line up again.	

 Tell children to finger-write the uppercase *N* in the air as you repeat the Letter Talk. Have them do the same for lowercase *n*. Have them practice writing uppercase *N* and then lowercase *n* several times on their *Write-on/Wipe-off Boards*.

 Have children turn to *Practice Book* page 19. Help children circle each uppercase *N* and underline each lowercase *n*. Have them trace the letters and write them on the lines.

Day 5

PRETEACH
High-Frequency Words

Write the high-frequency word *the* on the board and on an index card. Point to and read the word *the* on the board. Have children say it with you. Say: **The door is closed.** Display the index card and say the word. Match the index card to the word on the board, say the word, and have children say it with you.

Write *the* on index cards, one for each child. Distribute the cards to children. Say the word, and have children point to the word and read it. Then write the high-frequency words *I, a,* and *the* on index cards for your use. Tell children that you will show them words, and when they see *the,* they should hold up their card and say the word. Hold up the index cards for *the, I,* and *a* in random order until children can consistently identify the word *the.* Keep the index cards for use in Lesson 4.

High-Frequency Words

a   I

the

RETEACH
Build Robust Vocabulary

Read to children the Student-Friendly Explanations for *feast, gusto,* and *prepare.* Then discuss each word, using the following examples.

feast
If you had a *feast* of your favorite foods, what would you eat first? What would you eat last?

gusto
Do you play on the playground with *gusto*? How do you show it?

prepare
How do you and your family *prepare* for a trip? What do you need?

VOCABULARY
Student-Friendly Explanations

feast A feast is a big meal with lots of different kinds of foods.

gusto When you do something with gusto, you do it with energy and excitement.

prepare When you prepare for something, you get ready to do it.

Grade K   37

LESSON 4

PHONEMIC AWARENESS
Word Segmentation

PHONICS
Preteach Relate *Nn* to /n/

HIGH-FREQUENCY WORDS
Reteach *the, I, my*

COMPREHENSION
Reteach Characters

BUILD ROBUST VOCABULARY
Reteach *feast, gusto, prepare*

Materials Needed:

Sound/Spelling Card *Nn* | Sounds of Letters CD | Word Builder and Word Builder Cards

Write-On/Wipe-Off Boards | Copying Master | Practice Book

Phonemic Awareness

Word Segmentation Remind children that a sentence is a group of words that tells about something. Say: **Listen carefully. *My dog runs*. I will say the sentence again and clap for each word in it.** Clap once for each word as you repeat it. Say: **The words in the sentence are *My . . . dog . . . runs*.**

Have children repeat these sentences after you and clap for each word.

She is tall.   **I like snow.**   **Sam and I played.**

PRETEACH

Phonics

 Relate *Nn* to /n/ Display *Sound/Spelling Card Nn*. Say: **This is *Nn*. The letter *n* stands for /n/, the sound at the beginning of *nine*.** Have children repeat the sound. Play /n/ on the *Sounds of Letters CD*.

Discriminate /n/ Tell children to listen for words beginning with /n/. Say: **If the word begins with /n/, raise your hands and say /n/. If the word does not begin with /n/, put your hands down.** Say the words *kite, nice, never, grape, boat,* and *night*. Tell children that /n/ is at the end of some words, such as *tin*. Have them say whether /n/ is at the beginning or end of these words: *in, no, fan, burn, not*.

 Identify Sound Position Distribute *Word Builder Card n* and a *Write-on/Wipe-off Board* to each child. Have children point to the heart shape on side B of the *Write-on/Wipe-off Board*. Explain that they will use the three boxes next to the heart. Draw three similar boxes on chart paper. Say: **I will say some words. If /n/ is at the beginning, put your letter *n* on the beginning box. If /n/ is at the end, put your letter *n* on the end box.** Model the activity using the word *pan*.

		n

Have children place their *n* cards in the appropriate box for these words:
      pin   **nap**   **ten**   **now**   **nut**

 Distribute *Copying Master* page 7. Have children trace the letter *N* and *n*. Then have children look at each picture and circle the letter *n*. (Children trace the *Nn* and circle letter *n* in each box.)

38   Lesson 4

Day 1

RETEACH

High-Frequency Words

Write *the* on the board. Point to and read the word. Ask children to point to a letter in the word and then count the letters. Write *the* on an index card. Match the word on the index card with the word *the* on the board.

Distribute to children the index cards for *the* used on Day 5 of Lesson 3. Say the word, and have children point to the word on their cards and read it. Then write the high-frequency words *I* and *my* on index cards for your use. Tell children that you will show them words, and when they see *the,* they should say the word and point to it on their card. Hold up the index cards for *the, I,* and *my* in random order until children consistently identify the word *the*.

High-Frequency Words

I   my

the

RETEACH

Comprehension

Characters Explain that a story tells about something that happens to the people or animals in it. Tell children that the people or animals in a story are called the characters. Then read the following story aloud to them.

> Fox wanted fresh berries to bring home for lunch. On the way to pick berries, Fox met Rabbit. "I want to go with you," Rabbit said. "But first I have to pick lettuce."
>
> After they picked lettuce, Rabbit wanted to bake bread. By the time they picked berries, it was too late to go home for lunch. Fox said, "Let's eat what we have." They had a big picnic with all their food. "Yum," Fox said.

Guide children to turn to page 20 in their *Practice Books*. Have them look at the pictures as you ask them to point to and name the animals in the story. Ask children to name the characters and tell what they are doing. Help them use the pictures to retell the story.

RETEACH

Build Robust Vocabulary

Go over the Student-Friendly Explanations for *feast, gusto,* and *prepare.* Then discuss each word, asking children the following questions.

feast
If you eat one apple, is that a *feast*? Why or why not?

gusto
Which would you do with *gusto*—play tag or brush your teeth?

prepare
How do you *prepare* to ride a bike?

VOCABULARY

Student-Friendly Explanations

feast A feast is a big meal with lots of different foods.

gusto When you do something with gusto, you do it with energy and excitement.

prepare When you prepare for something, you get ready to do it.

Grade K   39

LESSON 4

PHONEMIC AWARENESS
Syllable Blending and Segmentation

PHONICS
Preteach Consonant *Pp*

HIGH-FREQUENCY WORDS
Reteach *the*

COMPREHENSION
Preteach Generate Questions

BUILD ROBUST VOCABULARY
Reteach *lonely, remind, preoccupied*

Materials Needed:

Phoneme Phone Sound/Spelling Card *Pp* Write-On/Wipe-Off Boards

Copying Master Photo Cards Practice Book

Phonemic Awareness

 Syllable Blending and Segmentation Review with children that words can be taken apart and put back together again. Say: **Listen as I say a word: *captain*. *Captain* has two parts: *cap . . . tain*.** Tell children to clap as you say each word part. Say: **Now listen as I put the word parts back together again: *captain*.**

Distribute the *Phoneme Phones*. Say the word *dinner* into a *Phoneme Phone*, and model how to use the mirror to look at your mouth position. Then ask children to do the same. Ask: **Does *dinner* have one part or two?** (two) **What are the two parts?** (din . . . ner) **Now put the word parts back together and say *dinner*.** (dinner) Repeat using the following words:

 summer winter paper pencil

PRETEACH

Phonics

 Consonant *Pp* Display *Sound/Spelling Card Pp*. Say: **This is the letter *p*.** Point to uppercase *P* and say: **This is uppercase *P*.** Point to lowercase *p* and say: **This is lowercase *p*.** Have children identify the letters.

Writing *P* and *p* Write *P* and *p* on the board. Have children identify the letters. Say: **Watch and listen as I write the letter *P*.** As you give the Letter Talk, trace the uppercase *P*. Do the same for lowercase *p*.

Letter Talk for *P*	**Letter Talk for *p***
1. Straight line down.	1. Straight line down.
2. Go to the top.	2. Go to the top.
3. Curved line out, down, and around until you touch the middle of the straight line.	3. Make a circle that goes around and touches the line.

 Repeat the Letter Talk, having children finger-write the uppercase *P* and lowercase *p* in the air. Then direct them to practice writing uppercase *P* and then lowercase *p* several times on their *Write-on/Wipe-off Boards*.

 Distribute *Copying Master 8*. Help children circle each uppercase *P* and underline each lowercase *p*. Have them trace the letters and write them on the lines.

Day 2

RETEACH
High-Frequency Words

 On the board, write the high-frequency word *the*. Display *Photo Card kangaroo* next to the word *the* to form the phrase *the ‹kangaroo›*. Read the phrase and have children repeat it. Replace *Photo Card kangaroo* with *Photo Card hammer*. Read the phrase. Have children repeat it. Continue with *Photo Cards boy, igloo,* and *pencil*.

Have children turn to *Practice Book* page 21 to review high-frequency words and practice newly learned words. Complete the page together.

High-Frequency Word
the

PRETEACH
Comprehension

Generate Questions Explain to children that asking questions as they read and looking for answers will help them understand and enjoy what they read. Create a chart with these column headings: *Question, Answer*. Recall the story about Fox and Rabbit from Day 1. Reread the story and pause to ask and record questions about each character. As children respond, record their responses on the chart under the *Answer* heading.

Question	Answer
What does Fox want to do?	

RETEACH
Build Robust Vocabulary

Read the Student-Friendly Explanations for the words *lonely, remind,* and *preoccupied*. Then discuss each word, prompting children with the following questions.

lonely
If you have a friend who is *lonely*, what can you do?

remind
Does someone *remind* you to brush your teeth? What does the person say?

preoccupied
Are you *preoccupied* before your birthday? Why or why not?

VOCABULARY
Student-Friendly Explanations

lonely When you are lonely, you are sad because you feel like you are all by yourself.

remind When you remind someone of something, you make them remember it.

preoccupied When you are preoccupied, you are always thinking about something else.

Grade K 41

LESSON 4

DAY AT A GLANCE — Day 3

PHONEMIC AWARENESS
Syllable Blending and Segmentation

PHONICS
Preteach Relate *Pp* to /p/

HIGH-FREQUENCY WORDS
Reteach *the*

COMPREHENSION
Reteach Characters

BUILD ROBUST VOCABULARY
Reteach *lonely, remind, preoccupied*

WRITING
Reteach Writing Trait: Organization

Materials Needed:

Write-On/Wipe-Off Boards   Sound/Spelling Card *Pp*   Sounds of Letters CD

Word Builder and Word Builder Cards   Photo Cards   Practice Book

Phonemic Awareness

Syllable Blending and Segmentation   Remind children that words are made up of parts. Draw two boxes on the board and model how to break a word into syllables. Say: *pic-nic.* Write a check mark in each box as you segment the syllables in the word again. Say: **I hear two word parts in this word. Now I'm going to blend the word parts together. Listen:** *picnic.*

Distribute three buttons or markers and a *Write-on/Wipe-off Board* to each child. Point to the heart shape on side B of the *Write-on/Wipe-off Board*. Tell children they will be working with the three boxes next to the heart. Say the words *brother, sister, uncle,* and *grandma,* segmenting and exaggerating the syllables as you say them. Tell children to place a button or marker in a box for each word part they hear. Have them count the number of syllables in each word and blend the syllables to say the word.

PRETEACH
Phonics

Relate *Pp* to /p/   Display *Sound/Spelling Card Pp*. Say: **What letter is this?** (p) **The letter p stands for /p/, the sound at the beginning of pencil. Say it with me.** Have children repeat the sound as you touch the letter on the card several times. Play the /p/ sound on the *Sounds of Letters CD,* and have children listen and repeat it.

 Discriminate /p/   Give each child a *Word Builder Card p*. Say: **If you hear the /p/ sound at the beginning of the word, hold up your card. If you don't, hide your card behind your back.** Say the words: *pool, game, play, van, run,* and *pot.* Explain that /p/ also appears at the end of some words, such as *map.* Have children indicate whether /p/ is at the beginning or at the end of the words: *jump, flap, pal, trap, pass,* and *pour.*

Write the following chant on the board: *Popping popcorn in the pot.* Read the chant aloud, tracking the print. Point to and read the *Pp* words. Have children repeat them, and then read the chant again.

RETEACH

High-Frequency Words

 On the board, write the word *the*. Hold *Photo Card ring* next to the word *the* to form the phrase *the ‹ring›*. Read the phrase aloud. Ask a child to find the word *the* in the phrase. Then read the phrase aloud with children.

Continue making phrases with other *Photo Cards,* such as *Photo Cards apple, hammer, tree,* and *watch*. Work with children to read the phrases aloud.

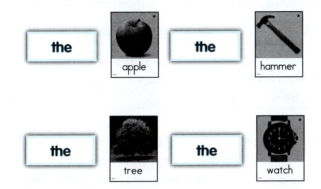

Write this phrase on the board and read it: *the _____*. Have children copy and complete the sentence with a picture.

Grade K

Day 3

RETEACH

Comprehension

 Characters Remind children that the characters in a story are the people or animals that the story is about. Have children listen as you read aloud the following story.

> Ruben and his sister Lucy rode their bikes to the park. Ruben wanted to show his sister something special. They went down the path to the pond. In the pond they saw a mother duck. The mother duck had six ducklings swimming behind her. Lucy wanted to pet the ducklings.
>
> Ruben said, "Don't touch the ducklings. The mother duck needs to protect her babies."
>
> So Lucy came up with a better idea. She decided to wave to them instead. "Hi," she whispered quietly.

Guide children to *Practice Book* page 22. Have children use the pictures to retell the story. Ask: **Who are the characters?** (Ruben and Lucy) **What are they doing?** (They are riding their bikes and looking at the mother duck and her ducklings in a pond.)

RETEACH

Build Robust Vocabulary

Read the Student-Friendly Explanations for *lonely*, *remind*, and *preoccupied*. Then ask children the following questions.

lonely
When might you be *lonely*—when playing with friends or thinking about a friend who's moved away? Why do you think so?

remind
Can stickers on a calendar *remind* you to do things? Why do you think so?

preoccupied
Do you think a drummer would be *preoccupied* with drumming or cooking?

VOCABULARY
Student-Friendly Explanations

lonely When you are lonely, you are sad because you feel like you are all by yourself.

remind When you remind someone of something, you make them remember it.

preoccupied When you are preoccupied, you are always thinking about something else.

Day 3

RETEACH

Writing

Writing Trait: Organization Remind children that a caption is a few words that tell about a picture, and when they write a caption, they should write it under the picture. Draw a picture of a sun on the chalkboard and a caption underneath, such as *The sun is hot*. Read the caption aloud.

Say: **Point to the caption. Is the caption below or above the picture?** (below) Point out how the caption tells about the picture.

Repeat with the following picture and captions. Read them aloud. Ask a volunteer to circle the caption that is written correctly and explain why it is correct. (Children should identify the caption written below the picture.)

Grade K   45

LESSON 4

DAY AT A GLANCE — Day 4

PHONEMIC AWARENESS
Word Segmentation/Syllable Blending and Segmentation

PHONICS
Reteach /n/n, /p/p

READING
Review /n/n, /p/p
Review High-Frequency Words

BUILD ROBUST VOCABULARY
Review feast, gusto, prepare, lonely, remind, preoccupied

WRITING
Reteach Captions

Materials Needed:

Phoneme Phone | Sound/Spelling Cards Nn, Pp | Word Builder and Word Builder Cards

Practice Book | Photo Cards

Phonemic Awareness

Word Segmentation/Syllable Blending and Segmentation Say a simple sentence that includes a child's name, such as *Marcus is a boy*. Repeat the sentence, guiding children to clap for each word. Have them count how many words are in the sentence.

Remind children how to segment spoken words into syllables. Explain that words are like puzzles, and that the word parts, or syllables, can be taken apart and put back together. Say: **I'm going to break apart one of the words I just said. Listen: *Mar-cus*. Now I'm going to blend the word parts together to say the word: *Marcus*.**

Distribute the *Phoneme Phones*. Say the word *suitcase*. Ask children to repeat the word while looking at the position of their mouths in the mirror. Ask: **Does *suitcase* have one part or two?** (two) **What are the two parts?** (suit-case) **Now blend the syllables, or word parts, to say the word.** (suitcase) Repeat with these words: *little, otter, rabbit, children, elbow*.

RETEACH
Phonics

 /n/n, /p/p Display *Sound/Spelling Card Nn*. Ask: **What sound do you hear at the beginning of *no*? What letter stands for /n/ at the beginning of *no*?**

Display *Sound/Spelling Card Pp*. Ask: **What sound do you hear at the beginning of *pin*? What letter stands for /p/ at the beginning of *pin*?**

Give each child a *Word Builder Card* for *n* and *p*. Tell them that you are going to say some words, and if the word begins with /n/, they should hold up their *n* card and say /n/. If you say a word that begins with /p/, they should hold up their *p* card and say /p/. Say the following words:

    nail   part   name   pen   pail   nest

Repeat, having children listen for the /n/ or /p/ sounds at the end of words:

    hop   can   ton   pup   lap   win

Day 4

REVIEW
Reading

/n/n, /p/p   Write the words *nap, nod, pin, pod,* and *pal* on the board. Point to the words and have children read them.

High-Frequency Words   Distribute index cards for *I, a, my,* and *the*. Hold up a card and read it aloud. Have children find the card in their pile, hold it up, and read it as a group. Continue until all the cards have been read. Repeat as needed.

   Have children turn to *Practice Book* pages 23–24. Help children cut and fold the book. Have children read the sentences to practice the newly learned words.

High-Frequency Words

a	I
my	the

REVIEW
Robust Vocabulary

Remind children of the Student-Friendly Explanations of *feast, gusto, prepare, lonely, remind,* and *preoccupied*. Then determine children's understanding of the words by asking the following questions.

- If you are at a *feast,* will you feel hungry afterward? Why or why not?
- If you play tag with *gusto,* would you smile or frown?
- If you *prepare* to plant some seeds, what do you think you need?
- Is it nice to get a hug if you feel *lonely*? Why or why not?
- Does someone need to *remind* you how to tie your shoes? Why or why not?
- Imagine you are *preoccupied* with drawing. Would you want to stop?

VOCABULARY
Student-Friendly Explanations

feast   A feast is a big meal with lots of kinds of different foods.

gusto   When you do something with gusto, you do it with energy and excitement

prepare   When you prepare for something, you get ready to do it.

lonely   When you are lonely, you are sad because you feel like you are all by yourself.

remind   When you remind someone of something, you make them remember it.

preoccupied   When you are preoccupied, you are always thinking about something else.

RETEACH
Writing

 Captions   Remind children that a caption tells about a picture. It is usually written below the picture. Show children a picture, such as *Photo Card helicopter*.

Tell children that together you will write a caption for the picture. Ask them to name words that tell about a helicopter. Record their ideas on chart paper. Then use children's ideas to write a caption about the helicopter picture. Invite them to write letters and words they know. Read the finished caption to the children.

Grade K   **47**

LESSON 4

DAY AT A GLANCE — Day 5

PHONEMIC AWARENESS
Rhyming Words

PHONICS
Preteach Consonant *Cc*

HIGH-FREQUENCY WORDS
Preteach *go*

BUILD ROBUST VOCABULARY
Reteach *appetite, savor, urgency*

Materials Needed:

Photo Cards   Sound/Spelling Card *Cc*   Write-On/Wipe-Off Boards

Practice Book

Phonemic Awareness

 Rhyming Words Tell children that words that sound the same at the end are rhyming words. Display *Photo Cards pan* and *van*. Say: **Listen to the two words: *pan, van*. I hear the same sound at the end of each word—/an/. That's how I know that the words rhyme.** Tell children that you are going to say two words. Have them listen to see if the two words sound the same at the end. Tell them to clap if the two words rhyme. You may wish to segment the beginning and ending sounds to make it easier for children to discriminate.

ran / fan	let / get	dog / frog
bar / bed	shed / shell	van / tan
frown / gown	torn / toad	jump / plump

PRETEACH
Phonics

 Consonant *Cc* Display *Sound/Spelling Card Cc*. Say: **This is the letter *c*. Say the name with me.** Point to uppercase *C* and say: **This is uppercase *C*.** Point to lowercase *c* and say: **This is lowercase *c*.** Have children identify the letters. (C, c)

Writing *C* and *c* Write *C* and *c* on the board and have children identify the letters. Say: **Watch as I write the letter *C*.** As you give the Letter Talk, trace the uppercase *C*. Do the same for lowercase *c*.

Letter Talk for *C*	**Letter Talk for *c***
1. Curve left, down, and around.	1. Curve left, down, and around.
2. Go to the bottom of the line and curve up.	2. Go to the bottom of the line and curve up.

 Have children finger-write the uppercase *C* in the air as you repeat the Letter Talk. Have them do the same for lowercase *c*. Have them practice writing uppercase *C* and then lowercase *c* several times on their *Write-on/Wipe-off Boards*.

 Have children turn to *Practice Book* page 25. Help children circle each uppercase *C* and underline each lowercase *c*. Have them trace the letters and write them on the lines.

Day 5

PRETEACH
High-Frequency Words

Write the high-frequency word *go* on the board and on an index card. Point to and read *go* on the board. Have children say it with you. Say: **I go to the park.** Display the index card. Say: **Go.** Match the index card to the word on the board, say the word, and have children say it with you.

Display *Photo Cards* *hill, igloo, ladder,* and *taxi*. Point to the word *go* and the picture *hill* and say: **I go to the hill.** Have the children repeat the sentence after you. Continue creating similar sentences with the *Photo Cards igloo, ladder,* and *taxi*. Have children repeat after you.

Write *go* on index cards, one for each child. Distribute the cards to children. Say the word, and have children point to the word and read it. Then write the high-frequency words *the* and *I* on index cards for your use. Tell children that you will show them words, and when they see *go,* they should say the word and point to it on their card. Hold up the index cards for *go, the,* and *I* in random order until children can consistently identify the word *go*. Save the index cards for use in Lesson 5.

PRETEACH
Build Robust Vocabulary

Introduce the Student-Friendly Explanations of *appetite, savor,* and *urgency*. Then discuss each word by asking the questions listed below.

appetite
If a dog has an *appetite*, does it want to eat right now or later?
What time of day do you have a big *appetite*? Why?

savor
What foods do you *savor* in the summertime? What foods do you *savor* in the winter?

urgency
Do you feel an *urgency* to come inside when it's cold and raining? Why or why not?

High-Frequency Words

go   I

the

VOCABULARY
Student-Friendly Explanations

appetite You have an appetite when you are hungry.

savor You savor something that you really enjoy and want to last for a long time.

urgency If you need to do something with urgency, you need to do it right away.

Grade K 49

LESSON 5

PHONEMIC AWARENESS
Rhyming Words

PHONICS
Preteach Relate *Cc* to /k/

HIGH-FREQUENCY WORDS
Reteach *go*

COMPREHENSION
Preteach Characters

BUILD ROBUST VOCABULARY
Reteach *appetite, savor, urgency*

Materials Needed:

Phoneme Phone

Sound/Spelling Card *Cc*

Word Builder and Word Builder Cards

Photo Cards

Copying Master

Practice Book

Phonemic Awareness

Rhyming Words Remind children that words that sound the same at the end are rhyming words. Say: **Listen to these two words: *sun, fun*. I hear the same sound at the end of each word—/un/. That's how I know that the words rhyme.** Have children repeat the words into their *Phoneme Phones*. Then say the word pairs below. Have children listen to see if the two words sound the same at the end. Tell them to stand if the two words rhyme.

    ran / fan   let / get   bar / bed

PRETEACH

Phonics

Relate *Cc* to /k/ Say the words *cat* and *coat* and have children repeat the words. Tell them that *cat* and *coat* begin with /k/. Have children say /k/ several times.

 Connect Letter and Sound Display *Sound/Spelling Card Cc*. Ask: **What is the name of this letter? The letter *c* can stand for /k/, the sound at the beginning of *cape*. Say /k/.** Have children repeat the sound as you touch the letter on the card several times.

Discriminate /k/ Give each child *Word Builder Card c*. Say: **If the word begins with /k/ hold up the card and say /k/. If the word does not begin with /k/, hold your card against your chest.** Say the words *cup, bread, fire, candy, cape,* and *cuddle.*

 Identify Beginning Sound Display the *Sound-Spelling Card Cc* and *Photo Cards cat, pig,* and *cow*. Say: **I am going to name some pictures. If the picture name begins with /k/, hold up your hand.** Model the activity using the words *cat, pig,* and *cow*.

Say: **Now I'm going to name some words. If the words begin with /k/, then say /k/.** Read the following words:

    table   run   cape   case

 Distribute *Copying Master 9*. Have children trace the letter *Cc*. Then have children identify each picture and circle the beginning letter of the picture name. (Children should circle letter *c* for *cow, cat, comb, cap, car.*)

50 Lesson 5

Day 1

RETEACH

High-Frequency Words

Write *go* on the board. Point to and read the word. Have children say it with you. Say: **I go to the zoo.** Display the index card for *go* from Day 5 of Lesson 4. Say: **Go.** Match the index card to the word on the board, say the word, and have children say it with you.

Display the words *go, I, a,* and *my* on separate pieces of chart paper. Use your index card for *go,* and create index cards for *a, I,* and *my.* Tell children that you will show them words. They should say the word and stand next to the matching word written on chart paper.

High-Frequency Words	
a	I
go	my

PRETEACH

Comprehension

  Characters Explain to children that the characters in a story are the people or animals that the story is about. Then read this story aloud to them.

Once there was an owl who lived in a tree. Owl was lonely and wanted a friend.

Fish came by, but she wanted to live in the water. The tree wasn't wet enough.

Worm came by, but he wanted to live in the ground. The tree wasn't dirty enough.

Then another owl flew by. She landed on the branch. She could see the whole forest. It was just right.

"Yay," said the first owl. "Now I have a friend!"

Guide children to turn to page 26 in their *Practice Books*. Have them look at the pictures as you ask them to point to and name the animals in the story. Have children use the pictures to retell the story.

PRETEACH

Build Robust Vocabulary

Read Student-Friendly Explanations for *appetite, savor,* and *urgency*. Then discuss each word, using the following examples.

appetite
Do you have a big *appetite* before you eat or after you eat? Why?

savor
Do you *savor* the same kinds of food as a bird? Why or why not?

urgency
If you hear a fire alarm at school, do you move slowly or with *urgency*? Why or why not?

VOCABULARY

Student-Friendly Explanations

appetite You have an appetite when you are hungry.

savor You savor something that you really enjoy and want to last for a long time.

urgency If you need to do something with urgency, you need to do it right away.

Grade K 51

LESSON 5

DAY AT A GLANCE
Day 2

PHONEMIC AWARENESS
Rhyming Words

PHONICS
Reteach /k/c, /n/n

HIGH-FREQUENCY WORDS
Reteach go

COMPREHENSION
Preteach Answer Questions

BUILD ROBUST VOCABULARY
Reteach aroma, surround, tradition

Materials Needed:

Phoneme Phone | Sound/Spelling Cards Cc, Nn | Sounds of Letters CD

Photo Cards | Word Builder and Word Builder Cards | Copying Master

Practice Book

Phonemic Awareness

Rhyming Words Remind children that words that sound the same at the end are rhyming words. Say: **Listen as I say two words: road, toad. The word toad rhymes with road. I hear the same sound at the end of each word—/ōd/.** Have children say the words. Explain that other words also sound the same at the end as road and toad. Say: **Listen to this word—load. The beginning sound is different, but it has the same ending sound as toad and road. Load rhymes with road and toad.** Ask children to say the words road, toad, and load with you. Segment the words as needed. Substitute other beginning sounds. Have children to say the new word and to tell whether it rhymes.

Have children sit in a circle, and distribute the *Phoneme Phones*. Say the words *can* and *tan*. Ask the children to repeat the words while looking at the position of their mouths in the mirror. Ask: **Do can and tan have the same ending sound?** (yes) **What is the ending sound?** (/an/) Repeat with these words: *hut/cut, town/gown, worn/torn, some/gum, dash/sash*.

RETEACH
Phonics

 Connect Letters and Sounds Display *Sound/Spelling Card Cc*. Ask: **What sound do you hear at the beginning of car?** /k/ **What letter stands for /k/ at the beginning of car?** (c) Display *Sound/Spelling Card Nn*. Ask: **What sound do you hear at the beginning of nine?** /n/ **What letter stands for /n/ at the beginning of nine?** (n) Then play the sound /k/ and /n/ from the *Sounds of Letters CD*, and have the children repeat the sounds.

 Discriminate /k/ and /n/ Display *Photo Cards cat, cow,* and *nest*. Tell children that they are going to sort the cards by their beginning sounds. Have children say each picture name and place the card beside the *Sound/Spelling Card* that stands for the sound at the beginning of its name.

  Identify /k/ and /n/ Give each child *Word Builder Cards c* and *n*. Tell children that you are going to say some words. Have children listen for the sound at the beginning of each word. Have children hold up the appropriate *Word Builder Card* and say its sound.

      cab   no   nine   coat   cart

Distribute *Copying Master 10*. Have children trace the letter *Cc*. Then identify the pictures with the children. Have them write the beginning letter of the picture name. (Children should write letter *c* for *car, crayon, camel*; letter *n* for *nail, nose*.)

Day 2

RETEACH
High-Frequency Words

  On the board, write the sentence *I go*. Point to each word as you read the sentence. Identify the period. Then reread the sentence with children.

Prepare index cards for the words *The, can, go,* and a period, and *Photo Card ant*. Use the cards to create the sentence frame *The _____ can go*. Complete the sentence with *Photo Card ant*. Read the sentence aloud twice. Then have children say *go* and point to it. Repeat the activity with other *Photo Cards*, such as *truck, zebra,* or *dog*.

Have children turn to *Practice Book* page 27 to review high-frequency words and practice newly learned words. Complete the page together.

High-Frequency Words

a	I
can	my
go	the

PRETEACH
Comprehension

Answer Questions Explain to children that answering questions when they read will help them understand what they read. Remind children that all stories have characters, or the people and animals that the story is about. Create a chart with the headings: *Question* and *Answer*. Recall the story about the owl from Day 1. Reread the story and pause to ask and record questions about each character. As children respond, record their responses on the chart under the *Answer* heading.

Question	Answer
What does Owl want?	He wants a friend.
What does Fish want?	He wants to live in the water.

RETEACH
Build Robust Vocabulary

Recall the Student-Friendly Explanations for *aroma, surround,* and *tradition*. Then discuss each word, using the following examples.

aroma
Which do you like better—the *aroma* of a fresh orange or the *aroma* of a chopped onion? Why?

surround
What might *surround* a polar bear in the winter? Why do you think so?

tradition
What is a bedtime *tradition* in your family?

VOCABULARY
Student-Friendly Explanations

aroma If something has an aroma, it has a good smell.

surround If something surrounds you, it is on all sides of you.

tradition A tradition is a special way of doing things that a family or group has done for a long time.

Grade K 53

LESSON 5

DAY AT A GLANCE — Day 3

PHONEMIC AWARENESS
Rhyming Words

PHONICS
Reteach /k/c, /p/p

HIGH-FREQUENCY WORDS
Reteach go

COMPREHENSION
Reteach Characters

BUILD ROBUST VOCABULARY
Reteach aroma, surround, tradition

WRITING
Reteach Writing Trait: Conventions

Materials Needed:

Sound/Spelling Cards Cc, Pp   Photo Cards   Word Builder and Word Builder Cards

Practice Book

Phonemic Awareness

Rhyming Words Ask children what we call words that have the same ending sound. (rhyming words) Say: **Listen to these two words: *fun, sun*. I hear the same sound at the end of each word. That means that they rhyme. Listen to this word—*bun*. The sound at the beginning of the word is different, but it has the same sound at the end.** *Bun* **rhymes with** *fun* **and** *sun*.

Tell children that you are going to say two words. Tell them to stand if the two words rhyme. Segment the beginning and ending sounds as needed. Help children name additional words in the same rhyming family.

an / in	good / wood	week / cheek
for / far	side / wide	dog / top
fur / purr	beg / bet	seal / meal
slam / sled	dream / read	hint / mint

RETEACH

Phonics

 Connect Letters and Sounds Display *Sound/Spelling Card Cc*. Ask: **What sound do you hear at the beginning of *cap*? What letter stands for /k/ at the beginning of *cap*?** Display *Sound/Spelling Card Pp*. Ask: **What sound do you hear at the beginning of *pencil*? What letter stands for /p/ at the beginning of *pencil*?**

 Discriminate /k/ and /p/ Display *Photo Cards cat, cow, pan, pencil,* and *pig* in random order. Tell children that they are going to sort the cards by their beginning sounds. Have children say each picture name and place the card beside the *Sound/Spelling Card* that stands for the sound at the beginning of its name.

Identify /k/ and /p/ Give each child *Word Builder Cards c* and *p*. Tell children that you are going to say some words. Have children listen for the sound at the beginning of each word. If the word starts with /k/, children should hold up alphabet card *c* and say /k/. If the word starts with /p/, children should hold up *Word Builder Card p* and say /p/.

| cop | carrot | pan | pillow |
| catch | pickle | camping | penguin |

Day 3

RETEACH

High-Frequency Words

 On the board, write the sentence *I go.* Point to each word as you read the sentence. Identify the period. Then reread the sentence with children.

Invite children to name some ways they can go—for example, *slow, fast, up,* or *down*. Have children act out those actions. Distribute index cards with the word *go* to children. Have them trace the word with a finger and repeat after you as they say the word.

Display *Photo Cards cat, ant, fish, frog, kangaroo, octopus,* and *rabbit*. Have each child select a picture and say that picture name. Then have children take turns saying *I go*, and following it with an example of how that animal or insect moves.

High-Frequency Words	
I	go

Grade K 55

Day 3

RETEACH
Comprehension

  Characters Remind children that the characters in a story are the people or animals that the story is about. Have children listen as you read aloud the following story.

> Ben and his dad went on a hike in the woods. Ben wanted to see animals. He saw trees and leaves, but he didn't see an animal. His dad said, "The animals are hiding. Squirrels hide in the trees. Mice hide in holes in old logs."
>
> Ben looked at the side of a tree. He saw scratches on the trunk. His dad said, "A deer was here. He scratched his antlers on the tree."
>
> Ben looked for more clues. He saw a nest in a tree. "This is fun," he said. "I can't see an animal, but I can see where they've been."
>
> Then a chipmunk ran across the trail. "Look! There's an animal! I just needed to be quiet and patient." Ben said.

Guide children to *Practice Book* page 28. Have children use the pictures to retell the story. Ask: **Who are the characters?** (Ben and his dad) **What are they doing?** (They are looking for animals in the woods.)

RETEACH
Build Robust Vocabulary

Read the Student-Friendly Explanations, and remind children of the meanings of *aroma, surround,* and *tradition.* Then discuss each word, using the following examples.

aroma
Do you think a flower store might have a nice *aroma*? Why or why not?

surround
Name three things you like to *surround* yourself with when you take a nap.

tradition
Name or sing a song that is a *tradition* in your family. Why do you like the song? When do you sing it?

VOCABULARY
Student-Friendly Explanations

aroma If something has an aroma, it has a good smell.

surround If something surrounds you, it is on all sides of you.

tradition A tradition is a special way of doing things that a family or group has done for a long time.

Day 3

RETEACH

Writing

Writing Trait: Conventions Remind children that when they write a sentence, the first word should always start with an uppercase letter. Have a volunteer write an uppercase letter on the board. Point out that a period usually comes at the end of a sentence. Have a volunteer write a period on the board. Then write the following sentences on the board. Read each sentence while tracking the print.

> the girls swim in the pool
> The girls swim in the pool.

Ask: **Which sentence begins with an uppercase letter?** (the second sentence) **Point to and name the word with the uppercase letter.** (Children should point to and read the high-frequency word *The.*) **Which sentence ends in a period? Point to the period.** (The second sentence; children should point to and name the period.) Point out how the second sentence is complete because it begins with an uppercase letter and ends with a period.

Write the following sentences on the board and repeat. Ask children to name which sentence begins with an uppercase letter and ends with a period. (Children should identify the first sentence.) Then have a volunteer add an uppercase letter and a period to the second sentence to correct it.

> They splash in the water.
> they splash in the water

Grade K 57

LESSON 5

DAY AT A GLANCE — Day 4

PHONEMIC AWARENESS
Rhyming Words

PHONICS
Reteach /k/c, /n/n, /p/p

READING
Review /k/c, /n/n, /p/p
Review High-Frequency Words

BUILD ROBUST VOCABULARY
Review appetite, savor, urgency, aroma, surround, tradition

WRITING
Reteach Writing Form: Sentences

Materials Needed:

Phoneme Phone | Sound/Spelling Cards Cc, Nn, Pp | Sounds of Letters CD

Photo Cards | Practice Book

Phonemic Awareness

Rhyming Words Remind children that words that sound the same at the end are rhyming words. Say: **I am going to say the name of a boy: Bill. Now I am going to change the beginning sound of the name. Listen: /w/ -ill. Will rhymes with Bill.**

Have children sit in a circle, and distribute the *Phoneme Phones*. Say the words *Jim* and *him*. Ask the children to repeat the words while looking at the position of their mouths in the mirror. Ask: **Do Jim and him have the same ending sound?** (yes) **What is the ending sound?** (/im/) Repeat with these names and word pairs, having children identify the word that rhymes with each of the names shown below:

Pete: *peel/meat*   Lin: *win/won*
Dan: *man/dab*   Carey: *cart/marry*

RETEACH
Phonics

 Connect Letters and Sounds Display *Sound/Spelling Card Cc*. Ask: **What sound do you hear at the beginning of cap? What letter stands for /k/ at the beginning of cap?** Repeat the procedure with *Sound/Spelling Cards Nn* and *Pp*.

Distribute *Phoneme Phones* to the group. Play the sounds /k/, /n/, and /p/ from the *Sounds of Letters* CD. Have children listen carefully as each sound is spoken. Have children repeat the sound they hear into their *Phoneme Phone*. Encourage children to note the position of their mouths as they repeat each sound into their phone.

 Discriminate /k/, /n/, and /p/ Pass out the *Photo Cards cat, cow, nest, pencil, pan,* and *pig*. Display the *Sound/Spelling Cards* for *Cc, Nn,* and *Pp* in an accessible location. Tell children that they will place the *Photo Cards* in a pile near the correct *Sound/Spelling Card* letter. Have children first show their *Photo Card*, say the name of the picture, and then place the card beneath or near the letter that stands for the sound at the beginning of its name.

Day 4

REVIEW
Reading

 /k/c, /n/n, /p/p Write the letters *c*, *n*, and *p* on the board. Point to a letter and have children identify the letter and its sound.

High-Frequency Words Distribute index cards for *I*, *my*, *the*, *a*, and *go*. Have a volunteer show a card. Read the word on the card with children. Have children find the card in their pile and add it to the discard pile. Then have the next child choose a word to show and read. Continue until all the cards have been read.

Have children turn to *Practice Book* pages 29–30. Have children read the sentences as a take-home book to practice the newly learned words.

REVIEW
Robust Vocabulary

Remind children of the Student-Friendly Explanations for *appetite*, *savor*, *urgency*, *aroma*, *surround*, and *tradition*. Then determine children's understanding of the words by asking the following questions.

- If you smelled a good *aroma*, how might that change your *appetite*?
- What is your favorite fruit to *savor*? Why?
- What do you need to do with *urgency*: answer a phone or read a book?
- What might *surround* you at the beach?
- How do you celebrate the *tradition* of Thanksgiving?

RETEACH
Writing

 Writing Form: Sentences Remind children that a sentence is a group of words that tells about something. Discuss how a sentence begins with an uppercase letter and often ends with a period. Show children pictures, such as *Photo Card girl* and *boy*.

Tell children that together you will write sentences. Ask them to dictate words about the pictures. Record their ideas on chart paper. Then use children's ideas to write sentences. Invite children to add letters and words they know, and correct punctuation. Read the finished sentences to children.

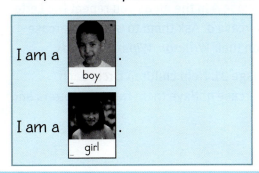

High-Frequency Words

a	my
go	the
I	

VOCABULARY
Student-Friendly Explanations

appetite You have an appetite when you are hungry.

savor You savor something that you really enjoy and want to last for a long time.

urgency If you do something with urgency, you need to do it right away.

aroma If something has an aroma, it has a good smell.

surround If something surrounds you, it is on all sides of you.

tradition A tradition is a special way of doing things that a family or group has done for a long time.

Grade K 59

LESSON 5

PHONEMIC AWARENESS
Alliteration

PHONICS
Preteach Short Vowel /a/a

HIGH-FREQUENCY WORDS
Review *I, a, go*

BUILD ROBUST VOCABULARY
Review *feast, appetite, aroma*

Materials Needed:

Sound/Spelling Card *Aa*   Write-On/Wipe-Off Boards   Practice Book

Phonemic Awareness

Alliteration   Remind children they have been learning about the sounds at the beginning of words. Explain that now they will listen for the same beginning sound in three words. Model for children how to tell whether the words all have the same beginning sounds. Say: **I am going to say three words:** *five, fun, fish.* **I hear the same sound at the beginning of** *five, fun, fish. Five, fun,* **and** *fish* **all begin with /f/. Listen: /f/ /ive/, /f/ /un/, /f/ /ish/.**

Tell children that you are going to say three words. Have them clap if all three words begin with the same sound. If children need additional help, suggest that children listen to only two words at a time. Then repeat the groups of words together.

two tiny turtles   big warm house
many mighty mice   cute cuddly cat
striped sleeping tiger   nine new neckties

PRETEACH

Phonics

Short Vowel /a/a   Display *Sound/Spelling Card Aa*. Say: **This is the letter** *a***. Say the name with me.** Point to uppercase *A* and say: **This is uppercase** *A***.** Point to lowercase *a* and say: **This is lowercase** *a***.** Have children identify the letters. (A, a)

Writing *A* and *a*   Write *A* and *a* on the board and have children identify the letters. Say: **Watch as I write the letter** *A* **so that everyone can read it.** As you give the Letter Talk, trace the uppercase *A*. Do the same for lowercase *a*.

Letter Talk for *A*	Letter Talk for *a*
1. Slant left.	1. Circle left.
2. Slant right.	2. Come around, up, and then
3. Straight across.	straight down.

Tell children to finger-write the uppercase *A* in the air as you repeat the Letter Talk. Have them do the same for lowercase *a*. Ask them to write uppercase *A* and then lowercase *a* several times on their *Write-on/Wipe-off Boards*.

Have children turn to *Practice Book* page 31. Help children circle each uppercase *A* and underline each lowercase *a*. Have them trace the letters and write them on the lines.

Day 5

REVIEW

High-Frequency Words

Write the words *I, a,* and *go* on the board and on separate index cards. Point to and read the words on the board. Have children say them with you. Point to yourself and say: ***I** am happy.* ***I** **go** to **a** park.* Display the index cards. Point to and say each word in turn. Then match the index cards to the words on the board. Say the words and have children say them with you. Match each index card to a word on the board, say the word, and have children say it with you.

Make and distribute index cards for the words *I, a,* and *go.* Have children find the word *I.* Have children point to the word and read it. Tell children that you will show them words and when they see *I,* they should say the word and point to it on their card. Hold up your set of index cards for *I, a,* and *go* until children consistently identify the word *I.* Then repeat the process with your index cards for *a* and *go.* Retrieve the index cards for use in Lesson 6.

High-Frequency Words

a	go
I	

REVIEW

Build Robust Vocabulary

Remind children of the Student-Friendly Explanations of *feast, appetite,* and *aroma.* Then discuss each word, using the following examples.

feast
If your family was having a *feast,* would you meet in the dining room or the bedroom? Tell why.

appetite
Do you have an *appetite* when you wake in the morning or after you eat breakfast? Why?

aroma
What might have an *aroma*: soup that is cooking in a pot or new pots for sale in a store? Why do you think so?

VOCABULARY
Student-Friendly Explanations

feast A feast is a big meal with lots of different kinds of foods.

appetite You have an appetite when you are hungry.

aroma If something has an aroma, it has a good smell.

Grade K 61

LESSON 6

PHONEMIC AWARENESS
Alliteration

PHONICS
Preteach Relate *Aa* to /a/

HIGH-FREQUENCY WORDS
Review *a, I, go*

COMPREHENSION
Review Make Predictions

BUILD ROBUST VOCABULARY
Review *prepare, urgency, lonely*

Materials Needed:

Sound/Spelling Card *Aa*   Word Builder and Word Builder Cards

Copying Master   Photo Cards   Practice Book

Phonemic Awareness

Alliteration Remind children that they have been listening for the same beginning sound in groups of words. Tell them that today they will listen for the same beginning sound in words that make sentences. Say: **Listen to this sentence:** *Big bunnies bounce.* **I hear /b/ at the beginning of each word in the sentence. Listen:** /b/ ig, /b/ unnies, /b/ ounce.

Have children say *yes* if all three words in the sentence begin with the same sound.

Henry has hamsters.	Paula likes oranges.
Catch the dog.	Wally watches whales.
Mice move meekly.	Draw a cat.
Lori laughs loudly.	Carry cakes carefully.

PRETEACH

Phonics

 Relate *Aa* to /a/ Display *Sound/Spelling Card Aa*. Ask: **What is the name of this letter?** (a) **The letter *a* can sometimes stand for /a/, the sound at the beginning of *alligator*.** Say /a/. Have children repeat the sound as you touch the letter on the card several times.

Discriminate /a/ Give each child *Word Builder Card a*. Say: **If the word begins with /a/, hold up the card and say /a/. If the word does not begin with /a/, put the card face-down.** Say the words *at, am, when, animal,* and *only.*

Tell children that /a/ can also come in the middle of some words, such as in *mad*. Follow the same procedure for the medial position. Use the words *can, van, get, log, cat,* and *family*. Then have children tell whether /a/ is in the beginning or middle of these words: *after, lap, brand, ask, camp,* and *sand.*

Distribute *Copying Master 11*. Have children trace the letter *A* or *a*. Then have children look at each picture and circle the letter that stands for the beginning sound of each picture name. (Circle letter *a* for *apples, ax, alligator*; circle letter *c* for *camel, cow.*)

62 Lesson 6

Day 1

REVIEW

High-Frequency Words

 Create or retrieve index cards with the words *I, a, go, can,* and a period. Use these index cards with *Photo Card rabbit* to build the following sentence:

| A | rabbit | can | go | . |

High-Frequency Words

a   I

go

REVIEW

Comprehension

  Make Predictions Remind children that they can make a prediction, or guess, about story events to help them understand and enjoy a story more. Read the story aloud:

> Jason wanted to make bread. He got out a cookbook in his kitchen. "It's too much trouble to read," he said. "I'll make it up as I go along."
>
> First, Jason added yeast to the water. Then he added some flour and let it rise. He pounded down the flour and added more water and flour.
>
> "Hmmm," he said. "I'm not sure that's going to be enough bread." He added more flour and more water. He poured it into the pan until it was at the top. Then he put the pan in the oven.
>
> When the bread was ready, he looked inside. "Oh, no," he said. "It looks like it's going to be too big for the pan!"

Confirm children's predictions about the story. Guide them to *Practice Book* page 32. Have them look at the pictures and circle what might happen next, recalling clues from the story.

REVIEW

Build Robust Vocabulary

Remind children of the Student-Friendly Explanations for *prepare, urgency,* and *lonely*. Then discuss each word, using the following examples.

prepare
Tell how you would *prepare* a peanut butter and jelly sandwich.

urgency
If you want to catch up with a friend, do you move with *urgency*? Why?

lonely
If you were feeling *lonely*, would you go and play with your friend or read a book? Why?

VOCABULARY

Student-Friendly Explanations

prepare When you prepare for something, you get ready to do it.

urgency If you do something with urgency, you need to do it right away.

lonely When you are lonely, you are sad because you feel like you are all by yourself.

Grade K 63

LESSON 6

DAY 2 — DAY AT A GLANCE

PHONEMIC AWARENESS
Alliteration

PHONICS
Reteach Blending /a/*a*, /t/*t*

HIGH-FREQUENCY WORDS
Review *my, the*

COMPREHENSION
Preteach Use Story Structure

BUILD ROBUST VOCABULARY
Review *gusto, surround, remind*

Materials Needed:

Word Builder and Word Builder Cards

Copying Master

Practice Book

Phonemic Awareness

Alliteration Remind children that they have been listening for sounds at the beginning of words. Tell them that they will listen for the same beginning sound in words that make sentences. Say: **Listen to this sentence:** *Laura likes lemons.* **I hear /l/ at the beginning of each word in the sentence. Listen: /L/ aura, /l/ ikes, /l/ emons.**

Say each sentence below. Have children raise their hand if all three words in the sentence begin with the same sound. Segment the initial sounds of words as needed.

Marvin mixes mud.	Jenny jumps joyfully.
George runs quickly.	Six sisters sit.
Lions like lollipops.	Bears burst balloons.

RETEACH
Phonics

Blending /a/*a*, /t/*t* Meet with children in a circle. As you read the following verse, have children echo you. Establish a rhythm and keep it going throughout the verse.

> We're going on a word hunt.
> What's this word?
> /c/ /a/ /t/
> Together say: cat!

Continue with the sounds /t/ /a/ /n/, (*tan*); /t/ /a/ /g*, (*tag*); /r/ /a/ /t/, (*rat*).

Word Blending Display the *Word Builder Cards a* and *t*, separated from each other. Point to each letter, and ask children to name it with you. Point to *a*. Say: **/a/**. Have children repeat the sound after you. Point to *t*. Say: **/t/**. Have children repeat the sound after you. Slide the *t* next to the *a*. Move your hand left-to-right under the letters and blend the sounds, elongating them: **/aat/**. Have children repeat after you. Model reading *at*. Then have children blend and read the word *at* with you. Write the word *at* on the board, and have children read it.

Distribute *Copying Master 12* for blending words with *a* and *t*. Have children trace each letter. Then have them name the picture and draw a line from the picture to the picture name. (Children draw line from dot by picture of sat to dot by word *sat*; children draw line from dot by picture of cat to dot by word *cat*.)

64 Lesson 6

Day 2

REVIEW
High-Frequency Words

 Practice Book 33 Distribute an index card with the word *the* to each child. Read the word aloud, then have children point to the word and read it aloud. Tell children that you will show them words and when they see *the*, they should hold up their word card and say *the*. Hold up index cards with the words *the, I, a,* and *my* until children consistently identify the word *the*. Repeat with the word *my*.

Have children turn to *Practice Book* page 33 to review high-frequency words and practice newly-learned words. Complete the page together.

High-Frequency Words
my   the

PRETEACH
Comprehension

Use Story Structure Remind children that they heard a story called "Too Much Bread." Read the story again. Help children identify details about the story, such as the characters. Begin a Story Map like the one shown below by writing the characters' names in the "who" box.

Who the story is about:	Where the story takes place:
Jason	Jason's kitchen
Story Events	
First: Jason wants to make bread without a recipe.	
Next: He keeps adding flour and water to the mix.	
Last: The bread becomes too big in the oven.	

Read the story again. Pause occasionally to fill in the chart. Discuss how remembering story details can help readers understand what is happening in a story.

REVIEW
Build Robust Vocabulary

Remind children of the Student-Friendly Explanations for *gusto, surround,* and *remind*. Discuss each word, using the following examples.

gusto
When you do something with *gusto*, are you tired or excited? Why do you think so?

surround
What *surrounds* you in your classroom? Explain.

remind
Does someone need to *remind* you of your birthday? Why or why not?

VOCABULARY
Student-Friendly Explanations

gusto When you do something with gusto, you do it with energy and excitement.

surround If something surrounds you, it is on all sides of you.

remind When you remind someone of something, you make them remember it.

Grade K

LESSON 6

PHONEMIC AWARENESS
Alliteration

PHONICS
Reteach Word Blending and Building

HIGH-FREQUENCY WORDS
Review *the, my*

COMPREHENSION
Review Make Predictions

BUILD ROBUST VOCABULARY
Review *savor, tradition, preoccupied*

WRITING
Reteach Writing Trait: Ideas

Materials Needed:

Word Builder and Word Builder Cards

Photo Cards

Practice Book

Phonemic Awareness

Alliteration Remind children they have been listening for the sounds at the beginning of words. Ask them to listen for the same beginning sound in three words. Say: **I am going to say three words:** *go, get, Gail.* **I hear the same sound at the beginning of** *go, get,* **and** *Gail. Go, get,* **and** *Gail* **all begin with the /g/ sound. Listen: /g/ o, /g/ et, /G/ ail.**

Tell children that you are going to say three words. Have them raise their hands if each word begins with the same sound. You may wish to segment the initial sound of each word if children need additional help.

dogs dig dirt	**one gray whale**
seven silly songs	**Hank has hens**

Word Segmentation Remind children that sentences are groups of words that tell about something. Sentences can be broken up into words. Model for children how to track words in spoken sentences and divide spoken sentences into words. Say: **I'm going to say a sentence:** *I see my kitten.* **Now I'm going to clap for each word as I say the sentence again.** *I . . . see . . . my . . . kitten.* Say the following sentences for children. Have them track the spoken words by clapping for each one.

Take out the trash.	**Play hopscotch with me.**
Cars stops at the light.	**Where is the library?**

RETEACH

Phonics

Word Blending and Building Distribute *Word Builders* and *Word Builder Cards m, a, p, c, t,* and *r.* As you place the *Word Builder Cards* into the *Word Builder,* tell children to place the same *Word Builder Cards* in their *Word Builder.*

Place the letters *m, a,* and *p* in the Word Builder with spaces between the letters. Point to *m.* Say: **/m/.** Have children repeat. Point to *a.* Say: **/a/.** Have children repeat. Slide *a* next to *m.* Slide your hand under *ma* and blend by elongating the sounds: **/maa/.** Have children do the same. Point to *p.* Say: **/p/.** Have children repeat. Slide *p* next to *ma.* Slide your hand under *map* and blend: **/maap/.** Have children do the same. Say *map* naturally. Have children repeat.

Build Words Have children build the word *pat* in their Word Builder as you build it in yours. Read the word and the write it on the board. Continue by saying:

- Change *p* to *c.* What word did you make? *(cat)*
- Change *c* to *r.* What word did you make? *(rat)*

66 Lesson 6

Day 3

REVIEW

High-Frequency Words

High-Frequency Words
my   the

Display an index card with the word *the* and *Photo Card pencil* to build the phrase *the [Photo Card pencil]*. Hold up a pencil and read the phrase as you track the print. Then have children read the phrase with you. Repeat the steps using the word *my,* and point to yourself and the pencil, as you say *my [Photo Card pencil]*.

Continue with the following phrases, using *Photo Cards hammer* and *elbow.*

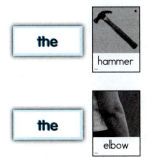

Point to each word as children read the phrases with you. Continue with other *Photo Cards* to build and read more phrases.

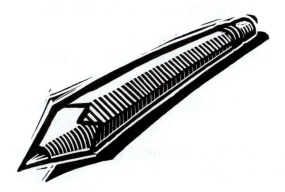

Grade K   67

Day 3

REVIEW
Comprehension

  Make Predictions Remind children that they can use clues in the words and pictures to make a prediction, or guess, about what might happen next in a story. Ask children to listen as you read aloud the beginning of a story.

> Vince and Harry wanted to race their toy cars. They made a ramp for the cars to go down. Vince thought that his car would win. "My car's bigger than your car," he said.
>
> Harry thought that his car would win. "My car's got more wheels than your car," he said. "It's got 10 wheels!"
>
> Then Teddy, Harry's younger brother, wanted to be in the race, too. He had a small car with four wheels. "Sure, you can race us, too," they said.

Discuss the story with children. Ask: **Who is the story about?** (Harry, Vince, and Teddy) **What do the boys want to do?** (They want to race their cars.) **What did you think would happen after Teddy asked to join the race?** (Possible response: I thought the boys would say yes.) **What clues helped you make that guess?** (Possible response: Each boy thinks he will win. The boys probably think they'll beat Teddy, too.)

Guide children to *Practice Book* page 34. Have children circle what they think might happen next in the story. Discuss the clues that helped them make their prediction.

REVIEW
Build Robust Vocabulary

Remind children of the Student-Friendly Explanations for *savor*, *tradition*, and *preoccupied*. Then discuss each word, using the following examples.

savor
Tell about a food that you *savor*. When did you last have it?

tradition
Name a *tradition* that your family has on a special holiday.

preoccupied
If you are *preoccupied* at school, might you be eating a snack or thinking about going home? Explain.

VOCABULARY
Student-Friendly Explanations

savor You savor something that you really enjoy and want to last for a long time.

tradition A tradition is a special way of doing things that a family or group has done for a long time.

preoccupied When you are preoccupied, you are always thinking about something else.

RETEACH

Writing

Writing Trait: Ideas Tell children that people get ideas for writing all around them. People make lists, draw pictures, and even talk to their friends to help them brainstorm ideas. Ask children to help you brainstorm a list of topics they would like to write about. Record children's ideas on chart paper.

> What We Can Write About
>
> dinosaurs
> foods
> dancers
> school

Read the list of ideas to children. Point out that brainstorming ideas helps a writer think about many different topics.

LESSON 6

PHONEMIC AWARENESS
Alliteration

PHONICS
Reteach Review /a/*a*

READING
Review /a/*a*
Review High-Frequency Words

BUILD ROBUST VOCABULARY
Review *gusto, perfectly, feast, tradition, prepare, talent, mellow, savor*

WRITING
Reteach Writing Form: News

Materials Needed:

Word Builder and Word Builder Cards

Practice Book pp. 35–36

Phonemic Awareness

Alliteration Remind children that they have been listening for the same beginning sound in groups of words. Tell them that they will listen for the same beginning sound in words that make sentences. Say: **Listen to this sentence:** *Busy bees buzz.* **I hear /b/ at the beginning of each word in the sentence. Listen: /b/ usy, /b/ ees, /b/ uzz.**

Say each sentence below. Have children raise their hands if all three words in the sentence begin with the same sound. You may wish to segment the initial sounds if children need assistance.

Snakes slither quietly.	Boys buy baseballs.
Red rabbits run.	Four foxes fight.

Word Segmentation Remind children that sentences can be broken up into words. Model for children how to track words in spoken sentences and divide spoken sentences into words. Say: **Listen to this sentence:** *I knit a scarf.* **Now I'm going to clap for each word as I say the sentence again. I . . . knit . . . a . . . scarf. The words in this sentence are *I, knit, a,* and *scarf.*** Say the following sentences for children. Have them track the spoken words by clapping for each one. Provide help as children name the words in each sentence.

Kim plants the seeds.	Lucy rides the bus.
The dog runs fast.	Watch out!
Bugs live under rocks.	Crows make nests.

RETEACH

Phonics

Review /a/*a* Write the word *cat* on the board. Model blending the sounds as you run a finger under each letter. Say: **/c/ /aa/ /t/. Say it with me: /c/ /a/ /t/. Cat.** Run a finger under the letters, having children read the word.

Read Words Use the *Word Builder Cards* to make more words in the *Word Builder*. Tell children that they are going to read the words by blending the sounds for each letter. Read each word. Then have children blend the sounds with you to read the word.

70 Lesson 6

Day 4

REVIEW
Reading

/a/a Review the /a/ sound with children. Have children listen for the /a/ sound in the following words: *cat, apple, ran,* and *land*.

Practice Book 35–36

High-Frequency Words Reuse or create index cards for *I, a, my, go,* and *the*. Distribute them to children. Reserve a set for your use. Ask children to take turns holding up a card. Read the card as a group. Have children hold up the matching card. Continue until all the cards have been read. Repeat as needed.

Have children turn to *Practice Book* pages 35–36. Help children cut and fold the book, and read it together. Have children take it home to read with their families.

High-Frequency Words

a	my
go	the
I	

REVIEW
Robust Vocabulary

Remind children of the Student-Friendly Explanations of *gusto, savor, perfectly, feast, tradition, prepare, talent,* and *mellow*. Then determine children's understanding of the words by asking the following questions.

- Do you *savor* your favorite food with *gusto*? Tell why.
- If you do something *perfectly*, did you make a lot of mistakes? Tell why or why not.
- What could you do to help *prepare* a *feast* with your family?
- What story or song is a *tradition* in your family? Can you share it with us?
- If you have a *talent* for playing drums, are you good at it or just learning?
- Is reading a book a *mellow* activity? How can you tell?

VOCABULARY
Student-Friendly Explanations

gusto When you do something with gusto, you do it with energy and excitement.

savor You savor something that you really enjoy and want to last for a long time.

perfectly If you do something perfectly, you do it in just the right way.

feast A feast is a big meal with lots of different kinds of foods.

tradition A tradition is a special way of doing things that a family or group has done for a long time.

prepare When you prepare for something, you get ready to do it.

talent If you are very good at doing something, you have a talent for it.

mellow When you are mellow, you feel gentle and relaxed.

RETEACH
Writing

Writing Form: News Review what news is and why people read newspapers and magazines, or watch the news on television. Point out that news tells about real people, places, and things that happen.

Write News Tell children that they will help you write some news about their community. Invite children to brainstorm ideas about people, places, or events. Decide on some news to write together. As you write, invite children to write any letters and words they know and to write punctuation at the end of sentences. Track the print as you read aloud the news.

> A New Park
> A new park just opened.
> It is close to our school.

Grade K 71

LESSON 6

DAY AT A GLANCE
Day 5

PHONEMIC AWARENESS
Rhyme Recognition

PHONICS
Preteach Word Blending

HIGH-FREQUENCY WORDS
Preteach *to*

BUILD ROBUST VOCABULARY
Reteach *sly, proceed, apparel*

Materials Needed:

Phoneme Phone   Sound/Spelling Card *Aa, Nn*

Word Builder and Word Builder Cards   Practice Book 37

Phonemic Awareness

Rhyme Recognition Remind children that words that have the same sound at the end are rhyming words. Guide children to recognize words that rhyme. Say: **Listen to these words: *joy, toy*. The words rhyme. They have the same ending sound, /oy/. Another word that rhymes with *joy* and *toy* is *boy*. Joy, toy,* and *boy* all rhyme. A word that does not rhyme with *joy* is *Jim*. *Joy* and *Jim* do not rhyme because the sounds at the ends of the words are not the same.**

Model for children how to look at the position of their mouth in a *Phoneme Phone* while saying *joy/toy* and *joy/Jim*. Then say each pair of words: **cat/can; him/dim; state/wait; at/bat; where/what; in/bin; far/fan; snap/tap; did/dad.** Now have children use the *Phoneme Phone* to look at the position of their mouth as they repeat the words. Children should raise their hands if the words rhyme and fold their arms if the words do not rhyme.

PRETEACH
Phonics

    Sounds in a Word Ask children to sit in a circle. Sing the following verse to the tune of "Old MacDonald." Have children echo you.

What is the word for these three sounds? /t/-/a/-/n/—*tan*! With a *tan, tan* here, and a *tan, tan* there. Here a *tan*, there a *tan*, everywhere a *tan, tan*. What is the word for these three sounds? /t/-/a/-/n/—*tan*!

Continue with these words:

/r/-/a/-/t/ *(rat)*   **/s/-/a/-/p/** *(sap)*   **/m/-/a/-/p/** *(map)*

Word Blending Display *Sound/Spelling Cards Aa* and *Nn*. Point to *a*. Ask: **What letter is this?** *(a)* **The letter *a* can stand for the sound /aa/. What does *a* stand for?** *(/aa/)* Explain that *a* can stand for the sound /a/, the sound at the beginning of *and*. Point to *n*. Ask: **What letter is this?** *(n)* **The letter *n* stands for the sound /nn/. What does *n* stand for?** *(/nn/)* Explain that *n* can stand for the sound /nn/, the sound at the beginning of *nice*.

Place the *Word Builder Cards a* and *n* into the *Word Builder*. Point to *a*. Say: **/aa/.** Have children name the letter and sound. Point to *n*. Say: **/nn/.** Have children name the letter and sound. Slide the *n* next to *a*. Move your hand under the letters and blend the sounds: **/aann/.** Have children repeat after you. Then have children blend and read the word *an* with you. Continue with the words *ran, tan, can,* and *pan*.

Have children turn to *Practice Book* page 37. Help children identify the pictures. Have them trace the letter *a* in each word.

72 Lesson 6

Day 5

PRETEACH

High-Frequency Words

Write the word *to* on the board. Point to and read *to*. Have children say it with you. Say: **Let's go *to* the playground.** Display an index card with the word *to*. Say: ***to*.** Match the index card to the word on the board, say the word, and have children say it with you.

Distribute an index card with the word *to* to each child. Have children point to the word and read it. Tell children that you will show them words, and when they see *to,* they should say the word and point to it on the card. Hold up index cards with the words *a, go, I,* and *to* in random order until children consistently identify the word *to.* Save the cards for use in Lesson 7.

RETEACH

Build Robust Vocabulary

Read the Student-Friendly Explanations for *sly, proceed,* and *apparel*. Then discuss each word, using the following examples.

sly
Does a *sly* fox sneak around a henhouse or enter it quickly? Tell why.

proceed
Should a car *proceed* at a red light? Why or why not?

apparel
Can you buy new *apparel* in a food store or a clothing store?

High-Frequency Word

to

VOCABULARY
Student-Friendly Explanations

sly Someone who is sly is tricky and sneaky.

proceed When you proceed, you go ahead with what you are doing.

apparel Someone's apparel is the clothes he or she wears.

Grade K 73

LESSON 7

DAY 1 AT A GLANCE

PHONEMIC AWARENESS
Rhyme Recognition and Production

PHONICS
Preteach Word Building

HIGH-FREQUENCY WORDS
Reteach *to*

COMPREHENSION
Reteach Beginning, Middle, Ending

BUILD ROBUST VOCABULARY
Reteach *sly, proceed, apparel*

Materials Needed:

Word Builder and Word Builder Cards

Write-On/Wipe-Off Boards

Copying Master

Photo Cards

Practice Book

Phonemic Awareness

Rhyme Recognition and Production Remind children that when words have the same sounds at the end, the words rhyme. Say: **Listen to these words: *get, net*. I hear the same sounds at the end of each word: *-et*. The two words rhyme. Say the words with me: *get, net*.**

Tell children you are going to say two words. Tell them to clap if the two words rhyme, and to put their hands behind their backs if the words do not rhyme. Segment the initial sounds to provide additional help.

    sun, fun   him, hen   cat, mat   tin, pen

PRETEACH
Phonics

Blend Phonemes Say: **I will say the sounds /n/-/a/-/p/. I can blend the sounds to say a word: /nn/-/aa/-/p/. The word is *nap*. Let's do another one: /p/-/a/-/t/—/p/-/aa/-/t/ The word is *pat*.**

Word Building Distribute *Word Builders* and *Word Builder Cards a, c, m, n, p, r, s,* and *t*. Review each letter name and sound. Then hold up letters at random and ask children to tell the letter name and sound.

Tell children that you will make a new word by changing one letter in the word. Say: **I will use the letters *n, a,* and *p* to make the word *nap*. Now you do the same. Blend the sounds with me: /n/-/a/-/p/, *nap*. If I take away the *n* and put *c* in its place, I have the word *cap*. Now you try it. Blend the sounds and say the word with me: /k/-/a/-/p/, *cap*.**

Build Words Have children continue with *map* in their *Word Builder*:

Change *m* to *t*. What word did you make? *(tap)*

Change *p* to *n*. What word did you make? *(tan)*

Continue with the words *can, man,* and *pan*. Then have children practice writing the words that they built on their *Write-On/Wipe-Off Boards*.

Distribute *Copying Master 13*. Have children trace the letters at the bottom of the page and cut them out. Help children identify the pictures. Then have them paste the letter *a* in the box to complete each picture name. (Children should add *a* to make *cap, nap, pan, cat*.)

74 Lesson 7

Day 1

RETEACH

High-Frequency Words

Write *to* on the board and read it with children. Then write these sentences on the board: *Go to the zoo. Go to the park. Go to school.* Read them aloud and have children repeat. Work with children to point to and read the word *to* in each sentence.

Write *go, to,* and *the* on index cards. Display them on the chalk ledge by Photo Card truck. Track the words as you read the sentence: *Go to the ‹truck›.* Have children repeat. Continue with Photo Cards *van* and *hill.*

High-Frequency Words

to

RETEACH

Comprehension

Beginning, Middle, Ending Remind children that every story has a beginning, a middle, and an ending. Then read this story aloud to them.

> Leeann and Cory played together every day. One day they were jumping rope on the playground. Leeann saw Amir sitting by himself. Amir was new to school and didn't have any friends.
>
> Leeann told Cory, "He lives near me. Let's say 'hi'."
>
> Amir was shy, but he said, "I like to play soccer. Do you?"
>
> "Yes!" the girls said. The three children played soccer until recess was over. The girls had a lot of fun and made a new friend.

Guide children to turn to page 38 in their *Practice Books*. Have them look at the pictures as you ask them to identify the beginning, the middle, and the ending of the story.

RETEACH

Build Robust Vocabulary

Remind children of the Student-Friendly Explanations for *sly, proceed,* and *apparel.* Then discuss each word, asking the following questions.

sly
Should you be *sly* while playing a game or brushing your teeth? Why?

proceed
Can a tall ship *proceed* under a short bridge? Why or why not?

apparel
What is good *apparel* for the snow—mittens or a sled? Why?

VOCABULARY

Student-Friendly Explanations

sly Someone who is sly is tricky and sneaky.

proceed When you proceed, you go ahead with what you are doing.

apparel Someone's apparel is the clothes he or she wears.

Grade K 75

LESSON 7

DAY AT A GLANCE — Day 2

PHONEMIC AWARENESS
Rhyme Recognition and Production

PHONICS
Reteach Word Building

HIGH-FREQUENCY WORDS
Reteach to

COMPREHENSION
Preteach Use Graphic Organizers

BUILD ROBUST VOCABULARY
Reteach announced, imaginary, precisely

Materials Needed:

Word Builder and Word Builder Cards   Write-On/Wipe-Off Boards   Copying Master

Photo Cards   Practice Book

Phonemic Awareness

Rhyme Recognition and Production Recite the rhyme "Jack and Jill": **Jack and Jill went up the hill to fetch a pail of water. Jack fell down and broke his crown and Jill came tumbling after.** Model for children how to recognize words that rhyme: Say: **I know that the words *Jill* and *hill* rhyme. They both have the same sounds at the end. Other words also have the same sounds at the end. Listen as I say words that rhyme with *Jill* and *hill*: will, mill, pill, Bill, fill.**

Say the following sentences for children:

On the *trail* I saw a *pail*.   **Ed and *Joe* ran in the *snow*.**

After each sentence, name word pairs from the sentence and ask children if they rhyme. Then name other words that rhyme with the rhyming word pair. Have children repeat the rhyming words with you.

RETEACH

Phonics

   Blend Phonemes Say the sounds in a word and work with children to name that word. Model an example. Say: **I will blend the sounds: /r/-/a/-/t/. The word is *rat*.** Tell children to "say the word" with you after each group of sounds that you say:

/a/-/n/ (an)   **/g/-/e/-/t/** (get)   **/m/-/e/-/n/** (men)

Word Building Distribute *Word Builders* and *Word Builder Cards a, c, m, n, p, s,* and *t*. Explain to children that when letters in words change, so do the sounds. Model word building, saying: **I will use the letters *c, a,* and *t* to make the word *cat*. Now you do the same. Blend the sounds with me: /k/-/a/-/t/, *cat*. If I take away the *t* and put *n* in its place, I have the word *can*. Now you try it. Blend the sounds and say the word: /k/-/a/-/n/, *can*.**

Build Words Have children continue with *pan* in their *Word Builder*:

Change *n* to *t*. What word did you make? (pat)

Change *p* to *m*. What word did you make? (mat)

Continue with the words *sat, sap, tap*. Then have children practice writing the words they built on their *Write-On/Wipe-Off Boards*.

Distribute *Copying Master 14*. Have children trace each letter. Then have them name the picture and draw a line from it to the picture name. (Children trace the *Aa* and *Pp*. Children draw line from dot by picture of *tap* to word *tap*; children draw line from picture of *map* to word *map*.)

76 Lesson 7

Day 2

RETEACH
High-Frequency Words

  Use index cards with the words *I, go, to, the* and one with a period to build the sentence frame below. Point to and read each word and have children repeat. Then place *Photo Card ladder* to complete the sentence, and have children read it aloud.

| I | go | to | the | ladder | . |

Repeat for *Photo Cards cat, lamp,* and *tree.*

Have children turn to *Practice Book* page 39 to review high-frequency words and practice newly learned words. Complete the page together.

PRETEACH
Comprehension

Use Graphic Organizers Remind children that people can use special drawings, or charts, to help them understand and remember what happens in stories. Create a chart with these row headings: *Beginning, Middle, Ending*. Reread the story about the girls and the boy on the playground from Day 1. Pause to have children name what happens in each part of the story. Record their responses on the chart.

Beginning	Leeann and Cory play together on the playground.
Middle	The girls talk to Amir.
End	The three children play soccer together.

RETEACH
Build Robust Vocabulary

Read the Student-Friendly Explanations for *announced, imaginary,* and *precisely*. Then ask children the following questions.

announced
If I *announced* snack time, would I want everyone to know, or would I want it to be a secret? Why?

imaginary
What are some things an *imaginary* animal might do?

precisely
If a line is drawn *precisely*, is the line straight or crooked?

High-Frequency Words

to

VOCABULARY
Student-Friendly Explanations

announced When you announce something, you tell people things you want them all to know.

imaginary Something that is imaginary is make-believe.

precisely If you do something precisely, you do it exactly as it should be done.

Grade K 77

LESSON 7

DAY AT A GLANCE — Day 3

PHONEMIC AWARENESS
Rhyme Recognition and Production

PHONICS
Preteach Phonogram *-am*

HIGH-FREQUENCY WORDS
Reteach *to*

COMPREHENSION
Reteach Beginning, Middle, Ending

BUILD ROBUST VOCABULARY
Reteach *announced, imaginary, precisely*

WRITING
Reteach Writing Trait: Voice

Materials Needed:

Photo Cards
Phoneme Phone

Write-On/Wipe-Off Boards
Practice Book

Phonemic Awareness

Rhyme Recognition and Production Tell children that they will play a game to practice making rhymes. Put the following *Photo Cards* in a bag: *egg, fish, hat, hill, lamp, nest, pig, ring, sun,* and *van*. Then model how to play the game. Say: **I will take a picture out of the bag. Next, I will say the name of the picture. Then I will say a rhyming word.** Choose a *Photo Card*, such as *Photo Card fish*. Say: *fish*. **What rhymes with** *fish*? **/d/-/ish/,** *dish*. *Fish* **and** *dish* **have the same ending sound.** *Fish* **and** *dish* **rhyme.**

Let each child take a card out of the bag and name the picture on the card. Have the rest of the group repeat the word. Help the child say a word that rhymes with the picture name. Distribute the *Phoneme Phones*. Model saying the picture name and a rhyming word. Have children use the *Phoneme Phone* to look at the position of their mouths as they repeat the rhyming words.

Blend Syllables Remind children that words are made up of parts and that they can put word parts together to say words. Guide children to identify syllables in spoken words, and to combine syllables to say words. Say: **Here are the parts of a word:** *be-fore*. **The word has two word parts. Now I am going to blend the word parts together to say the word:** *before*. Read these syllables aloud, clapping as you say each syllable. Have children count the number of syllables and blend them together to say the word:

| play-ing | gar-den | bro-ken |
| draw-ing | hap-py | sis-ter |

PRETEACH

Phonics

Identify Rhyming Words Remind children what rhyming words are. Say: **Listen to these words:** *ram, Sam*. *Ram* **and** *Sam* **both have /am/.** *Ram* **and** *Sam* **rhyme. What are the words?** (*ram, Sam*) **Do they rhyme?** (yes) Continue with these word pairs:

| ham, Pam | ram, rat | Sam, Pam |
| jam, tap | Pam, ran | am, Sam |

78 Lesson 7

Phonogram –am Write the word *am* on the board. Track the print as you read the word. Have children repeat after you. Then write the word *Sam*. Track the print as you read the word. Have children repeat after you. Ask how the two words are the same. (They both have /am/; they rhyme.) Say: **The words *am* and *Sam* are in the *-am* word family because they both end in *-am*.** Continue by writing the words *ram* and *Pam*.

Distribute *Write-on/Wipe-off Boards*. Write these words on the board: *ham, map,* and *Sam*. Have children read the words with you and copy those words in the *-am* word family on their *Write-on/Wipe-off Boards*. Have them underline *–am* in each word.

RETEACH

High-Frequency Words

 Use index cards for *I, go, to,* the *Photo Card hill,* and a card with a period to build the sentence *I go to the hill*. Point to each word and have children read the sentence with you.

Replace *Photo Card hill* with *Photo Card helicopter*. Read the new sentence with children. Continue, using the *Photo Cards taxi, tree, truck,* and *van*. Have children read the sentences until they can read them fluently.

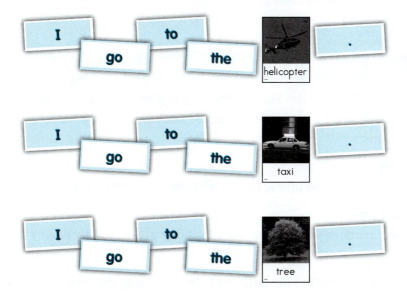

High-Frequency Words

to

Day 3

RETEACH

Comprehension

  Beginning, Middle, Ending Remind children that stories have a beginning, middle, and an ending. Have children listen for the beginning, middle, and ending as you read this story:

> Tess the little turtle didn't like his shell. It was too big for him. All the other turtles had shells that fit just right. Tess's shell rattled when he walked. It was so loose that sometimes he even needed to use suspenders to hold it on.
>
> Tess looked everywhere for a new shell. He found a snail shell. It was far too small. He found an eggshell. It was much too fragile. He found a hollow log. That would just look silly. Tess decided to rest for a while. Winter was coming, and he was getting sleepy. Tess took a long, long nap.
> When it began to get warm again, Tess slowly opened one eye. Then he opened another. He gave a big stretch. His shell didn't rattle. It wasn't loose. Tess had grown big, and his shell fit perfectly.

Guide children to *Practice Book* page 40. Have them look at the pictures and retell what happens in the beginning, the middle, and the ending of the story. Ask: **In the beginning of the story you met the character. Who is he?** (Tess the turtle) **What happens in the middle?** (Tess searches all over for a new shell.) **Does the story have a happy ending?** (Possible response: yes, Tess grows into his shell.)

RETEACH

Build Robust Vocabulary

Remind children of the Student-Friendly Explanations for *announced*, *imaginary*, and *precisely*. Then discuss each word, using the following questions.

announced
If your parents had dinner ready, what would be *announced*? Say the words.

imaginary
Can an *imaginary* friend get you a birthday present? Why or why not?

precisely
If someone says that his birthday is in the winter, did he tell you the day *precisely*? Why or why not?

VOCABULARY

Student-Friendly Explanations

announced When you announce something, you tell people things you want them all to know.

imaginary Something that is imaginary is make-believe.

precisely If you do something precisely, you do it exactly as it should be done.

RETEACH

Writing

Writing Trait: Voice Tell children that in their writing, they can show others who they are. Explain that one way to let their writing sound familiar is to use words that they would normally use when they talk to someone.

Remind children that they heard a story about a turtle named Tess who wanted a new shell because his didn't fit. You may wish to reread the story. Then invite children to pretend they meet Tess. Have them use words to say what they might say to him. Model by saying: **This is what I would say to him: "Tess, I like your shell, even if it's too big." Those words sound like I'm talking to someone. It sounds like me.** Write down children's words on the chart paper, with the child's name next to each quotation. Read the dialogue aloud. Reinforce to children that their comments are in their own words, or voice, and that this makes their writing sound as if they were actually speaking.

> Now your shell fits just right. (Luis)
> That's a great shell, Tess. (Emma)

Day 3

Grade K 81

LESSON 7

PHONEMIC AWARENESS
Rhyme Recognition and Production

PHONICS
Preteach Phonogram -at

READING
Review Phonogram -at
Review High-Frequency Words

BUILD ROBUST VOCABULARY
Review announced, apparel, imaginary, precisely, proceed, sly

WRITING
Reteach Writing Form: Sentences About Me

Materials Needed:

Write-On/ Wipe-Off Boards

Practice Book

Phonemic Awareness

Rhyme Recognition and Production Tell children that today they will be playing a rhyming word game. Say: **I will say two words. If the words rhyme, help me think of another word that rhymes with the two words. If the words do not rhyme, say, "They don't rhyme."** Model an example. Say: **Listen to these two words:** *get, net*. *Get* **and** *net* **end with the /et/ sound, so they rhyme. I will say another word:** *let*. **Now I will say all three rhyming words:** *get, net, let*. Play the game with the following pairs of words. Segment the initial sounds as necessary:

| dip, lip | bat, mat | fin, fan |
| bun, sun | hat, ham | cot, lot |

Syllable Blending Remind children that they can blend word parts together to say words. Model how to count the syllables in the word *summer* and blend them together. Then have children continue with the following words:

ci-ty (2)   **pa-per** (2)   **can-dy** (2)   **hap-pi-ly** (3)

RETEACH

Phonics

Identify Rhyming Words Remind children that two words that have the same middle and ending sounds are called rhyming words. Rhyming words are in the same word family. Say: **Listen to these words:** *mat, pat*. *Mat* **and** *pat* **both have /at/.** *Mat* **and** *pat* **rhyme. Both words are in the** *-at* **family. What are the words?** (*mat, pat*) **Do the words rhyme?** (yes) Read the following pairs of words and have children tell you whether they rhyme: *sat, rat*; *cat, can*; *mat, hat*.

Phonogram *-at* Write the word *at* on chart paper. Track the print as you read the word. Have children read the word. Repeat with the word *sat*. Point out that both words have /at/ and that they rhyme. Say: **The words** *at* **and** *sat* **are in the** *-at* **word family because they both end in** *-at*. Continue with the words *mat* and *rat*. Have volunteers trace the letters *–at* in the words on the chart paper.

Distribute *Write-on/Wipe-Off Boards* to children. Write these words on the board: *cat, can, Dan,* and *bat*. Read the words with children. Have them copy these words in the *-at* word family on their *Write-on/Wipe-off Boards*.

82   Lesson 7

Day 4

REVIEW: Reading

Phonogram -at Write *mat* on chart paper. Run a finger under the letters as you blend the sounds. Say: /m/ /a/ /t/, *mat*. Say it with me: /m/ /a/ /t/, *mat*. Repeat with the word *hat*.

High-Frequency Words Distribute index cards with the words *I, a, my, go,* and *to* written on them. Ask children to listen to the word you say, find the matching card, and hold it up. Continue until all the cards have been matched correctly.

Have children turn to *Practice Book* pages 41–42. Have children cut and fold the book, and read it together. Have children take it home to read with their families.

High-Frequency Words
to

REVIEW: Robust Vocabulary

Remind children of the Student-Friendly Explanations for *announced, apparel, imaginary, precisely, proceed,* and *sly*. Then determine children's understanding of the words by asking the following questions.

- If you are *sly*, do you say *precisely* what you mean? Why or why not?
- Can you *proceed* through an *imaginary* door? Why or why not?
- What kind of *apparel* is good when it's raining outside?
- If you *announced* that it's time for dessert, do you whisper or say it loudly? Why?

RETEACH: Writing

Writing Form: Sentences About Me Review with children that sentences that tell something about them, can be about many different topics. Model how to think of something to share about yourself. Say: **What special thing do I know how to do? I know how to play the piano. What am I proud of? I am proud of a picture I drew. What is something about myself that others might not know? I once rode in a helicopter.**

Invite children to dictate sentences about themselves. Record their ideas on chart paper. Invite them to write letters or sounds that they know. Point out how each sentence begins with an uppercase letter and ends with a period. Then read the sentences to the group.

> I have a cat named Sam.
> I can play drums.
> I am proud of my mom.

VOCABULARY: Student-Friendly Explanations

announced When you announce something, you tell people things you want them all to know.

apparel Someone's apparel is the clothes he or she wears.

imaginary Something that is imaginary is make-believe.

precisely If you do something precisely, you do it exactly as it should be done.

proceed When you proceed, you go ahead with what you are doing.

sly Someone who is sly is tricky and sneaky.

LESSON 7

PHONEMIC AWARENESS
Onset/Rime Blending

PHONICS
Preteach Consonant *Dd*

HIGH-FREQUENCY WORDS
Preteach *like*

BUILD ROBUST VOCABULARY
Reteach *active, gigantic, voyage*

Materials Needed:

Sound/Spelling Card *Dd*   Write-On/Wipe-Off Boards

Practice Book

Phonemic Awareness

Onset/Rime Blending Remind children that words are made up of parts. **Say: Listen as I say a word in parts: /k/ -at, /k/-at, cat.** Continue with the name *Sam*. **Say: Repeat what I say: /ss/-am. The word is Sam.**

Have children follow the same procedure, using the following sounds and words. Ask them to repeat the sounds and then blend the parts to say words:

/m/-at (*mat*)   /t/-in (*tin*)   /b/-at (*bat*)   /d/-ad (*dad*)   /k/-ap (*cap*)
/P/-am (*Pam*)   /r/-at (*rat*)   /p/-en (*pen*)   /s/-it (*sit*)

PRETEACH

Phonics

 Consonant *Dd* Display *Sound/Spelling Card Dd*. **Say: This is the letter *d*. Say the name with me.** Point to uppercase *D* and say: **This is uppercase *D*.** Point to lowercase *d* and say: **This is lowercase *d*.** Have children identify the letters. (D, d)

Writing *D* and *d* Write *D* and *d* on the board and have children identify the letters. **Say: Watch as I write the letter *D* so that everyone can read it.** As you give the Letter Talk, trace the uppercase *D*. Do the same for lowercase *d*.

Letter Talk for *D*	Letter Talk for *d*
1. Straight line down.	1. Straight line down, up, and around.
2. Go to the top of the line.	
3. Draw a curved line out, down, and around.	

Tell children to finger-write the uppercase *D* in the air as you repeat the Letter Talk. Have them do the same for lowercase *d*.

 Distribute *Write-on/Wipe-off Boards* to children. Ask them to write uppercase *D* and then lowercase *d* several times on their *Write-on/Wipe-off Boards*.

 Have children turn to *Practice Book* page 43. Help children circle each uppercase *D* and underline each lowercase *d*. Have them trace the letters and write them on the lines.

Day 5

PRETEACH

High-Frequency Words

Write the word *like* on the board. Point to and read *like*. Have children say it with you. Say: **I like my job.** Display an index card with the word *like*. Say: *like*. Match the index card to the word on the board, say the word, and have children say it with you.

Distribute an index card with the word *like* to each child. Have children point to the word and read it. Tell children that you will show them words, and when they see *like,* they should say the word and point to it on the card. Hold up index cards with the words *go, I, my,* and *like* in random order until children consistently identify the word like. Retrieve the cards for use in Lesson 8.

RETEACH

Build Robust Vocabulary

Tell children the Student-Friendly Explanations *active, gigantic,* and *voyage*. Then discuss each word, using the following examples.

active
Are you *active* when you run or when you nap? Why do you think so?

gigantic
What might be *gigantic* to an ant? To an elephant?

voyage
Do you need to pack a lot or a little for a *voyage*? Why do you think so?

High-Frequency Words

| go | I |
| like | my |

VOCABULARY
Student-Friendly Explanations

active If you are active, you are doing something in a busy way.

gigantic Something that is gigantic is very, very big.

voyage If you go on a voyage, you go on a trip to a place far away.

Grade K 85

LESSON 8

PHONEMIC AWARENESS
Onset/Rime Blending

PHONICS
Preteach Relate *Dd* to /d/

HIGH-FREQUENCY WORDS
Reteach *like*

COMPREHENSION
Reteach Beginning, Middle, Ending

BUILD ROBUST VOCABULARY
Reteach *active, gigantic, voyage*

Materials Needed:

Sound/Spelling Card *Dd*   Word Builder and Word Builder Cards   Write-On/Wipe-Off Boards

Copying Master   Practice Book   Sounds of Letters CD

Phonemic Awareness

Onset/Rime Blending Tell children that you will play a game with them. You will say a word in two parts and they will blend the parts together to say the word. Say: **I am thinking of word. It begins with /d/. It ends with *ig*. The word is *dig*. Now you try it. I am thinking of a new word. It begins with /f/. It ends with *un*. What is the word?** (*fun*) Ask children to follow the same procedure with the following words: /f/-og (*fog*), /k/-id (*kid*), /m/-ud (*mud*), and /b/-ad (*bad*). Make sure children blend the words parts to say each word.

PRETEACH
Phonics

  Relate *Dd* to /d/ Display *Sound/Spelling Card Dd* and play the /d/ sound on the *Sounds of Letters CD*. Ask: **What is this letter? The letter *d* stands for /d/, the sound at the beginning of *dinner*.** Say /d/. Have children repeat the sound as you touch the letter on the card several times.

Discriminate /d/ Give each child *Word Builder Card d*. Say: **If the word begins with /d/, hold up the card and say /d/. If the word does not begin with /d/, put the card behind your back.** Say the words *pass, dark, dog, dull, sap, Dan, glad*.

Tell children that /d/ can also come at the end of words such as *pad*. Follow the same procedure for the final position. Use the words *lad, sat, bad, pat, and dad*. Then have children tell whether they hear the /d/ sound at the beginning or end of these words: *road, dot, doll, bed, dog, Ned, and den*.

 Identify Sound Position Distribute *Word Builder Card d* and a *Write-on/Wipe-off Board* to each child. Explain that they will be working on the three boxes next to the heart. Draw three similar boxes on chart paper, and say: **I am going to say some words. If /d/ is at the beginning of the word, put your letter *d* on the beginning box. If /d/ is at the end, put your letter *d* on the last box.**

 Model the activity using the word *dog*. Continue with the following words: *door, food, Ted, end, and doll*. Distribute *Copying Master* page 15. Have children trace the letter *D* and *d*. Help children identify each picture. Then have children circle the letter that stands for the beginning sound of the picture name. (Children should circle letter *d* for *dog, door, duck, donkey, dollar*)

86 Lesson 8

Day 1

RETEACH

High-Frequency Words

Write *like* on the board and read it with children. Then write *go, to, my,* and *like* on index cards. Tell children that you will hold up index cards. When they see the word *like,* they should read the word and give the thumbs-up sign. If they don't see the word, they should make the thumbs-down sign. Continue cycling through the cards several times.

High-Frequency Words	
go	like
ny	to

RETEACH

Comprehension

Beginning, Middle, Ending Remind children that every story has a beginning, middle, and ending. Then read this story aloud.

Once upon a time a little ant went for a walk with his brothers and sisters. He followed them in a straight line up and down the rocks. Then he smelled something good to eat. He decided to find out what it was. He walked over some grass and up a tall piece of wood. It seemed like a tree but it was different from a tree. It was a picnic table. At the top of the table, he saw a big plate of cupcake crumbles. It smelled delicious. He wanted to find his brothers and sisters so they could eat some, too. As soon as he turned around to call their names, he realized that he was alone. He did not know what to do next.

Guide children to turn to page 44 in their *Practice Books*. Have them look at the pictures as you ask them to identify the events that happen in the beginning, the middle, and the ending of the story.

RETEACH

Build Robust Vocabulary

Remind children of the Student-Friendly Explanations for *active, gigantic,* and *voyage*. Then discuss each word, using the following examples.

active
What does an *active* puppy like to do? Can you show us?

gigantic
If you had a *gigantic* bowl of ice-cream, could you share it with many people? Why or why not?

voyage
Would a trip to school be a *voyage*? Why or why not?

VOCABULARY

Student-Friendly Explanations

active If you are active you are doing something.

gigantic Something that is gigantic is very, very big.

voyage If you go on a voyage, you go on a trip to somewhere far away.

Grade K 87

LESSON 8

DAY AT A GLANCE — Day 2

PHONEMIC AWARENESS
Onset/Rime Blending

PHONICS
Reteach Blending /d/*d*, /a/*a*

HIGH-FREQUENCY WORDS
Reteach *like*

COMPREHENSION
Reteach Use Story Structure

BUILD ROBUST VOCABULARY
Reteach *gasped, glum, whimper*

Materials Needed:

Photo Cards   Word Builder and Word Builder Cards   Practice Book

Write-On/Wipe-Off Boards   Copying Master

Phonemic Awareness

 Onsets/Rime Blending Remind children that words are made up of parts. Tell them to listen as you say a word in two parts. Have them think about the word you are saying. Hold up *Photo Card hill*. Say: **First I'll say /h/. Next, I'll say *ill*. I'll blend the word parts together to say the word: *hill*. Say the word with me: *hill*.** Repeat with *Photo Cards cow, dog,* and *fish*.

Say the following word parts. Repeat each of the following onset and rime pairs several times. /s/-*at* (*sat*), /k/-*art* (*cart*), /l/-*og* (*log*), /b/-*ox* (*box*), /y/-*ak* (*yak*), /r/-*ope* (*rope*). Have children blend the parts and say the word.

RETEACH

Phonics

Blending /d/*d*, /a/*a* Have children sit in a circle. **We're going on a word hunt. What's this word? /D/-/a/-/d/ Together: *dad*!** Have children echo you. Establish a rhythm and keep it going throughout the verse. Continue for the words /s/-/a/-/d/ (*sad*), /m/-/a/-/d/ (*mad*), and /p/-/a/-/d/ (*pad*).

Word Blending Place the *Word Builder Cards a* and *d* in the *Word Builder*. Point to *a*. Say /aa/. Have children name the letter and sound. Point to *d*. Say /d/. Have children name the letter and sound. Slide the *d* next to *a*. Move your hand under the letters and blend the sounds: /aad/. Have children repeat after you. Then have children blend and read the word *ad* with you.

Continue with the words *mad, sap, pad,* and *nap*. Then have children practice writing the words they built on their *Write-On/Wipe-Off Boards*.

Distribute *Copying Master 16*. Have children trace *Aa* and *Dd*. Help them identify the picture and have them draw a line from the picture to the correct picture name. (Children should connect picture of *dad* word *dad*; picture of *sad* to word *sad*.)

RETEACH

High-Frequency Words

Use index cards with the words *I, like, my,* and card with a period to build the sentence frame: *I like my _____.* Point to each word as you read the sentence. Reread it with children. Ask a volunteer to point to the word *like*. Place the *Photo Card cat* to complete the sentence, and have children read the sentence to you.

Replace *Photo Card cat* with *Photo Card rabbit*. Help children read the sentence. Repeat with the *Photo Cards* for *drum, hammer, pencil, truck, van,* and *watch*.

88 Lesson 8

Have children turn to *Practice Book* page 45 to review high-frequency words and practice newly-learned words. Complete the page together.

RETEACH

Comprehension

 Use Story Structure Recall the story about the little ant and the picnic table from Day 1. Ask children who the story is about. (a little ant and his brothers and sisters) Remind them that the animals or people in stories are the characters. Ask: **Where does the story take place?** (a picnic table) Tell children that the setting is where a story happens.

Record the characters and setting in a story map. Remind children that a story has a beginning, middle, and an ending. Reread the story from Day 1 and pause to have children tell what happens in each part of the story. Record their responses in the story map.

Characters	Setting
little ant, his brothers and sisters	the picnic table
Beginning: Little ant smells something good.	
Middle: He climbs up a picnic table and finds cupcake crumbs.	
End: He leaves to tell his brothers and sisters about the crumbs.	

RETEACH

Build Robust Vocabulary

Tell children the Student-Friendly Explanations for *gasped, glum,* and *whimper.* Then discuss each word, using the following examples.

gasped
If someone *gasped*, what might it sound like?

glum
Some people feel *glum* on a rainy day. Explain why.

whimper
Who might *whimper*, a hungry baby or a ticklish baby? Why do you think so?

High-Frequency Words

I   like

my

VOCABULARY

Student-Friendly Explanations

gasped When you gasp, you take a short, quick breath because you are surprised.

glum Someone who feels glum is sad and quiet.

whimper When someone whimpers, they make a quiet, crying sound.

LESSON 8

DAY AT A GLANCE — Day 3

PHONEMIC AWARENESS
Onset/Rime Blending
Rhyme Recognition

PHONICS
Preteach Word Blending and Building

HIGH-FREQUENCY WORDS
Reteach *like*

COMPREHENSION
Reteach Beginning, Middle, Ending

BUILD ROBUST VOCABULARY
Reteach *gasped, glum, whimper*

WRITING
Reteach Writing Trait: Ideas

Materials Needed:

Phoneme Phone | Word Builder and Word Builder Cards | Write-On/Wipe-Off Boards

Photo Cards | Practice Book

Phonemic Awareness

Onset/Rime Blending Tell children that you will play a game with them. You will say a word in two parts and they will blend the parts together to say the word. Say: **I am thinking of word. It begins with /g/. It ends with *um*. What is the word?** (*gum*)

Repeat the game, using these word parts: /b/-*ed* (*bed*); /g/-*ot* (*got*); /h/-*at* (*hat*); /m/-*itt* (*mitt*); /r/-*un* (*run*); /f/-*ish* (*fish*); /s/-*ail* (*sail*); /w/-*et* (*wet*); /n/-*ut* (*nut*). Repeat the onsets and rimes several times.

Rhyme Recognition Remind children that words that sound the same at the end are called rhyming words. Say: **Listen as I say two words: *ball, call*. I hear the same sound at the end of each word. The two words rhyme.** Say the following sets of words: *cot/dot; melt/felt; wall/wait; oat/own; toe/sew; lid/low*. Have children use the Phoneme Phone to look at the position of their mouth as they repeat each pair of words. Ask children to clap if the words rhyme.

PRETEACH
Phonics

Word Blending and Building

Blend Words Distribute *Word Builders* and *Word Builder Cards a, c, d, m, n, p, s,* and *t*. Review each letter name and sound. Then hold up letters at random and ask children to tell the letter name and sound.

Explain to children that you are going to show them how a word can change when the letters in the word change. Say: **Use your *Word Builder* and *Word Builder Cards* to make new words with me. I will use the letters *p, a,* and *d* to make the word *pad*. Now you do the same. Blend the sounds with me: /p/-/a/-/d/, *pad*. If I take away the *d* and put *n* in its place, I have the word *pan*. Now you try it. Blend the sounds and say the word with me: /p/-/a/-/n/, *pan*.**

90 Lesson 8

Day 3

 Build Words Have children continue with pan in their Word Builder:

- **Change *p* to *m*. What word did you make?** (*man*)
- **Change *n* to *p*. What word did you make?** (*map*)

Continue with the words *tap, tan,* and *cap.* Then have children practice writing the words they built on their *Write-On/Wipe-Off Boards.*

RETEACH
High-Frequency Words

 Use index cards with the words *I, like, the,* and a card with a period to build the sentence frame below. Point to and read each word and have children repeat it. Ask a volunteer to point to the word *like.* Then place *Photo Card sandwich* to complete the sentence, and have children read it aloud: **I like the** *sandwich*

High-Frequency Words

I	like
my	

Grade K 91

Day 3

RETEACH

Comprehension

  Beginning, Middle, Ending Remind children that stories have a beginning, middle, and an ending. Have children listen as you read aloud the following story.

Courtney wanted to make a special breakfast for her mother. She helped her dad in the kitchen. She added pancake mix into a bowl. They added water and an egg. Courtney carefully stirred it. "Good job," her dad said.

When the pan was hot, her dad poured the pancake batter into the pan. He made a big circle in the center and two smaller circles on top. "It looks like a panda bear," Courtney said. "You made a panda-bear pancake!"

When her mom saw the pancake she smiled. "This is the best breakfast ever," she said.

Guide children to *Practice Book* page 46. Have them look at the pictures and choose the one in each row that tells about the beginning, the middle, or the ending. Have them retell what happened in each part of the story.

RETEACH

Build Robust Vocabulary

Remind children of the Student-Friendly Explanations for *gasped, glum,* and *whimper.* Then discuss each word, using the following examples.

gasped
If you *gasped* when you saw a friend, were you surprised or were you bored? Tell why.

glum
How can you make a *glum* friend feel better?

whimper
What's the difference between a dog's *whimper* and a dog's bark? Show us.

VOCABULARY

Student-Friendly Explanations

gasped When you gasp, you take a short, quick breath because you are surprised.

glum Someone who is glum feels sad and quiet.

whimper When someone whimpers, they make a quiet, crying sound.

Day 3

RETEACH

Writing

Writing Trait: Ideas Tell children that when they write, they should picture in their minds what they see or hear. They can also think about how they feel about what they are writing about. Sharing their ideas will make their writing more interesting.

Remind children that they heard a story about a girl and her dad who make pancakes for her mom. You may wish to reread the story. Then invite children to add another sentence to the story to tell what happens next. Model by saying, **I think about how the characters are feeling in the story. I think Courtney's mom is happy. I think that Courtney is probably happy, too. I'll add that idea to the story and tell why she is happy. What ideas can you add to the story?**

Write down children's words on the board or on chart paper. Work with them to add enough information to form complete sentences. Read the sentences aloud. Praise children for their ideas and what they've added to the story.

Grade K

LESSON 8

PHONEMIC AWARENESS
Onset/Rime Blending
Rhyme Recognition and Production

PHONICS
Reteach Review /d/d

READING
Review Words with Consonant *Dd*
Review High-Frequency Words

BUILD ROBUST VOCABULARY
Review *active, gigantic, voyage, gasped, glum, whimper*

WRITING
Reteach Writing Form: Sentences

Materials Needed:

Sound/Spelling Card *Dd, Pp*   Photo Cards   Practice Book

Phonemic Awareness

Onset/Rime Blending Have children sit in pairs. Tell them you will play a game. Say: **I am going to whisper a word part to each partner. You will say the word parts aloud.** Whisper /s/ to one partner and *at* to the other. Have partners repeat the word parts aloud. They can repeat several times as needed. Then ask the group to blend the parts together to say the word. (*sat*)

Follow the same procedure, using the following words: /m/-*et* (*met*), /s/-*and* (*sand*), /l/-*ick* (*lick*), /r/-*ace* (*race*), /w/-*ill* (*will*), /b/-*end* (*bend*). Have children repeat the word parts several times and then name the word.

Rhyme Recognition and Production Remind children that words that sound the same at the end are called rhyming words. Say: **Listen as I say some silly words that rhyme:** *get/wet, neat/feet.* **Now I will say some more silly words. Stand up if they rhyme.** Encourage children to name other words that rhyme with them. Use the following word pairs: fat/fish, round/hound, love/dove, nose/grows, owl/towel, pet/pup

RETEACH
Phonics

 Connect Letters and Sounds Display *Sound/Spelling Card Dd*. Ask: **What sound do you hear at the beginning of** *deer***? What letter stands for /d/ at the beginning of** *deer***?** Display *Sound/Spelling Card Pp*. Ask: **What sound do you hear at the beginning of** *paper***? What letter stands for /p/ at the beginning of** *paper***?**

 Discriminate /d/ and /p/ Display the *Sound/Spelling Cards*. Display *Photo Cards dog, pan, pencil,* and *pig.* Tell children that they are going to place each card beside the letter that stands for the sound at the beginning of its name.

Model by holding up *Photo Card pig.* Say: **This is a pig.** *Pig* **begins with /p/. The letter** *p* **stands for the sound /p/. I'll put the pig card next to the card for** *p***.** Continue with the remaining cards.

94 Lesson 8

Day 4

REVIEW

Reading

Read Words with Consonant *Dd* Write on the board *dad*, *mad*, and *sad*. Model sounding out and blending each word. Then read each word naturally. Finally, have children practice reading the words.

Practice Book 47–48

Review High-Frequency Words Reuse or create index cards for *I, like, my,* and *to*. Hold up each card and read it. Then shuffle the cards and randomly display each card, having children read each word.

Have children turn to *Practice Book* pages 47–48. Have children read the sentences as a take-home book to practice the newly-learned words.

REVIEW

Robust Vocabulary

Remind children of the Student-Friendly Explanations for *active, gigantic, voyage, gasped, glum,* and *whimper*. Then determine children's understanding of the words by asking the following questions.

- **If someone in a story *gasped*, do you think they saw a *gigantic* elephant or a tiny ladybug? Why?**
- **If you went on a *voyage* to outer space, would you feel *glum* or excited? Why?**
- **Who is more *active*: a girl playing soccer or a girl resting on a sofa?**
- **If you heard your puppy *whimper*, what would you do?**

RETEACH

Writing

Writing Form: Sentences Tell children that they are going to write sentences with you about something they like to do outside. Ask children to brainstorm ideas by dictating action words or phrases, such as *play, jump, chase my dog, throw a ball*. Write the words on chart paper and suggest that children include them in the sentences you write together.

As children dictate sentences, point out that the first word in a sentence begins with an uppercase letter, and that sentences usually end with a period. As you write and read their sentences, point out words that may be familiar to children, and demonstrate how to map sounds to letters, such as the sounds in *dog*.

> I play with my sister.
> I chase my dog.

High-Frequency Words

I	like
my	to

VOCABULARY

Student-Friendly Explanations

active If you are active, you are doing something in a busy way.

gigantic Something that is gigantic is very, very big.

voyage If you go on a voyage, you go on a trip to a place far away.

gasped When you gasp, you take a short, quick breath because you are surprised.

glum Someone who feels glum is sad and quiet.

whimper When someone whimpers, he or she makes a quiet, crying sound.

Grade K

LESSON 8

PHONEMIC AWARENESS
Onset/Rime Blending

PHONICS
Preteach Word Blending

HIGH-FREQUENCY WORDS
Preteach *he*

BUILD ROBUST VOCABULARY
Reteach *proceed, announced, gasped*

Materials Needed:

Sound/Spelling Card *Aa, Tt* | Word Builder and Word Builder Cards | Practice Book

Phonemic Awareness

Blend Onsets and Rimes Remind children that words are made up of parts. Tell children to listen as you say a word in two parts. Say: **First I'll say: /t/. Next, I'll say: *an*. Then I will blend the parts together to say a word: /t/-*an*, *tan*. Let's do one together. Repeat what I say: /p/-*in*. Say the word: *pin*.**

Follow the same procedure, using the following sounds and words: /p/-*ail* (*pail*), /r/-*un* (*run*), /s/-*at* (*sat*) /B/-*en* (*Ben*), /d/-*og* (*dog*), /k/-*up* (*cup*), /l/-*ap* (*lap*), /g/-*ood* (*good*), /r/-*ain* (*rain*)

PRETEACH

Phonics

Sounds in a Word Have children sit in a circle. Sing the following verse to the tune of "Old MacDonald." As you sing, have children echo after you. **What is the word for these three sounds? /k/-/a/-/t/, *cat*! With a *cat*, *cat* here, and a *cat*, *cat* there. Here a *cat*, there a *cat*. Everywhere a *cat*, *cat*. What is the word for these three sounds? /k/-/a/-/t/, *cat*!** Continue for the words /m/-/a/-/t/ (*mat*), /s/-/a/-/p/ (*sap*), and /k/-/a/-/n/ (*can*). Restate the sounds that were blended to make each word. For example, say: **We blended /m/-/a/-/t/ to make the word *mat*; /mm/-/a/-/t/, *mat*. We blended /s/-/a/-/p/. What word did we make?** (*sap*)

Display *Sound/Spelling Cards a* and *t*. Point to *a*. Ask: **What letter is this?** (*a*) **The letter *a* stands for the sound /aa/. What does *a* stand for?** (/a/) Remind children that *a* can stand for the sound /a/, the sound at the beginning of *apple*. Point to *t*. Ask: **What letter is this?** (*t*) **The letter *t* stands for the sound /t/. What does *t* stand for?** (/t/) Remind children that *t* can stand for the sound /t/, the sound at the beginning of *table*.

Blend More Words Place the *Word Builder Cards c, a,* and *n* in the *Word Builder*. Point to *c*. Say: **/k/.** Have children name the letter and sound. Point to *a*. Say:
/aa/. Have children name the letter and sound. Slide the *a* next to *c*. Point to *n*. Say: **/nn/.** Have children name the letter and sound. Slide the *n* next to *ca*. Move your hand under the letters and blend the sounds: **/kaann/.** Then say the sounds a little more quickly, again having children repeat them after you, until you say the word *can*. Repeat for the words *rat, map,* and *tan*.

 Have children turn to *Practice Book* page 49. Help children identify the pictures. Have them trace the letter *a* in each word.

Day 5

PRETEACH

High-Frequency Words

Write the word *he* on the board. Point to and read *he*. Have children say it with you. Point to a boy in the room. Say: **He is nice.** Display an index card with the word *he*. Say: **he.** Match the index card to the word on the board, say the word, and have children say it with you.

Distribute an index card with the word *he* to each child. Have children point to the word and read it. Tell children that you will show them words, and when they see *he,* they should say the word and point to it on the card. Hold up index cards with the words *he, go, like, my,* and *to* in random order until children consistently identify the word *he*. Retrieve the cards for use in Lesson 9.

RETEACH

Build Robust Vocabulary

Remind children of the Student-Friendly Explanations for *proceed, announced,* and *gasped.* Then discuss each word, using the following examples.

proceed
Can you *proceed* down a path if a log is in the way? Why or why not?

announced
If a teacher *announced* that it's time to cleanup, did she whisper or talk loudly?

gasped
If someone yawned and someone else *gasped*, did they make the same sound? Show your answer.

High-Frequency Words	
go	he
like	my
to	

VOCABULARY

Student-Friendly Explanations

proceed To proceed means to go forward.

announced If someone announced something, they would say it so everyone would hear it.

gasped When you gasp, you take a short, quick breath.

Grade K

DAY AT A GLANCE — Day 1

LESSON 9

PHONEMIC AWARENESS
Onset/Rime Blending

PHONICS
Preteach Word Building

HIGH-FREQUENCY WORDS
Reteach *he*

COMPREHENSION
Reteach Characters

BUILD ROBUST VOCABULARY
Reteach *sly, imaginary, active*

Materials Needed:

Photo Cards   Word Builder and Word Builder Cards   Write-On/Wipe-Off Boards

Copying Master 17   Practice Book 50

Phonemic Awareness

 Onset/Rime Blending Tell children that you will play a game with them. You will say a word in two parts and they will blend the parts together to say the word. Say: **I am thinking of word. It begins with /g/. It ends with *ame*. The word is *game*. Now you try it. I am thinking of another word. It begins with /l/. It ends with *og*. What is the word?** (*log*) Display *Photo Cards* box, boy, cow, fish, and milk. Hold up *Photo Card* box. Say: **/b/-*ox*, *box*.** Have children repeat. Then place the *Photo Card* face down and say the word again, pronouncing the onset and then the rime. Have children follow your example as they blend the word parts to say the names of the remaining *Photo Cards*.

PRETEACH — Phonics

Blend Words Distribute *Word Builders* and *Word Builder Cards* *a, c, d, m, n, p, r, s,* and *t*. Review each letter name and sound with children. Say: **Use your *Word Builder* and *Word Builder Cards* to make new words with me. I will use the letters *c, a,* and *p* to make the word *cap*. Now you do the same. Blend the sounds with me: /k/-/a/-/p/, *cap*. If I take away the *c* and put *t* in its place, I have the word *tap*. Now you try it. Blend the sounds and say the word with me: /t/-/a/-/p/, *tap*.**

Build Words Have children continue with *nap* in their *Word Builder*:

- Change *n* to *r*. What word did you make? (*rap*)
- Change *p* to *n*. What word did you make? (*ran*)

 Continue with the words *man, mat,* and *cat*. Then have children practice writing the words they built on their *Write-On/Wipe-Off Boards*.

 Distribute *Copying Master* page 17. Have children trace the letters at the bottom of the page and cut them out. Help children identify the pictures. Then have children paste the letter *a* in the box to complete each picture name. (*nap, can, cat, pan*)

98   Lesson 9

Day 1

RETEACH

High-Frequency Words

Write *he* on the board and read it with children. Then write these sentences on the board: *He is five. He likes toys. He has a dog.* Read them aloud and have children repeat. Work with children to point to and read the word *he* in each sentence.

Write *go, he, like* and *to* on index cards. Tell children that you will hold up index cards. When they see the word *he,* they should read the word and point to a boy in the group. If they don't see the card, they should fold their arms. Cycle through the cards several times.

High-Frequency Words

go	he
like	to

RETEACH

Comprehension

Characters Remind children that the people or animals in a story are called the characters. Then read this story aloud to them. Model how to figure out who the characters are.

One morning Little Wolf's mom told him that he would stay up late that night. Usually he went to bed early with the other wolves, but tonight would be different. So that night, he stayed up.

"What's so special about tonight?" he asked.

"Wait and see," they said.

Little Wolf looked up but all he could see were clouds in the night sky. Then the clouds moved and he saw a big yellow moon. The wolves lifted their heads and howled. Little Wolf howled, too.

Have children turn to *Practice Book* page 50. Have them identify which picture shows characters from the story and who they are. Ask them to retell what the characters do and say in the story.

RETEACH

Build Robust Vocabulary

Remind children of the Student-Friendly Explanations for *sly, imaginary,* and *active*. Then discuss each word, using the following examples.

sly
If you were in a story, who would you rather meet—a *sly* fox or an honest fox? Why?

imaginary
If you visited an *imaginary* land, could you see rainbow bridges? Why or why not?

active
If a bat is *active* at night, is it flying or sleeping? Why do you think so?

VOCABULARY
Student-Friendly Explanations

sly Someone who is sly is tricky and sneaky.

imaginary Something that is imaginary is not real. It is make-believe.

active If you are active you are doing something.

Grade K   99

LESSON 9

PHONEMIC AWARENESS
Onset/Rime Blending

PHONICS
Reteach Word Building

HIGH-FREQUENCY WORDS
Reteach *he*

COMPREHENSION
Preteach Summarize

BUILD ROBUST VOCABULARY
Reteach *apparel, voyage, whimper*

Materials Needed:

Word Builders/ Word Builder Cards | Write-On/ Wipe-Off Boards | Copying Master

Photo Cards | Practice Book

Phonemic Awareness

Blend Onsets and Rimes   Remind children that words are made up of parts. Tell them to listen as you say a word in two parts. Have them think about the word you are saying. Say: **First I'll say /b/. Next, I'll say *oat*. I'll blend the word parts together to say the word: *boat*. Say the word with me: *boat*.** Model blending the following word parts several times, increasing the pace each time: /n/-ut *(nut)*, /b/-ook *(book)*, /n/-est *(nest)*, /k/-oat *(coat)*, /t/-ime *(time)*, /b/-ird *(bird)* Then ask children to blend the parts and name each word.

RETEACH

Phonics

How Are They Different?   Tell children that they will be listening to words to tell how they are different. For example, say: **What is the first sound in *Dan*?** (/d/) **What is the first sound in *tan*?** (/t/) **How are *Dan* and *tan* different?** (They have different beginning sounds.) **What is the ending sound in *cat*?** (/t/) **What is the ending sound in *can*?** (/n/) **How are *cat* and *can* different?** (They have different ending sounds.) **Which sound is different in *tap* and *nap*?** (the beginning sounds)

Blend Words   Distribute *Word Builders* and *Word Builder Cards a, c, d, m, n, p, s,* and *t*. Review each letter name and sound. Then hold up letters at random and ask children to tell the letter name and sound.

Explain to children that you are going to show them how a word can change when the letters in the word change. Say: **Use your *Word Builder* and *Word Builder Cards* to make new words with me. I will use the letters *m, a,* and *p* to make the word *map*. Now you do the same. Blend the sounds with me: /m/-/a/-/p/, *map*. If I take away the *p* and put *d* in its place, I have the word *mad*. Now you try it. Blend the sounds and say the word with me: /m/-/a/-/d/, *mad*.**

Build Words   Have children continue with *sad* in their *Word Builder*:

- Change *d* to *p*. What word did you make? (*sap*)
- Change *s* to *t*. What word did you make? (*tap*)

Continue with the words *nap, cap,* and *can*. Then have children practice writing the words they built on their *Write-On/Wipe-Off Boards*.

Distribute *Copying Master* page 18. Help children name each picture and read the word choices below each picture. Then have children circle the word that names the picture and write the word. (*tap, map, nap, cat*)

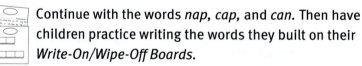

100 Lesson 9

Day 2

RETEACH

High-Frequency Words

  Use index cards with the words *He, can, go, to, the,* and a card with a period to build the sentence frame: *He can go to the _____.* Track each word as you read the sentence. Reread it with children. Ask a volunteer to point to the word *he*. Then complete the sentence with *Photo Card hill*. Read the sentence with children.

Have children turn to *Practice Book* page 51 to review high-frequency words and practice newly learned words. Complete the page together.

High-Frequency Words	
go	he
the	to

PRETEACH

Comprehension

Summarize Recall the story about the Little Wolf from Day 1. Tell children that a story summary tells what a story is about in a couple of sentences. Explain that summarizing may help the reader remember the story better.

Begin a Beginning, Middle, and Ending Chart. Say: **When I summarize a story, I tell what happens in the beginning, middle, and the end of the story.**

As you reread the story from Day 1, pause occasionally to summarize and record what happened at the beginning, middle, and end of the story.

In the beginning,	Little Wolf is told that he can stay up late.
In the middle,	he stays up late.
At the end,	all the wolves howl at the moon.

RETEACH

Build Robust Vocabulary

Remind children of the Student-Friendly Explanations for *apparel, voyage,* and *whimper*. Then discuss each word, using the following examples.

apparel
Would you have the same *apparel* for the beach and for school? Why or why not?

voyage
What is a *voyage*—a trip to the moon or a trip to the park? Why do you think so?

VOCABULARY
Student-Friendly Explanations

apparel Apparel is another word for clothing.

voyage If you go on a voyage, you go on a trip to somewhere far away.

whimper When someone whimpers, they make a quiet crying sound.

Grade K

LESSON 9

DAY AT A GLANCE — Day 3

PHONEMIC AWARENESS
Onset/Rime Blending

PHONICS
Preteach Phonogram -ap

HIGH-FREQUENCY WORDS
Reteach he

COMPREHENSION
Reteach Characters

BUILD ROBUST VOCABULARY
Reteach gigantic, glum, glum, precisely, complained

WRITING
Reteach Writing Trait: Word Choice

Materials Needed:

Phoneme Phone

Write-On/ Wipe-Off Boards

Photo Cards

Practice Book

Phonemic Awareness

Blend Onsets and Rimes Remind children that words are made up of parts. Tell them to listen as you say a word in two parts. Have them think about the word you are saying. Say: **First I'll say /k/. Next, I'll say *up*. I'll blend the word parts together to say the word: *cup*. Say the word with me: *cup*.**

Give each child a *Phoneme Phone*. Model using the *Phoneme Phone* to look at your mouth as you blend the parts to say: **b/-ook** (*book*). Have children use the *Phoneme Phones* to blend the word parts to say each word. Repeat the onsets and rimes several times.

/f/-**in** (*fin*)	/p/-**at** (*pat*)	/v/-**an** (*van*)
/g/-**oose** (*goose*)	/t/-**ub** (*tub*)	/w/-**olf** (*wolf*)
/k/-**orn** (*corn*)	/w/-**in** (*win*)	/h/-**ot** (*hot*)

PRETEACH
Phonics

Identify Rhyming Words Say the words *lap* and *tap,* and have children repeat them. Say: **The words *lap* and *tap* rhyme because they both end with /ap/.** Then tell children that you are going to say pairs of words. If the words rhyme, children should clap. If the words do not rhyme, children say nothing. Use the following pairs of words.

| **gap, tap** | **sap, sat** | **nap, cab** |
| **rap, gap** | **lap, cap** | **map, man** |

For additional reinforcement, tell children to listen for *-ap* in the following words. Have them tap their toes each time they hear *-ap*. Say: ***gap, nap, cat, tap, map, sat, lap, ran.***

Produce Rhymes Then tell children you are going to say a word. They should think of a word that rhymes with it, raise their hand, and say the rhyming word when you call on them. Use the following words: *bat*, *tan*, *tap*.

Day 3

 Read Words with -ap Write the word *cap* on the board. Track the print as you read the word. Have children repeat after you. Then write the word *sap*. Track the print as you read the word. Have children repeat after you. Ask how the two words are the same. (They both have /ap/; they rhyme.) Say: **The words *cap* and *sap* are in the -ap word family because they both end in *ap*.** Continue with the words *tap* and *map*.

Distribute *Write-on/Wipe-off Boards*. Write these words on the board: *gap, nap, rat, sap, tap, tin*. Have children read the words and circle the letters *ap*. Have them copy those words in the *-ap* word family on their *Write-on/Wipe-off Boards*.

High-Frequency Words	
he	ran
the	to

RETEACH

High-Frequency Words

Use index cards with the words *He, ran, to, the* and a card with a period to build the sentence frame shown below. Point to and read each word and have children repeat it. Ask a volunteer to point to the word *He*. Then place *Photo Card van* to complete the sentence, and have children read it aloud:

Replace *Photo Card van* with *Photo Card taxi*. Point to each word as children read the sentence with you. Repeat for *Photo Cards helicopter, hill, truck,* and *tree*.

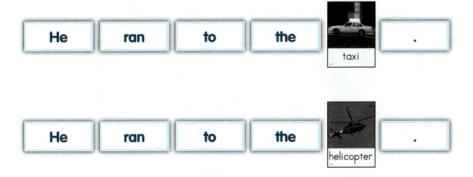

Grade K 103

Day 3

RETEACH

Comprehension

  Characters Remind children that the characters in a story are the people or animals that the story is about. Have children listen as you read aloud the following story.

Early Saturday morning, Billy and his brother Dylan waited on Main Street. In the distance they could hear the sound of marching drums. Soon marchers walked past. They played trumpets and pounded their drums. Dancers twirled and kicked their legs. They threw candy into the crowd.

"Look, I got a piece," Billy shouted.

"Hey, there's our teacher," Dylan called. He waved at Ms. Rodriguez. She sat in the front seat of a car decorated with flowers. She was in the parade as the Best Teacher of the Year. She waved back and smiled.

Guide children to *Practice Book* page 52. Have them look at the pictures and circle the characters. Have them retell what the characters do in the story. Ask: **In the beginning of the story you meet two characters. Who are they?** (Billy and Dylan) **Who do they see in the parade?** (They see trumpet players, drummers, dancers, and their teacher, Ms. Rodriguez.)

Day 3

RETEACH

Build Robust Vocabulary

Remind children of the Student-Friendly Explanations for *precisely, gigantic, glum,* and *complained.* Then discuss each word, using the following examples.

precisely
If you know your telephone number *precisely*, can you say it without any mistakes? Why or why not?

gigantic
What animals would seem *gigantic* to an ant? Can you name some?

glum
What word means almost the same thing as *glum: happy* or *sad*? Can you show the glum feeling on your face?

complained
Would you rather play with a friend who *complained* a lot or who laughed a lot? Why?

VOCABULARY
Student-Friendly Explanations

precisely Precisely means exactly.

gigantic Something that is gigantic is very, very big.

glum When you feel glum, you feel sad.

complained If you complained about something, you told how it makes you unhappy.

RETEACH

Writing

Writing Trait: Word Choice Tell children that when they write a caption, they should use words that tell about the main thing that is happening in the picture. This helps the reader get a good understanding of what the picture is mostly about.

Remind children that they heard a story about two boys who went to a parade. Reread the story. Then invite children to draw a picture about the story. Choose one of the pictures, and say: **I want to write a caption for this picture. What words can I use to tell someone what the picture is mostly about?**

Write down children's words on the board or on chart paper. Work with them to add enough information to form complete sentences. Read the captions aloud. Point out how they tell about the parade.

Grade K 105

LESSON 9

DAY AT A GLANCE — Day 4

PHONEMIC AWARENESS
Onset/Rime Blending

PHONICS
Reteach Phonogram -an

READING
Review Words with Phonograms -ap, -an
Review High-Frequency Words

BUILD ROBUST VOCABULARY
Review proceed, voyage, gasped, active, glum, imaginary

WRITING
Reteach Writing Form: Caption Sentences

Materials Needed:

Photo Cards   Write-On/Wipe-Off Boards   Practice Book pp. 53–54

Phonemic Awareness

 Blend Onsets and Rimes Tell children that you will play a game with them. You will say a word in two parts and they will blend the parts together to say the word. Say: **I am thinking of a word. It begins with /h/. It ends with *at*. The word is *hat*. Now you try it. I am thinking of another word. It begins with /t/. It ends with *op*. What is the word? It is *top*.**

Place *Photo Cards* of various CVC words on the chalk ledge, such as *box, cat, dog, fox, pan, pig,* and *van*. Say the onset and then the rime of one of the words. Have children point to the corresponding picture and then say the word. Continue until all of the words have been said.

RETEACH
Phonics

Identify Rhyming Words Say the words *tan* and *can,* and have children repeat them. Say: **The words *tan* and *can* rhyme because they both end with /an/.** Then say the words *can* and *cat*. Say: **The words *can* and *cat* do not rhyme. They have different ending sounds.** Tell children that you are going to say pairs of words. If the words rhyme, children should give the thumbs-up sign. If the words do not rhyme, children should give the thumbs-down sign. Use the following pairs of words.

ran, tan	map, man	can, pan
Dan, dad	tan, man	Nan, nap

Read Words with *-an* Write the word *an* on chart paper. Track the print as you read the word. Have children repeat after you. Then write the word *tan*. Track the print as you read the word. Have children repeat after you. Ask how the two words are the same. (They both have /an/; they rhyme.) Explain to children that the only difference in these two words are that they have different beginning letters and sounds.

 Distribute *Write-on/Wipe-off Boards*. Write these words on the board: *man, Nan, tan, pat, pan, lap, can*. Have children read the words. Call on a volunteer to circle the letters *-an* in the words on the board. Have children copy the words in the *-an* word family on their *Write-on/Wipe-off Boards*.

106 Lesson 9

Day 4

REVIEW
Reading

 Read Words with Phonograms -ap, -an Write these words on chart paper. Track the print and read them together: *map, tap, nap, man, tan, can*.

Review High-Frequency Words Reuse or create index cards for *he, like, my,* and *the*. Display the cards. Read each card aloud, tracking the word as you read it. Have children repeat the words after you. Then shuffle the cards and randomly display each word, having children read each word. Continue until all the words have been correctly identified.

Have children turn to *Practice Book* pages 53–54. Have children read the sentences as a take-home book to practice the newly-learned words.

REVIEW
Robust Vocabulary

Remind children of the Student-Friendly Explanations for *proceed, voyage, gasped, active, glum,* and *imaginary*. Then determine children's understanding of the words by asking the following questions.

- Would you *proceed* on a *voyage* in a leaky boat? Why or why not?
- If a boy in a story *gasped* at the sight of a giant mouse, is he in an *imaginary* story or a real story? Why do you think so?
- If you are *active* outside with friends, do you think you are happy or *glum*? Why?

RETEACH
Writing

Writing Form: Caption Sentences Tell children that they are going to write sentences with you about a person who is special to them. Ask: **Who is special to you? Why is that person special to you?** List children's responses on the board. After the list is complete, reread children's responses.

Draw a picture on the board of someone who is special to you. Model writing a caption. Say: **I am going to write a sentence that tells about the picture. I will tell why this person is special to me.** Write a caption underneath, such as, *My sister is funny*.

Invite a volunteer to draw a picture on chart paper of someone who is special to him or her. As a group, write a caption sentence for the picture. Encourage them to use words from the board. Read the caption aloud. Point out the period at the end of the sentence. Elicit how the words in the caption help the reader get a good understanding of what the picture is mostly about.

> My dad reads to me.

High-Frequency Words

he	like
my	the

VOCABULARY
Student-Friendly Explanations

proceed To proceed means to go forward

voyage If you go on a voyage, you go on a trip to a place far away.

gasped When you gasp, you take a short, quick breath.

active If you are active you are doing something.

glum When you feel glum, you feel sad.

imaginary Something that is imaginary is not real. It is make-believe.

LESSON 9

DAY AT A GLANCE
Day 5

PHONEMIC AWARENESS
Phoneme Isolation

PHONICS
Preteach Short Vowel /i/i

HIGH-FREQUENCY WORDS
Preteach come
Review go, like, my, the

BUILD ROBUST VOCABULARY
Preteach squabble, mischief, uproar

Materials Needed:

Photo Cards   Sound/Spelling Card Ii   Practice Book

Phonemic Awareness

 Phoneme Isolation Remind children that words are made of sounds. Point out that they can listen for the beginning sound in a word. Display *Photo Cards rabbit, ladder,* and *box.* Say: **Listen as I say a word: rabbit. Rabbit. I hear /rr/ at the beginning.** Say the word again, emphasizing the beginning consonant, /rr/. Repeat the activity with the words *ladder* and *box.* Emphasize the initial sound to help children better isolate the phoneme. Then, say each of the following words:

| for (/f/) | now (/n/) | day (/d/) | each (/ē/) | inch (/i/) |
| at (/a/) | come (/k/) | igloo (/i/) | gold (/g/) | if (/i/) |

Have volunteers identify the initial sound they hear at the beginning of each word.

PRETEACH

Phonics

 Short Vowel /i/i Display *Sound/Spelling Card Ii.* Say: **This is the letter i. Say the name with me.** Point to uppercase *I* and say: **This is uppercase I.** Point to lowercase *i* and say: **This is lowercase i.** Have children identify the letters. (I, i)

Writing *I* and *i* Write *Ii* on the board and have children identify the letters. Say: **Watch as I write the letter I.** As you give the Letter Talk, trace the uppercase *I.* Do the same for lowercase *i.*

Letter Talk for *I*	Letter Talk for *i*
1. Straight line down.	1. Straight line down.
2. Go to the top.	2. Dot above the line.
3. Straight line across.	
4. Go to the bottom.	
5. Straight line across.	

108 Lesson 9

Practice Book 55

Guided Practice Have children finger-write the uppercase *I* in the air as you repeat the Letter Talk. Do the same for lowercase *i*. Then, have children turn to *Practice Book,* page 55. Have children circle each uppercase *I* and underline each lowercase *i*. Then have them practice writing each letter.

PRETEACH
High-Frequency Words

Write the word *come* on the board. Say the word. Have children repeat the word, point to the word, and read it. Then write on the board the words *go, like, my,* and *the*. Read each word to children, and have them repeat that word and point to the correct word. Tell children that you will point to words, and when you point to the word *come,* they should say it and point to the word also. Randomly point to *go, like, my, the,* and *come* until children consistently identify *come*.

High-Frequency Words

come	go
like	my
the	

PRETEACH
Build Robust Vocabulary

Read the Student-Friendly Explanations for the words *squabble, mischief,* and *uproar*. Then discuss each word by asking children the following questions.

squabble
What does it look like when two children *squabble* over a toy?

mischief
Which do you think is more likely to get into *mischief*: a turtle or a puppy? Why?

uproar
Would you be more likely to hear an *uproar* on the playground or in an office building? What might cause the uproar?

VOCABULARY
Student-Friendly Explanations

squabble If you squabble with someone, you argue about something that is not very important.

mischief If you get into mischief, you cause trouble by playing tricks on people.

uproar An uproar is a lot of noise and fussing made by someone who is upset about something.

Day 5

Grade K 109

LESSON 10

PHONEMIC AWARENESS
Phoneme Isolation

PHONICS
Preteach Short Vowel /i/*i*

HIGH-FREQUENCY WORDS
Reteach *come*
Review *a*

COMPREHENSION
Reteach Draw Conclusions

BUILD ROBUST VOCABULARY
Reteach *squabble, mischief, uproar*

Materials Needed:

Phoneme Phone · Sound/Spelling Card *Ii* · Sounds of Letters CD

Word Builder and Word Builder Cards · Copying Master · Photo Cards

Practice Book

Phonemic Awareness

Phoneme Isolation Show children how to identify and isolate the initial sound in a word. Say: **Listen as I say a word: *inch*.** Elongate /ii/ as you say /iinch/, and have children repeat /iinch/. Model using the *Phoneme Phone* to look at the position of your mouth as you say the word. Have children do the same. **The beginning sound in *inch* is /i/. Say /i/. Now listen as I say another word: *can*. I hear /k/ at the beginning. /kan/.** Continue with the following words. Have children use the *Phoneme Phone* to look at the position of their mouth as they repeat each word and name the sound they hear at the beginning:

| **lamp** (/l/) | **watch** (/w/) | **rock** (/r/) | **most** (/m/) | **dog** (/d/) |
| **tree** (/t/) | **bird** (/b/) | **violet** (/v/) | **in** (/i/) | **pear** (/p/) |

PRETEACH
Phonics

Relate *Ii* to /i/ Display *Sound/Spelling Card Ii*. Say: **One sound that the letter *i* may stand for is /i/, the sound at the beginning of *ill*. Say /i/.** Have children repeat the sound as you touch the card several times. Play the /i/ sound from the *Sounds of Letters CD*.

 Give each child a *Word Builder Card i*. Say: **If the word begins with /i/, hold up the card and say /i/. If the word does not begin with /i/, hold your card behind your back.** Say the words *in, is, my, did, inch, it, pit, insect,* and *pin*. Tell children that /i/ may also be heard in the middle of words like *big*. Follow the same procedure for the medial position, using the words *rag, sip, wig, ten, flap,* and *dig*. Then have children tell whether /i/ is at the beginning or middle of these words:

with   ill   give   flip   inside   invent

 Distribute *Copying Master 19*. Have children identify each picture and circle the letter that stands for the beginning sound of each picture name. (Children should circle letter *i*: *igloo, iguana, inch*; letter *m*: *mitt* and *milk*.)

Day 1

RETEACH

High-Frequency Words

 Write the word *come* on the board. Say the word, and have children repeat it and point to the word. Show *Photo Card dog*. Write on the board *A _____ can come*. Tell children to imagine there is a party for the animals. Have a volunteer point to *come* as you read the sentence frame. Complete the sentence with *Photo Card dog*. Read the sentence to children. Have children point to the sentence and read it. Then have them take turns completing the sentence starter with other animals that could be invited to the party.

High-Frequency Words	
a	come

PRETEACH

Comprehension

Draw Conclusions Remind children that the author of a story sometimes puts clues in a story to help the reader understand things the author doesn't say. Then read this story aloud to them.

Tanya ran down the stairs to the kitchen. Her father was at the stove making pancakes. He turned around and flashed a big smile at her. "It's your day, Tanya! I'm making your favorite breakfast—pancakes!"

"Thank you, Daddy!" Tanya said, and hugged him. Then she asked, "When can I open the package that came in the mail from Grandma?"

Her father chuckled, "Tonight, after your mother and I get home from work, okay?"

Tanya nodded happily and started to set the table for breakfast. She knew it was going to be a great day.

 Guide children to *Practice Book* page 56. Have them look at the pictures and draw conclusions based on them. Ask: **What happened when Tanya woke up? What did she do when she went downstairs? Which package do you think came from Grandma? Why?**

PRETEACH

Build Robust Vocabulary

Talk about the Student-Friendly Explanations of *squabble, mischief,* and *uproar*. Then discuss each word, using the following examples.

squabble
Would you be more likely to *squabble* over sharing a vegetable or a dessert?

mischief
Do you have a friend or a sibling with whom you sometimes get into *mischief*? What happens when you do?

uproar
Can one child make an *uproar*? Tell why or why not.

VOCABULARY
Student-Friendly Explanations

squabble If you squabble with someone, you argue about something that is not very important.

mischief If you get into mischief, you cause trouble by playing tricks on people.

uproar An uproar is a lot of noise and fussing made by someone who is upset about something.

Grade K 111

LESSON 10

DAY AT A GLANCE — Day 2

PHONEMIC AWARENESS
Phoneme Isolation

PHONICS
Preteach Blending /i/i, /t/t

HIGH-FREQUENCY WORDS
Reteach come
Review a, to, the

COMPREHENSION
Preteach Make Inferences

BUILD ROBUST VOCABULARY
Preteach tend, soggy, wobble

Materials Needed:

Word Builder and Word Builder Cards

Copying Master

Photo Cards

Practice Book 57

Phonemic Awareness

Phoneme Isolation Tell children that you will say three words that all have the same beginning sound, and then they will name the first sound they hear in the words. Say: **Listen for the beginning sound of these words: cold, cat, cane. I hear /k/ at the beginning of cold, cat, and cane. Say the sound: /k/.** Repeat the activity, asking volunteers to identify the initial sound of the words in of the following sets:

sold, sad, sink (/s/)	**goat, get, gap** (/g/)	**ill, it, is** (/i/)
just, jump, jet (/j/)	**hill, has, her** (/h/)	**key, king, key** (/k/)

RETEACH
Phonics

Blend Sounds Clap your hands to get a steady rhythm going. Then, in time with the beat, say: **We're going on a word hunt. What's this word? /p/ /i/ /n/ Together: pin!** Have children echo you. Continue for the words /b/ /i/ /g/ (**big**), /d/ /i/ /d/ (**did**), /h/ /i/ /m/ (**him**).

 Blending /i/i, /t/t Place the Word Builder Cards i and t in the Word Builder. Point to i. Say /ii/. Have children name the letter and sound. Point to t. Say /t/. Have children name the letter and sound. Slide the t next to i. Move your hand under the letters and blend the sounds: /iit/. Have children repeat after you. Then have children blend and read the word it with you. Continue with the words sit, bit, fit, and kit.

 Distribute *Copying Master 20* to review short /i/i with children. Help children identify the pictures. Children should write the letter *i* for *inch, iguana, igloo, insects,* and *ill*.

RETEACH
High-Frequency Words

Use *Photo Card tree*, the words *A, can, come, to,* and *the* on index cards, and the period card to build the sentence frame shown. Point to each word as you read the sentence. Reread it with children. Ask a volunteer to point to the word *come*. Place the *Photo Card frog* to complete the sentence, and have children read the sentence with you.

| A | frog | can | come | to | the | tree | . |

Day 2

Practice Book 57 — Replace the *frog* card with *Photo Card fox*. Point to each word and have children read the new sentence with you. Repeat with the cards for *ant, boy, girl,* and *rabbit.* Have children turn to *Practice Book,* page 57 to review high-frequency words and practice newly-learned words. Complete the page together.

High-Frequency Words

a	come
the	to

PRETEACH
Comprehension

Make Inferences Explain that good readers use what they already know and clues from the author to figure out details in a story that the author did not directly say. Recall the story about Tanya's morning from Day 1. Copy the chart below onto chart paper. Ask: **What do you already know about birthdays?** Record some responses in the What I Know column. Say: **The Text Clues column is for clues that the author may give about Tanya's special day. Let's read to find clues that will help us understand more about her day.**

As you read, help children make inferences by focusing on clues in the selection. Add the clues and inferences to the graphic organizer.

What I Know +	Text Clues =	Inferences
It can be exciting to have a birthday.	Tanya is very excited to start the day.	Tanya has been waiting for this day and is happy it is here.
Some families celebrate with special meals.	Tanya's father says he is making her favorite breakfast.	This family celebrates birthdays by having special meals.
Relatives who live far away may send gifts.	Tanya has received a package from her grandma.	The package is a birthday gift.

RETEACH
Build Robust Vocabulary

Remind children of the Student-Friendly Explanations of *tend, soggy,* and *wobble.* Then discuss each word, using the following examples.

tend
Would you be more likely to *tend* to a scratched knee, or to a television? How?

soggy
How might a rainy day make something turn *soggy*?

wobble
What makes a table or chair *wobble* on a flat floor? Is there a way to fix it?

VOCABULARY
Student-Friendly Explanations

tend When you tend to something, you take care of it.

soggy Something that is soggy is so wet that it's squishy.

wobble When things wobble, they move from side to side in an unsteady way.

Grade K 113

LESSON 10

PHONEMIC AWARENESS
Phoneme Isolation

PHONICS
Reteach Word Blending and Building

HIGH-FREQUENCY WORDS
Reteach come
Review the, to

COMPREHENSION
Reteach Draw Conclusions

BUILD ROBUST VOCABULARY
Reteach tend, soggy, wobble

WRITING
Preteach Writing Trait: Organization

Materials Needed:

Word Builder and Word Builder Cards

Write-On/Wipe-Off Boards

Photo Cards

Practice Book

Phonemic Awareness

Phoneme Isolation   Tell children that you will say two words that have the same beginning sound, and then they will name the first sound they hear in the words. Say: **Listen for the beginning sound of these words: cold, cat. I hear /k/ at the beginning of cold and cat. Say the sound: /k/.** Repeat the activity, asking volunteers to identify the initial sound of the following pairs of words:

sold, sad (/s/)   **goat, get** (/g/)   **it, is** (/i/)

jump, jet (/j/)   **hill, has** (/h/)   **key, king** (/k/)

Syllable Segmentation   Remind children that they have been working with beginning sounds and that they have also worked with word parts, or syllables. Remind them how to segment words into syllables. Say: **Insect. I can break the word into parts: in-sect. Say the word parts with me: in-sect.** Have children listen to the words you say, and divide them into syllables:

in-vent (invent)   **tur-key** (turkey)   **be-low** (below)

hap-py (happy)   **in-to** (into)   **a-gree** (agree)

RETEACH
Phonics

Blend Words   Distribute *Word Builders* and *Word Builder Cards a, i, n, p, s,* and *t*. Review each letter name and sound. Then hold up letters at random and ask children to say the letter name and sound.

Explain to children that you are going to show them how a word can change when the letters in the word change. Say: **Use your *Word Builder* and *Word Builder Cards* to make new words with me. I will use the letters *s*, *i*, and *p* to make the word *sip*. Now you do the same. Blend the sounds with me: /s/-/i/-/p/, *sip*. If I take away the *p* and put *t* in its place, I have the word *sit*. Now you try it. Blend the sounds and say the word with me: /s/-/i/-/t/, *sit*.**

Build Words   Have children continue with *tip* in their *Word Builder*:

Change the *p* to *n*. What word did you make? (*tin*)

Change the *t* to *p*. What word did you make? (*pin*)

Continue with the words *pan, pat,* and *sat.* Then have children practice writing the words they built on their *Write-on/Wipe-off Boards*.

114 Lesson 10

Day 3

RETEACH

High-Frequency Words

Write the words *come, to,* and *the* on the board. Say the words and have children repeat after you. Then point to each word randomly, and have children say the word as you point to it. Continue until they identify all words correctly and consistently.

Write the sentence frame *Come to the _____* on the board. Complete the sentence frame with *Photo Card helicopter*. Point to each word as you read the sentence. Reread it with children. Ask a volunteer to point to the word *come*. Continue with the following sentences. Point to each word in a sentence and have children read the sentence.

High-Frequency Words

come   the

to

Grade K 115

Day 3

RETEACH
Comprehension

  Draw Conclusions Remind children that the author of a story sometimes puts clues in a story to help the reader understand things the author doesn't say. Have children listen as you read aloud the following story:

> Raul decided to make his grandfather a card. He used a blue crayon to draw himself in the card. He used a green crayon to draw his grandfather in the big bed at the hospital. Raul took the card to his mother and handed her the orange crayon. "Please help me write 'Get well soon,'" he said.
>
> His mother looked at the orange crayon in her hand. "You want to write that with an orange crayon?" she asked.
>
> "Yes," replied Raul. "Orange is happy. I want him to be happy."
>
> "Ah," said his mother. She took Raul's hand and gently wrapped his fingers around the crayon. She put her hand around his hand and said, "We'll write the words together."

Pause as you read to help children draw conclusions. Then discuss the story.

What kind of card is this? (a Get Well card for someone who is sick) **How do you know?** (the message is "Get Well Soon" and the picture is of someone in a hospital bed)

Guide children to *Practice Book,* page 58. Have them look at the pictures as you ask them to identify which picture makes sense for the story, based on the clue the author has provided. Have them tell which clues in the story helped them decide on the correct pictures.

RETEACH
Build Robust Vocabulary

Remind children of the Student-Friendly Explanations of *tend, soggy,* and *wobble*. Then discuss each word, using the following examples.

tend
Tell what you might do if you were *tending* to a plant.

soggy
Do you mind *soggy* cereal? How can you keep cereal from getting soggy?

wobble
Can you stand on one foot and not *wobble*? Tell why or why not.

VOCABULARY
Student-Friendly Explanations

tend When you tend to something, you take care of it.

soggy Something that is soggy is so wet that it's squishy.

wobble When things wobble, they move from side to side in an unsteady way.

RETEACH

Writing

Writing Trait: Organization Remind children that when they write a list, they need to organize the items by writing each item below the next on a new line. Explain that it is also helpful to the reader to have a title that tells the reader what the list is about.

Write the following title on chart paper: *Things We Like*. Then ask children to name things that they like. If children get stuck, contribute something you like that could help children think of new categories of things they like (e.g., food, colors, pets, activities, seasons). Think aloud as you work to model writing each item on a new line. Clarify for children that it is each item and not each word that goes on a new line. Model by saying: **I just wrote spaghetti and meatballs. Now I want to write apple pie. Apple pie is a new item on my list, so it goes on the next line. Apple pie is two words, but both words go on the same line because they tell about the same thing.**

Grade K **117**

LESSON 10

PHONEMIC AWARENESS
Phoneme Isolation

PHONICS
Reteach Short Vowel /i/*i*

READING
Review Short Vowel /i/*i*
Review High-Frequency Words

BUILD ROBUST VOCABULARY
Review squabble, mischief, uproar, tend, soggy, wobble

WRITING
Preteach Writing Form: Lists

Materials Needed:

Phoneme Phone | Word Builder and Word Builder Cards | Write-On/Wipe-Off Boards

Practice Book

Phonemic Awareness

Phoneme Isolation Remind children that they can listen for the beginning sound in a word. Say: **Listen for the beginning sound of these words: *bat, band, bill*. I hear /b/ at the beginning of *bat, band,* and *bill*. Say the sound: /b/.** Repeat the activity, using each of the following sets of words and the *Phoneme Phones*.

cat, cold, can (/k/)   **nut, nine, nest** (/n/)   **doll, dad, dip** (/d/)

part, pin, pest (/p/)   **led, love, leaf** (/l/)   **mom, make, men** (/m/)

Remind children that they have been working with the beginning sounds in words. They have also worked with word parts called syllables. Say: ***Happy**. I can break the word into parts: **hap-py**. Say the word parts with me: **hap-py**.* Have children listen to the words you say, and divide them into syllables:

cen-ter (center)   **chil-i** (chili)   **far-ther** (farther)

fa-vor (favor)   **goal-ie** (goalie)   **men-u** (menu)

RETEACH

Phonics

Blend Sounds Write the word *pin* on an index card and hold it up for children to see. Model blending the sounds as you run a finger under each letter. Say: **/p/ /ii/ /nn/. Say it with me. /p/ /i/ /nn/. *Pin*.** Run a finger under the letters, having children read the word.

 Read Words Display the following *Word Builder Cards*: *a, i, n, p, s, t*. Use the *Word Builder Cards* to make more words. Tell children that they are going to read the words by blending the sounds for each letter. Have children blend the sounds to read each word.

Write Words Give children *Write-on/Wipe-off Boards*. Have children write words made using the *Word Builder Cards*. Invite them to read the words they have written to classmates.

118 Lesson 10

Day 4

REVIEW
Reading

Short Vowel /i/i Write the word *sits* on an index card. Have children blend the sounds to read the word.

High-Frequency Words Write the word *come* on the board. Point to and read the word. Have children repeat.

Then have children turn to *Practice Book,* pages 59–60. Help children cut and fold it into a book. Have children read the sentences to practice the skills.

REVIEW
Robust Vocabulary

Remind children of the Student-Friendly Explanations of *squabble, mischief, uproar, tend, soggy,* and *wobble.* Then determine children's understanding of the words by asking the following questions.

- **Which word better describes a group of barking puppies all trying to get the same dog bone: *mischief* or *uproar*? Why?**
- **Which word better describes a carboard box in the rain: *soggy* or *squabble*? Explain.**
- **Which word better describes caring for a living thing: *tend* or *wobble*? Why?**

RETEACH
Writing

Writing Form: Lists Remind children that people write lists often and for many reasons. Brainstorm reasons people write lists. (grocery lists, wish lists, to-do lists, lists of ideas, lists of things they don't want to forget)

Tell children that together you will write a list of things children have learned about or learned to do so far this year. Record the list on chart paper. Invite children to write letters and words they know. Then read the finished list, tracking the print as you read.

> What We Have Learned This Year
> writing letters
> plants need sun
> plants need water

VOCABULARY
Student-Friendly Explanations

squabble If you squabble with someone, you argue about something that is not very important.

mischief If you get into mischief, you cause trouble by playing tricks on people.

uproar An uproar is a lot of noise and fussing made by someone who is upset about something.

tend When you tend something, you take care of it.

soggy Something that is soggy is so wet that it's squishy.

wobble When things wobble, they move from side to side in an unsteady way.

LESSON 10

PHONEMIC AWARENESS
Phoneme Isolation

PHONICS
Preteach Consonant *Gg*

HIGH-FREQUENCY WORDS
Preteach *here*

BUILD ROBUST VOCABULARY
Preteach *anxious, huddle, moans*

Materials Needed:

Photo Cards   Sound/Spelling Card *Gg*   Write-On/Wipe-Off Boards

Practice Book

Phonemic Awareness

Phoneme Isolation Remind children that words are made of sounds. Point out that they can listen for the ending sound in a word. Display *Photo Cards ant, lamp, milk,* and *pig.* Say: **Listen as I say a word: *ant*. I hear /t/ at the end.** Say the word again, emphasizing the ending consonant, /t/. Repeat the activity with the words *lamp, milk,* and *pig.* Emphasize the final sound to help children better isolate the phoneme.

Then, say each of the following words:

cat (/t/)	**slip** (/p/)	**sun** (/n/)
sock (/k/)	**off** (/f/)	**broom** (/m/)

Have volunteers identify the final sound they hear at the end of each word.

PRETEACH
Phonics

I spy Display *Photo Cards milk, sun, rabbit, tiger, nest,* and *pencil.* Point to each card and have children name the picture. After all cards have been identified, say: **Let's play "I Spy." I'll give clues and you tell me which picture I'm looking at. I spy a picture that begins with /t/.** (tiger) Continue the activity, offering the initial sound as the first clue.

Consonant *Gg* Display *Sound/Spelling Card Gg.* Say: **This is the letter *g*. Say the name with me.** Point to uppercase *G* and say: **This is uppercase *G*.** Point to lowercase *g* and say: **This is lowercase *g*.** Have children identify the letters. (G, g)

Writing *G* and *g* Write *Gg* on the board and have children identify the letters. Say: **Watch as I write the letter *G*.** As you give the Letter Talk, trace the uppercase *G*. Do the same for lowercase *g*.

Letter Talk for *G*	Letter Talk for *g*
1. Circle left.	1. Circle left.
2. Stop at the dotted line.	2. Straight line down.
3. Straight line across.	3. Curve to the left.

120 Lesson 10

Guided Practice Have children use their Write-on/Wipe-off Board to write uppercase G as you repeat the Letter Talk. Repeat with lowercase g. Then have children turn to *Practice Book* page 61. Have children circle each uppercase G and underline each lowercase g. Then have them practice writing each letter.

PRETEACH
High-Frequency Words

Write the high-frequency word *here* on index cards, and distribute one to each child. Say the word. Have children repeat the word, point to the word, and read it. Tell children that you will show them words, and when they see *here*, they should say it and point to their card. Write high-frequency words *go, my, the,* and *to* on index cards. Randomly hold up the cards for *go, my, the, to,* and *here* until children consistently identify *here*. Randomly choose 8 *Photo Cards*, shuffle them, and place them in a pile face down. Write on the board *Here is a _____* and read the sentence starter aloud to the class. Have volunteers take the top card, look at it, and then read the sentence, using name of the *Photo Card* in the blank. As children say *here,* have them point to *here* on the board. Then, have the volunteer place the *Photo Card* on the bottom of the pile and choose the next volunteer. Continue until every child has had a chance to be the volunteer, or as time permits.

High-Frequency Word

here

PRETEACH
Build Robust Vocabulary

Remind children of the Student-Friendly Explanations of *anxious, huddle,* and *moans.* Then discuss each word, using the following examples.

anxious
Would you be more likely to feel *anxious* before going to the dentist or before watching a favorite show? Tell why.

huddle
Would you be more likely to sit in a *huddle* while playing a game or while doing homework? Tell why.

moans
Would you be more likely to *moan* if it were sunny outside or if it were rainy? Tell why.

VOCABULARY
Student-Friendly Explanations

anxious If you feel anxious, you feel nervous or afraid that something is going to happen.

huddle (n.) A huddle is a group of people or animals that are close together in a circle.

moans When someone moans, he or she is sad or mad, and makes a long, low sound.

Grade K 121

LESSON 11

PHONEMIC AWARENESS
Phoneme Isolation

PHONICS
Preteach Consonant *Gg*

HIGH-FREQUENCY WORDS
Reteach *here*

COMPREHENSION
Preteach Draw Conclusions

BUILD ROBUST VOCABULARY
Reteach *anxious, huddle, moans*

Materials Needed:

Photo Cards   Sounds of Letters CD   Sound/Spelling Card *Gg*

Word Builder and Word Builder Cards   Copying Master   Practice Book

Phonemic Awareness

Phoneme Isolation Tell children to listen for the final sound at the end of a word you say. Model how to identify and isolate the ending sound in words. Say: **Listen as I say a word:** *dream*. **I hear /m/ at the end.** /dreamm/. **Now listen as I say another word:** *drop*. **I hear /p/ at the end.** /drop/. **Next, say each of the following words:** *hot* (/t/), *flap* (/p/), *tan* (/n/), *week* (/k/), *half* (/f/), *pig* (/g/).

PRETEACH

Phonics

 Relate Gg to /g/ Say the words *give* and *gate* and have children repeat them. Tell children that *give* and *gate* begin with /g/. Play the /g/ sound from the *Sounds of Letters CD*. Have children say /g/ several times. Display *Sound/Spelling Card Gg*. Say: **The letter *g* can stand for /g/, the sound at the beginning of *gave*. Say /g/.** Have children repeat the sound as you touch the card several times. Give each child *Word Builder Card g*. Say: **If the word begins with /g/ hold up the card and say /g/. If the word does not begin with /g/, hold your card behind your back.** Say the words *mad, grape, red, gift, green,* and *go*. Tell children that /g/ may also be heard at the end of words, like *big*. Follow the same procedure for the final position, using the words *rag, stamp, wag, tan, flip,* and *dog*. Then have children tell whether /g/ is at the beginning or end of these words:

bug	gap	gust	tag	game	shrug	wig
leg	girl	brag	gap	peg	glue	good

 Distribute *Copying Master 21*. Have children identify each picture and circle the letter that stands for the beginning sound of each picture name. (Children should circle *g* for *girl, goat, gate, gloves, guitar*.)

122 Lesson 11

Day 1

RETEACH

High-Frequency Words

Write the word *here* on an index card for each child and distribute. Say the word and have children repeat it. Write on the board *Here is my _____*. Show *Photo Card hat*. Point to and read each word in the sentence, completing the sentence with the word *hat*. Have children match their word *here* to the word in the sentence. Repeat with other *Photo Cards*, having children match their index card *here*.

High-Frequency Word

here

PRETEACH

Comprehension

Draw Conclusions Tell children that the author may put clues in a story to help the reader understand things the author doesn't say. Then read this story aloud to them.

> Emily sighed. She was bored. Now that Ben was at school all morning, she had nothing to do. She found a sunny spot on the living room rug and lay down on the warm carpet. She put her paws over her eyes and went to sleep. She woke up to the sound of the school bus chugging up the steep street she lived on. The door suddenly burst open and Emily jumped up, barking for joy. Ben was home! Now they could play all afternoon.

Guide children to turn to *Practice Book* page 62. Have them look at the pictures as you ask them to identify which picture makes sense for the story, based on the clues the author has provided. (apple: dog looking sad; star: dog snoozing in sunny spot; fish: dog barking excitedly)

PRETEACH

Build Robust Vocabulary

Remind children of the Student-Friendly Explanations of *anxious*, *huddle*, and *moans*. Then discuss each word, using the following examples.

anxious
Why might someone feel *anxious* when trying to learn how to do something new?

huddle
In football, the team will often get in a *huddle* to plan what they will do next. Why might it help them to be in a *huddle*?

moans
What are some reasons you might *moan*?

VOCABULARY
Student-Friendly Explanations

anxious If you feel anxious, you feel nervous or afraid that something is going to happen.

huddle (n.) A huddle is a group of people or animals that are close together in a circle.

moans When someone moans, he or she is sad or mad, and makes a long, low sound.

Grade K 123

LESSON 11

DAY AT A GLANCE — Day 2

PHONEMIC AWARENESS
Phoneme Isolation

PHONICS
Preteach Consonant *Ff*

HIGH-FREQUENCY WORDS
Preteach *this*

COMPREHENSION
Preteach Monitor Comprehension: Reread

BUILD ROBUST VOCABULARY
Preteach *productive, idle, scrumptious*

Materials Needed:

Photo Cards   Phoneme Phone   Sound/Spelling Card *Ff*

Write-On/Wipe-Off Boards   Copying Master   Practice Book

Phonemic Awareness

Phoneme Isolation Remind children that words are made of sounds and that they have been listening for the ending sound in words. Display *Photo Cards box, dog, ladder,* and *octopus.* Say: **Listen as I say a word: *box.* I hear /ks/ at the end.** Say the word again, emphasizing the ending sound, /ks/. Model using the *Phoneme Phone* to look at the position of your mouth as you say the word. Repeat the activity with the words *dog, ladder,* and *octopus.* Then say each of the following words. Have children use the *Phoneme Phone* to look at the position of their mouth as they repeat each word and name the sound they hear at the end of each word.

man (/n/)   tag (/g/)   tub (/b/)   hop (/p/)   pass (/s/)

PRETEACH
Phonics

Consonant *Ff* Display *Sound/Spelling Card Ff.* Say: **This is the letter *f*. Say the name with me.** Point to uppercase *F* and say: **This is uppercase *F*.** Point to lowercase *f* and say: **This is lowercase *f*.** Have children identify the letters. (F, f) Write *F* and *f* on the board and have children identify the letters. Say: **Watch as I write the letter *F* so that everyone can read it.** As you give the Letter Talk, trace the letters.

Letter Talk for *F*	Letter Talk for *f*
1. Straight line down.	1. Curve left and down.
2. Go to the top.	2. Go to the middle.
3. Straight line across.	3. Straight line across.
4. Go to the middle.	
5. Straight line across.	

Guided Practice Have children finger-write the letters in the air as you repeat the Letter Talk. Then guide them to write the letter on their Write-on/Wipe-off Boards. Have them practice writing the letter on their boards several times. Distribute Copying Master 22. Have children circle each uppercase *F* and underline each lowercase *f*. Then have them trace each letter and practice writing it on the line.

124 Lesson 11

Day 2

PRETEACH
High-Frequency Words

Practice Book 63 Distribute index cards with the high-frequency word *this* written on it. Say the word and have children repeat it. Then have them point to the word and read it. Tell children that you will show them words, and when they see the word *this*, they should say the word and point to it. Randomly hold up index cards with the following high-frequency words printed on them: *I, like, he, come,* and *this*. Continue until children consistently identify the word *this*. Write on the board the sentence starter *Look at this* _____ and read it aloud to the class. Have children brainstorm words that could complete the sentence. List their responses on the board. Then have children turn to *Practice Book* page 63 to review high-frequency words. Complete the page together.

High-Frequency Word
this

PRETEACH
Comprehension

Focus Strategy **Monitor Comprehension: Reread** Explain that even good readers can get confused when reading a story. Remind children that they can reread the parts that are confusing. Recall the story about Emily's morning from Day 1. Copy the following onto chart paper.

Possible responses shown.

What I Don't Understand or Remember	What I Found Out After Rereading
Who is "she" in the first sentence? Who is Ben?	Emily is the character lying down on the rug. Ben is someone Emily misses.
Why did she wake up?	She woke up because a noisy school bus was driving by.

PRETEACH
Build Robust Vocabulary

Introduce the Student-Friendly Explanations of *productive, idle,* and *scrumptious*. Then discuss each word, using the following examples.

productive and idle
When is a good time to be *productive*? When might it be a good time to be *idle*?

scrumptious
What food is cooked in your home that is *scrumptious*? What is it about this food that makes it taste so good?

VOCABULARY
Student-Friendly Explanations

productive When you are productive you are making or doing something.

idle When you are idle, you are not doing anything.

scrumptious Something that is scrumptious tastes very, very good.

Grade K 125

LESSON 11

DAY AT A GLANCE — Day 3

PHONEMIC AWARENESS
Phoneme Isolation Final

PHONICS
Reteach Relate *Ff* to /f/

HIGH-FREQUENCY WORDS
Reteach *this*

COMPREHENSION
Reteach Draw Conclusions

BUILD ROBUST VOCABULARY
Reteach *productive, idle, scrumptious*

WRITING
Reteach Writing Trait: Ideas

Materials Needed:

Phoneme Phone | Photo Cards | Sounds of Letters CD

Sound/Spelling Card *Ff* | Word Builder and Word Builder Cards

Write-On/Wipe-Off Boards | Practice Book

Phonemic Awareness

Phoneme Isolation: Final Remind children that they can listen for the ending sound in a word. Say the following rhyme: **Listen carefully with each ear, and then say the ending sound you hear:** *rug, tag*–/g/. Repeat the rhyme, using the following pairs of words. Have children repeat each pair of words and name the ending sound.

sink, junk (/k/)	**tan, men** (/n/)	**bed, sad** (/d/)
mop, cup (/p/)	**cat, sit** (/t/)	**him, ham** (/m/)

Then model using the *Phoneme Phone* to look at the position of your mouth as you repeat each word. Have children do the same and name the sound they hear at the end.

Remind children that they have been working with ending sounds and that they have also learned how to blend word parts to say a word. Say: **First I'll say: /s/. Next I'll say *eed*. Then I will blend the parts together to say a word. /s/–*eed*, *seed*.** Have children repeat the following sounds and then blend the parts together to make the words:

/r/–ink (*rink*)   /h/–um (*hum*)   /d/–ig (*dig*)   /l/–ock (*lock*)

RETEACH

Phonics

  Relate *Ff* to /f/ Say the words *fresh* and *fly* and have children repeat the words. Tell them that *fresh* and *fly* begin with /f/. Play the sound of *f* from the *Sounds of Letters CD*. Have children repeat /f/ several times. Display *Sound/Spelling Card Ff*. Ask: **What is the name of this letter? The letter *f* stands for /f/, the sound at the beginning of *fresh*. Say /f/.** Have children repeat the sound as you touch the letter on the card several times. Give each child a *Word Builder Card f*. Say: **If the word begins with /f/ hold up the card and say /f/. If the word does not begin with /f/, hold your card behind your back.** Say the words *job, fork, found, pail,* and *float*.

Tell children that /f/ may also be heard at the end of words, such as *cuff*. Follow the same procedure for the final position, using the words *leaf, sniff, tan, flip,* and *calf*. Then have children tell whether /f/ is at the beginning or end of these words: *half, free, first, leaf, fade,* and *chief*.

126 Lesson 11

Day 3

 Give each child a *Write-on/Wipe-off Board*. Explain to children that they will be working with the three boxes next to the heart on side B of the *Write-on/Wipe-off Board*. Draw the boxes on chart paper. Display *Photo Cards fish* and *fox*. Also display a sketch of a leaf or a wolf drawn on an index card. Tell children: **I am going to say some words. If /f/ is at the beginning of the word, put your letter *f* on the first box. If /f/ is at the end of the word, put your letter *f* on the last box.** Model the activity using *fish, fox, leaf,* and *wolf*. Then say the following words, and have children place their *Word Builder Cards* on the appropriate box: *if, four, food, cliff, find*.

RETEACH
High-Frequency Words

Distribute to children index cards with the following words printed on them: *this, a, go, he,* and *my*. Say each word. Have children repeat the word and hold up the correct card. Guide children in tracing the word *this* on their index card. Have them say each letter as they trace it.

Show *Photo Card watermelon*. Ask children to say the picture name. Then use index cards with the words *this, is,* and *a* printed on them, *Photo Card watermelon,* and a period card to build the sentence frame shown below. Point to each word as you read the sentence. Ask children to read the sentence with you.

Invite children to take turns choosing another *Photo Card* to complete the sentence and reading their new sentence aloud.

High-Frequency Word

this

Day 3

RETEACH
Comprehension

 Draw Conclusions Remind children that the author of a story sometimes puts clues in a story to help the reader understand things the author doesn't say. Have children listen as you read aloud the following story:

> Milo climbed into the rocket, closed the flaps, and sat down. He turned his attention to the controls. He checked the gauges and put on his headphones. With the flip of a switch, he calls ground control. "Astronaut Hughes to ground control, do you read me?" "We read you Astronaut Hughes," came the reply. Then there was a loud gasp! "Oh, no! Watch out Astronaut Hughes! It's a—" Suddenly the rocket was knocked on its side and a large dog poked its head through the cardboard flaps to lick Milo's face enthusiastically. "Abort Mission! Abort Mission!" Milo giggled between licks. His brother was trying to pull the big dog off the crushed rocket, but was laughing too hard to have much success.

Discuss the story with children. Then guide children to *Practice Book* page 64. Have them look at the pictures and identify which picture would make sense in the story, based on the clue the author has provided. Ask these questions:

What is the rocket made out of? (a cardboard box) **What clues tell you so?** (closing the flaps, cardboard flaps)

Who was "ground control"? (Milo's brother)

Were the headphones and controls real or pretend? (pretend) **How do you know?** (cardboard boxes don't have rocket controls)

Have them tell which clues in the story helped them decide on the correct pictures. (apple: boy climbing into cardboard box; star: dog leaping on box; fish: two laughing boys and happy dog)

RETEACH
Build Robust Vocabulary

Remind children of the Student-Friendly Explanations of *productive, idle,* and *scrumptious*. Then discuss each word, using the following examples.

productive
Where are you more *productive*—at a desk, or on the floor? Why?

idle
Are you being *idle* if you are helping dry dishes? Why or why not?

scrumptious
If you could plan a meal of *scrumptious* foods, what foods would you include?

VOCABULARY
Student-Friendly Explanations

productive When you are productive you are making or doing something.

idle When you are idle, you are not doing anything.

scrumptious Something that is scrumptious tastes very, very good.

Day 3

RETEACH

Writing

Writing Trait: Ideas Remind children that the topic of a piece of writing is the main idea. Explain that a writer might have many ideas to write about. Remind children that once they know what their main idea, or topic, will be, they should be sure that all their sentences are about that idea in some way. Explain that pictures can also help to tell ideas about something. Show pictures from books the class is familiar with. Have volunteers offer details about the pictures, and then discuss how those details support the main idea.

Point out that good writers want to write something that is interesting to the reader. One way to do this is to think of what questions the reader will have about the topic. When you answer the reader's questions, you make the topic interesting to the reader. Write the following sentences on chart paper:

> Kate walked.
>
> Kate walked out onto the cold, dark porch.

Say: **Both sentences are about the same person and that the same person is doing the same action in both sentences, but one of the sentences contains more information for the reader. Which sentence is more interesting to read?** (the second sentence) **Why?** (Possible response: It has more ideas; It has more details; It helps you picture the scene better.)

Name a topic. Have children say sentences about that topic. Record their sentences on chart paper. Talk about each sentence, and work with the group to make the sentences answer questions the reader might have.

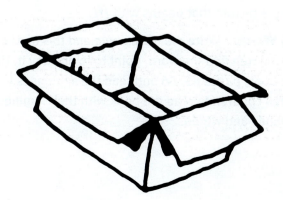

Grade K **129**

LESSON 11

PHONEMIC AWARENESS
Phoneme Isolation

PHONICS
Reteach Consonant /g/g, /f/f

READING
Review /g/g, /f/f
Review High-Frequency Words

BUILD ROBUST VOCABULARY
Review anxious, huddle, moans, productive, idle, scrumptious

WRITING
Reteach Writing Form: Poster

Materials Needed:

Phoneme Phone   Sound/Spelling Card Gg, Ff   Word Builder and Word Builder Cards

Photo Cards   Practice Book

High-Frequency Word

here   this

Phonemic Awareness

Phoneme Isolation Remind children that they can listen for the ending sound in a word. Say: **Listen carefully and then say the ending sound you hear: cat, pit-/t/.** Continue with the following words. Have children use the *Phoneme Phone* to look at the position of their mouth as they repeat each word and name the ending sound they hear.

    bank, sunk (/k/)   **pan, ton** (/n/)   **bad, said** (/d/)   **map, top** (/p/)

Onset/Rime Blending Remind children that they have been working with the ending sounds in words. They have also learned how to blend word parts to say a word. Say: **First say /s/. Next say and. Then I blend the parts together to say a word. /s/-and, sand.** Have children repeat the following sounds and then blend the parts together to make the words: /c/-an (*can*), /l/-ine (*line*), /h/-int (*hint*), /d/-ish (*dish*), /g/-et (*get*).

RETEACH
Phonics

 Consonant /g/g, /f/f Display *Sound/Spelling Card Gg*. Ask: **What sound do you hear at the beginning of *green*? What letter stands for the /g/ sound at the beginning of *green*?** Repeat with *Sound/Spelling Card Ff* and the word *friend*.

Next, give children *Word Builder Cards g* and *f*. Say: **I am going to say some words. If the word begins with the /g/ sound, hold up the *g* card and say /g/. If the word begins with the /f/ sound, hold up the *f* card and say /f/.** Say the following words for children: *flash, game, gold, fair, gas, fast*. Continue the activity, having children identify the ending sound in these words: *self, whiff, egg, wolf, half, bag*.

REVIEW
Reading

 /g/g, /f/f Write the letters *Gg* and *Ff* on the board. Have children identify each letter and its sound. Help children create the book on *Practice Book* pages 65–66. Have them circle the picture that begins with /g/ and box the picture that begins with /f/.

High-Frequency Words Write the words *here* and *this* on the board. Say each word. Have children find the word, point to it, and say it. Have children return to *Practice Book,* pages 65–66 and read the sentences to practice the skill. Encourage children to read the book with their families to practice newly-learned sounds and words.

REVIEW

Robust Vocabulary

Remind children of the Student-Friendly Explanations of *anxious, huddle, moans, productive, idle,* and *scrumptious*. Then determine children's understanding of the words by asking the following questions.

- **If a friend says he or she feels** *anxious,* **what would you do to help your friend?**
- **Would you be more likely to** *huddle* **together with friends on a hot day or a cold day? Why?**
- **Why might you want to go tell an adult if you heard** *moans* **coming from a pet?**
- **Would you want a day at school to be** *productive* **or** *idle?* **Why?**
- **What might you tell someone who made you something** *scrumptious* **to eat? Why?**

RETEACH

Writing

Writing Form: Poster Remind children that a poster is a sign that uses words and pictures to tell about something. Indicate posters in the classroom, and have children tell what each poster is about. Explain that a poster may tell only the main idea and rely on the picture to give the reader some details.

Tell children that together you will make a poster about classrooms. Have children suggest important details of the classroom. Help children sort and develop their ideas, prompting them to discern between important details (such as a whiteboard and markers) from less important details (such as staples). Record their ideas on chart paper. Then use children's ideas to write a sentence about their classroom. Invite them to write letters and words they know. Read the finished sentence to the children. Decide as a class what to show as the poster's illustration. Have volunteers add portions of the picture until it is complete.

> Our classroom is the perfect place to learn.

VOCABULARY

Student-Friendly Explanations

anxious If you feel anxious, you feel nervous or afraid that something is going to happen.

huddle (n.) A huddle is a group of people or animals that are close together in a circle.

moans When someone moans, he or she is sad or mad, and makes a long, low sound.

productive When you are productive you are making or doing something.

idle When you are idle, you are not doing anything.

scrumptious Something that is scrumptious tastes very, very good.

Grade K **131**

LESSON 11

DAY AT A GLANCE
Day 5

PHONEMIC AWARENESS
Phonemic Isolation

PHONICS
Preteach Word Blending

HIGH-FREQUENCY WORDS
Review like, come, I, to, the

BUILD ROBUST VOCABULARY
Reteach squabble, anxious, uproar

Materials Needed:

Photo Cards | Phoneme Phone | Sound/Spelling Cards *Ii, Nn*

Word Builder and Word Builder Cards | Practice Book

Phonemic Awareness

 Phonemic Isolation Display *Photo Cards fish, cat, box, sun, nest.* Say: **Name the sound you hear in the middle of the words I say. Listen as I do the first one.** Hold up *fish*. Say: **The first word is *fish*, /fiish/.** Have children repeat the sounds. Ask: **What is the middle sound in the word /ff/-/ii/-/sh/?** The middle sound is /ii/. **What is the word?** (fish) **What is the middle sound?** (/ii/) Hold up the *Photo Card cat* and have children name the picture. Give each child a *Phoneme Phone*. Have children elongate the picture name, look at their mouth position, and identify the middle sound. If children have difficulty, have them listen to the sound on the *Phoneme Phone*. Ask whether this is the same middle sound as in *cat*. Continue with the remaining *Photo Cards*.

PRETEACH

Phonics

 Have children sit in a circle. Explain that you will blend sounds to say words. Say the following verse, and have children echo you. Say: **We're going on a Word Hunt. What's this word? /b/-/i/-/g/?** Together: **big!** Continue with the words *bit, tin,* and *did*. Then review the sounds you blended to make each word.

Display *Sound/Spelling Cards Ii* and *Nn*. Point to *Ii*. Ask: **What letter is this?** (i) Tell children that *i* can stand for the sound /i/, the sound at the beginning of *igloo*. Point to *n*. Ask: **What letter is this?** (n) **The letter n stands for the sound /nn/. What does n stand for?** (/nn/) Tell children that *n* stands for the sound /nn/, the sound at the beginning of *noodle*.

 Word Blending Display the *Word Builder Cards i* and *n*. Point to *i*. Say /ii/. Have children name the letter and sound. Point to *n*. Say /nn/. Have children name the letter and sound. Slide the *n* next to *i*. Move your hand under the letters and blend the sounds: /iinn/. Have children repeat after you.

Then have children blend and read the word *in* with you. Continue with the words *tin, fin, big,* and *rip*.

Have children turn to *Practice Book* page 67. Help children identify the pictures. Have them trace the letter *i* in each word.

132 Lesson 11

Day 5

REVIEW
High-Frequency Words

 Write the following words on index cards and distribute them: *like, come, I, to,* and *the.* Say each word, and have the children repeat that word and hold up the correct card. Show the *Photo Card hill.* Ask children to say the picture name. Then use the index word cards, the *Photo Card,* and a period card to build the sentence frame shown below. Point to each word as you read the sentence. Then have children read the sentence with you.

Replace *Photo Card hill* with *tree.* Point to each word as you read the sentence. Point to each word again as children read the sentence aloud. Repeat with other index word card and *Photo Card* combinations.

RETEACH
Build Robust Vocabulary

Read the Student-Friendly Explanations for the words *squabble, anxious,* and *uproar.* Then discuss each word by asking children the following questions.

squabble
If two children *squabble* over one toy, do they want to play with the toy together, or does one child want to play with the toy alone? Explain.

anxious
If someone is acting *anxious,* is the person happy or is the person worried about something?

uproar
Would you be more likely to hear an *uproar* at a circus or at a library? What might cause the uproar?

High-Frequency Words

come	I
like	the
to	

VOCABULARY
Student-Friendly Explanations

squabble If you squabble with someone, you argue about something that is not very important.

anxious If you feel anxious, you feel nervous or afraid that something is going to happen.

uproar An uproar is a lot of noise and fussing made by someone who is upset about something.

Grade K 133

LESSON 12

PHONEMIC AWARENESS
Phoneme Isolation

PHONICS
Preteach Word Building

HIGH-FREQUENCY WORDS
Review come, to, a, he, my, the

COMPREHENSION
Reteach Beginning, Middle, Ending

BUILD ROBUST VOCABULARY
Reteach mischief, idle, productive

Materials Needed:

Phoneme Phone | Word Builder and Word Builder Cards | Write-On/Wipe-Off Boards

Copying Master | Photo Cards | Practice Book

Phonemic Awareness

Phoneme Isolation Tell children to listen for the middle sound in the middle of a word you say. Show them how to identify the middle sound. Say: **Listen as I say this word: sit. Now repeat after me, sit. What is the middle sound in sit?** (/i/) **Listen as I say another word: can, /kaan/. I hear /a/ in the middle of can.**

Give each child a *Phoneme Phone*. Say the word *cat*. Have children elongate the sounds in *cat* while looking at their mouth position in the mirror. Ask the children to identify the middle sound. Continue in the same way with the words *pet, tip, pup, sock,* and *ham*.

PRETEACH

Phonics

Word Building Distribute *Word Builder Cards a, d, g, i, n, p, s,* and *t*. Review each letter name and sound. Then hold up letters at random and ask children to tell the letter name and sound.

Explain to children that you are going to show them how a word can change when the letters in the word change. Say: **Use your *Word Builder Cards* to make new words with me. I will use the letters *b, i,* and *g* to make the word *big*. Now you do the same. Blend the sounds with me: /b/-/i/-/g/, *big*. If I take away the *i* and put *a* in its place, I have the word *bag*. Now you try it. Blend the sounds and say the word with me: /b/-/a/-/g/, *bag*.**

Build Words Have children continue with *bag* in their *Word Builder*:

Change the *b* to *t*. What word did you make? (*tag*)

Change the *g* to *p*. What word did you make? (*tap*)

Continue with the words *sap, sip, dip*. Then have children practice writing the words they built on their *Write-On/Wipe-Off Boards*.

Distribute *Copying Master 23*. Have children trace the letters at the bottom of the page and cut them out. Help children identify the pictures. Then have children paste *a* or *i* in the box to complete each picture name. (*pig, lip, cat, rip*)

134 Lesson 12

Day 1

REVIEW
High-Frequency Words

Distribute index cards for the words *come, to,* and *my.* Say each word. Have children repeat each word and hold up the correct card. Show *Photo Card igloo.* Ask children to say the picture name. Then use the index word cards, a period card, an index card *can,* and the *Photo Card* to build the sentence shown below. Point to each word as you read the sentence. Ask children to read the sentence with you. Continue with other *Photo Card* combinations.

| Come | to | my | | . |

High-Frequency Words

come   my

to

RETEACH
Comprehension

Beginning, Middle, Ending Remind children that every story has a beginning, a middle, and an ending. Then read this story aloud to them.

> Matt has two new puppies. The puppies follow Matt and do everything he does. One day Matt ran outside. The dogs ran outside. Matt jumped in a puddle. The dogs jumped in the puddle too. So Matt gave the puppies a bath. They shook and splashed all over Matt. "This time I followed the dogs. They had a bath, and then I got a bath too," Matt laughed.

Guide children to turn to *Practice Book* page 68. Have them look at the pictures to retell what happened in the beginning, the middle, and the ending of the story.

RETEACH
Build Robust Vocabulary

Remind children of the meanings of *mischief, idle,* and *productive.* Then discuss each word, using the following examples.

mischief
What are some things a puppy might do to cause *mischief*?

idle and productive
Tell me whether the character is being *idle* or *productive*:
- The bees were busy making honey.
- Grasshopper was lying on his couch daydreaming.

VOCABULARY
Student-Friendly Explanations

mischief If you get into mischief, you cause trouble by playing tricks on people.

idle A person or thing that is idle is not doing anything.

productive When you are productive, you are making or doing something useful.

Grade K 135

LESSON 12

DAY AT A GLANCE — Day 2

PHONEMIC AWARENESS
Phoneme Isolation

PHONICS
Reteach Word Building

HIGH-FREQUENCY WORDS
Review here, this, a, come, go, to

COMPREHENSION
Preteach Graphic Organizers

BUILD ROBUST VOCABULARY
Reteach moans, glum, tend

Materials Needed:

Photo Cards | Phoneme Phone | Word Builder and Word Builder Cards

Write-On/Wipe-Off Boards | Copying Master | Practice Book

Phonemic Awareness

Phoneme Isolation Remind children that they have been listening for middle sounds in words. Review how to identify and isolate the middle sound in a word. Display *Photo Cards* *fox*, *sun*, *hill*, *nest*, and *pan*. Hold up *Photo Card fox*. Say: **Listen as I say the picture name: *fox*, /foks/. I hear /o/ in the middle of *fox*. Now you repeat the word I say and name the sound you hear in the middle.** Give each child a *Phoneme Phone*. Hold up *Photo Card sun*. Say *sun* into a *Phoneme Phone*, emphasizing the middle sound, and modeling for children the correct mouth position. Then have children name the picture while looking at their mouth position in the mirror. Have children repeat the word. Continue in the same way with remaining *Photo Cards*.

RETEACH

Phonics

Word Blending Distribute *Word Builder Cards* *a, d, g, i, n, p, s,* and *t*. Explain to children that when letters in words change, so do the sounds.

Have the children following along as you model word building. Say: **Use your *Word Builder Cards* to make new words with me. I will use the letters *m*, *a*, and *t* to make the word *mat*. Now you do the same. Blend the sounds with me: /m/-/a/-/t/, *mat*. If I take away the *m* and put *f* in its place, I have the word *fat*. Now you try it. Blend the sounds and say the word with me: /f/-/a/-/t/, *fat*.**

Build Words Have children continue with *fat* in their *Word Builder*:

Change the *a* to *i*. What word did you make? (*fit*)

Change the *f* to *p*. What word did you make? (*pit*)

Continue with the words *pat, sat, sit*. Then have children practice writing the words they built on their *Write-on/Wipe-off Boards*.

Distribute *Copying Master 24* to review building words with short *a* and *i*. Help children name each picture. Then have children circle the word that names the picture and write the word on the line. (*hip, sit, nap, pin*)

136 Lesson 12

Day 2

RETEACH

High-Frequency Words

Practice Book 69 Show an index card with the word *here*. Say the word, and have children point to it and repeat it. Repeat the steps with the word *this* on an index card. Randomly show both words, and have children say the words correctly and consistently.

Create and distribute index cards for the following words: *here, this, a, come, go,* and *to*. Have children sit in a circle. Give each child one word card. At your signal, have them pass their cards around the circle until you tell them to stop. Ask: **Who has the word *here*?** The child with the word *here* should stand and read the word. Repeat with the rest of the words.

Have children turn to *Practice Book* page 69 to review high-frequency words. Complete the page together.

High-Frequency Words	
a	come
go	here
this	to

PRETEACH

Comprehension

 Graphic Organizers Explain that writing down important things about a story can help you remember and understand a story better. Remind children that all stories have a beginning, a middle, and an ending. Create a chart with these row headings: *Beginning, Middle,* and *Ending*. Recall the story about Matt and his puppies from Day 1. Reread the story. Then ask children to name what happens in each part of the story as you write their responses on the chart under the correct heading.

Beginning	Matt's puppies followed him outside.
Middle	
Ending	

RETEACH

Build Robust Vocabulary

Remind children of the Student-Friendly Explanations for *moans, glum,* and *tend*. Then discuss each word, using the following examples.

glum, moans
Would you *moan* if you felt *glum* or happy? Tell why.

tend
What are some ways you can *tend* to a pet?

VOCABULARY

Student-Friendly Explanations

moans When someone moans, he or she is sad or mad and makes a long, low sound.

glum Someone who feels glum is sad and quiet.

tend When you tend something, you take care of it.

Grade K 137

LESSON 12

DAY AT A GLANCE — Day 3

PHONEMIC AWARENESS
Phoneme Isolation: Medial
Phoneme Isolation: Initial

PHONICS
Preteach Phonogram -it

HIGH-FREQUENCY WORDS
Review he, to, a, go, my, the, too

COMPREHENSION
Reteach Beginning, Middle, Ending

BUILD ROBUST VOCABULARY
Reteach scrumptious, feast, soggy

WRITING
Preteach Writing Trait: Word Choice

Materials Needed:

Phoneme Phone   Write-On/Wipe-Off Boards   Photo Cards

Practice Book

Phonemic Awareness

Phoneme Isolation: Medial   Tell children to listen carefully as you say two words: *ham, cat. Ham* and *cat* have the same middle sound /a/. Listen as I say two more words: *pet, sat. Pet* and *sat* do not have the same middle sound: /e/, /a/.

Have children sit in a circle, and distribute the *Phoneme Phones*. Say the words *tin* and *sip*. Ask the children to repeat the words while looking at the position of their mouths in the mirror. Ask: **Do *tin* and *sip* have the same middle sound?** (yes) **What is the sound?** (/i/) Repeat with these words, having children identify the medial sound:

  sun, bug   cup, cap   ran, pan   fit, dig   tan, pet

Phoneme Isolation: Initial   Remind children that words are made up of sounds. They have been listening for the middle sounds in words. Now they should listen for the beginning sound. Say: ***Sun*. I hear /s/ at the beginning of *sun*. What is the word?** (sun) **What is the beginning sound?** (/s/)

Have children identify the beginning sound in the following words:

  map   fix   nap   wig   girl   boy   jet

PRETEACH — Phonics

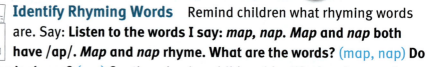

Identify Rhyming Words   Remind children what rhyming words are. Say: **Listen to the words I say: *map, nap. Map* and *nap* both have /ap/. *Map* and *nap* rhyme. What are the words?** (map, nap) **Do the words rhyme?** (yes) Continue having children identify rhyming words using these word pairs:

  sun, sit   pit, mitt   cab, bed   men, ten   an, can

Phonogram -it   Write the word *bit* on the board. Track the print as you read the word. Have children repeat after you. Then write the word *hit*. Track the print as you read the word. Have children repeat after you. Ask how the two words are the same. (They both have /it/; they rhyme.) Say: **The words *bit* and *hit* are in the *-it word* family because they both end in *-it*.** Continue with the words *kit* and *lit*.

Distribute *Write-on/Wipe-off Boards*. Write these words on chart paper: *hit, bit, ran, lit, nap*. Have children read the words and copy those words in the *-it* word family on their *Write-on/Wipe-off Boards*.

138 Lesson 12

RETEACH

High-Frequency Words

High-Frequency Words	
a	the
go	to
he	my

Distribute index cards for *he, to, a, go, my,* and *the* to children. As you say each word, have children repeat the word and hold up the correct card. Show *Photo Card hill.* Ask children to say the picture name. Then use the index card words, a period card, an index card with the word *can,* and *Photo Card hill* to build the first sentence shown below. Point to each word as you read the sentence. Ask children to read the sentence with you.

He can go to the hill .

Then continue with the following sentences. Point to each word and have children read the sentences aloud.

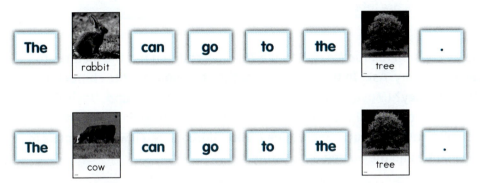

The rabbit can go to the tree .

The cow can go to the tree .

Write the following sentence frame on the board: *He can go to the _____* . Have children copy and complete the sentence with a word or a picture.

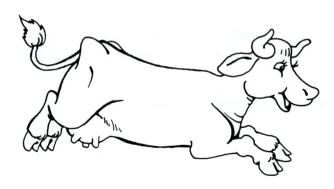

Grade K 139

Day 3

RETEACH

Comprehension

Beginning, Middle, Ending Remind children that every story has a beginning, a middle, and an ending. Have children listen for the beginning, middle, and ending as you read aloud the following story.

Practice Book 70

> Maya and Josh are very excited because they are going to a potluck picnic. Grandpa and Grandma are going. They call Uncle Chris, Aunt Julie, and their cousins, Ellie and Michael. They will come too.
>
> Everyone takes a different food. They rush to meet at the park.
>
> Maya and Josh's family is the first to arrive at the park. They bring tuna fish sandwiches and crunchy carrot sticks. Next come Grandpa and Grandma. They bring plates, cups, and sweet lemonade to drink. Then, Aunt Julie and Uncle Chris arrive. They bring creamy potato salad. Ellie and Michael carry huge bunches of grapes.
>
> All the food is on the table. Now it's time to eat! This family thinks potluck picnics are lots of fun.

Guide children to *Practice Book* page 70. Have children use the pictures to retell the story. Ask: **In the beginning of the story you met the characters. Who are they?** (Maya, Josh, their parents, Grandma, Grandpa, Uncle Chris, Aunt Julie, and cousins Ellie and Michael) **What are they doing?** (They are going to have a potluck picnic.) Then ask children to retell what happens in the middle and the ending of the story.

RETEACH

Build Robust Vocabulary

Talk about the Student-Friendly Explanations for the words *scrumptious*, *feast*, and *soggy*. Then discuss each word, asking children the following questions.

scrumptious
Which would you consider *scrumptious*: a chocolate cupcake loaded with frosting, or a glass of water?

feast
Which would you be more likely to see at a *feast*: a computer, or a table piled with fresh bread, warm spaghetti, and spicy meatballs?

soggy
What are some reasons your socks might get *soggy*?

VOCABULARY
Student-Friendly Explanations

scrumptious Something that is scrumptious tastes very, very good.

feast A feast is a big meal with lots of different kinds of foods.

soggy Something that is soggy is so wet that it is squishy.

Day 3

PRETEACH

Writing

Writing Trait: Word Choice Remind children that when they write a sentence, a story, or a poem, it is important to use just the right words that tell about ideas, feelings, or actions. This way the reader gets a better idea of what the writing is about. Write the following sentences on the board. Read each sentence while tracking the print.

> Maya and Josh are going to a picnic.
> Maya and Josh are very excited because they are going to a potluck picnic.

Ask: **Who are these sentences about? Where are Maya and Josh going? Which sentence tells about the character's feelings?** (the second sentence: very excited) **Which sentence gives more ideas about the picnic?** (the second sentence: a potluck picnic) Point out how the second sentence has better ideas. It gives the reader more information about what is happening.

Repeat with the following sentences. Ask children to explain which sentence has better word choices and why:

> They bring sandwiches and carrot sticks.
> They bring tuna fish sandwiches and crunchy carrot sticks.

Grade K **141**

LESSON 12

PHONEMIC AWARENESS
Phoneme Isolation: Medial
Phoneme Isolation: Initial

PHONICS
Preteach Phonogram *-ip*

READING
Review Phonogram *-it*, *-ip*
Review High-Frequency Words

BUILD ROBUST VOCABULARY
Review *tend, soggy, wobble, squabble, scrumptious, huddle*

WRITING
Reteach Writing Form: Poems

Materials Needed:

Phoneme Phone Write-On/Wipe-Off Boards Practice Book

Phonemic Awareness

 Phoneme Isolation: Medial Tell children to listen carefully as you say two words: *set, bed*. *Set* and *bed* have the same middle sound: /e/. What is the middle sound? (/e/)

Have children sit in a circle, and distribute the *Phoneme Phones*. Say the words *win* and *lip*. Ask the children to repeat the words while looking at the position of their mouths in the mirror. Ask: **Do *win* and *lip* have the same middle sound?** (yes) **What is the middle sound?** (/i/) Repeat with these words: *had, mat; top, rock; ten, pet; sun, mud; pig, sit*.

Phoneme Isolation: Initial Remind children that words are made up of sounds. They have been listening for the middle sounds in words. Now they should listen for the beginning sound. Say: ***Cut*. I hear /k/ at the beginning of *cut*. What is the word?** (cut) **What is the beginning sound?** (/k/) Have children identify the beginning sound in the following words: *bag, sip, fox, dog, lap, hot*.

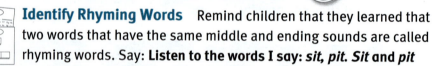

PRETEACH

Phonics

Identify Rhyming Words Remind children that they learned that two words that have the same middle and ending sounds are called rhyming words. Say: **Listen to the words I say: *sit, pit*. *Sit* and *pit* both have /it/. *Sit* and *pit* rhyme. What are the words?** (sit, pit) **Do the words rhyme?** (yes) Read the following word pairs and have children tell you whether they rhyme: *bit/fit, hit/hot, mitt/kit*.

Phonogram *-ip* Write the word *dip* on the board. Track the print as you read the word. Have children repeat after you. Then write the word *nip*. Track the print as you read the word. Have children repeat after you. Ask how the two words are the same. (They both have /ip/; they rhyme.) Say: **The words *dip* and *nip* are in the *-ip* word family because they both end in *-ip*.** Continue with the words *tip* and *rip*.

Distribute *Write-on/Wipe-off Boards*. Write these words on chart paper: *hip, pit, sip, lip, cat*. Have children read the words and practice copying those words in the *-ip* word family on their *Write-on/Wipe-off Boards*.

142 Lesson 12

Day 4

REVIEW
Reading

Phonogram -it, -ip Review the *-it* and *-ip* word families. Write the following words on the board. Have children read each word and identify if the word belongs in the *-it* or *-ip* family: *sip, Pip, nip, kit, sit, hip.*

Practice Book 71–72

High-Frequency Words Distribute to children index cards for the words *I, like, be, come, here,* and *this.* Play "Show and Tell." As you say each word, have children find the corresponding word card, show the word to you, and say the word. Repeat until each word has been identified correctly.

Have children turn to *Practice Book* page 71–72. Help them cut out and fold the book. Encourage them to read it at home.

High-Frequency Words

be	come
here	I
like	this

REVIEW
Robust Vocabulary

Tell children that they have been learning some interesting words. Remind children of the Student-Friendly Explanations for *tend, soggy, wobble, squabble,* and *huddle.* Then determine children's understanding of the words by asking the following questions.

- **If you scraped your knee, how might your mom *tend* to you?**
- **If it is a rainy day, how can you keep your feet from getting *soggy*?**
- **If the chair legs *wobble*, would you sit on the chair? Explain.**
- **When might you and a brother or sister *squabble*?**
- **Name the most *scrumpious* food you can think of.**
- **During what kinds of activities would you get into a *huddle*?**

VOCABULARY
Student-Friendly Explanations

tend When you tend something, you take care of it.

soggy Something that is soggy is so wet that it's squishy.

wobble When things wobble, they move from side to side in an unsteady way.

squabble If you squabble with someone, you argue about something that is not very important.

scrumptious Something that is scrumptious tastes very, very good.

huddle A huddle is a group of people or animals that are close.

RETEACH
Writing

Writing Form: Poems Remind children that a poem often has rhyming words and describes things.

Tell children that together you will write a poem about summer. Ask them to name words that describe summer. Record their word choices on chart paper. Then use children's ideas to write a poem about summer. Invite them to write letters and words they know. Read the finished poem to the children.

> **I Like Summer**
> I like to play.
> I think it is fun.
> I like to swim
> And to feel the hot sun.

Grade K 143

LESSON 12

PHONEMIC AWARENESS
Phoneme Isolation

PHONICS
Preteach Consonant *Bb*

HIGH-FREQUENCY WORDS
Preteach *me*

BUILD ROBUST VOCABULARY
Preteach *fading, perhaps, prefer*

Materials Needed:

Photo Cards   Sound/Spelling Card *Bb*

Write-On/ Wipe-Off Boards   Practice Book

Phonemic Awareness

Phoneme Isolation: Identify Initial Sounds Remind children that they have been listening for sounds in the beginning, middle, and end of words. Today they will be listening for sounds in the beginning of words. Show *Photo Card frog*. Say: **Frog. I hear /f/ at the beginning of frog. What is the word?** (frog) **What is the beginning sound?** (/f/) Have children sit in a circle. Display *Photo Cards hammer, egg, ring, tree,* and *zipper.* Have children say each picture name, then identify the beginning sound.

PRETEACH

Phonics

Consonant *Bb* Display *Sound/Spelling Card Bb*. Say: **The name of this letter is *b*. Say the name with me.** (*b*) Point to the uppercase *B* on the *Sound/Spelling Card*. Say: **This is the uppercase *B*.** Point to the lowercase *b*. Say: **This is the lowercase *b*.** Point to the *Sound/Spelling Card* again. Ask: **What is the name of this letter?** (*b*)

Writing *B* and *b* Model how to write the letter *B* and *b*. Say: **Watch as I write the letter *B*.** As you give the Letter Talk, trace the uppercase *B*. Do the same for lowercase *b*. As you write *B* on the board, say:

Letter Talk for *B*	Letter Talk for *b*
1. Straight line down.	1. Straight line down.
2. Go to the top of the line.	2. Circle around and touch the bottom line.
3. Curved line out, down, and around.	
4. Touch the middle of the straight line.	
5. Curved line out, down, and around.	
6. Touch the bottom of the line.	

Have children take turns writing the uppercase *B* and lowercase *b* in the air with their fingers. Then have children practice writing upper and lower case *B* on their *Write-on/ Wipe-off Boards* several times. Encourage them to use the *Sound/Spelling Card* as their model. Then have children turn to page 73 in their *Practice Book* to write and identify *Bb*.

144 Lesson 12

Day 5

PRETEACH

High-Frequency Words

Write the word *me* on the board. Point to and read *me*. Say: **Come with *me*.** Then display an index card with the word *me* written on it. Say: ***me***. Match the index card *me* with the word on the board. Say *me* and have children repeat several times.

Have children say sentences that use the word *me*. Write their sentences on chart paper. Then read each sentence, holding up the index card *me* as you say the word. You may wish to read a sentence frame, such as *Come with me to _____*. Have children join in and say the word *me* with you.

Distribute to children index cards with these words written on them: *me, my, he, here, to,* and *go*. Have children work in pairs. One child should say a word, while the other finds the word and displays it. Allow children to play several rounds.

High-Frequency Words

go	me
he	my
here	to

PRETEACH

Build Robust Vocabulary

Read aloud to the children the Student-Friendly Explanations for *fading, perhaps,* and *prefer*. Then discuss each word, using the following examples:

fading
If I leave a towel in the sun for a long time, the color starts to fade. If something is *fading*, what do its colors look like?

perhaps
If you say, "*Perhaps* it will snow today," would that mean that it will snow, or that it might snow?

prefer
I *prefer* to wear t-shirts in the summer. Would you prefer to wear a t-shirt or a sweater in the summer? Why?

VOCABULARY
Student-Friendly Explanations

fading When something is fading, it is becoming lighter and harder to see.

perhaps If you say perhaps something will happen, maybe it will and maybe it won't happen.

prefer If you prefer something, you like it more than another thing.

Grade K 145

LESSON 13

DAY 1

PHONEMIC AWARENESS
Phoneme Isolation Final

PHONICS
Reteach Relate *Bb* to /b/

HIGH-FREQUENCY WORDS
Reteach *me*

COMPREHENSION
Preteach Note Details

BUILD ROBUST VOCABULARY
Reteach *fading, perhaps, prefer*

Materials Needed:

Photo Cards — Phoneme Phone — Sound/Spelling Card *Bb*

Sounds of Letters CD — Word Builder and Word Builder Cards — Write-On/Wipe-Off Boards

Copying Master — Practice Book

Phonemic Awareness

 Phoneme Isolation: Identify Final Sounds Explain to children that they will be listening for final sounds of words. Show *Photo Card box*. Say: **This is a box. I hear /ks/ at the end of box. /boks/ What is the word?** (*box*) **What is the sound at the end of box?** (/ks/)

Have children sit in a circle. Display *Photo Cards dog, lamp, sun,* and *tree*. Give one child the *Phoneme Phone* to use. Ask the child to select a *Photo Card*. Say the picture name, elongating the sound at the end of the word. Then have the child say the picture name and look at the position of the mouth in the mirror he or she repeats the word and names the ending sound. Have the child pass the *Phoneme Phone* to the next child and repeat.

PRETEACH

Phonics

 Relate *Bb* to /b/ Display *Sound/Spelling Card Bb*. Ask: **What is the name of this letter?** (*b*) **The letter *b* stands for the /b/ sound.** Have children listen as you introduce the /b/ sound, using the *Sounds of Letters CD*. Then say: **The letter *b* stands for the /b/ sound.** Say: **/b/.** Have children repeat several times.

  Listen for /b/ Give each child a *Word Builder Card b* and a *Write-on/Wipe-off Board*. Have children find the heart on Side 2 of the board. They will use the three boxes next to the heart and the *Word Builder Card b*. Tell children: **Listen to the word I say: book. Now you say the word, book. I hear the /b/ sound at the beginning of book. So let's put our *b* in the first box on the board. The word book begins with /b/. Let's do another word.** Repeat using the word *cab* and place the *b* in the end box on the board. Have children do the same. Continue by having children say the following words and place the letter *b* in the correct position on their boards. Use the words *bear, bug, web, bat, cab, belt, cub,* and *bed*.

 Guided Practice Distribute *Copying Master 25* to children. Have them trace the letter *Bb* and then circle the letter that stands for the sound at the beginning of each picture. (Children should circle *b* for the *bed, bus,* and *bug*; they should circle *m* for *mouse* and circle *r* for *ring*.)

RETEACH

High-Frequency Words

Distribute index cards *me, my, he, like, to,* and *go* to children. Display the words. Say one of the words aloud: **my.** Use it in a sentence: **This is my dog.** Have a child volunteer to match his or her word card *my* with the one displayed. Then have children read the word. Ask a volunteer to use the word in a sentence. Continue this activity using all of the words.

PRETEACH

Comprehension

  Note Details Explain to children that every story has details. Details are the words and pictures that help a reader understand what the story is about. Then read this story aloud to them.

> One hot and sunny morning, Cat went down to the pond. Cat was going to find some lunch. Cat could see lots of goldfish darting around in the water. He would soon have a tasty treat. So Cat found a nice cool spot in the shade under the apple tree. He sat in the grass and put his pole over the water and waited. Before long Cat was sound asleep. The goldfish had fun tugging on his pole to try to awaken him, but Cat kept sleeping. The fish got tired, so they swam away. All of a sudden an apple fell from the tree. Plop! It hit Cat on the head and woke him up. Startled, Cat immediately checked his pole. But there were no fish. Cat ate the juicy red apple instead and soon fell back to sleep.

Guide children to turn to page 74 in their *Practice Books.* Have them circle the picture in each pair that identifies the story detail. Ask: **What is Cat going to do at the pond?** (Cat will fish.) **Where does Cat sit to fish?** (in the shade under the apple tree) **What does Cat eat for lunch?** (a juicy, red apple) Encourage children to tell details about the picture that they circled.

RETEACH

Build Robust Vocabulary

Remind children of the Student-Friendly Explanations of *fading, perhaps,* and *prefer.* Then discuss each word, using the following examples.

fading
If the moon is *fading* behind a cloud, is the moon easier or harder to see?

perhaps
If I say, "*Perhaps* we'll have pizza for lunch today," does it mean we will or we might have pizza?

prefer
What games do you *prefer* to play on the playground?

Day 1

High-Frequency Words

go	me
he	my
like	to

VOCABULARY
Student-Friendly Explanations

fading When something is fading, it is becoming lighter and harder to see.

perhaps If you say perhaps something will happen, maybe it will and maybe it won't happen.

prefer If you prefer something, you like it more than another thing.

Grade K   147

LESSON 13

DAY AT A GLANCE — Day 2

PHONEMIC AWARENESS
Phoneme Isolation Final

PHONICS
Preteach Consonant *Kk*

HIGH-FREQUENCY WORDS
Preteach *for*

COMPREHENSION
Preteach Generate Questions

BUILD ROBUST VOCABULARY
Preteach *warn, whirl, property*

Materials Needed:

Sound/Spelling Card *Kk* — Write-On/Wipe-Off Boards — Copying Master

Practice Book

Phonemic Awareness

Phoneme Isolation: Final Remind children they have been listening to sounds at the beginning and end of words. Tell the children that you are going to say some words. Ask them to listen for the sound at the end of each word you say. Say: **I am going to say a word:** *big*. **/big/ I hear /g/ at the end of the word** *big*. **Now listen as I say another word:** *him*. **/himm/. I hear /m/ at the end of** *him*. Then say the following words. Emphasize the final sound. Have children repeat each word and name the sound they hear at the end.

cat (/t/)   **tan** (/n/)   **duck** (/k/)

tip (/p/)   **sad** (/d/)   **tub** (/b/)

PRETEACH

Phonics

 Consonant *Kk* Display *Sound/Spelling Card Kk*. Say: **The name of this letter is *k*. Say the name with me.** (*k*) Point to the uppercase *K* on the *Sound/Spelling Card*. Say: **This is the uppercase *K*.** Point to the lowercase *k*. Say: **This is the lowercase *k*.** Point to the *Sound/Spelling Card* again. Ask: **What is the name of this letter?** (*k*)

Write K and k Say: **Watch as I write the letter *K*.** As you give the Letter Talk, trace the uppercase *K*. Use the same modeling for lowercase *k*.

Letter Talk for *K*	Letter Talk for *k*
1. Straight line down.	1. Straight line down.
2. Slant left and down.	2. Slant left and down.
3. Slant right and down.	3. Slant right and down.
K	k

 Have children use their fingers to practice writing uppercase *K* in the air as you repeat the Letter Talk. Then repeat with lowercase *k*. Distribute *Write-on/Wipe-off Boards*. Have children practice writing upper and lower case *K* on the boards several times using *Sound/Spelling Card Kk* as their model. Then distribute *Copy Master 26*, and help children to identify and write the letter *Kk*.

148 Lesson 13

Day 2

PRETEACH
High-Frequency Words

Practice Book 75 Write the word *for* on the board. Point to and read *for*. Have children say it with you. Say: **The gift is *for* you.** Write the word *for* on an index card. Match the card to the word on the board, say the word, and have children say it with you. Then prepare index cards with the following words on them: *for, to, the, here, like*.

Have children sit in a circle. Give each child one index card. At your signal, have them pass their cards around the circle until you tell them to stop. Ask: **Who has the word *for*?** The child with the word *for* should stand and read the word. Repeat with the rest of the words.

Have children turn to *Practice Book* page 75 to review high-frequency words and practice newly-learned words. Complete the page together.

High-Frequency Words

for	to
here	the
like	

PRETEACH
Comprehension

Generate Questions Explain to children that asking questions when reading can help them to better understand the information in the story. Recall the story about Cat from Day 1. Reread the first sentence, and model asking questions about Cat. Say: **I wonder why Cat is going down to the pond.** As you continue reading, pause to allow children to ask questions. Record their questions on a chart.

Questions	Answers
Why is Cat going down to the pond?	

Guide children to answer those questions as you continue reading, and record them in the chart.

RETEACH
Build Robust Vocabulary

Read the Student-Friendly Explanations for *warn, whirl,* and *property*. Then discuss each word, using the following examples.

warn
What are some ways you might *warn* someone?

whirl
What is more likely to *whirl*, a merry-go-round or a desk?

property
What is your *property*, your book bag or the classroom table? Why?

VOCABULARY
Student-Friendly Explanations

warn If you warn someone, you let him or her know that something dangerous might happen.

whirl When things whirl, they spin around in circles.

property Something that belongs to you is called your property.

Grade K 149

LESSON 13

PHONEMIC AWARENESS
Phoneme Isolation Medial

PHONICS
Preteach Relate *Kk* to /k/

HIGH-FREQUENCY WORDS
Reteach *for*

COMPREHENSION
Reteach Note Details

BUILD ROBUST VOCABULARY
Reteach *warn, whirl, property*

WRITING
Reteach Writing Trait: Conventions

Materials Needed:

Phoneme Phone   Sound/Spelling Card Kk   Sounds of Letters CD

Word Builder and Word Builder Cards   Write-On/Wipe-Off Boards   Photo Cards

Practice Book

Phonemic Awareness

Phoneme Isolation: Medial Tell children to listen carefully as you say two words. Say the first word, and elongate the medial sound: **bat. I hear /a/ in the middle. /baat/. Now listen as I say another word: can. I hear /a/ in the middle. /caan/. I hear /a/ in the middle of both bat and can.**

Have children sit in a circle, and distribute *Phoneme Phones*. Say the words *bug* and *gum*. Ask children to repeat the words while looking at the position of their mouths in the mirror. Ask: **Do bug and gum have the same middle sound?** (yes) **What is the sound?** (/u/) Repeat using these words:

pot, box (/o/)   *pup, cup* (/u/)

lid, sick (/i/)   *hen, pen* (/e/)

PRETEACH

Phonics

 Relate *Kk* to /k/ Display *Sound/Spelling Card Kk*. Ask: **What is the name of this letter?** (*k*) **The letter *k* stands for the /k/ sound.** Have children listen as you introduce the sound of *k*, using the *Sounds of Letters CD*. Have children repeat the sound they hear on the CD. Then say: **The letter *k* stands for the /k/ sound. Say /k/.**

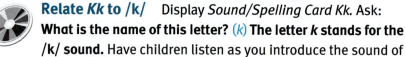 Distribute *Word Builder Card k*. Tell children to listen for the /k/ sound as you say some words, and to show their *k* card if they hear the /k/ sound. Model by saying the word *cap* and holding up *Word Builder Card k*. Have children listen for the /k/ sound in these words: *car, cat, got, sun, cold,* and *kick*. Tell children that the /k/ sound can also be at the end of words. Have children listen for the /k/ sound at the end of these words: *take, mat, make, back, son*.

 Discriminate /k/ Give each child the *Word Builder Card k* and a *Write-on/Wipe-off Board*. Have children find the heart on Side 2 of the board. They will use the three boxes next to the heart and the letter card *k*. Tell children: **Listen to the word I say: *kick*. Now you say the word *kick*. I hear the /k/ sound at the beginning of *kick*. So let's put our *k* in the first box on the board. The word *kick* begins with /k/. Let's do another word.** Repeat using the word *yak* and place the *k* in the end box on the board. Have children do the same. Continue by having children say the following words and use the letter to show the position on their boards. Use the words *book, kit, kick, dark, kid, keep, rake*.

150 Lesson 13

Day 3

RETEACH

High-Frequency Words

Prepare and distribute index cards for the words *for, me,* and *the* to children. Say each word, use it in a sentence, and have children hold up the correct card. Have volunteers use the word in a sentence. Continue with the rest of the cards until children orrectly identify each of them.

Prepare index cards for the word *is* and a period mark. Use these cards along with the high-frequency index cards and the *Photo Card box* to build the first sentence frame shown below. Point to each word as you read the sentence aloud to the children. Ask children to read the sentence with you.

Then continue with the following sentences. Point to each word as you read each sentence aloud. Encourage children to read along with you.

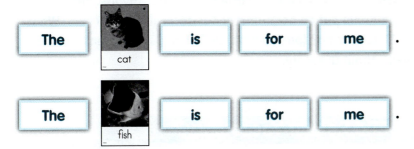

Write the following sentence frame on the board: *The ____ is for me.* Have children copy and complete the sentence with a word or a picture.

High-Frequency Words

for	the
me	

Grade K **151**

Day 3

RETEACH

Comprehsion

  Note Details Remind children that details in a story are the words and pictures that give a reader more clues to understand what the story is about. Read the following story aloud, pausing to point out details to the children.

> Annie arrived at Mrs. Lynn's classroom at exactly eight o'clock. She waved goodbye to her dad. It was her first day of kindergarten, and she was very excited. First, Annie unpacked her new supplies. She put her new folders, crayons, and pencils in her desk. Next, Annie colored her nametag. She added stickers for decoration. Last, Annie and her friend Marie helped Mrs. Lynn pass out snacks to the other children. Everyone ate delicious cookies, drank lots of milk, and made new friends. It was a great first day!

Guide children to *Practice Book* page 76. Have children use the pictures to recall details from the story. Ask: **What time did Annie arrive at school?** (eight o'clock) **What supplies did Annie bring?** (folders, crayons, and pencils) **What did Annie put on her nametag for decoration?** (stickers) **What did Annie help Mrs. Lynn do?** (pass out snacks) Then ask children to name additional details about the story.

RETEACH

Build Robust Vocabulary

Remind children of the meanings of *warn*, *whirl*, and *property*. Then discuss each word by asking children the following questions.

warn
What are some things you might say to *warn* someone about matches?

whirl
If you were watching a ballerina, would she be more likely to *whirl* or crawl? Why?

property
How do you treat something that is your *property*?

VOCABULARY

Student-Friendly Explanations

warn If you warn someone, you let him or her know that something dangerous might happen.

whirl When things whirl, they spin around in circles.

property Something that belongs to you is called your property.

152 Lesson 13

Day 3

RETEACH

Writing

Writing Trait: Conventions Remind children that every question, like other sentences, must begin with a capital letter. Point out that we use a question mark at the end to show that the sentence asks a question. Draw a large question mark on chart paper.

Say: **I am going to ask you a question.** *Do you enjoy reading?* Write the question on chart paper. Say: **This is a question. It begins with a capital letter and ends with a question mark.** Point to the capital letter and circle the question mark. Invite children to finger trace a question mark in the air as you model how to form it.

Write the following sentences on chart paper. Read each sentence aloud to the children.

> where did Annie go
>
> does Annie unpack her supplies
>
> who is Annie's teacher

Ask: **What is missing in each of these sentences?** (capital letters, question marks) Ask volunteers to add a capital letter and a question mark to each sentence. Remind children that question sentences always begin with a capital letter and end with a question mark. Have volunteers suggest other questions and record them on the chart paper. Ask children to help you show that these are questions by adding the correct punctuation to each.

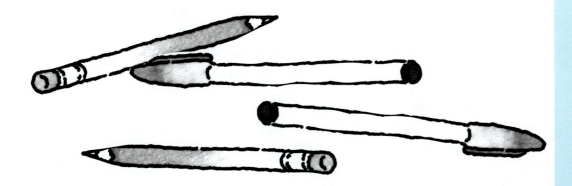

Grade K 153

LESSON 13

DAY AT A GLANCE — Day 4

PHONEMIC AWARENESS
Phoneme Isolation: Medial

PHONICS
Reteach Review /b/*b*, /k/*k*

READING
Review /b/*b*, /k/*k*
Review High-Frequency Words

BUILD ROBUST VOCABULARY
Review *fading, perhaps, prefer, warn, whirl, property*

WRITING
Reteach Writing Form: Questions

Materials Needed:

Photo Cards

Sound/Spelling Cards *Bb, Kk*

Word Builder and Word Builder Cards

Practice Book

Phonemic Awareness

Phoneme Isolation: Medial Display the *Photo Cards fox*, and *sun*. Tell children that they will listen for sounds in the middle of words. Say: **I am going to say a word:** *fox.* **I hear /o/ in the middle of** *fox.* **/fox/. Now listen as I say another word:** *sun.* **I hear /u/ in the middle.** Repeat the words, segmenting each into three sounds to help children hear the medial sound.

Display *Photo Cards fox* and *sun*. Say: **I am going to say some words that have the same middle sound as** *fox* **or** *sun.* **Point to the card that has the same middle sound.** Say the following words, one at a time. When children point to a card, ask them to say the middle sound of the word.

| box | rub | dot | pug |
| run | top | bug | cut |

RETEACH

Phonics

Review /b/*b*, /k/*k* Display *Sound/Spelling Card Bb*. Ask: **What sound do you hear at the beginning of** *ball*? **What letter stands for the /b/ sound at the beginning of** *ball*? Repeat the process with *Sound Spelling Card Kk* and the word *kite*.

Discriminate /b/*b* and /k/*k* Distribute *Word Builder Card b* and *k* to children. Say the following words aloud and have children hold up either the *b* or *k Word Builder Card* to show what sound they hear at the beginning of each word.

| big | bite | kit | king | bug | best | keep |

Then have children listen for words ending with the sounds /k/ and /b/. Have them hold up the correct *Word Builder Card* for the following words:

| look | tuck | lab | cub | rack | bib |

Day 4

REVIEW
Reading

Review /b/*b*, /k/*k* Review the /b/ and /k/ sounds. Write the words *bug* and *kid* on the board, and help children blend the sounds to read the words. Have children name other words that begin with each sound.

Practice Book 77–78

Review High-Frequency Words Distribute index cards for *me, for, like, to, here,* and *the* to children. Explain that you will play "Match." As you say and display each word, have children find the corresponding index card, say the word, and display the card back to you. Repeat until each word has been identified correctly.

Have children turn to *Practice Book* page 77 and 78. Help children cut and fold the book. Encourage them to read it at home.

High-Frequency Words

for	me
here	the
like	to

REVIEW
Robust Vocabulary

Remind children of the Student-Friendly Explanations of *fading, perhaps, prefer, warn, whirl,* and *property*. Then determine children's understanding of the words by asking the following questions.

- If I said *perhaps* we will go on a field trip, does that mean we will, won't, or we might?
- If the color of your jacket was *fading*, how might it look?
- What *property* in your bedroom is most important to you? Why?
- Do you *prefer* muffins or donuts? Why?
- Give an example of how you might *warn* a friend if you thought he or she might fall off a chair.
- Show what it looks like to *whirl*.

VOCABULARY
Student-Friendly Explanations

fading When something is fading, it is becoming lighter and harder to see.

perhaps If you say perhaps something will happen, maybe it will and maybe it won't happen.

prefer If you prefer something, you like it more than another thing.

warn If you warn someone, you let him or her know that something dangerous might happen.

whirl When things whirl, they spin around in circles.

property Something that belongs to you is called your property.

RETEACH
Writing

Writing Form: Questions Remind children that question sentences ask something. Tell children that together you will write questions about gym class. Record their ideas on chart paper. Invite them to assist you in writing letters and words they know. Remind children that when they write a question, they should begin it with a capital letter and end it with a question mark.

> What sport will we learn this week?

Read each question to the children. Review with children how they can tell that these sentences are questions.

Grade K 155

LESSON 13

DAY AT A GLANCE
Day 5

PHONEMIC AWARENESS
Phoneme Identity: Initial

PHONICS
Preteach Word Blending

HIGH-FREQUENCY WORDS
Preteach where, here, me, for, this, he, the

BUILD ROBUST VOCABULARY
Preteach arrives, creeps, nestle

Materials Needed:

Sound/Spelling Card *Ii, Nn*   Word Builder and Word Builder Cards   Practice Book

Photo Cards

Phonemic Awareness

 Phoneme Identity: Initial   Remind children they have listened for sounds in words. Today they will listen for beginning sounds in words. Display *Photo Cards helicopter* and *hill*. Say: **Listen as I say these two words: helicopter, hill. I hear /h/ at the beginning of each word. The sound at the beginning of each word is the same. I will say the words again: /h/ /elicopter/, /h/ /il/.** As you say each word, elongate the beginning sound. Have children repeat the words. Say: **What sound is the same in helicopter and hill?** (/h/) Follow the same procedure with these words: *top, toe* (/t/); *bag, bed* (/b/); *dog, doll* (/d/); *sun, sip* (/s/). Have children tell which sound is the same in each set of words and name the sound.

PRETEACH
Phonics

 Sounds in a Word   Have children sit in a circle. Explain that you will blend sounds to say words. Say the following verse, and have children echo your words. Say: **We're going on a Word Hunt. What's this word? /d/-/i/-/p/? Together: dip!** Continue with the words *rip* and *lip*. Review the sounds blended to make each word.

Display *Sound/Spelling Cards Ii* and *Nn*. Point to and name *i*. Say: **The letter *i* stands for the sound /ii/. What does *i* stand for?** (/ii/) Tell children that *i* stands for the sound /i/ at the beginning of *itch*.

 Word Blending   Display the *Word Builder Cards i* and *n*. Point to *i*. Say: **/ii/.** Have children name the letter and sound. Point to *n*. Say: **/nn/.** Have children name the letter and sound. Slide the *n* next to *i*. Move your hand under the letters and blend the sounds: **/iinn/.** Have children repeat after you. Then have children blend and read the word *in* with you. Continue with the words *pin, tin,* and *rip*.

Have children turn to *Practice Book* page 79. Help children identify the pictures on this page. Then have the children trace the letter *i* in each word.

Day 5

PRETEACH

High-Frequency Words

Write the word *where* on the board. Point to and read *where*. Say: **Where should we go?** Then display an index card with the word *where* written on it. Say: *where*. Match the index card *where* with the word on the board. Say *where* and have children repeat several times.

Have children say sentences that use the word *where*. Write their sentences on chart paper. Then read each sentence, holding up the index card *where* as you say the word. You may wish to read a sentence frame, such as *Where do I _____?* Have children join in and say the word *where* with you.

Distribute to children index cards with these words written on them: *where, here, me, for, this, he,* and *the*. Have children work in pairs. One child should say a word, while the other finds the word and displays it. Allow children to play several rounds.

High-Frequency Words

for	the
he	this
here	where
me	

PRETEACH

Build Robust Vocabulary

Tell children of the Student-Friendly Explanations for *arrives, creeps,* and *nestle*. Then discuss each word, using the following examples.

arrives
When your teacher *arrives* at school, she prepares her lesson plans. What do you do when you arrive at school?

creeps
When someone *creeps* across the classroom floor, are they running or moving slowly?

nestle
Would it be nicer to *nestle* in a warm blanket or on a hardwood floor? Explain your answer.

VOCABULARY
Student-Friendly Explanations

arrives Arrives is another word for comes.

creeps When something creeps, it moves very slowly along the ground.

nestle When you nestle, you snuggle up next to something or someone.

Grade K 157

LESSON 14

Day 1 — Day at a Glance

PHONEMIC AWARENESS
Phoneme Identity: Initial

PHONICS
Preteach Word Building

HIGH-FREQUENCY WORDS
Reteach *where, the*

COMPREHENSION
Preteach Details

BUILD ROBUST VOCABULARY
Reteach *arrives, creeps, nestle*

Materials Needed:

Phoneme Phone | Word Builder and Word Builder Cards | Write-On/Wipe-Off Boards

Copying Master | Photo Cards | Practice Book

Phonemic Awareness

Phoneme Identity: Initial Remind children that they listen for the same sound in words. Model how to identify the same sound. Say: **I will say two words: *net, new*. I hear /n/ at the beginning of each word. The sound at the beginning of *net* and *new* is the same.**

Give each child a *Phoneme Phone*. Say the words *wet* and *wool*. Have children use the *Phoneme Phone* to elongate the sounds of each word as they look at their mouth position in the mirror. Ask the children to identify the common beginning sound they hear in *wet* and *wool*. (/w/) Continue in the same way with the following word groups: *pet, put* (/p/); *sock, set* (/s/); *tip, tug* (/t/); *ran, roll* (/r/); *dog, dig* (/d/).

PRETEACH
Phonics

Word Blending Distribute *Word Builders* and *Word Builder Cards* *b, p, i, n, r, s, f,* and *t*. Review each letter name and each letter sound. Then hold up the letters at random and ask children to tell you the letter name and sound.

Explain to children that you will show them how a word can change when the letters in the word change. Say: **Use your *Word Builder* and *Word Builder Cards* to make new words with me. I will use the letters *b, i,* and *n* to make the word *bin*. Now, you do the same. Blend the sounds with me: /b/-/i/-/n/, *bin*. If I take away *b* and put *t* in its place, I have the word *tin*. Now, you try it. Blend the sounds and say the word with me: /t/-/i/-/n/, *tin*.** The words *bin* and *tin* both end in *–in*. The words *bin* and *tin* rhyme.

  Build Words Have children continue with *tin* in their *Word Builder*:

Change the *n* to *p*. What word did you make? (*tip*)

Change the *t* to *r*. What word did you make? (*rip*)

Continue with the words *sip, sin, fin*. Then have children practice writing the words that they built on their *Write-on/Wipe-off Boards*.

Distribute *Copying Master* 27. Have children trace the letters at the bottom of the page and cut them out. Help children identify the pictures and paste *i* or *a* in the box to complete each picture name. (*pin, map, tag, pig*)

158 Lesson 14

Day 1

RETEACH

High-Frequency Words

 Distribute index cards *where* and *the* to the children. Say each word, and have children repeat and hold up the correct card. Show *Photo Card fox*. Ask children to name the picture. Then use the word cards, a question mark card, an index card with *is*, and the picture to build the sentence frame below. Point to each word as you read the sentence with children. Continue with other sentences.

| Where | is | the | fox | ? |

High-Frequency Words

| the | where |

PRETEACH

Comprehension

  Details Remind children that the details of a story are the small parts in the words and pictures that help a reader understand the story. Then read this story aloud to them.

> Dave loves animals. His favorite animals are monkeys. One day Dave went to the zoo to see the monkeys. When he arrived at their cage, Dave noticed that one monkey was very sad. Dave decided he wanted to cheer up the monkey. Dave began to sing and dance and wave his arms for the monkey. Suddenly, the sad monkey began to jump up and down. His sad face turned very happy as he watched Dave. Dave felt so good when he saw this. He knew he had made the monkey very happy!

Guide children to *Practice Book* page 80. Have them identify the picture pairs and circle the picture that tells story details. Ask: **Where is Dave going?** (the zoo) **What is Dave's favorite animal?** (the monkey)

RETEACH

Build Robust Vocabulary

Remind children of the Student-Friendly Explanations for *arrives, creeps,* and *nestle*. Then discuss each word, using the following examples.

arrives
When your principal *arrives* at school, what might he or she do first?

creeps
Which of these characters *creeps*?
- Harry the Spider
- Daisy the Dog
- Susan the Snail

nestle
- Are you more likely to *nestle* on the couch or in a tree? Explain.

VOCABULARY
Student-Friendly Explanations

arrives Arrives is another word for comes.

creeps When something creeps, it moves very slowly along the ground.

nestle When you nestle, you snuggle up next to something or someone

Grade K 159

LESSON 14

DAY AT A GLANCE — Day 2

PHONEMIC AWARENESS
Phoneme Identity: Initial

PHONICS
Reteach Word Building

HIGH-FREQUENCY WORDS
Reteach do, go, me, for, to, he, my

COMPREHENSION
Preteach Answer Questions

BUILD ROBUST VOCABULARY
Preteach slumbering, delight, blustery

Materials Needed:

Photo Cards | Phoneme Phone | Word Builder and Word Builder Cards

Write-On/Wipe-Off Boards | Copying Master | Practice Book

Phonemic Awareness

 Phoneme Identity: Initial Remind children that they have been listening for the same sounds in groups of words. Review how to identify and isolate the same sound in a group of words. Display *Photo Cards pan, pencil,* and *pig*. Say: **Listen as I say the picture names: pan, pencil, pig. I hear the /p/ sound at the beginning of each word. The sound at the beginning of pan, pencil, and pig is the same.** Give each child a *Phoneme Phone*. Hold up *Photo Cards taxi, tiger,* and *tree*. Have children name the picture while looking at his or her mouth position in the mirror. Have children repeat the words and tell which sound is the same. (/t/)

RETEACH

Phonics

Word Building Distribute the *Word Builder and Word Builder Cards i, a, f, h, n, t, s,* and *p*. Explain to the children that when letters in words change, the sounds in the words also change. Have the children follow along as you model word building. Say: **Use your Word Builder and Word Builder Cards to make new words with me. I will use the letters p, i,** and **n to make the word pin. Now, you do the same. Blend the sounds with me: /p/-/i/-/n/, pin. If I take away the p and put f in its place, I have the word fin. Now, you try it. Blend the sounds and say the word with me: /f/-/i/-/n/, fin.**

Build Words Have children continue with *fin* in their *Word Builder*. Say: **Change the f to t. What word did you make?** (tin) **Change the n to p. What word did you make?** (tip)

Continue with the words *tap, nap,* and *sap*. Then have children practice writing the words that they built on their *Write-On/Wipe-Off Boards*. Distribute *Copying Master 28* to the children. Help children name each picture and read the word choices below each picture. Then have children circle the word that names the picture and write the word. (pig, lip, sit, pin)

160 Lesson 14

Day 2

RETEACH
High-Frequency Words

Practice Book 81 Distribute *do* index card to each child. Have children point to the word and read it. Then ask children to repeat the word. Say the word again, having children repeat the word and hold up the card.

Use index cards *do, go, me, for, to, he,* and *my*. Have children sit in a circle. Give each child one word card. At your signal, have them pass their cards around the circle until you tell them to stop. Ask: **Who has the word *do*?** The child with the word *do* should stand and read the word. Repeat with the rest of the words.

Have children turn to *Practice Book* page 81 to review high-frequency words and practice newly-learned words. Complete the page together.

High-Frequency Words

do	me
for	my
go	to
he	

PRETEACH
Comprehension

Answer Questions Explain that asking and answering questions while reading a story helps you understand and enjoy a story. Remind children that many stories have details. Recall the story about Dave and the sad monkey from Day 1. Reread the story and pause to note details. Have children ask and answer questions about details in the story. Record their questions and answers on chart paper.

Question	Answer
What is Dave's favorite animal?	Dave's favorite animal is a monkey.
Where does Dave go in the story?	Dave goes to the zoo.

PRETEACH
Build Robust Vocabulary

Tell children the Student-Friendly Explanations for *slumbering, delight,* and *blustery*. Then discuss each word, using the following examples.

slumbering
When you are *slumbering*, where are you?

delight
What would *delight* you more, going to the zoo or going home?

blustery
When the weather is *blustery*, are the leaves more likely to stay on the trees or fall off the trees?

VOCABULARY
Student-Friendly Explanations

slumbering If you are slumbering, you are sleeping.

delight If something makes you feel delight, it makes you feel very happy.

blustery When the weather outside is blustery, it is very windy.

Grade K 161

LESSON 14

PHONEMIC AWARENESS
Phoneme Identity: Initial

PHONICS
Preteach Phonogram -in

HIGH-FREQUENCY WORDS
Reteach do, where, I, me, he, the

COMPREHENSION
Reteach Details

BUILD ROBUST VOCABULARY
Reteach slumbering, delight, blustery

WRITING
Reteach Writing Trait: Voice

Materials Needed:

Photo Cards   Write-On/Wipe-Off Boards   Practice Book

Phonemic Awareness

 Phoneme Identity: Initial Tell children to listen carefully to the following sentence. Say: **Carol can count.** Tell the children that the beginning sound of each word is the same. Say: **All of the words begin with the /c/ sound.** Ask: **Which sound is the same in each word of the sentence?** (/c/) Repeat the sentence emphasizing the /c/ sound at the beginning of each word. Display the *Photo Card hammer*. Guide the children in creating a sentence where each word has the same beginning sound as *hammer*. Help them create similar sentences using *Photo Cards frog, pig,* and *rabbit*. Encourage them to identify the initial sound of each word in the sentences they create. Record the sentences on chart paper.

Phoneme Isolation: Final Remind children that words are made up of sounds. Tell them that they will listen for ending sounds in words. Say: **dig. I hear /g/ at the end of *dig*. What is the word?** (dig) **What is the ending sound?** (/g/) The word *dig* ends in the /g/ sound. Repeat the activity with the children, using the word *pin* and the ending sound /n/. Have children identify the ending sound in the following words: *big, rat, had, web,* and *tin*.

PRETEACH

Phonics

 Identify Rhyming Words Remind children that rhyming words have the same ending sounds. Say: **Listen to the words I say: spin, thin. Spin and thin both have /in/. Spin and thin rhyme. What are the words?** (spin, thin) **Do the words rhyme?** (yes) Continue with these word pairs: *fin/tin; sit/sun; rat/bad; win/grin*. Ask children if each word pair rhymes. If the words rhyme, ask children to identify the sound they hear in both words.

Phonogram -in Write the word *pin* on the board. Track the print as you read the word. Have children repeat after you. Then write the word *win*. Track the print as you read the word. Have children repeat after you. Then say both words, *pin* and *win*. Ask: **How are the words *pin* and *win* the same?** (They both have /in/; they rhyme.) Say: **The words *pin* and *win* are in the -in word family because they both end in -in. The words *pin* and *win* rhyme.** Continue with the words *bin* and *tin*. Encourage children to recognize that rhyming words belong in the same word family.

Distribute *Write-on/Wipe-off Boards*. Write these words on the board: *fat, pin, run, sin, shin*. Have children read the words and copy those words in the *-in* word family on their *Write-on/Wipe-off Boards*.

162 Lesson 14

Day 3

RETEACH
High-Frequency Words

High-Frequency Words	
do	the
I	where

Distribute index cards for *do, where,* and *the* to children. As you say each word, have children repeat the word and hold up the correct card. Show *Photo Card drum*. Ask children to say the picture name. Then use the words, a question mark card, and the picture to build the first sentence frame shown below. Point to each word as you read the sentence. Ask children to read the sentence with you.

Then continue with the following sentences. Point to each word and have children read the sentences aloud.

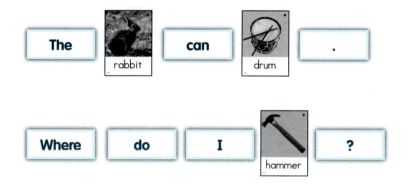

Write the following sentence frame on the board: *Where do I ____?* Have children copy and complete the sentence with a word or a picture.

Continue by changing the *Photo Card* to create new phrases. Invite volunteers to read them.

Grade K   163

Day 3

RETEACH

Comprehension

  Details Remind children that details are the small parts of a story that help a reader understand and enjoy a story. Have children listen as you read aloud the following story.

> Megan and Ellie are very excited because they are going to the lake. They pack their bathing suits and towels. Megan finds her sand toys in the basement. Ellie applies lots of sunscreen. Both girls rush to the car. When they arrive at the lake, the girls run toward the lake. First, they swim to the raft. Next, they catch a frog. Afterward, the girls relax on the shore and build a large sandcastle. The sun begins to go down, so then Megan and Ellie pack their things and travel home. They cannot wait until their next trip to the lake!

Guide children to *Practice Book* page 82. Have children use the pictures to retell the story. Ask: **Where are Megan and Ellie going in the story?** (the lake) **What do they do at the lake first?** (swim to the raft) **What do the girls build on shore?** (A large sandcastle) Then ask children to retell more details that they remember from the story.

RETEACH

Build Robust Vocabulary

Remind children of the Student-Friendly Explanations for *slumbering*, *delight*, and *blustery*. Then discuss each word, using the following examples.

slumbering
Which would you do while you were *slumbering*: dream or ride your bike?

delight
Which would give you more *delight*: riding on a roller coaster or sitting in a cold room?

blustery
What are you more likely to do on a *blustery* day: fly a kite or lay on a sandy beach?

VOCABULARY
Student-Friendly Explanations

slumbering If you are slumbering, you are sleeping.

delight If something makes you feel delight, it makes you feel very happy.

blustery When the weather outside is blustery, it is very windy.

RETEACH

Writing

Writing Trait: Voice Remind the children that you use words like *you* and *your* when you talk to someone else. Also, you use words like *me* and *my* when you talk about yourself. Write the following sentence pair on the board. Read each sentence while tracking the print.

> Megan and Ellie are very excited because they are going to the lake. Ellie applies lots of sunscreen.

Ask the children to pretend that Megan and Ellie were standing in their classroom. Tell the children to brainstorm a variety of questions that they would like to ask the girls. Model by writing the following questions on chart paper:

> What is <u>your</u> favorite thing to do at the lake?
> Do <u>you</u> catch frogs in the water or on shore?

Encourage children to think of more questions for Megan and Ellie. Record their questions on chart paper, and underline the words *you* and *your*.

LESSON 14

PHONEMIC AWARENESS
Phoneme Identity: Initial
Phoneme Isolation: Final

PHONICS
Preteach Phonogram *-ig*

READING
Review *-ig, -in*
Review High-Frequency Words

BUILD ROBUST VOCABULARY
Review *arrives, creeps, nestle, slumbering, delight, blustery*

WRITING
Reteach Interview Questions

Materials Needed:

Phoneme Phone | Write-On/Wipe-Off Boards | Practice Book

Phonemic Awareness

Phoneme Identity: Initial Explain to children that they will listen for beginning sounds in words. Say: **cake, cut. I hear the /c/ sound at the beginning of the words** *cake* **and** *cut*. **What are the words?** (cake, cut) **What sound is the same in each word?** (/c/).

Have children sit in a circle, and distribute the *Phoneme Phones*. Say the words *bug* and *ball*. Ask the children to repeat the words while looking at the position of their mouths in the mirror. Ask: **Do** *bug* **and** *ball* **have the same sound?** (yes) **What is the same sound in each word?** (/b/) Repeat with these word pairs: *mat/mug, pop/pack, ton/team, sit/send,* and *kick/keep.*

Phoneme Isolation: Final Remind children that words are made up of sounds. They have listened for the beginning sound in words. Now, they will listen for the ending sound in words. Say: **pet. I hear /t/ at the end of** *pet*. **What is the word?** (pet) **What is the final sound?** (/t/) **The word** *pet* **ends in the /t/ sound.** Repeat this process with the following words: *hit, bud, fig, ran,* and *cub.* Have children identify the final sound in each word.

PRETEACH
Phonics

Identify Rhyming Words Tell children that words with the same middle and ending sounds are rhyming words. Say: **Listen:** *fig, dig*. *Fig* **and** *dig* **both have /ig/.** *Fig* **and** *dig* **rhyme. Both words are in the *-ig* word family. What are the words?** (fig, dig) **Do the words rhyme?** (yes) **What is their word family?** (*-ig*) Read these word pairs and have children tell if they rhyme: *rig/pig, twig/pan, pig/pen, wig/dig.*

Phonogram *-ig* Write the words *dig* and *big* on the board. Track the print as you read each word. Have children repeat after you. Say: ***Dig* and *big* are in the *-ig* word family because they both end in *-ig*.** Continue with the words *wig* and *pig.*

Distribute *Write-on/Wipe-off Boards*. Write these words: *cat, twig, pin, rig.* Track the print as you read each word. Have children repeat. Have them copy the words in the *-ig* word family on their *Write-on/Wipe-off Boards.*

Day 4

REVIEW
Reading

 Review -ig, -in Review the -ig and -in sounds. Write the words *pig* and *pin* on the board. Ask children to blend the sounds with you as you run a finger under each letter. Say: /p/ /i/ /g/. **Say it with me.** /p/ /i/ /g/. Repeat the process with *pin*.

Review High-Frequency Words Distribute the index cards for *where, do, here, I,* and *go* to children. Explain that you will play "Show and Tell." As you say each word, have children find the corresponding word card, show the word to you, and say the word. Repeat until each word has been identified correctly.

Have children turn to *Practice Book* pages 83 and 84. Help children cut and fold the book. Encourage them to read it at home.

REVIEW
Robust Vocabulary

Remind children of the Student-Friendly Explanations for *arrives, creeps, nestle, slumbering, delight,* and *blustery.* Then determine children's understanding of the words by asking the following questions.

- **Would it *delight* you to *nestle* on the couch and watch a good movie?**
- **If a spider *creeps* across your room, is the spider moving slow or fast?**
- **On a *blustery* day, are you more likely to lose your hat or lose your dog?**
- **If you are *slumbering*, do you prefer to be in bed or on the couch?**
- **When your mom *arrives* at school, is she usually early or late?**

RETEACH
Writing

Writing Form: Interview Questions Remind children that question sentences ask something. In an interview, you ask questions to find out about someone else's life. Tell the children they are going to pretend to interview the President of the United States. Point out that by asking the President questions, they can gather information about the President, our government, and our country. As a group, brainstorm a list of interview questions. Record these questions on chart paper. Invite the children to help you with the chart, using letters and words that they know. Read the finished questions to the children.

> How did you become the President?
> How many people live in our country?
> What is your favorite state to visit?

VOCABULARY
Student-Friendly Explanations

arrives Arrives is another word for comes.

creeps When something creeps, it moves very slowly along the ground.

nestle When you nestle, you snuggle up next to something or someone.

slumbering If you are slumbering, you are sleeping.

delight If something makes you feel delight, it makes you feel very happy.

blustery When the weather outside is blustery, it is very windy.

LESSON 14

PHONEMIC AWARENESS
Phoneme Categorization: Initial

PHONICS
Preteach Short Vowel /o/o

HIGH-FREQUENCY WORDS
Preteach *you, come, like, my, here*

BUILD ROBUST VOCABULARY
Reteach *whirl, blustery, prefer*

Materials Needed:

Sound/Spelling Card *Oo*   Practice Book   Write-On/Wipe-Off Boards

---

Phonemic Awareness

Phoneme Categorization: Initial Review for children the meaning of the words *different* and *same*, using sets of classroom objects. Tell children that now they will listen for beginning sounds. Say: **I'll say some word pairs. If both words begin with the same sound, say *same*. If the words begin with different sounds, say *different*.** Model the first example: *man, mat.* **I hear /m/ at the beginning of both words. They both begin with the same sound: /m/. Now you try some.** Say these pairs of words, emphasizing the initial sound: *lid, kid; hat, hot; dig, dog; cab, zip; vet, van.*

Tell children to listen for the different beginning sound in a group of words. Say: **I will say three words. One word has a different beginning sound:** *band, fan, bib.* **I hear /b/ at the beginning of *band* and *bib*. I hear /f/ at the beginning of *fan*. *Fan* begins with a different sound.** Say each set of words. Have children repeat each set of words and name the word with a different beginning sound.

zero, zest, bat (bat)   **trace, bang, bale** (trace)   **gift, nice, glue** (nice)

PRETEACH

Phonics

Short Vowel *Oo* Display *Sound/Spelling Card Oo*. Say: **This is the letter *o*. Say the name with me.** Point to uppercase *O* and say: **This is uppercase *O*.** Point to lowercase *o* and say: **This is lowercase *o*.** Have children identify the letters. (O, o)

Writing *O* and *o* Write *Oo* on the board and have children identify the letters. Say: **Watch as I write the letter *O*.** As you give the Letter Talk, trace the uppercase *O*. Do the same for lowercase *o*.

Letter Talk for *O*	Letter Talk for *o*
1. Make a large circle.	1. Make a small circle.
2. Circle around and close.	2. Circle around and close.

Guided Practice Have children finger-write the uppercase *O* in the air as you repeat the Letter Talk. Do the same for lowercase *o*. Then, have children turn to *Practice Book* page 85. Have children circle each uppercase *O* and underline each lowercase *o*. Then have them practice writing each letter.

168 Lesson 14

Day 5

PRETEACH
High-Frequency Words

In advance, write *you, come, like, my,* and *here* on index cards. Write the word *you* on the board. Point to and read *you*. Have children say it with you. Say: **I like you.** Point to the word on the board again and say *you* again. Write on the board *come, like, my,* and *here*. Read each word to children, and have them repeat that word and point to the correct word. Tell children that you will show them words, and when they see *you*, they should say it and point to the word on the board. Shuffle the index cards and then randomly show one to children, going through the stack of cards several times until children consistently identify *you*.

Distribute *Write-on/Wipe-off Boards* to children. Have them copy the word *you* on their board and practice writing it several times.

High-Frequency Words

come	my
here	you
like	

RETEACH
Build Robust Vocabulary

Read to children the Student-Friendly Explanations for *whirl, blustery,* and *prefer*. Then discuss each word, asking children the following questions.

whirl
If a fan *whirls*, what is it doing?

blustery
What do the trees look like on a *blustery* day?

prefer
What kind of weather do you *prefer*? Why?

VOCABULARY
Student-Friendly Explanations

whirl When things whirl, they spin around in circles.

blustery When the weather outside is blustery, it is very windy.

prefer If you prefer something, you like it better than something else.

Grade K   169

LESSON 15

PHONEMIC AWARENESS
Phoneme Categorization: Initial

PHONICS
Preteach Relate *Oo* to /o/*o*

HIGH-FREQUENCY WORDS
Reteach *you*

COMPREHENSION
Reteach Draw Conclusions

BUILD ROBUST VOCABULARY
Reteach *fading, arrives, slumbering*

Materials Needed:

Sounds of Letters CD   Sound/Spelling Card *Oo*   Word Builder and Word Builder Cards

Write-On/Wipe-Off Boards   Photo Cards   Copying Master

Practice Book

Phonemic Awareness

Phoneme Categorization: Initial Say: **Listen to these words: *wink, sand, wish*. I hear /w/ at the beginning of *wink* and *wish*. I hear /s/ at the beginning of *sand*. So the sound at the beginning of *sand* is different.** Say each set of words. Have children repeat each set of words and name the word that has a different beginning sound.

crab, shin, shift (crab)   **dog, dish, cat** (cat)   **wind, red, wink** (red)

blue, bush, mail (mail)   **snake, scab, gold** (gold)   **inch, room, rake** (inch)

PRETEACH

Phonics

 Relate *Oo* to /o/ Play the /o/ sound from the *Sounds of Letters CD*. Say the words *odd* and *on,* and have children repeat them. Explain that *odd* and *on* both begin with /o/. Have children say /o/ several times. Display *Sound/Spelling Card Oo*. Say: **One sound that the letter *o* may stand for is /o/, the sound at the beginning of *odd*. Say /o/.** Have children repeat the sound as you touch the card several times.

 Give each child a *Word Builder Card o*. Say: **If the word begins with /o/ hold up the card and say /o/. If the word does not begin with /o/, hold your card behind your back.** Say the words *odd, bin, ox, October,* and *dim*. Tell children that /o/ may also be heard in the middle of words like *log*. Follow the same procedure, using the words *pop, sat, fin,* and *rock*.

  Give each child a *Write-on/Wipe-off Board*. Tell children that they will work with the three boxes next to the heart on side B. Draw the boxes on chart paper. Display *Photo Cards box* and *otter*. Tell children: **I will say some words. If /o/ is at the beginning of the word, put your letter *o* on the first box. If /o/ is in the middle of the word, put your letter *o* on the middle box.** Model the activity using *box* and *otter*. Then say the following words, and have children place *Word Builder Cards* on the appropriate box: *frog, odd, rock, often, ox,* and *clock*.

Distribute *Copying Master 29*. Have children trace the *Oo,* and circle the letter for the beginning sound of each picture. (Children should circle *o* for *ostrich, octopus; k* for *kite; m* for *mitt; t* for *top*.)

Day 1

RETEACH

High-Frequency Words

Write the word *you* on the board. Say the word, and have children repeat it and point to the word. Write on the board: *You hit.* Read the sentence with the group, and invite a volunteer to pantomime hitting a ball. Have the volunteer point to *you* as you read the sentence again. Repeat the activity with other action words children can read such as *ran, sat,* and *tap*.

High-Frequency Word

you

RETEACH

Comprehension

Draw Conclusions Remind children that sometimes readers must figure out things in a story for themselves. Then read this story aloud to them.

> Ben had been watching the water dragon sit on the piece of green netting for ten minutes before he saw it move. Ben thought it was asleep until it suddenly opened its eyes and dropped into the small pond below. Ben watched in delight as the water dragon rapidly flicked its tail back and forth in the water to swim from one end of the pond to the other. The water dragon climbed quickly onto the rocks at the shallow end of the pond and looked around. A nearby cricket sensed the danger and tried to leap away, but it hit the glass wall and bounced back into the pond. The water dragon leaped and swallowed the cricket in one gulp. "Eeeewwww," said Ben, but he couldn't stop watching the water dragon.

Guide children to *Practice Book* page 86. Have them use clues in the story to draw conclusions about which illustrations most likely match the lizard and story setting.

RETEACH

Build Robust Vocabulary

Remind children of the Student-Friendly Explanations of *fading, arrives,* and *slumbering*. Then discuss each word, using the following examples.

fading
Do you have clothing on which the color is *fading*? What does it look like?

arrives
If I say that the principal *arrives* at 7:00 in the morning, what does the principal do at that time?

slumbering
If you are *slumbering*, are you being productive or idle? Explain.

VOCABULARY

Student-Friendly Explanations

fading When something is fading, it is becoming lighter and harder to see.

arrives If a person arrives somewhere, he or she have just come to that place.

slumbering If you are slumbering, you are sleeping.

LESSON 15

PHONEMIC AWARENESS
Phoneme Categorization

PHONICS
Preteach Blending /o/o, /t/t

HIGH-FREQUENCY WORDS
Preteach look, you, where, come, like

COMPREHENSION
Reteach Reread

BUILD ROBUST VOCABULARY
Reteach perhaps, warn, property

Materials Needed:

Phoneme Phone   Word Builder and Word Builder Cards

Copying Master   Practice Book

Phonemic Awareness

Phoneme Categorization Tell children that today they will say sentences that have three words. Two of the words will begin with the same sound. Tell children to listen for the word that has a different beginning sound. Use *a Phoneme Phone*, and emphasize the initial sounds. Say: **Seven snakes rattle. I hear /s/ at the beginning of seven and snakes. I hear /r/ at the beginning of rattle. Rattle begins with a different sound.** Continue with the following sentences. Have children use the *Phoneme Phone* to look at the position of their mouth as they repeat the sentence and name the word that begins with a different sound.

Birds sing songs. (birds)   **Five fish swim.** (swim)

Don't scold snakes. (don't)   **Brian toasts bread.** (toasts)

Big boats float. (float)   **Kites can't roll.** (roll)

PRETEACH

Phonics

  Blending /o/o, /t/t Clap your hands to get a steady rhythm going. Then, in time with the beat, say: **We're going on a word hunt. / What's this word? / /h/ /o/ /t/ /** Together: **hot!** Have children echo you. Continue for the words /p/ /o/ /t/ (pot), /g/ /o/ /t/ (got), /l/ /o/ /t/ (lot).

Word Blending Place the *Word Builder Cards* d, o, and t in the *Word Builder*. Point to d and say /d/. Point to o and say /o/. Slide the o next to the d. Move your hand under the letters and blend the sounds, elongating them: /doo/. Have children blend the sounds after you. Point to t. Say /t/. Have children repeat the sound. Slide the t next to the do. Slide your hand under dot and blend the sounds. Have children blend the sounds as you slide your hand under the word. Then have children read the word *dot* along with you. Continue with the words *hot, got,* and *not*.

Distribute *Copying Master 30* to review building words with short vowel /o/o and /t/t with children. (Children should trace Oo, write o for *octupus, ostrich, ox*; trace o in *top, pot*.)

172 Lesson 15

Day 2

PRETEACH
High-Frequency Words

Practice Book 87 In advance, write *look, you, where, come,* and *like* each on an index card. Say: *look*. **Look** at this pencil. **Look** at the desk. Write the word *look* on the board. Point to and read *look*. Have children say it with you.

Have children sit in a circle, and distribute the index cards with high-frequency words, giving one to each child. Tell children that you will say a word. If they have that word, they should stand, show their card, and read the word. Ask: **Who has the word *where*?** Continue with the rest of the words until children consistently identify all words correctly.

Have children turn to *Practice Book,* page 87 to review high-frequency words and practice newly-learned words. Complete the page together.

High-Frequency Words

come	where
like	you
look	

RETEACH
Comprehension

 Monitor Comprehension: Reread   Remind children that rereading can help them keep track of information as they read. Recall the story about the water dragon from Day 1. Read the story and then discuss it with children. Then ask the following questions, modeling how to reread the story for information.

- **How long had Ben been watching the water dragon at the start of the story?** (10 minutes)
- **Can water dragons swim?** (yes) **What part of their body do they use to move through the water?** (their tail)
- **What is one food that water dragons eat?** (crickets)
- **What was Ben's reaction to seeing the water dragon eat the cricket?** (He did not like it, but he was interested in the water dragon)

RETEACH
Build Robust Vocabulary

Remind children of the Student-Friendly Explanations of *perhaps, warn,* and *property*. Then discuss each word, using the following examples.

perhaps
How would it make you feel if I said, *"Perhaps* we will have a party tomorrow?"

warn
How could you *warn* someone that it was raining very hard outside if you didn't both speak the same language? Show me.

property
Name some *property* that a fire fighter has. A doctor?

VOCABULARY
Student-Friendly Explanations

perhaps If someone says perhaps something will happen, it means that it may or may not happen.

warn If you warn someone, you let that person know that something dangerous is going to happen.

property Something that belongs to you is called your property.

Grade K   173

LESSON 15

DAY AT A GLANCE
Day 3

PHONEMIC AWARENESS
Phoneme Categorization
Phoneme Isolation: Medial

PHONICS
Preteach Word Blending

HIGH-FREQUENCY WORDS
Reteach *look, I, the*

COMPREHENSION
Reteach Draw Conclusions

BUILD ROBUST VOCABULARY
Reteach *creeps, nestle, delight*

WRITING
Reteach Writing Trait: Conventions

Materials Needed:

Word Builder and Word Builder Cards

Write-On/Wipe-Off Boards

Photo Cards

Practice Book

Phonemic Awareness

Phoneme Categorization Say: **I am going to say three words: ring, sea, right. Two of these words have the same beginning sound. Which one has a different beginning sound?** (sea) Have children repeat each set of words and name the word that has a different beginning sound.

plum, pole, surf (surf)   **shoe, dish, shine** (dish)   **rack, rink, wink** (wink)

sore, bus, sun (bus)   **mint, socks, sink** (mint)   **pale, mail, mall** (pale)

If children have difficulty identifying the sound that is different at the beginning of words, say two words at a time. Then have them tell whether the initial sounds in the pairs of words are the same or different.

Phonem Isolation: Medial Have children listen for and name the sound they hear in the middle of these words.

had (/a/)	**get** (/e/)	**mitt** (/i/)	**back** (/a/)
mop (/o/)	**fit** (/i/)	**run** (/u/)	**cut** (/u/)
man (/a/)	**pet** (/e/)	**sip** (/i/)	**last** (/a/)

PRETEACH

Phonics

 Word Blending Distribute *Word Builders* and *Word Builder Cards o, a, p, r, n, c,* and *t*. Review each letter name and sound. Then hold up letters at random and ask children to say the letter name and sound.

Explain to children that you are going to show them how a word can change when the letters in the word change. Say: **Use your *Word Builder* and *Word Builder Cards* to make new words with me. I will use the letters *r, o,* and *t* to make the word *rot*. Now you do the same. Blend the sounds with me: /r/-/o/-/t/, *rot*. If I take away the *r* and put *p* in its place, I have the word *pot*. Now you try it. Blend the sounds and say the word with me: /p/-/o/-/t/, *pot*.**

Build Words Have children continue with *pot* in their *Word Builder*:

Change the *p* to *n*. What word did you make? (not)

Change the *n* to *c*. What word did you make? (cot)

Change the *o* to *a*. What word did you make? (cat)

Continue with the words *cap, nap,* and *tap*. Then have children practice writing the words they built on their *Write-On/Wipe-Off Boards*.

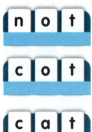

174 Lesson 15

Day 3

RETEACH
High-Frequency Words

 Display *Photo Cards fish, octopus,* and *otter*. Write on the board the sentence frame *Look at the _____*. Ask a volunteer to point to *look* in the sentence. Complete the sentence frame with *Photo Card fish*. Point to each word, and have children read the sentence aloud. Then continue with the following sentences, adding or changing words and *Photo Cards* as needed. Point to each word and have children read the sentence aloud.

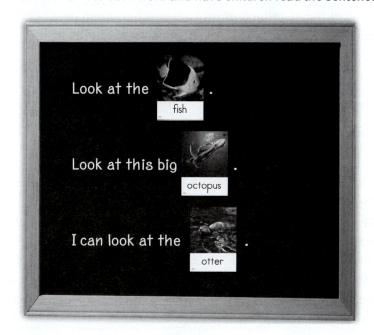

Reread the sentence frame on the board: *Look at the ____*. Have children copy and complete the sentence with a picture.

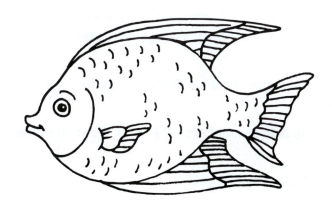

High-Frequency Words

I   the

look

Grade K   175

Day 3

RETEACH
Comprehension

  Draw Conclusions Remind children that authors put clues in the story to help readers understand things they don't say. Tell children that when we figure out what an author doesn't tell us, we are drawing conclusions. Read the following story aloud, pausing to guide children toward clues in the story.

> Kate stared at the building that was her new home and held her Dad's hand tighter. She counted the windows up the side of the building: 1, 2, 3, 4, 5! She remembered her mother telling her that they lived on the fifth floor. "How are we ever going to get up there?" she asked.
>
> Her father smiled and said, "We'll take the elevator, Kate."
>
> "Oh, yeah," she sighed with relief, glad they weren't going to have to walk up five flights of stairs.
>
> Her father gently tugged on her hand and they walked up the big stairs in front of the building. Her father opened one of the large glass doors and they walked through together. There was a short hallway and then another set of glass doors. On the other side of the glass doors was a long hallway with rows of small mailboxes on the wall and four elevator doors. At the other end of the hallway was another little girl. Her mother was getting mail. Kate waved shyly. The girl waved back. Kate decided that this place might be okay.

Guide children to *Practice Book* page 88. Have children use clues from the text to identify the correct building and add missing details.

RETEACH
Build Robust Vocabulary

Recall the Student-Friendly Explanations for the words *creeps, nestle,* and *delight.* Then discuss each word, asking children the following questions.

creeps
Pretend to *creep* around a corner. Show me how you might move.

nestle
What kind of an animal might *nestle*? Into what does it nestle?

delight
What kinds of things *delight* you?

VOCABULARY
Student-Friendly Explanations

creeps When something creeps, it moves very slowly along the ground.

nestle When you nestle, you crawl up next to something.

delight If you feel delight, you are very happy or pleased about something.

176 Lesson 15 •

Day 3

RETEACH

Writing

Writing Trait: Conventions Tell children that sentences that show strong feeling are called exclamations. Brainstorm with children exclamations people might say, and list them on the board.

This is fun!
No!
It's my birthday!

Read the exclamations to the children expressively and with excitement. Then say: **It's my birthday! Listen to my voice—can you hear how excited I am? When I write an exclamation, I want my readers to know I'm excited. I write a special mark at the end of my sentence, like this.**

Show children the exclamation points in the sentences you wrote. Explain that exclamations always end with exclamation points. Ask children to name additional exclamations. Record their responses without the exclamation point on chart paper. Remind children that sentences always start with an uppercase letter and point out the uppercase letter that begins each sentence you record. Invite children to write the exclamation point for the sentence they contributed.

It's my birthday!
It is so cold outside!
I can see my breath!
That's a pretty shirt!

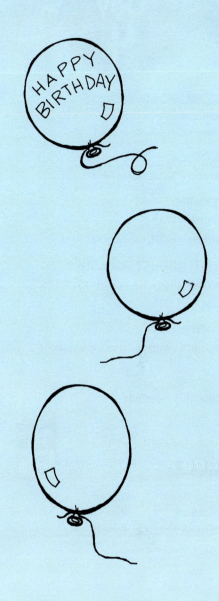

Grade K   177

LESSON 15

PHONEMIC AWARENESS
Phoneme Categorization
Phoneme Isolation: Medial

PHONICS
Reteach Short Vowel /o/o

READING
Review /o/o
Review High-Frequency Words

BUILD ROBUST VOCABULARY
Review soggy, warn, blustery, nestle, wobble

WRITING
Preteach Writing Form: Exclamations

Materials Needed:

Word Builder and Word Builder Cards

Write-On/ Wipe-Off Boards

Practice Book 89–90

Phonemic Awareness

Phoneme Categorization   Say: **I am going to say three words: leaf, bone, and lap. Two of these words have the same beginning sound. Which one has a different beginning sound?** (bone) Have children repeat each set of words and name the word that has a different beginning sound.

rod, rip, sing (sing)   **dim, long, leg** (dim)   **bit, bun, toad** (toad)

zoo, zip, moon (moon) **sun, line, lift** (sun)   **fin, clocks, fox** (clocks)

Phoneme Isolation: Medial   Tell children to listen for the sound in the middle of words. Have children name the medial sound in these words:

hip (/i/)	**pond** (/o/)	**robe** (/ō/)	**kiss** (/i/)
sag (/a/)	**fun** (/u/)	**wig** (/i/)	**hot** (/o/)
run (/u/)	**wet** (/e/)	**fetch** (/e/)	**box** (/o/)

RETEACH

Phonics

 Short Vowel /o/o   Write the word *not* on an index card and hold it up for children to see. Model blending the sounds as you run a finger under each letter. Say: **/nn/ /oo/ /t/. Say it with me. /nn/ /oo/ /t/. Not.** Run a finger under the letters, having children read the word.

Read Words   Use the *Word Builder Cards* to make more words. Tell children that they are going to read the words by blending the sounds for each letter. Have children blend the sounds to read each word.

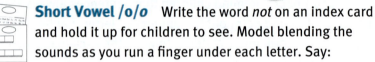

Write Words   Display the following *Word Builder Cards* for children: *a, i, o, n, p, s, t*. Give children *Write-On/Wipe-Off Boards*. Have children write words using the letters. Invite them to read the words they have written to classmates.

REVIEW

Reading

Apply Phonics /o/o Write the words *pot, nod, on, top,* and *dog* on the board. Point to the words and have children read them. Write *you* and *look* on index cards. Show them several times, reading each word. Then show them randomly and have children read them. Repeat until children identify them correctly.

Practice Book 89–90

Have children turn to *Practice Book* pp. 89–90. Help children cut out and fold the book. Read the sentences with children. Have children take the book home to read with their families.

REVIEW

Robust Vocabulary

Tell children that they have been learning some interesting words. Remind children of the Student-Friendly Explanations of *soggy, warn, blustery, nestle,* and *wobble*. Then determine children's understanding of the words by asking these questions.

- Can ground be *soggy*? What does it feel like when it's soggy?
- If the news *warns* you about the weather, does that usually mean good weather or bad weather is coming?
- How does a *blustery* day make you feel? Show how you might look.
- How might a dog look when it *nestles*?
- What makes a table *wobble*? How might you fix it?

PRETEACH

Writing

Writing Form: Exclamations Remind children that exclamations show a lot of feeling. Tell children that when they write exclamations, their sentence should begin with an uppercase letter and end with an exclamation point.

Tell children that together you will write an exclamation. Have children brainstorm exclamations they could say about their class. Record their ideas on chart paper. Then use children's ideas to write a final exclamation summarizing the way the class feels about itself. Invite children to write letters and words they know. Read the finished exclamation to children. Post the finished exclamation on a bulletin board and have children contribute drawings to go with the exclamation.

> Our class is smart, funny, and terrific!

High-Frequency Words

look   you

VOCABULARY

Student-Friendly Explanations

soggy Something that is soggy is so wet that it's squishy.

warn If you warn someone, you let that person know that something dangerous is going to happen.

blustery When the weather outside is blustery, it is very windy.

nestle When you nestle, you crawl up next to something.

wobble When things wobble, they move from side to side in an unsteady way.

Grade K **179**

LESSON 15

PHONEMIC AWARENESS
Phoneme Identity: Final

PHONICS
Preteach Consonant *Ll*

HIGH-FREQUENCY WORDS
Preteach *one*

BUILD ROBUST VOCABULARY
Preteach *load, bound, steep*

Materials Needed:

Sound/Spelling Card *Ll*   Write-On/Wipe-Off Boards   Practice Book

Phonemic Awareness

Phoneme Identity: Final   Tell children that today they will be listening for the sound that is the same in groups of words that you will say. Model the process. Say: **I am going to say three words:** *him, jam, gum*. **The sound at the end of** *him, jam,* **and** *gum* **is the same. The ending sound of** *hum, jam,* **and** *gum* **is /m/. Let's use these words:** *met, sat, pot*. **The sound at the end of** *met, sat,* **and** *pot* **is the same, /t/.**

Say each set of words below. Provide support as you name words. Add emphasis to the final sound as you say the words in a set. Have children repeat each set of words, adding a similar emphasis to the final sounds. Have them tell which sound is the same in each set of words (beginning, middle, or ending) and then name the sound.

| lick, sock, rake (/k/) | rug, dog, tag (/g/) | cop, rap, sip (/p/) |
| hall, mill, seal (/l/) | sit, fat, hut (/t/) | ran, ton, fin (/n/) |

PRETEACH

Phonics

Consonant *Ll*   Display *Sound/Spelling Card Ll*. Say: **This is the letter *l*. Say the name with me.** Point to uppercase *L* and say: **This is uppercase *L*.** Point to lowercase *l* and say: **This is lowercase *l*.** Have children identify the letters. (*L, l*)

Writing *L* and *l*   Write *L* and *l* on the board and have children identify the letters. Say: **Watch as I write the letter *L*.** As you give the Letter Talk, trace the uppercase *L*. Do the same for lowercase *l*.

Letter Talk for *L*	Letter Talk for *l*
1. Straight line down.	1. Straight line down.
2. Straight line to the right.	

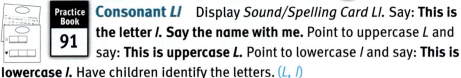

Tell children to finger-write the uppercase *L* in the air as you repeat the Letter Talk. Have them do the same for lowercase *l*. Distribute *Write-on/Wipe-off Boards* to children. Ask them to write uppercase *L* and then lowercase *l* several times on their *Write-on/Wipe-off Boards*.

Have children turn to *Practice Book* page 91. Help children circle each uppercase *L* and underline each lowercase *l*. Have them trace the letters and write them on the lines.

180 Lesson 15

Day 5

RETEACH
High-Frequency Words

Write the word *one* on the board. Point to and read *one*. Hold up one finger. Have children say it with you. Say: **I have *one* book.** Write *one* on an index card and display it. Say: *one*. Match the index card to the word on the board, say the word, and have children say it with you.

one

Have children point to the word and read it. Write the words *here, the, you,* and *for* on index cards. Tell children that you will show them words, and when they see *one*, they should say the word and point to it on the board. Hold up index cards in random order until children consistently identify the word *one*.

PRETEACH
Build Robust Vocabulary

Tell children the Student-Friendly Explanations for *load, bound,* and *steep*. Then discuss each word, using the following examples.

load
When you *load* a grocery cart, do you fill it or empty it?

bound
Imagine you are on a space ship. Where would you be *bound* for?

steep
Why might you be out of breath after walking up a *steep* hill?

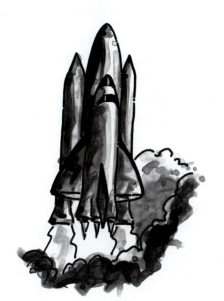

High-Frequency Words

for	here
one	the
you	

VOCABULARY
Student-Friendly Explanations

load When you load things, you put them into something.

bound When you are going somewhere, you are bound for that place.

steep When something is steep, it is hard to climb because of the way it goes up.

Grade K 181

LESSON 16

PHONEMIC AWARENESS
Phoneme Identity: Final

PHONICS
Preteach Relate *Ll* to /l/

HIGH-FREQUENCY WORDS
Reteach *one*

COMPREHENSION
Preteach Setting

BUILD ROBUST VOCABULARY
Reteach *load, bound, steep*

Materials Needed:

Phoneme Phone

Sound/Spelling Card *Ll*

Sounds of Letters CD

Word Builder and Word Builder Cards

Copying Master

Photo Cards

Practice Book

Phonemic Awareness

Phoneme Identity: Final Remind children that they have been listening for sounds that are the same in groups of words. Say: **Listen for the sound that is the same in these three words: *sit, mat, cut*. The ending sound in *sit, mat,* and *cut* is the same. They end with /t/.**

Distribute the *Phoneme Phones*. Model using the *Phoneme Phone,* showing the position of your mouth as you say *sit, mat,* and *cut*. Have children use the *Phoneme Phone* to look at the position of their mouths as they repeat each set of words after you. Tell which sound is the same, and name the sound.

bad, need, sled (/d/)   wall, real, full (/l/)   rake, kick, pack (/k/)

cap, mop, hip (/p/)   rag, dog, hug (/g/)   bus, this, yes (/s/)

PRETEACH

Phonics

   Relate *Ll* to /l/ Play the /l/ sound from the *Sounds of Letters CD.* Say the words *ladder* and *lamp* and have children repeat them. Tell children that *ladder* and *lamp* begin with /l/. Have children say /l/ several times.

Connect Letter and Sound Display *Sound/Spelling Card Ll.* Say: **The letter *l* can stand for /l/, the sound at the beginning of *ladder*. Say /l/.** Have children repeat the sound as you touch the card several times.

Discriminate /l/ Give each child a *Word Builder Card l.* Say: **If the word begins with /l/ hold up the card and say /l/. If the word does not begin with /l/, hold your card behind your back.** Say the words *lemon, lovely, melon, set,* and *luck*. Tell children that /l/ may also be heard at the end of words like *sell*. Follow the same procedure for the final position, using the words *rug, wall, sit, stuff, hill,* and *pull*.

 Distribute *Copying Master* page 31. Have children trace each letter. Then have them look at each picture and circle the letter that stands for the beginning sound of each picture name. (Children circle letter *l* in each box: *lips, lamp, log*. Children circle letter *g* in box *gate*. Children circle letter *s* in box *sock*.)

182 Lesson 16

Day 1

RETEACH
High-Frequency Words

Write the word *one* on the board. Say the word, and have children repeat it and point to the word. Write on the board: *I have one ____.* Complete the sentence with *Photo Card apple*. Read the sentence with the group and invite a volunteer to tell how many apples are described. (one) Have the volunteer point to *one* as you read the sentence again. Repeat the activity with other *Photo Cards,* having children point to the word *one* on the board each time they say the word.

High-Frequency Words

have	I
here	one

RETEACH
Comprehension

Setting Tell children that the setting of a story is where and when the story takes place. Read aloud the following story for children:

Katya and her family went camping one Saturday. In the morning, Katya woke up and felt cool air on her face. The sun shone through the small tent and made the tent glow. Katya was alone. She could hear her sister laughing outside with her parents. The smell of bacon drifted through the tent. "Yum," Katya said. She was hungry, so she got ready and stepped out of the tent. Outside, she saw huge green trees around the campsite. She was happy to be outdoors on a beautiful morning.

Guide children to *Practice Book* page 92. Have them look at the pictures as you reread the story. Have children circle the picture in the first row that shows when the story takes place. Have them circle the picture in the second row that shows where the story takes place. Have them use the pictures to retell the story.

RETEACH
Build Robust Vocabulary

Remind children of the Student-Friendly Explanations for *load, bound,* and *steep*. Then discuss each word, using the following examples.

load
What special things in your home would you *load* into a box?

bound
If you are *bound* for school, are you going to it or leaving it?

steep
Which is *steep*—a playground slide or a merry-go-round?

VOCABULARY
Student-Friendly Explanations

load When you load things, you put them into something.

bound When you are going somewhere, you are bound for that place.

steep When something is steep, it is hard to climb because of the way it goes up.

Grade K 183

LESSON 16

DAY AT A GLANCE — Day 2

PHONEMIC AWARENESS
Phoneme Identity: Final

PHONICS
Preteach Consonant *Hh*

HIGH-FREQUENCY WORDS
Preteach *see*

COMPREHENSION
Preteach Use Story Structure

BUILD ROBUST VOCABULARY
Preteach *drooped, joyous, thrill*

Materials Needed:

Sound/Spelling Card *Hh*   Copying Master   Practice Book

Write-On/Wipe-Off Boards

Phonemic Awareness

Phoneme Identity: Final   Tell children that you are going to say groups of words, and children are to listen for the sound that is the same in all the words. Model an example for children. Say: **Listen for the sound that is the same in these three words: *hog, bag, rig*. Say the words with me: *hog, bag, rig*. I hear /g/ at the end of each word. The ending sound of *hog, bag,* and *rig* is the same, /g/.** As you say each set of words, repeat or elongate the ending sound. Have children say the ending sound after you. Point out that the ending sound is the same in each set of words.

year, car, roar (/r/)	his, bus, likes (/s/)	got, bat, set (/t/)
from, Tim, ram (/m/)	lock, kick, back (/k/)	tell, cool, mill (/l/)

PRETEACH — Phonics

Consonant *Hh*   Display *Sound/Spelling Card Hh*. Say: **This is the letter *h*. Say the name with me.** Point to uppercase *H* and say: **This is uppercase *H*.** Point to lowercase *h* and say: **This is lowercase *h*.** Have children identify the letters. (*H, h*)

Writing *H* and *h*   Write *H* and *h* on the board and have children identify the letters. Say: **Watch as I write the letter *H*.** As you give the Letter Talk, trace the letters.

Letter Talk for *H*	Letter Talk for *h*
1. Straight line down.	1. Straight line down.
2. Straight line down line.	2. Halfway up the line again; curve to the right and down.
3. Short line across to connect the lines.	

Tell children to finger-write the uppercase *H* in the air as you repeat the Letter Talk. Have them do the same for lowercase *h*. Distribute *Write-on/Wipe-off Boards* to children. Ask them to write uppercase *H* and then lowercase *h* several times on their *Write-on/Wipe-off Boards*.

Give children *Copying Master* page 32. Have children circle each uppercase *H* and underline each lowercase *h*. Then have them trace each letter and practice writing it on the line.

Day 2

PRETEACH: High-Frequency Words

Write the word *see* on the board. Point to and read *see*. Have children say it with you. Say: **I see one desk.** Write *see* on an index card and display it. Say: *see*. Match the index card to the word on the board, say the word, and have children say it with you. Write the words *go, he, like,* and *where* on index cards. Tell children that you will show them words, and when they see *see*, they should say the word and point to it on the board.

Have children turn to *Practice Book* page 93 to review High-Frequency Words and practice newly-learned words. Complete the page together.

High-Frequency Words

go	see
he	where
like	

PRETEACH: Comprehension

Use Story Structure Tell children that paying attention to the beginning, middle, and ending of a story can help them better understand the story. Recall the story about Katya's camping trip from Day 1. Copy the Story Map below onto chart paper. Reread the story and complete the chart together.

Katya's Camping Trip
Beginning
Katya wakes up in a tent.
Middle
Katya smells bacon cooking.
End
Katya goes outside and feels happy.

PRETEACH: Build Robust Vocabulary

Tell children the Student-Friendly Explanations for *drooped, joyous,* and *thrill*. Then discuss each word, using the following examples.

drooped
If an apple tree branch *drooped,* do you think it is heavy with apples? Why or why not?

joyous
Would you feel *joyous* if you won a race? Why?

thrill
Which would be more likely to give you a *thrill*—riding a horse or walking a dog? Why?

VOCABULARY: Student-Friendly Explanations

drooped If something drooped, it bent or hung down because it was weak.

joyous When you feel joyous, you feel very, very happy.

thrill When you do something exciting that makes you a little tingly, you get a thrill.

Grade K 185

LESSON 16

DAY AT A GLANCE — Day 3

PHONEMIC AWARENESS
Phoneme Identity: Final

PHONICS
Preteach Relate *Hh* to /h/

HIGH-FREQUENCY WORDS
Reteach *one, see*

COMPREHENSION
Reteach Setting

BUILD ROBUST VOCABULARY
Reteach *drooped, joyous, thrill*

WRITING
Reteach Writing Trait: Word Choice

Materials Needed:

Sounds of Letters CD | Sound/Spelling Card *Hh* | Word Builder and Word Builder Cards

Photo Cards | Practice Book

Phonemic Awareness

Phoneme Identity: Final Remind children that they have been listening for the sound that is the same in a group of words. Say: **Listen for the sound that is the same in these three words:** *dog, big, egg*. **Say the words with me:** *dog, big, egg*. **I hear /g/ at the end of each word. The sound at the end of** *dog, big,* **and** *egg* **is the same, /g/.** Follow the same procedure, using the following sets of words. Have children tell which sound is the same. Then have them name the sound.

back, rock, sick (/k/)	**tub, cab, rob** (/b/)	**up, leap, cap** (/p/)
bed, good, had (/d/)	**leg, bag, dog** (/g/)	**if, half, leaf** (/f/)

Repeat the procedure for the following sets of words. Have children repeat the words and tell which sound is the same. (beginning) Then have them name the sound that is the same in each set.

put, page, pat (/p/)	**dim, doll, dad** (/d/)	**wide, wash, well** (/w/)
bed, bush, big (/b/)	**sad, sell, sun** (/s/)	**tub, talk, time** (/t/)

PRETEACH

Phonics

Relate *Hh* to /h/ Play the sound of *h* from the *Sounds of Letters CD*. Say the words *hat* and *hill* and have children repeat the words. Tell them that *hat* and *hill* begin with /h/. Have children say /h/ several times.

Connect Letter and Sound Display *Sound/Spelling Card Hh*. Ask: **What is the name of this letter? The letter *h* stands for /h/, the sound at the beginning of *hat*. Say /h/.** Have children repeat the sound as you touch the letter on the card several times.

Discriminate and Identify /h/ Give each child a *Word Builder Card* for *h*. Tell children that you will show them some pictures. Explain that children should tell what the picture shows and hold up their *Word Builder Card h* if the word begins with /h/. Randomly hold up the *Photo Cards* for *frog, girl, hammer, hat, helicopter, hill,* and *kangaroo*. Display the cards whose names begin with *h* after they have been identified. When children have identified all the *Photo Cards* whose names begin with *h*, point to and say the names of the pictures displayed.

186 Lesson 16

RETEACH

High-Frequency Words

High-Frequency Words	
I	see
one	

Write the words *one, see, I,* and a period on index cards. Then use the index cards and *Photo Card otter* to build the first sentence frame shown below. Point to each word as you read the sentence. Ask children to read the sentence with you.

Then continue with the following sentences. Point to each word and have children read the sentences aloud. Use a *Photo Card* to complete each sentence.

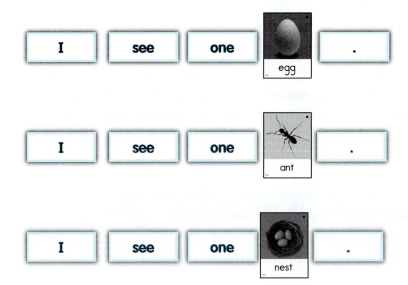

Grade K **187**

Day 3

RETEACH

Comprehension

  Writing Trait: Setting Remind children that the setting of a story is where and when the story happens. Explain that they will listen to a story. Ask children to pay attention to words and pictures that tell where and when the story happens. As you read aloud the following story, pause at appropriate points to ask children about the story's setting.

After school, Raul walked through the big double doors of the library. On the way to the children's room, he said hello to Ms. Miller, his favorite librarian. She smiled and winked at him. In the children's room, his older sister was lying on a bench and reading a chapter book. When Raul reached the bench, he dropped his backpack and hopped up next to her.

She sat up and gave him a hug, "Hi, Squirt. How was school?"

"It was great!" he replied. He hopped back off the bench and looked for a good book to read.

Guide children to *Practice Book* page 94. Have children look at the pictures as you reread the story. Have children discuss where and when the story takes place and circle the appropriate pictures. Have them use the pictures to retell the story.

RETEACH

Build Robust Vocabulary

Remind children of the Student-Friendly Explanations for *dropped*, *joyous*, and *thrill*. Then discuss each word, using the following examples.

drooped
If you had a plant that *drooped*, would you want to do something special for it or not? Why?

joyous
What are some ways you might make your parents feel *joyous*?

thrill
Name an animal that would give you a *thrill* if you saw it in the wild. Tell why.

VOCABULARY

Student-Friendly Explanations

drooped If something drooped, it bent or hung down because it was weak.

joyous When you feel joyous, you feel very, very happy.

thrill When you do something exciting that makes you a little tingly, you get a thrill.

PRETEACH

Writing

Writing Trait: Word Choice Remind children that it is important, when writing, to choose words that will tell someone exactly what they need to know. Write the following sentences on the board.

> Bring that to me.
> Go to my desk and bring me the red marker.

Read aloud the first sentence to children and ask what the writer wants you to bring. Point out that there is not enough information to know. Then read aloud the second sentence and have children tell what the writer wants them to bring and where it is located. Elicit that the second sentence gives more details. Tell children that together, you will write a sentence telling someone what to do. Direct children's attention to the first sentence on the board. Have children suggest a classroom item to write about in the sentence. Model rewriting the sentence. Say: **I want someone to bring me the stapler. Currently my sentence says,** *Bring that to me.* **The word** *that* **could mean anything in the classroom! I will replace the word** *that* **with** *stapler*. Read the revised sentence aloud. Then create additional sentences using the same pattern with children.

Grade K **189**

LESSON 16

PHONEMIC AWARENESS
Phoneme Identity: Final

PHONICS
Reteach Consonants /l/*l*, /h/*h*

READING
Review /l/*l*, /h/*h*
Review *one, see*

BUILD ROBUST VOCABULARY
Review *load, bound, steep, drooped, joyous, thrill*

WRITING
Reteach Writing Form: Commands

Materials Needed:

Sound/Spelling Card *Ll, Hh* — Word Builder and Word Builder Cards

Photo Cards — Practice Book pp. 95–96

Phonemic Awareness

Phoneme Identity: Final Remind children that they have been listening for the sound that is the same in a group of words. To reinforce the lesson, focus on two words. Say: **Listen for the sound that is the same in two words: *hat, cute*. Say the words with me: *hat, cute*. I hear /t/ at the end of each word. The sound at the end of *hat* and *cute* is the same, /t/.** Follow the same procedure, using the following pairs of words. Have children tell which sound is the same. Then have them name the sound.

| **hid, sad** (/d/) | **win, pan** (/n/) | **fill, call** (/l/) |
| **dip, sleep** (/p/) | **rake, week** (/k/) | **ham, plum** (/m/) |

Repeat the procedure for the following pairs of words. Have children repeat the words and tell which sound is the same. (beginning) Then have them name the sound that is the same in each set.

| **girl, gas** (/g/) | **dog, dish** (/d/) | **will, wash** (/w/) |
| **ball, bench** (/b/) | **red, ring** (/r/) | **seed, sink** (/s/) |

RETEACH

Phonics

Consonants /l/*l*, /h/*h* Display *Sound/Spelling Card Ll*. Ask: **What sound do you hear at the beginning of *leaf*?** (/l/) **What letter stands for the /l/ sound at the beginning of *land*?** (*l*) Repeat the process with *Sound/Spelling Card Hh*, using the word *horse*.

Discriminate /l/*l* and /h/*h* Give children *Word Builder Cards l* and *h*. Randomly display one of the following *Photo Cards: ladder, lamp, hammer, hat, helicopter,* and *hill*. Have children name the picture and hold up the letter card that represents the sound they hear at the beginning of the word. Finally, follow the same procedure, but use spoken words. Say: **I am going to say some words. If the word begins with the /l/ sound, hold up the *l* card and say /l/. If the word begins with the /h/ sound, hold up the *h* card and say /h/.** Say the following words for children:

| hit | lame | last | hose | loop |
| heat | less | hair | help | lip |

190 Lesson 16

Day 4

REVIEW
Reading

Practice Book 95–96

Review /l/l, /h/h Review the /l/ and /h/ sounds. Write the words *lip* and *hat* on the board, and read and blend the sounds for the children. Then have children name other words that begin with each sound.

Write the words *one, my, here, the,* and *where* on index cards. Distribute index cards with the word *one* to each child. Tell children that you will show them words, and when they see *one*, they should say the word, point to it on their card, and then hold up one finger. If they do not see the word, they should put their card behind their backs. Hold up index cards in random order until children consistently identify the word *one*.

Have children turn to *Practice Book* pages 95–96. Have children read the sentences as a take-home book to practice the newly-learned words.

REVIEW
Robust Vocabulary

Remind children of the Student-Friendly Explanations for *load, bound, steep, drooped, joyous,* and *thrill*. Then determine children's understanding of the words by asking the following questions.

- **What do you look like when you are *joyous*?**
- **If someone had a surprise birthday party for you, would you feel *thrilled* or bored? Explain.**
- **If a train is *bound* for the top of a *steep* hill, is it going up or going down?**
- **If you *loaded* too many heavy blocks into a paper bag, what might happen?**
- **If your dog's tail *drooped*, what does it look like?**

VOCABULARY
Student-Friendly Explanations

load When you load things, you put them into something.

bound When you are going somewhere, you are bound for that place.

steep When something is steep, it is hard to climb because of the way it goes up.

drooped If something drooped, it bent or hung down because it was weak.

joyous When you feel joyous, you feel very, very happy.

thrill When you do something exciting that makes you a little tingly, you get a thrill.

RETEACH
Writing

Writing Form: Commands Remind children that a command is a sentence that tells someone what to do. Explain that when writing commands, it is important to choose words that will tell someone exactly what to do. Tell children they are going to write a command with you. Tell them to think about a command that you might say in the classroom. Write their ideas on the board. Together, write a command on chart paper or a sentence strip, having volunteers contribute any known letters and punctuation.

> Put away your books.

Grade K 191

LESSON 16

DAY AT A GLANCE — Day 5

PHONEMIC AWARENESS
Phoneme Categorization: Final

PHONICS
Preteach Word Blending

HIGH-FREQUENCY WORDS
Preteach what
Review you, do, see

BUILD ROBUST VOCABULARY
Preteach fantasy, jolly, versatile

Materials Needed:

Sound/Spelling Card
Gg, Oo, Tt

Word Builder and Word Builder Cards

Practice Book 97

Photo Cards

Phonemic Awareness

Phoneme Categorization: Final Tell children that you will be saying groups of words, and they will be listening for the word with a different ending sound. Say: **Here are three words: hot, kit, pan. Hot and kit have the sound /t/ at the end. Pan ends with /n/. The sound at the end of pan is different. Pan is the word with a different ending sound.** Repeat the process using the following sets of words. Emphasize the final sounds of the words. Have children repeat each set of words in the same manner and name the word in each set that has a different ending sound.

pin, won, bed (bed)   sit, hat, rug (rug)   nod, call, will (nod)

rip, bad, cop (bad)   dress, miss, got (got)   week, hen, sick (hen)

PRETEACH

Phonics

Have children sit in a circle. As you say the following verse, have children echo you. Establish a rhythm and keep it going through the verse. Say: **We're going on a word hunt. What's this word? /d/-/o/-/g/ Together: dog!** Continue with the words *hat, hug,* and *dot.* Then review the sounds you blended to make each word.

Word Blending Display *Sound/Spelling Cards g, o,* and *t.* Point to *g.* Have children name the letter and the sound. Point to *o.* Have children name the letter and the sound. Slide the *o* next to the *g.* Point to t. Have children name the letter and the sound. Slide the *t* next to the letters *go.* Move your hand left-to-right under the letters and blend the sounds, elongating them: /goot/. Have children repeat after you.

Distribute to children *Word Builder* and *Word Builder Cards.* Place the *Word Builder Cards p, o,* and *t* in the *Word Builder.* Point to *p.* Say: **/p/.** Have children name the letter and sound. Point to *o.* Say: **/o/.** Have children name the letter and sound. Slide the *o* next to p. Point to *t.* Say: **/t/.** Have children name the letter and sound. Slide the *t* next to the letters *po.* Move your hand under the letters and blend the sounds: /pot/. Have children repeat after you. Then have children blend and read the word *pot* with you. Continue with the words *not, hot, hop,* and *pop.*

Have children turn to *Practice Book* page 97. Help children identify the pictures. Have them trace the letter *o* in each word.

Day 5

PRETEACH
High-Frequency Words

 Write the word *what* on the board and on an index card. Point to the board and read *what*. Have children say it with you. Say: **What is my name?** Display the index card *what*. Say: **what**. Match the index card to the word on the board, say the word, and have children say it with you. Have children repeat the word *what* as you point to it several times. On the board, write the question, *What do you see?* Read the question with children. Point to *Photo Card elephant* and ask: **What do you see?** Have children give the answer. Then invite children to take turns choosing a *Photo Card* and asking the question, pointing to the word *what* on the board as they say *what*.

High-Frequency Words

do	what
you	see

PRETEACH
Build Robust Vocabulary

Tell children of the Student-Friendly Explanations of *fantasy, jolly,* and *versatile*. Then discuss each word, using the following examples.

fantasy
Which is more of a *fantasy,* being a princess or being a student at a new school?

jolly
What kinds of activities make you feel *jolly*? Why?

versatile
Is a pair of scissors *versatile*? Why or why not?

VOCABULARY
Student-Friendly Explanations

fantasy A fantasy is something you think of or daydream about that couldn't really happen.

jolly Someone who is jolly is cheerful and always in a good mood.

versatile Something that is versatile can be changed easily so that it can be used in different ways.

Grade K 193

LESSON 17

DAY AT A GLANCE — Day 1

PHONEMIC AWARENESS
Phoneme Categorization: Final

PHONICS
Preteach Word Building

HIGH-FREQUENCY WORDS
Reteach *what*

COMPREHENSION
Reteach Setting

BUILD ROBUST VOCABULARY
Reteach *fantasy, jolly, versatile*

Materials Needed:

Word Builders and Word Builder Cards · Write-On/Wipe-Off Boards

Copying Master · Practice Book

Phonemic Awareness

Phoneme Categorization: Final Tell children to listen to the sound at the end of each word you say and to tell you which word has a different ending sound. Say: **mitt, bun, bat. I hear /t/ at the end of *mitt*, /n/ at the end of *bun*, and /t/ at the end of *bat*. The sound at the end of *bun* is different.** Use the following sets of words. Segment the ending sounds as needed. Have children repeat each set of words, and then name the word that has a different ending sound.

bed, lid, mat (*mat*)   **fed, top, nap** (*fed*)   **cup, dog, tap** (*dog*)
mop, can, fin (*mop*)   **sat, men, kit** (*men*)   **neck, log, rag** (*neck*)

PRETEACH

Phonics

Word Building Distribute *Word Builders* and *Word Builder Cards* *d, f, g, h, i, n, o, p, r, s,* and *t*. Review each letter name and sound. Then hold up letters at random and ask children to tell the letter name and sound.

Explain that a word can change when the letters in the word change. Say: **Use your *Word Builder* and *Word Builder Cards* to make new words with me. I will use the letters *g, o,* and *t* to make the word *got*. Now you do the same. Blend the sounds with me: /g/-/o/-/t/, *got*. If I take away the *g* and put *p* in its place, I have the word *pot*. Now you try it. Blend the sounds and say the word with me: /p/-/o/-/t/, *pot*.**

Build Words Have children continue with *rot* in their *Word Builder*:

- Change the *t* to *d*. What word did you make? (*rod*)
- Change the *r* to *n*. What word did you make? (*nod*)

 Continue with the words *not, hot, hit,* and *fit*. Then have children practice writing the words they built on their *Write-On/Wipe-Off Boards*. Distribute *Copying Master* page 33. Have children trace each word and blend the sounds to read each picture name. Then have children cut out each word and paste it below the matching picture. (*cot, mop, pot, top.*)

Day 1

RETEACH

High-Frequency Words

Write the word *what* on the board. Have children point to the word and read it aloud. Then ask children to point to the word on the board as they ask a question that begins with the word *what,* such as: *What is that?*

RETEACH

Comprehension

Setting Remind children that the setting of a story is where and when the story takes place. Then read this story aloud to them.

> **Maya and Marissa's Morning**
>
> Maya and Marissa climbed onto the tall stools in the kitchen. Their father poured cereal into two bowls and gave one to each girl. It was morning and their father was washing some dishes before work. The bright sun made the soap bubbles sparkle in the sink. Maya carefully poured herself some orange juice. Marissa started eating. Every morning before school they enjoyed this quiet time together in the kitchen.

Guide children to *Practice Book* page 98. Have children use the pictures to identify the two settings in the story.

RETEACH

Build Robust Vocabulary

Remind children of the Student-Friendly Explanations of *fantasy, jolly,* and *versatile.* Then discuss each word, using the following examples.

fantasy
Which is more likely to be a *fantasy*: living in a castle or living in an apartment building?

jolly
Name a person you know who is *jolly*. How does this person act?

versatile
How is a chair *versatile*? Explain.

High-Frequency Word

what

VOCABULARY

Student-Friendly Explanations

fantasy A fantasy is something you think of or daydream about that couldn't really happen.

jolly Someone who is jolly is cheerful and always in a good mood.

versatile Something that is versatile can be changed easily so that it can be used in different ways.

Grade K 195

LESSON 17

DAY AT A GLANCE
Day 2

PHONEMIC AWARENESS
Phoneme Categorization: Final

PHONICS
Reteach Word Building

HIGH-FREQUENCY WORDS
Preteach two
Reteach a, go, he, this

COMPREHENSION
Preteach Summarize

BUILD ROBUST VOCABULARY
Preteach agreed, contribute, spontaneously

Materials Needed:

Phoneme Phone | Word Builders/Word Builder Cards | Write-On/Wipe-Off Boards

Copying Master 34 | Practice Book 99

Copying Master | Practice Book

Phonemic Awareness

Phoneme Categorization: Final Tell children that you are going to say groups of three words, and that they are to say which of the words has a different ending sound. Say: **hen, tag, pig. I hear /n/ at the end of hen. I hear /g/ at the end of tag and pig. Hen has a different ending sound than tag and pig.** Continue, using the following sets of words. Elongate or repeat the ending sounds in words to help children discriminate the differences in them. Model using the *Phoneme Phone* as you say the groups of words. Have children use the *Phoneme Phone* to look at the position of their mouths as they repeat each set of words and name the word that ends with a different sound.

| rub, dab, big (*big*) | wig, sack, peck (*wig*) | doll, call, sit (*sit*) |
| pan, bed, tin (*bed*) | lid, fed, has (*has*) | cat, fin, ton (*cat*) |

RETEACH
Phonics

Word Building Distribute *Word Builders* and *Word Builder Cards a, g, h, i, o, p, r, t,* and *w*. Explain to children that when letters in words change, so do the sounds. Have children following along as you model word building. Say: **Use your Word Builder and Word Builder Cards to make new words with me. I will use the letters h, o, and p to make the word hop. Now you do the same. Blend the sounds with me: /h/-/o/-/p/, hop. If I take away the h and put t in its place, I have the word top. Now you try it. Blend the sounds and say the word with me: /t/-/o/-/p/, top.**

Build Words Have children continue with *tip* in their *Word Builder*:

- Change the *t* to *r*. What word did you make? (*rip*)
- Change the *p* to *g*. What word did you make? (*rig*)

 Continue with the words *rag, wag,* and *tag*. Then have children practice writing the words that they built on their *Write-On/Wipe-Off Boards*. Distribute *Copying Master* page 34. Have children name the pictures, circle the words that name the pictures, and then write the words. (Children circle and write the word *pot, cat, hat,* and *mop*.)

Day 2

PRETEACH
High-Frequency Words

Practice Book 99 Write the word *two* on an index card and on the board. Point to the board and read *two*. Have children say it with you. Say: **I have *two* eyes.** Display the index card. Say: *two*. Match the index card to the word on the board, say the word, and have children say it with you. Tell children that you will show them words, and when they see *two*, they should say the word and point to it on the board. Create index cards for the words *a, this, he,* and *go,* shuffle the cards, and show each card to children until they consistently identify the word *two*. Finally, have children turn to *Practice Book* page 99. Complete the page together.

High-Frequency Words	
a	this
go	two
he	

RETEACH
Comprehension

 Summarize Remind children that when they read, it helps to stop and think about what has happened so far in the story. This helps them better understand and remember the story. Have children recall the story from Day 1. Say: **When I read, I pay attention to important things that happen. Sometimes I write down these parts as I read.**

Characters (Maya and Marissa)	**Setting** (a kitchen)
Beginning (Maya and Marissa sit at stools in the kitchen)	
Middle (Their father pours them cereal.)	
Ending (Maya and Marissa eat their cereal.)	

During Reading As you read the story aloud, pause occasionally to summarize what has happened to that point. Record your observations in the chart. Invite volunteers to write any known letters, words, or punctuation.

RETEACH
Build Robust Vocabulary

Tell children of the Student-Friendly Explanations of *agreed, contribute,* and *spontaneously*. Then discuss each word, using the following examples.

agreed
If you and a friend *agreed* to play hopscotch, are you going to play the same game? Why or why not?

contribute
How do you *contribute* to chores at home?

spontaneously
If you laugh *spontaneously,* do you think about it first? Why or why not?

VOCABULARY
Student-Friendly Explanations

agreed If two people agreed, they felt the same way or thought the same thing.

contribute When you contribute, you give or add a part along with others.

spontaneously When you do something spontaneously, you do it right at that moment without planning.

Grade K 197

LESSON 17

DAY AT A GLANCE — Day 3

PHONEMIC AWARENESS
Phoneme Categorization: Final

PHONICS
Preteach Phonogram -ot

HIGH-FREQUENCY WORDS
Reteach what, two
Review where, do, I, see

COMPREHENSION
Reteach Setting

BUILD ROBUST VOCABULARY
Reteach agreed, contribute, spontaneously

WRITING
Preteach Writing Trait: Organization

Materials Needed:

Phoneme Phone

Word Builders and Word Builder Cards

Write-On/Wipe-Off Boards

Practice Book

Phonemic Awareness

Phoneme Categorization Tell children that you are going to listen for the word that has a different ending sound. Say: **I will say three words to you. One word is not like the other two: hit, sat, rub. Which word does not belong?** (rub) Repeat the process, using the following sets of words. Have children use the *Phoneme Phone* to look at the position of their mouths as they repeat each set of words and name the word that ends with a different sound.

pin, cat, ran (ran)	**sit, mat, log** (log)	**tip, dog, rap** (dog)
tan, hip, sap (tan)	**read, bid, van** (van)	**cup, mad, hip** (mad)

Tell children that now you want them to listen for a word that has a different beginning sound. Model an example. Say: **sat, sip, hen. Say the words with me. Which word does not belong?** (hen) Have children repeat each set of words and name the word that begins with a different sound.

zip, zap, cut (cut)	**run, gas, rip** (gas)	**lip, tub, tan** (lip)
hop, sad, hat (sad)	**mitt, man, cup** (cup)	**Ben, mop, bad** (mop)

PRETEACH
Phonics

Identify Rhyming Words Say the words *not* and *got*, and have children repeat them. Ask how the two words are the same. (They both have /ot/; they rhyme.) Tell children you are going to say pairs of words. If the words rhyme, they are to say "They rhyme." If the words do not rhyme, they are to say nothing. Use the following words:

hot, tot	**sip, not**
tab, top	**lot, cot**
pot, not	**cap, dot**

Read Words with -ot Write the word *got* on the board. Track the print as you read the word. Have children repeat after you. Then write the word *hot*. Track the print as you read the word. Have children repeat after you. Ask how the two words are the same. (They both have /ot/; they rhyme.) Say: **The words *not* and *hot* are in the -ot word family because they both end in -ot.** Continue with the words *pot* and *dot*.

Have children work with the *Word Builders* and *Word Builder Cards* d, g, l, n, o, p, t, and c. Guide them in blending and building the words *dot, got, lot, tot,* and *cot*. After children read each word, have them write it on the *Write-on/Wipe-off Board*.

198 Lesson 17

Day 3

RETEACH

High-Frequency Words

Display index cards with the high-frequency words *what, two, where, do, I,* and *see* written on each index card. As you say each word, have children repeat the word and point to the correct card.

High-Frequency Words	
do	two
I	what
see	where

RETEACH

Comprehension

Practice Book 100

Setting Remind children that the setting of a story is where and when the story happens. Have children listen as you read aloud the following story.

> David pulled on his jacket and hat and got in line. The class was lining up in the school hallway. Mrs. Robinson was taking them out to the new playground.
>
> Mrs. Robinson led the class down the hall and out the big double doors to the new playground. As soon as they were through the doors, most of the children cheered and ran toward the new equipment. But David stood and looked at the playground carefully. The ground was covered with a huge, red and yellow rubber mat. There were tire swings, monkey bars, three slides, and a climbing area. David yelled happily, too, and started to run toward the tallest slide.

Guide children to *Practice Book* page 100. Have children use the pictures to tell when and where the story takes place.

Grade K **199**

Day 3

VOCABULARY
Student-Friendly Explanations

agreed If two people agreed, they felt the same way or thought the same thing.

contribute When you contribute, you give or add a part along with others.

spontaneously When you do something spontaneously, you do it right at that moment without planning it.

RETEACH
Build Robust Vocabulary

Remind children of the Student-Friendly Explanations of *agreed, contribute,* and *spontaneously.* Then discuss each word, using the following examples.

agreed
If you and a friend *agreed* to play with blocks, are you going to play with cars instead? Why or why not?

contribute
What are some ways in which you *contribute* to the classroom?

spontaneously
Is it safe to *spontaneously* run into the street? Why or why not?

200 Lesson 17

Day 3

PRETEACH
Writing

Writing Trait: Organization Tell children that when writing directions, it is important to write the steps in the correct order. The words *first, next,* and *then* can help a reader follow the steps. Explain that it is also helpful to the reader to begin each new direction on a new line.

Write the following title on chart paper: *Snack Time*. Read it aloud. Then ask children to tell you how to get ready for snack time. Ask questions to prompt responses in order.

> <u>Snack Time</u>
>
> First, we put our things away.
> Then we wash our hands.
> Finally, we pass out snacks.

Record children's responses. Then read the directions aloud. Point out that the steps are in order. Ask volunteers to explain why it is so important that the steps are in order.

Grade K 201

LESSON 17

DAY AT A GLANCE — Day 4

PHONEMIC AWARENESS
Phoneme Categorization: Final

PHONICS
Preteach Phonogram -op

READING
Review Phonogram -ot, -op
Review High-Frequency Words

BUILD ROBUST VOCABULARY
Review *fantasy, jolly, versatile, agreed, contribute, spontaneously*

WRITING
Preteach Writing Form: Directions

Materials Needed:

Write-On/
Wipe-Off
Boards

Practice
Book

Phonemic Awareness

Phoneme Categorization Tell children that they are going to listen for the word that has a different ending sound. Say: **I will say three words to you. One word is not like the other two: sip, ran, fun. Which word does not belong?** (*sip*) Repeat the process, using the following words. Have children repeat each set of words and name the word that has a different ending sound.

| **wig, fun, rag** (*fun*) | **dad, wig, leg** (*dad*) | **hill, rap, fell** (*rap*) |
| **hip, top, can** (*can*) | **nip, ten, cap** (*ten*) | **dot, get, rug** (*rug*) |

Remind children that they can also listen for a word with a different beginning sound in a group of words. Model an example. Say: **tap, fog, tin. Say the words with me. Which word has a different beginning sound?** (*fog*) Use the process above and the following sets of words, having children listen for the word with a different beginning sound.

| **cup, bed, bat** (*cup*) | **dad, dot, men** (*men*) | **win, car, wed** (*car*) |
| **dog, can, dip** (*can*) | **rug, pot, pan** (*rug*) | **man, mitt, hop** (*hop*) |

RETEACH
Phonics

Identify Rhyming Words Say the words *cop*, *sap*, and *pop*, and have children repeat them. Say: **Cop and pop rhyme because they both end with /op/. Sap does not rhyme with cop and pop because it ends with /ap/.** Tell children that you are going to say sets of words. They should tell you the words that rhyme in each set of words. Use the following words: *rip/tip; pin/pick; hop/top; log/fog*.

Read Words with *-op* Write the word *pop* on the board. Track the print as you read the word. Have children repeat after you. Then write the word *hop*. Track the print as you read the word. Have children repeat after you. Ask how the two words are the same. (They both have /op/; they rhyme.) Say: **The words *pop* and *hop* are in the *-op* word family because they both end in *-op*.** Continue with the words *top* and *bop*.

Distribute *Write-on/Wipe-off Boards*. Write these words on the board: *bop, hop, map, mop, hot, top,* and *pop*. Have children read the words and copy those words in the *-op* word family on their *Write-on/Wipe-off Boards*.

Day 4

REVIEW
Reading

 Apply Phonics /o/o Write the word *pop* on the board. Model blending the sounds as you run a finger under each letter. Say: /p/-/o/-/p/. **Say it with me:** *Pop!* Run a finger under the letters as children read the word.

High-Frequency Words Write *what* and *two* on the board. Have children read the words. Point to each word several times, having children read it each time.

Have children turn to *Practice Book* pages 101–102. Have children read the sentences as a take-home book to practice the newly-learned words.

REVIEW
Robust Vocabulary

Tell children that they have been learning some interesting words. Remind children of the Student-Friendly Explanations of *agreed, contribute, spontaneously, fantasy, jolly,* and *versatile*. Then determine children's understanding of the words by asking the following questions.

- If you were *spontaneously jolly,* would you be laughing all of a sudden or crying all of a sudden?
- If someone *contributed* to a story, did they tell more or end it?
- How is a piece of paper *versatile*? What can you do with it?
- If you and a friend *agreed* to meet at the park and then you decided not to go, how would your friend feel? Why?
- Which is more of a *fantasy*: seeing a dancing rabbit or a sleeping rabbit? Why?

PRETEACH
Writing

Writing Form: Directions Point out that to write directions to make something, you must fully understand how make it. Model making cinnamon toast, as children prompt you on each step. Ask: **First, I toast the bread. Now what do I spread on the bread?** After you have described making cinnamon toast, have the group review the steps in order. Record each step on chart paper. Invite them to help you to write letters and words that they know. Read the finished directions to children.

> How to Make Cinnamon Toast
> First, toast the bread.
> Then spread butter on the toast.
> Finally, sprinkle sugar and cinnamon on the toast.

VOCABULARY
Student-Friendly Explanations

agreed If two people agreed, they felt the same way or thought the same thing.

contribute When you contribute, you give or add a part along with others.

spontaneously When you do something spontaneously, you do it right at that moment without planning it.

fantasy A fantasy is something you think of or daydream about that couldn't really happen.

jolly Someone who is jolly is cheerful and always in a good mood.

versatile Something that is versatile can be changed easily so that it can be used in different ways.

Grade K 203

LESSON 17

DAY AT A GLANCE
Day 5

PHONEMIC AWARENESS
Phoneme Identity

PHONICS
Preteach Consonant Ww

HIGH-FREQUENCY WORDS
Review *for, me, the*

BUILD ROBUST VOCABULARY
Review *drooped, jolly, joyous, spontaneously*

Materials Needed:

Photo Cards   Sound/Spelling Card *Ww*   Practice Book

Phonemic Awareness

Phoneme Identity   Display *Photo Cards cat, pan, fish,* and *pig*. Say: **Name the sound you hear in the middle of the words I say. Listen as I do the first one.** Hold up *Photo Card cat* and read it. Have children repeat the word. Elongate the medial sound of *cat* and say: **The middle sound is /a/.** Repeat with *Photo Card pan*. Then say: **The sound in the middle of these words is the same. It is /a/. What is the sound?** (/a/) Continue with the Photo Cards *fish* and *pig* and the middle sound /i/.

PRETEACH

Phonics

I Spy   Display the *Photo Cards boy, hammer, kangaroo,* and *milk*. Point to each card and have children name the picture. Say: **Let's play "I Spy." I'll give clues and you name the picture. I spy a picture that begins with /hhhh/ and shows a tool.** (hammer) Repeat with the remaining photo cards, offering the initial sound as the first clue.

Consonant Ww   Display *Sound/Spelling Card Ww*. Point to the uppercase *W* and say: **This is uppercase W.** Point to lowercase *w* and say: **This is lowercase w.** Have children identify the letters. (W, w)

Writing W and w   Write *W* and *w* on the board and have children identify the letters. Say: **Watch as I write the letter W so that everyone can read it.** As you give the Letter Talk, trace the uppercase *W* and lowercase *w*.

Letter Talk for *W*	Letter Talk for *w*
1. Slanted line down.	1. Shorter slanted line down.
2. Slanted line up.	2. Slanted line up.
3. Slanted line down.	3. Slanted line down.
4. Slanted line up again.	4. Slanted line up again.

Guided Practice   Have children finger-write the uppercase *W* in the air as you repeat the Letter Talk. Do the same for lowercase *w*. Then have children turn to *Practice Book* page 103. Help children circle the uppercase *W* and underline the lowercase *w*. Then have them trace the letters and practice writing the letters on the lines.

Day 5

REVIEW
High-Frequency Words

 Write the high-frequency words *for, me,* and *the* and the word *is* on index cards. Say each word, and hold up the card as the children repeat the word. Show *Photo Card box* and have children say its name. Then use the index cards, the *Photo Card*, and a period card to build the sentence frame shown below. Point to each word as you read the sentence. Then have children read the sentence to you.

| The | box | is | for | me | . |

Repeat using other *Photo Cards*.

REVIEW
Build Robust Vocabulary

Read the Student-Friendly Explanations of *drooped, jolly, joyous,* and *spontaneously.* Then discuss each word, using the following examples.

drooped
Would you walk under a tree if the branches *drooped*? Why or why not?

jolly
Which will make you feel *jolly*, going to the circus or going to the dentist? Why?

joyous
What would make your friends feel *joyous*? Why?

spontaneously
Where would you do something *spontaneously*, in a park or in a museum? Why?

High-Frequency Words

for   me
the

VOCABULARY
Student-Friendly Explanations

drooped If something drooped, it bent or hung down because it was weak.

jolly When you are jolly, you feel cheerful and happy.

joyous When you feel joyous, you feel very, very happy.

spontaneously When you do something spontaneously, you do it in the moment and without thinking about it first.

Grade K 205

LESSON 18

PHONEMIC AWARENESS
Phoneme Identity

PHONICS
Preteach Relate Ww to /w/

HIGH-FREQUENCY WORDS
Reteach one, see
Review do, here, you, my, I

COMPREHENSION
Reteach Beginning, Middle, Ending

BUILD ROBUST VOCABULARY
Review steep, gigantic, blustery

Materials Needed:

Sound/Spelling Card Ww   Sounds of Letters CD   Word Builders and Word Builder Cards

Photo Cards   Copying Master   Practice Book

Phonemic Awareness

 Phoneme Identity   Remind children they can listen for the middle sound in words. Say: **Listen as I say two words: sit, fix. Listen again: /siiiit/, /fiiiiks/. What is the middle sound in these words?** (/i/)

Ask children to identify the middle sound in *bed* and *sell*. (/e/) Repeat this activity with following the words:

bat, ram (/a/)   lid, pin (/i/)   box, fox (/o/)
joke, rope (/ō/)   trim, sit (/i/)   trash, tap (/a/)
met, fed (/e/)   kite, might (/ī/)

PRETEACH

Phonics

Relate Ww to /w/   Say the words *wave* and *wish* and have children repeat the words. Tell them that *wave* and *wish* both begin with the /w/ sound. Have children repeat /w/ several times.

  Connect Letter and Sound   Display *Sound/Spelling Card Ww*. Ask: **What is the name of this letter?** (w) **The letter *w* can stand for the beginning sound of *water*. Say /w/.** Ask children to repeat the sound as you play the /w/ sound on the *Sounds of Letters CD*.

Discriminate /w/   Give each child *Word Building Card w*. Say: **If the word I say begins with /w/, hold up the card and say /w/. If the word does not begin with /w/, hold your card behind your back.** Say the words *wade, wing, pale, junk, want,* and *wet*.

Identify /w/   Tell children you will show them pictures. They will raise their hand if the name begins with the /w/ sound. Show *Photo Card watch*. Say: **watch. Say the name with me: watch. Is the /w/ sound at the beginning of *watch*?** (yes) Repeat with *Photo Cards taxi* and *watermelon*.

 Distribute *Copying Master 35*. Have children trace *Ww*. Then have them circle the letter that names the beginning sound in each picture. (Children should circle *w* for *web, wagon, worm*; *g* for *girl*; *f* for *flag*.)

Day 1

REVIEW
High-Frequency Words

Write high-frequency words on index cards to make the sentence frame: *Do you see one _____ ?* Read it aloud to children and have them find *one* and *see* in the question. Complete the question with *Photo Card tiger*. Point to each word and reread the completed question. Have children read it after you. Repeat the activity with other *Photo Cards*. You can vary the activity using additional index cards for *here* and *I* to make: *Here is one _____ . I see one _____ .*

| Do | you | see | one | tiger | ? |

High-Frequency Words

do	eye
here	my
one	see
you	

RETEACH
Comprehension

Beginning, Middle, Ending   Remind children that a story has a beginning, a middle, and an ending. Then read this story aloud to them.

> Jan wants to buy a new fish for her tank. She goes to the pet store with her mom. They look at all of the fish. Jan sees red fish and blue fish. She watches a striped fish swim fast. Her mom points to two tiny fish. Jan sees one fish with a giant tail. Finally, Jan chooses a small orange and yellow fish. "I can't wait to take my new fish home!" Jan says.

Guide children to turn to page 104 in their *Practice Books*. Have them look at the pictures as you ask them to identify the events that happen in each part of the story. Have children retell what happened in the beginning, middle, and ending of the story.

RETEACH
Build Robust Vocabulary

Read the Student-Friendly Explanations to remind children of the meanings of *steep*, *gigantic*, and *blustery*. Then talk about each word by asking the following questions.

steep
What do you look like when you climb something *steep*?

gigantic
Which would you say is *gigantic*, a mountain or an ant hill? Tell why.

blustery
Would it be easy to keep a hat on your head on a *blustery* day? Why or why not?

VOCABULARY
Student-Friendly Explanations

steep Steep describes mountains or hills with high sides.

gigantic Something that is gigantic is very, very big.

blustery When the weather outside is blustery, it is very windy.

Grade K 207

LESSON 18

DAY AT A GLANCE — Day 2

PHONEMIC AWARENESS
Phoneme Identity

PHONICS
Preteach Consonant *Xx*

HIGH-FREQUENCY WORDS
Review *do, here, what, to*

COMPREHENSION
Preteach Use Graphic Organizers

BUILD ROBUST VOCABULARY
Review *joyous, jolly, delight*

Materials Needed:

 Phoneme Phone
 Photo Cards
 Sound/Spelling Card *Xx*
 Copying Master 36
 Practice Book 105

Phonemic Awareness

Phoneme Identity Remind children that they have been listening for middle sounds in words. Say: **Listen for the sound that is the same in these two words: *bun, mutt*. Say each word with me: *bun, mutt*. The sound /u/ is the same in the middle of each word.** Give each child a *Phoneme Phone*. Say the word *sock*. Have children repeat the sounds in *sock* while looking at his or her mouth position in the mirror. Ask children to identify the middle sound that is the same in the following words:

tot, rob, sock (/o/)   lake, make, wake (/ā/)   set, wet, men (/e/)
rib, kick, fin (/i/)   beak, meat, week (/ē/)   tub, mud, fun (/u/)

PRETEACH

Phonics

  I Spy Display *Photo Cards girl, hill, sun,* and *van*. Point to each card and have children name the picture. Say: **Let's play "I Spy." I'll give clues and you name the picture. I spy a picture that ends with /l/ and shows a person.** (girl) Continue the activity, offering the final sound as the first clue, and a second clue if needed.

Consonant *Xx* Display *Sound/Spelling Card Xx*. Say: **This is the letter *x*. Say the name with me.** Point to the uppercase *X* and say: **This is uppercase X.** Point to lowercase *x* and say: **This is lowercase x.** Have children identify the letters. (*X, x*)

Writing *X* and *x* Write *X* and *x* on the board and have children identify the letters. Say: **Watch carefully as I write the letter X.** As you give the Letter Talk, trace the uppercase *X* and then the lowercase *x*.

Letter Talk for *X*	Letter Talk for *x*
1. Slanted line down to the right.	1. Draw a shorter slanted line down to the right.
2. Slanted line down to the left.	2. Slanted line down to the left.

Guided Practice Have children finger-write the uppercase *X* in the air as you repeat the Letter Talk. Have them do the same for lowercase *x*. Then give children *Copying Master 36*. Help children circle the uppercase *X* and underline the lowercase *x*. Then have them trace the letters and practice writing the letters on the lines.

Day 2

REVIEW
High-Frequency Words

Practice Book 105

Display an index card for *what*. Have children point to the word and read it. Repeat with the index word card *two*. Then ask children to repeat the words. Say each word again, having children repeat the word as you hold up the index card.

Use index word cards *what, two, do,* and *here*. Have children sit in a circle. Give each child one word card. At your signal, have them pass their cards around the circle until you tell them to stop. Ask: **Who has the word *what*?** The child with the word *what* should stand and read the word. Repeat with the rest of the words.

Have children turn to *Practice Book* page 105 to review high-frequency words and practice newly-learned words. Complete the page together.

High-Frequency Words

do	here
two	what

PRETEACH
Comprehension

Use Graphic Organizers Explain that writing down the important things about a story can help you remember and understand a story. Create a Problem/Solution Chart. Explain that in many stories a character has a problem to figure out. Recall the story about Jan and her new fish from Day 1. Reread the story and pause to note what the problem is and how the characters figure it out. Ask children to name the problem and solution as you write their responses on a chart under the correct heading.

Who?	Jan and her mother
Problem?	Jan wants a fish.
Solution?	Jan and her mom buy a fish.

REVIEW
Build Robust Vocabulary

Read the Student-Friendly Explanations for *joyous, jolly,* and *delight*. Then discuss each word, using the following examples.

joyous
Is *joyous* more like feeling unhappy or glad? Why?

jolly
Would you giggle or whine if you felt *jolly*? Tell why.

delight
What is something that might cause you to feel *delight*?

VOCABULARY
Student-Friendly Explanations

joyous When you feel joyous, you are very happy.

jolly If you feel jolly, you are happy.

delight If something makes you feel delight, it makes you feel very happy.

Grade K 209

LESSON 18

DAY AT A GLANCE — Day 3

PHONEMIC AWARENESS
Phoneme Identity

PHONICS
Preteach Relate *Xx* to /ks/

HIGH-FREQUENCY WORDS
Review *two, what*

COMPREHENSION
Reteach Beginning, Middle, Ending

BUILD ROBUST VOCABULARY
Reteach *spontaneously, agreed, complained*

WRITING
Reteach Writing Trait: Voice

Materials Needed:

Phoneme Phone | Sound/Spelling Card *Xx* | Sounds of Letters CD

Word Builder and Word Builder Cards | Photo Cards | Practice Book

Phonemic Awareness

Phoneme Identity Tell children you're going to say three words and that they should listen to find the two words with the same middle vowel sound. Say: **hip, deck, dill. Listen again and then tell me which two words have the same middle vowel sound.** Say *hip, deck,* and *dill* again, but this time elongate the middle vowel sound. (hip, dill) Ask: **What is their middle vowel sound?** (/i/) Continue the activity using the following word sets:

man, pan, pot (/a/)	kite, knit, sip (/i/)	pup, blue, mud (/u/)
June, hop, Tom (/o/)	bed, leg, lid (/e/)	oad, foam, pop (/ō/)
mix, fox, fix (/i/)	seed, meet, met (/ē/)	red, bug, fun (/u/)

Spiral Review Remind children that they have also learned how to listen for beginning sounds in words. Say *my, map, miss,* and ask children to repeat them with you. Say: **I hear the /m/ sound at the beginning of each word. It is the same for each word.** Have children identify the beginning sound in the following words:

cute, code, cape (/k/)	vine, vet, vote (/v/)
me, my, mine (/m/)	yes, yellow, yak (/y/)
fig, frog, from (/f/)	jump, jack, jar (/j/)

PRETEACH

Phonics

Relate *Xx* to /ks/ Tell children they can listen for the sounds at the end of words. Say: **Listen to these words: *fix* and *tax*. They end with /ks/.** Have children repeat the words. Ask: **What sound do the words end with?** (/ks/) **Is it the same sound?** (yes)

  Connect Letter and Sound Display *Sound/Spelling Card Xx*. Say: **This is the letter *x*. The letter *x* stands for the /ks/ sound at the end of *fix*. What letter is this?** (*x*) **What sound does *x* stand for?** (/ks/) Play the /ks/ sound on the *Sounds of Letters CD*. Have children listen carefully to the sound and repeat it several times.

210 Lesson 18

Day 3

 Discriminate /ks/ Give children *Word Builder Card x*. Say the word *fax* and tell children this word ends with the /ks/ sound. Say: **If the word ends with /ks/, hold up the card and say /ks/. If the word does not end with /ks/, hold your card behind your back.** Say *hid, six, tax, tip*. Have children decide whether each ends with the /ks/ sound.

RETEACH
High-Frequency Words

Distribute the index cards for *two* and *what* to children. As you say each word, have children repeat the word and hold up the correct card. Show *Photo Card box*. Ask children to say the picture name. Then say: **I have one** *box*. **If you gave me another** *box*, **I will have** *two*. **How many would I have?** (two) Have children hold up the index card *two*. Say: **If you gave me a** *box*, **I might ask you, "What did you give to me?"** Ask children to hold up the index card *what*. Then ask children to hold up the index cards *two* and *what* each time they hear you say the words. Then say several sentences that include *two* and *what* as children listen and hold up the appropriate card.

High-Frequency Words

two   what

Grade K 211

Day 3

RETEACH

Comprehension

 Beginning, Middle, Ending Remind children that a story has a beginning, middle, and ending. Read aloud the story below, and have children listen carefully to the beginning, the middle, and the ending.

> Kathy looks out the window as soon as she wakes up. She sees snow everywhere! She is so excited! It's a snow day. There is no school today. Kathy can play in the snow all day.
>
> Kathy quickly eats her breakfast. She gets dressed in her warmest clothes. Then Kathy puts on her coat, snowpants, and boots. Next, she pulls on her warm hat and her thickest gloves. Mom wraps a soft scarf around her neck.
>
> Kathy opens the door and turns to Mom. "I think I am ready for fun in the snow!" Kathy says, as she runs out the door into the snowy yard.

Guide children to *Practice Book* page 106. Have children use the pictures to retell the story. Ask: **What happens in the middle of the story?** (Kathy gets ready to go outside. She eats breakfast, puts on warm clothes and her coat, snowpants, and boots. She puts on a warm hat and gloves. Mom gives her a scarf.)

RETEACH

Build Robust Vocabulary

Remind children of the Student-Friendly Explanation of *spontaneously*, *agreed*, and *complained*. Then gauge children's understanding through their responses to the following questions.

spontaneously
Have you ever *spontaneously* visited a friend? What happened?

agreed
What is something that you *agreed* to with your family? Explain.

complained
If a person *complained*, would he or she smile or frown? Why?

VOCABULARY
Student-Friendly Explanations

spontaneously When someone does something spontaneously, he or she does it without making a plan first.

agreed If someone has agreed to something, it means he or she will do it.

complained If you complained, you told about something that makes you unhappy.

Day 3

RETEACH

Writing

Writing Trait: Voice Remind children it is important to use their own words in their writing. Using their own words will make their writing sound like they are talking to the reader.

Draw on the board a 3-row chart. Label the first row *red,* the second row *blue,* and the third row *green*.

Ask children to name things for each color. Record their responses in the chart.

Red
roses, stop signs, stop lights

Blue
the sky, water, blueberries

Green
grass, trees, frogs,

Read aloud the responses and then have volunteers dictate a sentence for each color using some of the phrases from the chart.

> Red is a stop sign.
> Blue is the sky.
> Green is grass.

Point out that the sentences, which are about something so ordinary that everyone knows what they are already, are interesting because they tell something about what the writer likes, thinks, and notices. Using their own words made even this common topic—colors—become interesting.

Grade K

LESSON 18

PHONEMIC AWARENESS
Phoneme Identity

PHONICS
Reteach Review /w/w, /ks/x

READING
Review /w/w, /ks/x
Review High-Frequency Words

BUILD ROBUST VOCABULARY
Review load, drooped, thrill, fantasy, versatile, contribute

WRITING
Reteach Writing Form: Story Response

Materials Needed:

Phoneme Phone   Sound/Spelling Card Ww, Xx   Write-On/Wipe-Off Boards

Practice Book

Phonemic Awareness

Phoneme Identity Remind children that they have been listening for the sound in the middle of words. Say: **Listen for the sound that is the same in these words:** *tin, mill*. **The middle sound is the same, /i/. What sound is the same in** *tin* **and** *mill***?** (/i/)

Have children sit in a circle. Distribute the *Phoneme Phones*. Say the words *bet* and *fell*. Ask children to repeat the words while looking at the position of their mouths in the mirror. Ask: **Do** *bet* **and** *fell* **have the same sound in the middle?** (yes) **What is the middle sound?** (/e/) Repeat with these word pairs: *tack, ran; hop, lock; mug, sun*.

Spiral Review Remind children that they have been listening for the same middle sound in words. Now they should listen for beginning sounds without using the *Phoneme Phone*. Say the words *vent* and *mad*. Have children repeat the words with you. Say: **I hear the /v/ sound at the beginning of** *vent*. **I hear the /m/ sound at the beginning of** *mad*. **The beginning sounds are different.** Say the following pairs of words and ask children to repeat them with you. Then ask them to identify the beginning sound of each word and tell if they are the same or different: *bad, bet* (/b/; same); *rob, lid* (/r/, /l/; different); *girl, got* (/g/; same).

RETEACH

Phonics

 Review /w/w, /ks/x Display *Sound/Spelling Card Ww*. Say the word *water*. Then say: **I hear the sound /w/ at the beginning of** *water*. **What is the word?** (water) **What sound do you hear at the beginning?** (/w/) **What letter stands for the /w/ sound?** (w) Repeat the process with *Sound/Spelling Card Xx* and the /ks/ sound and letter *x* at the end of the word *mix*.

Discriminate /w/w and /ks/x Distribute *Write-on/Wipe-off Boards*. Write the following words on the board: *tax, win, fix, wit*. Read each word aloud and then have children read each word. Have children copy the words that end with the /ks/ sound at the top of their *Write-on/Wipe-off Boards*. (*tax, fix*) Then ask children to copy the words that begin with the /w/ sound at the bottom of their *Write-on/Wipe-off Boards*. (*win, wit*)

REVIEW

Reading

 /w/w, /ks/x Write the letters w and x on the board. Point to the letters and have children identify each letter and its sound. Say the words *well* and *warm*. Have children name the sound they hear at the

214 Lesson 18

beginning of the words. (/w/) Then say the words *ax* and *fix*. Have children name the sound they hear at the end of the words. (/ks/)

Distribute index cards for high-frequency words *one, see, two,* and *what* to children. Tell children that you will play "Show and Tell." Say each word, and have children find the corresponding word card, show the word, and read the word aloud. Repeat until each word is identified correctly several times.

Have children turn to *Practice Book* pages 107–108. Help children cut and fold the book. Explain that they will read this book with their family at home.

REVIEW Build Robust Vocabulary

Remind children of the Student-Friendly Explanations of *load, drooped, thrill, fantasy, versatile,* and *contribute.* Then determine children's understanding of the words by asking the following questions.

- **What would you *load* into a bag to take to the beach?**
- **If a dog's ears *drooped*, did they stand up tall or bend down low?**
- **Do you feel a *thrill* when you win a game? Tell why.**
- **Is a flying school bus a *fantasy*? Why?**
- **Can you play with a *versatile* toy in one way or many ways? Why?**
- **What might you *contribute* to a used toy sale?**

RETEACH Writing

Writing Form: Story Response Remind children that a story response gives their thoughts about a story and tells about it in their own words.

Tell children that together you will write a response to the story about Jan and her new fish. Prompt children with the following questions: **Would you tell a friend to read this story? Why or why not? Do you know someone who has a pet fish? What was your favorite part of the story?** Record children's ideas on chart paper. Then use their ideas to write a story response on the chart paper. Invite volunteers to add letters or punctuation.

Read the finished story response to the children. Point out that the story response uses the words they would use if they were talking to the reader.

> I like this story. It is fun to get a new pet. I like fish. I have a red one and a black one.

High-Frequency Words

one	see
two	what

VOCABULARY
Student-Friendly Explanations

load When you load things, you put them into something.

drooped If something drooped, it bent or hung down because it was weak.

thrill When you do something exciting that makes you a little tingly, you get a thrill.

fantasy A fantasy is something you think of or daydream about that couldn't really happen.

versatile Something that is versatile can change easily from one thing to another or can be used in many ways.

contribute When you contribute, you give or add a part along with others.

Grade K 215

LESSON 18

PHONEMIC AWARENESS
Phoneme Categorization: Medial

PHONICS
Preteach Word Blending

HIGH-FREQUENCY WORDS
Preteach up

BUILD ROBUST VOCABULARY
Preteach contrast, meander, tidy

Materials Needed:

Photo Cards | Word Builder and Word Builder Cards | Practice Book

Phonemic Awareness

 Phoneme Categorization: Medial Display *Photo Cards fish, hat, hill, pig, sun, van.* Tell children that they will listen for words that have different middle sounds in them. Say: **The first word is hat. The middle sound is /a/.** Repeat with *pig* and *van.* (/i/, /a/) Ask: **What is the middle sound in hat and van?** (/a/) **What is the middle sound in pig?** (/i/) **The word that has a different middle sound is pig, /i/.** Repeat with *fish, hill,* and *sun.* Have children tell which word has a different middle sound. (sun, /u/)

Say the following sets of words. Have children repeat the words and name the word that has a different middle sound: *pet, ham, tack* (pet, /e/); *lock, wet, ten* (lock, /o/); *pin, wag, dig.* (wag, /a/)

PRETEACH

Phonics

Sounds in a Word Have children sit in a circle. Explain that you will blend sounds to say words. Say the following verse in a rhythmic way, and have children echo you. Say: **What is the word for these three sounds? /d/ /o/ /t/ Dot!** Repeat the verse with the words /t/ /o/ /p/ (top) and /d/ /o/ /g/ (dog).

Word Blending Place the *Word Builder Cards o* and *n* in the *Word Builder.* Point to *o.* Say: **/o/.** Have children name the letter and sound. Point to *n.* Say: **/nn/.** Have children name the letter and sound. Slide the *n* next to *o.* Move your hand under the letters and blend the sounds, elongating them: **/oonn/.** Have children repeat after you. Then have children blend and read the word *on* with you. Continue with the words *tot, log, not,* and *hot.*

 Have children turn to *Practice Book* page 109. Help children identify the pictures. Have them trace the letter *o* in each word.

216 Lesson 18

Day 5

PRETEACH
High-Frequency Words

Write the high frequency word *up* on an index card. Then write the same word on the board. Point to the word *up*. Read the word and have children say it with you. Say: **A jet flies *up* high in the sky.** Display index card *up* and match it to the word *up* on the board. Have children say the word with you.

Distribute an index card to each child with the word *up* and have children read the word. Tell children that you will show them words and they should raise their *up* index card when they see the word *up*. Then display index cards for high-frequency words *do, for, go, see,* and *up* randomly until children consistently and accurately identify the word *up*.

PRETEACH
Build Robust Vocabulary

Tell children that they are going to be learning three new words: *contrast, meander,* and *tidy*. Then discuss each word, using the following examples.

contrast
How would you *contrast* an elephant with a mouse?

meander
If you were to *meander* through a park, would you walk slowly and look around, or would you run? Tell why.

tidy
What would you do first to *tidy* the classroom?

High-Frequency Words

do	for
go	see
up	

VOCABULARY
Student-Friendly Explanations

contrast When you contrast things, you tell how they are different.

meander If you meander, you walk along slowly without a special place to go.

tidy To tidy a place means to make it neat.

Grade K **217**

LESSON 19

Day 1

PHONEMIC AWARENESS
Phoneme Categorization: Medial

PHONICS
Reteach Word Building

HIGH-FREQUENCY WORDS
Reteach up

COMPREHENSION
Preteach Reality/Fantasy

BUILD ROBUST VOCABULARY
Reteach contrast, meander, tidy

Materials Needed:

Word Builder and Word Builder Cards

Write-On/Wipe-Off Boards

Copying Master

Photo Cards

Practice Book

Phonemic Awareness

Phoneme Categorization: Medial Tell children to listen for the middle sound that is different in words. Show them how to name a word that has a different middle sound. Say: **I will say three words: *bat, bin, bit*. *Bin* and *bit* both have the /i/ sound in the middle. *Bat* has the /a/ sound in the middle. *Bat* has a different middle sound than *bin* and *bit*.**

Say the word *lid* slowly. Show children how to elongate the sounds in *lid*. Ask children to identify the middle sound. (/i/) Continue in the same way with the words *fix* and *gab*. Have children identify the word that has a different middle sound. (*gab*) Repeat with the following sets of words: *pack, pen, pad* (*pen*); *hug, lot, rob* (*hug*); *mud, cut, dog* (*dog*); *wed, sag, hen* (*sag*).

RETEACH
Phonics

Word Building Distribute *Word Builders* and *Word Builder Cards a, h, m, n, o, p,* and *t*. Review each letter name and sound. Then hold up letters at random, having children identify the letter name and sound.

Explain to children that you are going to show them how a word can change when the letters in the word change. Say: **Use your *Word Builder* and *Word Builder Cards* to make new words with me. I will use the letters *t, o,* and *p* to make the word *top*. Now you do the same. Blend the sounds with me: /t/-/o/-/p/, *top*. If I take away the *p* and put *n* in its place, I have the word *ton*. Now you try it. Blend the sounds and say the word with me: /t/-/o/-/n/, *ton*.**

Build Words Have children continue with *ton* in their *Word Builder*:

Change the *o* to *a*. What word did you make? (*tan*)

Change the *n* to *p*. What word did you make? (*tap*)

 Continue with the words *nap, map,* and *mop*. Then have children practice writing the words they built on their *Write-On/Wipe-Off Boards*.

 Distribute *Copying Master 37*. Have children trace the letters at the bottom of the page and cut them out. Help children identify the pictures. Then guide children to paste *o* or *i* in the box to complete each picture name. (*pin, mop, sit, pot*)

Day 1

RETEACH
High-Frequency Words

Distribute an index card for *up*. Say the word, and have children repeat it and hold up the card. Show *Photo Card tree*. Ask children to say the picture name. Write index cards for the words *look, at,* and *the* and review the words. Then use the index cards, a period card, and the *Photo Card tree* to build the sentence frame shown below. Point to each word as you read the sentence. Ask children to read the sentence with you. Continue with other *Photo Card* combinations.

High-Frequency Words

at	look
the	up

PRETEACH
Comprehension

  Reality/Fantasy Remind children that some stories are real because the events in the story could really happen, while some are make-believe, or fantasy, because the events in the story could not really happen. Then read this story aloud to them.

Paul and his pet dinosaur, Tiny, take a walk. Tiny is so excited that he starts to run. Paul holds on tight to the giant leash so Tiny doesn't run away! When Tiny slows down, Paul says, "Let's play at the playground." So Paul hops on Tiny's head. Tiny lifts Paul up to the top of the big slide. Whee! Down goes Paul. Again and again, Tiny lifts him up. Again and again, Paul slides down. At the end of the day, Paul and Tiny walk home, smiling. They think about all the fun they had.

Guide children to turn to page 110 in their *Practice Books*. Have them look at the pictures as you ask them to identify the events that happen in the story. Have them decide if the events could or could not happen in real life.

RETEACH
Build Robust Vocabulary

Remind children of the Student-Friendly Explanations of *contrast, meander,* and *tidy*. Then discuss each word, using the following examples.

contrast
If someone asked you to *contrast* winter and summer, what would you say?

meander
Would a person being chased by a tiger *meander*? Tell why.

tidy
If you had to *tidy* your bedroom, would you need a broom? Tell why or why not.

VOCABULARY
Student-Friendly Explanations

contrast When you contrast things, you tell how they are different.

meander If you meander, you walk along slowly without a special place to go.

tidy To tidy a place means to make it neat.

Grade K 219

LESSON 19

DAY AT A GLANCE — Day 2

PHONEMIC AWARENESS
Phoneme Categorization: Medial

PHONICS
Reteach Word Building

HIGH-FREQUENCY WORDS
Preteach *down*

COMPREHENSION
Preteach Summarize

BUILD ROBUST VOCABULARY
Preteach *famished, modify, unfortunate*

Materials Needed:

Photo Cards | Word Builder and Word Builder Cards | Write-On/Wipe-Off Boards

Copying Master | Practice Book

Phonemic Awareness

Phoneme Categorization: Medial Remind children that they have been listening for different sounds in the middle of words. Review how to identify the middle sounds and how to name a word with a different middle sound. Display Photo Cards *fish, pig, cat, hat, box,* and *van*. Say: **Listen as I say these picture names: fish, pig, cat. Fish and pig have the /i/ sound in the middle. Cat has the /a/ sound in the middle. Cat has a different middle sound than fish and pig. Which word has a different middle sound?** (cat) Repeat with the words *hat, box,* and *van*. Have children name the word that has a different middle sound. (box)

RETEACH

Phonics

Model Word Building Distribute *Word Builders* and *Word Builder Cards a, b, f, g, i, n, p, t,* and *w*. Explain to children that when letters in words change, so do the sounds. Have the children following along as you model word building. Say: **Use your Word Builder and Word Builder Cards to make new words with me. I will use the letters w, a, and g to make the word wag. Now you do the same. Blend the sounds with me: /w/-/a/-/g/, wag. If I take away the w and put n in its place, I have the word nag. Now you try it. Blend the sounds and say the word with me: /n/-/a/-/g/, nag.**

Build Words Have children continue with *nag* in their *Word Builder*:

Change the n to t. What word did you make? (tag)

Change the g to p. What word did you make? (tap)

Continue with the words *tip, tin, bin,* and *fin*.

Then have children practice writing the words they built on their *Write-on/Wipe-off Boards*. Distribute *Copying Master 38* to review building words with short *a* and *i* with children. Help children name each picture, read the word choices, and circle the word that names the picture and write the word. (*pin, tag, lip, rag*)

220 Lesson 19

Day 2

RETEACH
High-Frequency Words

Practice Book 111 Write index cards for high-frequency words *down, here, like, this,* and *what*. Display the card for *down*. Have children point to the word and read it. Then ask children to repeat the word as you hold up the card. Use index word cards *here, like, this,* and *what*. Have children stand in a circle. As you show each word, have children say the word. Tell them that when they read aloud the word *down*, they should sit down. Read words aloud several times until children consistently read and correctly react to the word *down*.

Have children turn to *Practice Book* page 111 to review high-frequency words and practice newly-learned words. Complete the page together.

High-Frequency Words

down	here
like	this
what	

PRETEACH
Comprehension

Summarize Explain that when you read a story, you can tell what happened in the story. Remind children that they should tell only the important things that happened in the story. Recall the story about Paul and his dinosaur from Day 1. Reread the story, having children complete each of the following phrases with a sentence or two: **At first, _____. Then, _____. In the end, _____.** (*Possible responses: At first, Paul and his dinosaur, Tiny, take a walk, and Tiny runs because he is excited. Then, Tiny helps Paul play on the slide. In the end, Paul and Tiny are happy as they walk home together.*) Record the responses on the board and read them together. Point out that these sentences tell the important things that happened in the story. Remind children that it helps to write down the important parts in their own words.

PRETEACH
Build Robust Vocabulary

Read aloud the Student-Friendly Explanations for *famished, modify,* and *unfortunate*. Then discuss each word, asking the following questions.

famished
If you were *famished*, would you eat breakfast or play a game? Why?

modify
If you *modify* something, do you make some changes or keep it the same?

unfortunate
Would you feel *unfortunate* if you found a dollar bill on the floor? Explain.

VOCABULARY
Student-Friendly Explanations

famished If you are famished, you are very hungry.

modify To modify something means to change it a little.

unfortunate If you are unfortunate, you have bad luck.

LESSON 19

DAY AT A GLANCE — Day 3

PHONEMIC AWARENESS
Phoneme Categorization: Medial

PHONICS
Preteach Phonogram -ox

READING
Review Phonogram -ox
Review High-Frequency Words

COMPREHENSION
Reteach Reality/Fantasy

BUILD ROBUST VOCABULARY
Reteach famished, modify, unfortunate

WRITING
Preteach Writing Trait: Word Choice

Materials Needed:

Phoneme Phone

Write-On/ Wipe-Off Boards

Photo Cards

Practice Book 112

Phonemic Awareness

Phoneme Categorization: Medial Tell children they will listen for words that have different middle sounds. Say: **I will say three words to you. One of the words is not like the other two.** *Hip, box, did.* **Which word does not belong?** Tell children that *box* does not belong.

Have children sit in a circle and distribute the *Phoneme Phone*. Repeat the rhyme with the following words: *duck, lit, sun;* (*lit*) *lad, less, let.* (*lad*) Ask children to repeat the groups of words while looking at the position of their mouths in the mirror to determine which word has a different middle sound.

Phoneme Identity: Final Remind children that words are made up of sounds. They have been listening for middle sounds in words. Now they will listen for ending sounds in words. Say: **I will say three words:** *bat, nut, jet.* **They all have the same sound at the end: /t/. Listen again:** *bat, nut, jet.* Have children repeat each set of words and name the ending sound that is the same in the following words:

dug, big, sag (/g/) *bad, lid, pod* (/d/);

less, gas, kiss (/s/) *hum, dim, ram* (/m/).

PRETEACH
Phonics

Identify Rhyming Words Remind children what rhyming words are. Say: **Listen to the words I say:** *set, met.* *Set* **and** *met* **both end with /et/.** *Set* **and** *met* **rhyme. What are the words?** (set, met) **Do the words rhyme?** (yes) Continue with these word pairs: *bug, dug;* (yes) *bin, ran;* (no) *ox, box.* (yes)

Read Words With -ox Write the word *box* and *ox* on the board. Track the print as you read each word. Have children repeat after you. Ask how the two words are the same. (Both words have /oks/; they rhyme.) Say: **The words** *box* **and** *ox* **are in the** *-ox* **word family because they both end in** *-ox.* Continue with the words *fox* and *lox*.

 Distribute *Write-on/Wipe-off Boards*. Write these words on the board: *ox, box, bin, fox, set.* Have children read the words and then have them copy the words that are in the *-ox* word family on their *Write-on/Wipe-off Boards.* (ox, box, fox)

222 Lesson 19

Day 3

REVIEW

Reading

Review Words with -ox Write these words on the board: *box, bat, fox, map*. Have children read the words and name which words are in the *-ox* word family.

High-Frequency Words Distribute index cards with the words *up* and *down* to children. As you say each word, have children repeat the word and hold up the correct card. Show *Photo Card fox*. Ask children to say the picture name. Remind children that *fox* is in the *-ox* word family. Show *Photo Card tree*. Ask children to say the picture name. Then use the word cards, a period card, and index cards with the words *the, is, in, on, a*, to build the first sentence frame shown below. Point to each word as you read the sentence. Ask children to read the sentence with you.

High-Frequency Words	
a	can
come	down
in	is
on	the
up	

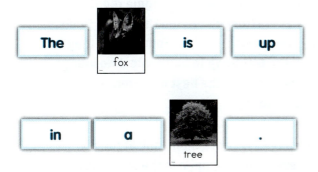

Then continue with the following sentence. Point to each word and have children read the sentence aloud.

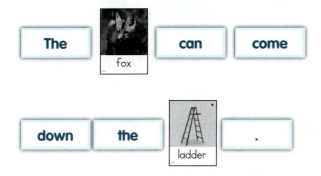

Grade K 223

Day 3

RETEACH

Comprehension

  Reality/Fantasy Remind children that some stories are real because the things that happen could happen in real life. Other stories are fantasy because the things that happen could not happen in real life. Have children listen as you read aloud the following story.

> Tom likes dinosaurs very much. He likes to read about dinosaurs and play with dinosaur toys. Today he is visiting the Field Museum with his family. He is very excited. He wants to learn more about dinosaurs. He wants to see dinosaurs! The first place that Tom, his sister Maggie, and his parents, walk to is the Hall of Dinosaurs. Tom is surprised to see huge dinosaur skeletons. He is a little scared when he stands next to one. He is small and it is so big! Maggie reads a sign that says dinosaur bones come from all around the world. Dad points out that some dinosaurs were smaller than Tom. Before they leave, Tom and Maggie stop in the Gift Shop to buy some dinosaur toys and books. Tom thinks this has been the best day ever. He learned so much about dinosaurs today.

Guide children to *Practice Book* page 112. Have them look at the pictures as you ask them to identify the events that happen in the story. Have them decide if the events could or could not happen in real life.

PRETEACH

Build Robust Vocabulary

Tell children the Student-Friendly Explanations for *famished*, *modify*, and *unfortunate*. Then discuss each word, asking children the following questions.

famished
Which word means almost the same as *famished*: *sad* or *starving*. Tell why.

modify
What could you do to *modify* your hair?

unfortunate
Which would make you feel *unfortunate*: losing a hat or finding a hat? Why?

VOCABULARY
Student-Friendly Explanations

famished If you are famished, you are very hungry.

modify To modify something means to change it a little.

unfortunate If you are unfortunate, you have bad luck.

Day 3

RETEACH

Writing

Writing Trait: Word Choice   Remind children that when they write it is important that they use words that will help give a reader a clear picture. Using the right words can help a reader have a clear idea of what a person in a story is like. Write the following sets of sentences on the board. Read each sentence aloud.

Tom is surprised to see huge dinosaur skeletons from long ago. He is a little scared when he stands next to one. He is small and it is so big!

Tom sees dinosaur skeletons. He stands next to one. The skeleton is big.
Ask children to explain which group of sentences has a better description of the character and why: *(The first group of sentences because it tells that Tom is surprised and scared, and that he is small.)*

Ask volunteers to supply other information that would help to describe the story. Ask: **What kind of dinosaur skeleton might Tom be looking at? How big might the skeleton be?**

Grade K   225

LESSON 19

PHONEMIC AWARENESS
Phoneme Categorization: Medial

PHONICS
Reteach Phonogram -ix

READING
Review Phonogram -ix
Review High-Frequency Words

BUILD ROBUST VOCABULARY
Review contrast, famished, meander, modify, tidy, unfortunate

WRITING
Reteach Writing Form: Description of a Person

Materials Needed:

Phoneme Phone

Write-On/ Wipe-Off Boards

Practice Book

Phonemic Awareness

Phoneme Categorization: Medial Tell children to listen for words that have different middle sounds. Say this rhyme: **I will say three words to you. One of the words is not like the two.** *Log, rat, map.* **Which word does not belong?** Tell children that *log* does not belong.

Have children sit in a circle and distribute the *Phoneme Phone*. Repeat the rhyme with the following words: *tab, cub, hug* (*tab*); *rod, cot, fed* (*fed*). Ask children to repeat the groups of words into the *Phoneme Phone*. Guide them to look at the position of their mouths in the mirror to determine which word has a different middle sound.

Phoneme Identity: Final Remind children that words are made up of sounds. They have been listening for middle sounds in words. Now they will listen for ending sounds in words. Say: **I will say three words:** *rap, tip, pup.* **They all have the same sound at the end:** /p/. **Listen again:** *rap, tip, pup.* Have children repeat each set of words and name the ending sound that is the same in the following words: *bid, led, sad* (/d/); *jab, rob, tub* (/b/); *hen, can, pin* (/n/); *wax, mix, fox* (/x/).

RETEACH
Phonics

Identify Rhyming Words Remind children what rhyming words are. Say: **Listen to these words:** *six, fix.* *Six* **and** *fix* **both have** /iks/. *Six* **and** *fix* **rhyme. What are the words?** (*six, fix*) **Do the words rhyme?** (*yes*) Continue with these word pairs: *wax, fax;* (*yes*) *dog, hog;* (*yes*) *fax, mix.* (*no*)

Read Words With -ix Write the words *mix* and *six* on the board. Track the print as you read the words. Have children repeat after you. Ask how the two words are the same. (Both words have /iks/; they rhyme.) Say: **The words** *mix* **and** *six* **are in the** *-ix* **word family because they both end in** *-ix*. Continue with the words *fix* and *mix*. (Both words have /iks/; they rhyme.)

Distribute *Write-on/Wipe-off Boards*. Write these words on the board: *mix, cat, fed, six, van, big.* Have children read the words and copy the words that are in the *-ix* word family on their *Write-on/Wipe-off Boards.* (*mix, six*)

226 Lesson 19

REVIEW

Reading

Practice Book 113–114

Review Words with -ix Write the words *fix* and *mix* on the board. Blend the words, tracking print as you read them. Have children read the words and tell how they are the same. Remind children that these words are in the *-ix* word family because they both end in *-ix*.

Review High-Frequency Words Create and distribute the index cards for the words *up* and *down*. Read the words with the children. Say: **I will say a sentence. If you hear the word *up*, hold the word card *up* high over your head. If you hear the word *down*, hold the word card *down* low at your side.** Say several sentences using the words *up* and *down*, such as *Look up at the sky.* and *The book is down there.* Have children listen to the sentences and respond appropriately.

Have children turn to *Practice Book* pages 113–114. Help children cut and fold the book. Explain that they will read this book with their family at home.

REVIEW

Build Robust Vocabulary

Remind children of the Student-Friendly Explanations of *contrast, famished, meander, modify, tidy,* and *unfortunate*. Determine children's understanding of the words by asking these questions.

- If you *contrast* a *tidy* room and a messy room, what would you say?
- If you were *famished*, would you *meander* to the dinner table? Why?
- If you *modify* a story, do you change words or keep them the same?
- Would it be *unfortunate* if it rained during a picnic? Tell why.

RETEACH

Writing

Writing Form: Description of a Person Remind children that when writing a person's description, they tell what the person looks and acts like. Discuss how using describing words helps tell the reader what the person is like.

Tell children that together you will write a description of a teacher. Write the teacher's name on chart paper. Ask children to tell what the teacher looks like, using describing words. Then ask them to share other words that tell about the teacher. Use the children's ideas write a description of the teacher. Have children to write letters or words they know. Read the finished description to the children.

> Mrs. Smith has brown hair.
> Mrs. Smith is helpful.

VOCABULARY

Student-Friendly Explanations

contrast When you contrast things, you tell how they are different.

famished If you are famished, you are very hungry.

meander If you meander, you walk along slowly without a special place to go.

modify To modify something means to change it a little.

tidy To tidy a place means to make it neat.

unfortunate If you are unfortunate, you have bad luck.

LESSON 19

PHONEMIC AWARENESS
Phoneme Isolation: Initial, Medial, Final

PHONICS
Preteach Short Vowel /e/e

HIGH-FREQUENCY WORDS
Preteach we

BUILD ROBUST VOCABULARY
Preteach treasure, sturdy, worth

Materials Needed:

Photo Cards   Sound/Spelling Cards   Practice Book

Phonemic Awareness

 Phoneme Isolation: Initial, Medial, Final Display *Photo Cards pig, watch, fish, cat, box, dog,* and *drum.* Remind children that words are made up of sounds. They can listen for beginning, middle, and end sounds. Say: **Name the sound you hear in the beginning of the words I say. Listen as I do the first one.** Hold up *pig.* Say: **The first word is *pig.* I hear /p/ at the beginning. What is the the word?** (*pig*) **What is the beginning sound?** /p/ Repeat with *Photo Cards witch* (/w/) and *fish* (/f/), having children identify the beginning sound. Then repeat the process with *Photo Cards cat* (/a/) and *box* (/o/), having children identify the middle sounds. Then have children identify the ending sounds in *Photo Cards dog* (/g/) and *drum* (/m/).

PRETEACH

Phonics

 Letter Naming Fluency Display *Sound/Spelling Cards w, x, l, h, b, k, g, f,* and *i.* Point to each letter and state letter name. Have children repeat the letter name. Then display the *Sound/Spelling Cards* in random order and ask children to identify each letter.

Short Vowel /e/e Display *Sound/Spelling Card Ee.* Say: **This is the letter e. Say the name with me: e.** Point to the uppercase *E* and say: **This is uppercase E.** Point to lowercase *e* and say: **This is lowercase e.** Have children identify the letters. (*E, e*)

Writing *E* and *e* Write *E* and *e* on the board and have children identify the letters. Say: **Watch as I write the letter *E* so everyone can read it.** As you give the Letter Talk, trace the uppercase *E.* Do the same for lowercase *e.*

Letter Talk for *E*	Letter Talk for *e*
1. Straight line down.	1. Curve left.
2. Line across at the top, at the middle, and at the bottom.	2. Straight across the middle.

Guided Practice Have children finger-write the uppercase *E* in the air as you repeat the Letter Talk. Have them do the same for lowercase *e.* Then have children turn to *Practice Book,* p. 115. Help children circle the uppercase *E* and underline the lowercase *e.* Then have them trace the letters and practice writing the letters on the lines.

Day 5

PRETEACH
High-Frequency Words

 Write the high-frequency words *we, the, here, see,* and *you* on index cards. Distribute the index cards to the children. Say each word, and have the children repeat that word and hold up the correct card. Show the *Photo Card ring*. Ask children to say the picture name. Use the index cards, the *Photo Card ring*, and a period card to build the sentence frame shown below. Point to each word as you read the sentence. Then have children read the sentence with you.

Replace *Photo Card ring* with *rabbit*. Point to each word as you read the sentence. Repeat with the following sentence frame:

| You | see | the | kangaroo | . |

High-Frequency Words

here	see
the	we
you	

PRETEACH
Build Robust Vocabulary

Remind children of the Student-Friendly Explanations of *treasure, sturdy,* and *worth*. Then discuss each word, using the following examples.

treasure
Describe a *treasure* you have at home. Why is it special to you?

sturdy
If a chair is *sturdy,* will it break or hold together when you sit down? Why?

worth
Name something you have made that is *worth* keeping.

VOCABULARY
Student-Friendly Explanations

treasure A treasure is something that is precious to someone.

sturdy Something that is sturdy is strongly built.

worth If something is worth a lot to someone, it is very important to that person.

Grade K 229

LESSON 20

DAY 1

PHONEMIC AWARENESS
Phoneme Identity: Initial, Final

PHONICS
Preteach Relate *Ee* to /e/

HIGH-FREQUENCY WORDS
Reteach *we*

COMPREHENSION
Reteach Reality/ Fantasy

BUILD ROBUST VOCABULARY
Reteach *treasure, sturdy, worth*

Materials Needed:

Phoneme Phone | Sound/Spelling Card *Ee* | Word Builder and Word Builder Cards

Copying Master | Photo Cards | Practice Book

Phonemic Awareness

 Phoneme Identity: Initial, Final Say: **Listen as I say two words: *leg, lock*. *Leg* and *lock* begin with /l/. What beginning sound is the same?** (/l/) **Listen as I say these words: *tug, wig*. *Tug* and *wig* end with /g/. What are the words?** (tug, wig) **What ending sound is the same?** (/g/)

Give each child a *Phoneme Phone*. Say *rid* and *rap*. Have children elongate the sounds in each word while looking at his or her mouth position in the mirror. Ask the children to identify the beginning sound. (/r/) Repeat with the following word pair: *wag, wed*. (/w/) Ask children to listen for the ending sound in these pairs: *tap, rip* (/p/); *pit, get* (/t/).

PRETEACH

Phonics

   Relate *Ee* to /e/ Say the words *elk* and *exit* and have children repeat the words. Tell them that *elk* and *exit* both begin with /e/.

Connect Letter and Sound Display *Sound/Spelling Card Ee*. Ask: **What is the name of this letter?** (e) **The letter *e* stands for the beginning sound of *elm*. Say /e/.** Have children repeat the the sound as you point to the letter.

Discriminate /e/ Give each child a *Word Builder Card e*. Say: **If the word begins with /e/, hold up the card and say /e/. If the word does not begin with /e/, hold your card behind your back.** Say *cold, elf, end,* and *wit*. Follow the same procedure for the medial position with *pen, ran, let,* and *hot*.

Identify Sound Position Give each child a *Write-on/Wipe-off Board*. Explain that children will work with the three boxes next to the heart on side B of the *Write-on/Wipe-off Board*. Draw the boxes on chart paper. Tell children: **I will say some words. If /e/ is at the beginning of the word, put your letter *e* in the first box. If /e/ is in the middle of the word, put your letter *e* on the middle box.** Then say the following words, and have children place their *Word Builder Card e* in the appropriate box: *beg, edit,* and *then*.

 Distribute *Copying Master 39*. Have children trace *Ee*. Have children look at each picture and circle the letter for the beginning sound of the picture name. (Children circle letter *e* for *egg, elephant, escalator*. Children circle letter *w* for *web, window*.)

230 Lesson 20

PRETEACH

High-Frequency Words

Write the high-frequency words *we, come, for,* and *to* on index cards. Write the word *we* on the board, and read it. Display the index card *we* and match it to the word on the board. Give a *we* index card to each child and have them read. Then tell children that you will show them words. When they see the word *we,* they should read it aloud with you and show thumbs up. If they do not see the word *we,* they should show their thumbs down. Hold up the index cards *we, come, for,* and *to* in random order until children accurately identify the word *we.*

High-Frequency Words	
come	for
to	we

RETEACH

Comprehension

  Reality/Fantasy Remind children that some stories are realistic because the things that happen could happen in real life. Some stories are make-believe because the things that happen could not really happen. Then read this story aloud to them.

> Ed Elephant is very sad. Giant tears roll down his grey cheeks. He lost his favorite pencil. The pencil is red with a blue stripe. It has a soft blue eraser on the top. "My pencil is gone forever!" Ed sobs.
>
> "I will help you find your pencil," Molly Monkey says. Together, they look around Ed's house. Ed looks under the green chair. Molly looks on the small brown shelf. She checks behind some dusty books.
>
> "Here is my pencil!" Ed yells. "It rolled behind the flower pot." Molly claps her hands. They are both glad Ed found his special pencil.

Guide children to turn to page 116 in their *Practice Books.* Have them look at the pictures as you ask them to identify the events that happen in the story. Have them decide if the events could or could not happen in real life.

RETEACH

Build Robust Vocabulary

Remind children of the Student-Friendly Explanations for *treasure, sturdy,* and *worth.* Then discuss each word, using the following examples.

treasure
Would a new piano be a *treasure* for a musician? Tell why.

sturdy
Which is more *sturdy,* a cardboard box or a metal box? Tell why.

worth
Would a camera be *worth* a lot to a photographer? Why?

VOCABULARY
Student-Friendly Explanations

treasure A treasure is something that is precious to someone.

sturdy Something that is sturdy is strongly built.

worth If something is worth a lot to someone, it is very important to that person.

Grade K 231

LESSON 20

PHONEMIC AWARENESS
Phoneme Identity: Medial

PHONICS
Preteach Blending /e/e, /t/t

HIGH-FREQUENCY WORDS
Preteach want

COMPREHENSION
Preteach Use Story Structure

BUILD ROBUST VOCABULARY
Reteach compliment, confer, mingle

Materials Needed:

Photo Cards   Write-On/Wipe-Off Boards   Word Builder and Word Builder Cards

Copying Master   Practice Book

Phonemic Awareness

 Phoneme Identity: Medial Remind children they have been listening for sounds that are the same in words. Review how to listen for the same middle sound. Display *Photo Cards* *pan*, *cat*, *fish*, and *pig*. Say: **Listen as I say these picture names: *pan*, *cat*. I hear /a/ in the middle of each word. What sound do you hear in the middle of *pan* and *cat*?** (/a/) Continue in the same way with *Photo Cards* *fish* and *pig*. Have children identify the same middle sound. (/i/) Then have children listen for the middle sound in these word pairs: *rub*, *fun* (/u/); *hem*, *fed* (/e/); *cot*, *mob* (/o/).

PRETEACH

Phonics

 Blend Phonemes Have children sit in a circle. Explain that you will blend sounds to say words. Say the following verse, and have children echo you. Say: **We're going on a Word Hunt. What's this word? /b/-/e/-/t/? Together: *bet*!** Continue with the words *met*, *den*, and *peg*.

Blending /e/e, /t/t Place the *Word Builder Cards* *p*, *e*, and *t* in *Word Builder*. Point to *p*. Say: /p/. Have children name the letter and sound. Point to *e*. Say: /e/. Have children name the letter and sound. Slide *e* next to *p*. Move your hand under the letters and blend the sounds: /ppee/. Have children repeat after you. Point to *t*. Say: /t/. Have children name the letter and sound. Slide *t* next to *pe*. Move your hand under the letters and blend the sounds: /ppeett/. Have children repeat after you. Then have children blend and read the word *pet* with you. Continue with *let* and *get*. Have children practice writing the words they built on their *Write-on/Wipe-off Boards*.

 Distribute *Copying Master 40*. Help children name each picture and read the word choices below each picture. Then have children circle the word that names the picture and write the word. (Children should write and circle *wet*, *net*, *pot*, *pet*.)

232 Lesson 20

Day 2

PRETEACH
High-Frequency Words

Practice Book 117

Write the high-frequency words *want, my, look, this,* and *where* on index cards. Then write the word *want* on the board. Point to the word *want*. Read the word and have children say it with you. Display the index card *want* and match it to the word *want* on the board. Have children say the word with you. Distribute an index card to each child with the word *want* and have children read the word. Then tell children that you will show them some words. When they see the word *want*, they should read it aloud with you and point to the word on their card. Hold up the index cards *want, my, look, this,* and *where* in random order until children accurately identify the word *want*.

Have children turn to *Practice Book* page 117 to review high-frequency words and practice newly-learned words. Complete the page together.

High-Frequency Words

look	my
this	where

PRETEACH
Comprehension

Use Story Structure Remind children that understanding who the character is and what the problem is helps you understand the story. Create a chart with these row headings: *Characters and Setting, Problem,* and *Solution*. Recall the story about Ed Elephant and his lost pencil from Day 1. Help children name Ed's problem and solution to complete the chart.

Characters and Setting:	Ed Elephant and Molly Monkey are in Ed's living room.
Problem:	Ed has lost his favorite pencil.
Solution:	Molly helps Ed look for the pencil. Ed finds his pencil.

RETEACH
Build Robust Vocabulary

Remind children of the Student-Friendly Explanations for *compliment, confer,* and *mingle*. Then discuss each word, using the following examples.

compliment
What *compliment* might you say about someone's shoes?

confer
When you *confer*, do you drink something or discuss something? Explain.

mingle
Would you *mingle* with people at a family party or when you sleep? Tell why.

VOCABULARY
Student-Friendly Explanations

compliment A compliment is something nice you say to someone else.

confer When you confer, you talk with others about what to do about something.

mingle When you mingle, you move around talking to different people who are gathered together.

Grade K 233

LESSON 20

DAY AT A GLANCE — Day 3

PHONEMIC AWARENESS
Phoneme Categorization: Initial, Final

PHONICS
Preteach Word Blending and Building

HIGH-FREQUENCY WORDS
Reteach *we, want*

COMPREHENSION
Reteach Reality/Fantasy

BUILD ROBUST VOCABULARY
Reteach *compliment, confer, mingle*

WRITING
Preteach Writing Trait: Word Choice

Materials Needed:

Photo Cards   Word Builder and Word Builder Cards

Write-On/Wipe-Off Boards   Practice Book

Phonemic Awareness

Phoneme Categorization: Initial, Final Display *Photo Cards boy, cat, box, fish, fox,* and *hat*. Have children listen for different beginning sounds. Say: **The first word is *boy*. The beginning sound is /b/.** Repeat with *box* and *cat*. (/b/, /c/) Ask: **What is the beginning sound in *boy* and *box*?** (/b/) **What is the beginning sound in *cat*?** (/c/) **Cat has a different beginning sound, /c/.** Repeat with *fish, fox,* and *hat*. (hat, /h/) Display *Photo Cards fox, box, sun, cat, cow,* and *hat*. Repeat the process, having children listen for the different ending sounds in the following word groups: *fox, box, sun* (/n/); *cat, cow, hat* (/w/).

Say the following sets of words. Have children repeat the words and name the word with a different beginning sound: *leg, pit, lad* (pit, /p/). Have children repeat the words and name the word that has a different ending sound: *tan, wig, rag* (tan, /n/); *deck, hit, rock* (hit, /t/).

PRETEACH

Phonics

 Blend Phonemes Tell children that you will play a game called "Say the Word." Say: **I will say the sounds in a word and you will say the word. I will do the first one for you. Listen: /m/ /a/ /n/. The word is *man*. What are the sounds?** (/m/ /a/ /n/) **What is the word?** (man) Continue with the following words: /r/ /i/ /p/ (rip); /n/ /e/ /t/ (net); /w/ /e/ /b/ (web).

Blend Words Distribute *Word Builders* and *Word Builder Cards b, e, l, o, p, s, t, w, h,* and *g*. Remind children that letters make sounds in words. Model word blending. Say: **Use your *Word Builder* and *Word Builder Cards* to make new words with me. I will use the letters *l, e,* and *t* to make the word *let*. Now you do the same. Blend the sounds with me: /l/ /e/ /t/, *let*. If I take away the *l* and put *g* in its place, I have the word *get*. Blend the sounds and say the word with me: /g/ /e/ /t/, *get*.**

Build Words Have children continue with *get* in their *Word Builder*:

Change the *e* to *o*. What word did you make? (got)

Change the *g* to *h*. What word did you make? (hot)

Continue with the words *pot, pet, set, wet,* and *bet*. Then have children practice writing the words they built on their *Write-on/Wipe-off Boards*.

234 Lesson 20

Day 3

RETEACH

High-Frequency Words

Write the high frequency words *we* and *want* on index cards. Then write the word *we* on the board. Point to the word *we*. Read the word and have children say it with you. Repeat with the word *want*. Display the high-frequency word index cards *we* and *want*, and match them to the words *we* and *want* on the board. Have children say the words with you.

Distribute the cards for *we* and *want* to children. As you say each word, have children read the word and hold up the correct card. Continue until children consistently read the words correctly.

On the board write *We want* _____. Have children take turns reading the sentence and filling in the blank. Point to each word as it is read.

Grade K 235

Day 3

RETEACH
Comprehension

Reality/Fantasy Remind children that some stories are real and some stories are make-believe. Talk about the difference between a realistic story and a fantasy story with the children. Have children listen as you read aloud the following story.

Practice Book 118

> Kira went to the store with her big brother to buy a gift for her mom. Kira looked at a pretty black hat with blue sparkles. She touched a fluffy pink scarf. Her brother pointed out a sparkly heart necklace. Kira liked all of these, but none were right for her mom. Kira saw shiny black pans and striped oven mitts. She checked out a big cookbook. Kira felt sad. She didn't think there was a gift for her mom anywhere. Then she saw the perfect gift! Soft fuzzy slippers were just what Mom needed! Slippers would make her sore feet feel better after a long day at work. Kira and her brother bought the slippers and headed home. Kira could hardly wait to give her mom this special gift.

Guide children to *Practice Book* page 118. Have them look at the pictures as you ask them to identify the events that happen in the story. Have them decide if the events could or could not happen in real life.

RETEACH
Build Robust Vocabulary

Remind children of the Student-Friendly Explanations for *compliment*, *confer*, and *mingle*. Then discuss each word, using the following examples.

compliment
Which is a *compliment*: *I can't wait for summer* or *I like your new jacket*?

confer
Would you rather *confer* with someone when you are asleep or awake? Why?

mingle
What are some things you would do if you were to *mingle* with other children right now?

VOCABULARY
Student-Friendly Explanations

compliment If you give a compliment, you tell someone that you like something about them.

confer When you confer, you talk with others about what to do about something.

mingle When you mingle, you move around talking to different people who are gathered together.

Day 3

PRETEACH

Writing

Writing Trait: Word Choice   Remind children that when they write a description, they need to choose words that help the reader get a clear picture of an object. Write the following sentences on the board. Read the sentences to children while tracking the print.

> Kira looked at a pretty black hat with blue sparkles.
>
> Kira looked at a hat.

Ask: What object is in both sentences? (a hat) **Which sentence gives the reader a clearer picture of the object? Why?** (The first sentence because it uses words that describe the hat.) Point out how the first sentence uses words that make it clear to the reader what the hat looked like. Repeat with the following sentences. Ask children to explain which sentence has a better description of the object:

Mom needs slippers.

Soft, fuzzy slippers were just what mom needed!

Explain to children that the second sentence is a better description of the object. Tell them that it contains words that give a clearer picture of the slippers. Have children name words that help them to picture the slippers. (*soft, fuzzy*)

Grade K   **237**

LESSON 20

PHONEMIC AWARENESS
Phoneme Categorization: Medial

PHONICS
Reteach Short Vowel /e/*e*

READING
Review Short Vowel /e/*e*
Review High-Frequency Words

BUILD ROBUST VOCABULARY
Review treasure, sturdy, worth, compliment, confer, mingle

WRITING
Reteach Writing Form: Description of a Thing

Materials Needed:

Word Builder and Word Builder Cards

Write-On/Wipe-Off Boards

Practice Book pp. 119–120

High-Frequency Words

we   want

Phonemic Awareness

Phoneme Categorization: Medial Remind children that they have listened for different sounds at the beginning and end of words. Tell them that they will listen for different sounds in the middle of words. Say: **The first word is *sick*. The middle sound is /i/.** Repeat with *big* and *red*. (/i/, /e/) Ask: **Does *sick* have the same middle sound as *big*?** (yes) **Do *sick* and *big* have the same middle sound as *red*?** (no) **Which word has a different middle sound: *sick*, *big*, or *red*?** (red) Continue with the following word groups: *pup, bun, fix* (fix); *ham, cat, hot* (hot); *miss, pin, rat* (rat).

RETEACH

Phonics

  Blend Sounds Place *Word Builder Cards n, e,* and *t* in the *Word Builder*. Point to *n*. Say: **/n/**. Have children name the letter and sound. Point to *e*. Say: **/e/**. Have children name the letter and sound. Slide *e* next to *n*. Move your hand under the letters and blend the sounds: **/nnee/**. Have children repeat after you. Point to *t*. Say: **/t/**. Have children name the letter and sound. Slide *t* next to *ne*. Move your hand under the letters and blend the sounds: **/nneett/**. Have children repeat after you. Then have children blend and read the word *net* with you.

Distribute *Write-on/Wipe-off Boards*. Write the word *pet* on the board. Say: **Write these letters on your *Write-on/Wipe-off Board*: p, e, t. Now point to the letter *p* and say the sound with me, /p/.** Repeat with *e* and *t*. Guide children to blend the sounds together to read the word *pet*. Repeat for *den, red, leg*.

REVIEW

Reading

Short Vowel /e/*e* Review the /e/ sound with children. Have children name the letter that stands for the beginning sound of the following words: *egg, elf,* and *end*.

 High-Frequency Words Distribute index cards for *we* and *want* to children. Use the word *we* in a sentence. When they hear the word *we*, children should hold up the *we* card. Continue with other sentences using *want* and *we*, having children hold up the appropriate index card.

Have children turn to *Practice Book* pages 119–120. Help children cut and fold the book. Explain that they will read this book with their family at home.

REVIEW

Robust Vocabulary

Remind children of the Student-Friendly Explanations for *treasure, sturdy, worth, compliment, confer,* and *mingle.* Then determine children's understanding of the words by asking the following questions.

- **Would you feel happy or sad if you found a *treasure*? Tell why.**
- **If a person built a *sturdy* table, would the table last a long time? Why?**
- **If you have something that has *worth*, do you throw it away or save it? Tell why.**
- **If someone gave you a *compliment* on your nice smile, what might that person say?**
- **What is something your friends might *confer* about?**
- **Would you *mingle* at a party or at a dentist's office? Why?**

RETEACH

Writing

Description of a Thing Remind children that a description can be sentences telling what something is like. Explain that a description of a thing tells what the thing looks like and what it does or how it is used.

Tell children that together you will write a description of something in the room. Have the children choose an object. Write the name of the object on chart paper. Ask children to describe the object. Prompt them with questions about the object if necessary. Record their ideas on chart paper. Then use children's ideas to write a description of the object. Invite children to help you write letters and words that they know. Read the finished description to the children.

```
                    A Globe
The globe is a _____ shape.
The globe feels _____.
There are _____ and _____ colors on the globe.
```

VOCABULARY
Student-Friendly Explanations

treasure A treasure is something that is precious to someone.

sturdy Something that is sturdy is strongly built.

worth If something is worth a lot to someone, it is very important to that person.

compliment If you give a compliment, you tell someone that you like something about them.

confer When you confer, you talk with others about what to do about something.

mingle When you mingle, you move around talking to different people who are gathered together.

Grade K 239

LESSON 20

PHONEMIC AWARENESS
Phoneme Blending

PHONICS
Preteach Word Blending

HIGH-FREQUENCY WORDS
Preteach *out*

BUILD ROBUST VOCABULARY
Reteach *treasure, worth, unfortunate*

Materials Needed:

Write-On/ Wipe-Off Boards

Sound/Spelling Cards *Rr, Ee, Dd*

Word Builder and Word Builder Cards

Practice Book

Phonemic Awareness

 Phoneme Blending Distribute *Write-on/Wipe-off Boards* and markers to each child. Explain to children that they will work on side B of *Write-on/Wipe-off Board* on the three boxes next to the heart. Say: **Listen as I say each sound: /m/ /e/ /n/, men.** Show children how to move markers into each box as they say each sound. Say: **What is each sound?** (/m/ /e/ /n/) **What is the word?** (men) Have children move markers in the same way as you say /t/ /a/ /p/, *tap*. Repeat with the following words:

| /k/ /u/ /t/ (cut) | /p/ /o/ /t/ (pot) | /d/ /i/ /g/ (dig) |
| /m/ /i/ /ks/ (mix) | /f/ /a/ /d/ (fad) | /w/ /e/ /t/ (wet) |

PRETEACH

Phonics

  Sounds in a Word Have children sit in a circle. Explain that you will blend sounds to say words. Say the following verse, and have children echo you.
Say: **We're going on a Word Hunt. What's this word? /w/ /e/ /t/? Together: wet!** Continue with the words *hop, pen,* and *vat*. Then review the sounds you blended to make each word.

Display *Sound/Spelling Cards r, e,* and *d*. Point to *r*. Ask: **What letter is this?** (r) **The letter *r* stands for the sound /r/. What does *r* stand for?** (/r/) Point to *e*. Ask: **What letter is this?** (e) **The letter *e* stands for the sound /e/. What does *e* stand for?** (/e/) Point to *d*. Ask: **What letter is this?** (d) **The letter *d* stands for the sound /d/. What sound does *d* stand for?** (/d/)

Word Blending Place the Word Builder Cards *r, e,* and *d* in Word Builder. Point to *r*. Say: **/r/.** Have children name the letter and sound. Point to *e*. Say: **/e/.** Have children name the letter and sound. Point to *d*. Say: **/d/.** Have children name the letter and sound. Slide the *e* next to *r*. Move your hand under the letters and blend the sounds: **/re/**. Have children repeat after you. Slide the *d* next to *re*. Move your hand under the letters and blend the sounds: **/red/**. Have children repeat after you. Then have children blend and read the word *red* with you. Continue with the words *fed, set, hen,* and *wed*.

Have children turn to *Practice Book* page 121. Help children identify the pictures, trace the letter *e* in each word, and blend sounds to read the words.

240 Lesson 20

Day 5

PRETEACH

High-Frequency Words

Write and distribute index cards for *out, down, like, two,* and *you.* Say each word, and have children repeat that word and hold up the correct card. Repeat this activity until children consistently identify the word *out* and the other words.

Then put together a deck of index cards containing two copies of each of the words: *out, down, like, two,* and *you.* Shuffle cards and deal each child three cards. Have children play *Go Fish.* When the game ends, have children read their word cards.

RETEACH

Build Robust Vocabulary

Remind children of the Student-Friendly Explanations for *treasure, worth,* and *unfortunate.* Then discuss each word, asking children the following questions.

treasure
What kinds of things might you find in a box filled with *treasure*? Why?

worth
What is *worth* more, a gift made by your friend or an empty box? Why?

unfortunate
Are you *unfortunate* if your painting wins a prize or gets ruined in the rain? Why?

High-Frequency Words

down	like
out	two
you	

VOCABULARY

Student-Friendly Explanations

treasure A treasure is something that is valuable to someone.

worth If an item has worth, it is very important to a person.

unfortunate If you are unfortunate, you have bad luck.

Grade K **241**

LESSON 21

DAY AT A GLANCE — Day 1

PHONEMIC AWARENESS
Phoneme Blending

PHONICS
Preteach Word Building

HIGH-FREQUENCY WORDS
Reteach *out*

COMPREHENSION
Reteach Setting

BUILD ROBUST VOCABULARY
Reteach *confer, mingle, tidy*

Materials Needed:

Write-On/
Wipe-Off
Boards

Word Builder and
Word Builder
Cards

Copying
Master

Practice
Book

Phonemic Awareness

Phoneme Blending Distribute *Write-on/Wipe-off Boards* and markers to each child. Explain that children will work on side B of *Write-on/Wipe-off Board* with the three boxes next to the heart. Say: **Listen as I say each sound: /m/ /o/ /p/, mop.** Show children how to move markers into each box as they say each sound. Say: **What is each sound?** (/m/ /o/ /p/) **What is the word?** (*mop*) Have children move markers in the same way as you say /l/ /e/ /t/, *let*. Repeat with the following words:

/h/ /i/ /t/ (*hit*)   /g/ /u/ /m/ (*gum*)

/t/ /a/ /n/ (*tan*)   /d/ /o/ /g/ (*dog*)

PRETEACH

Phonics

  Word Building Distribute *Word Builders* and *Word Builder Cards a, d, e, h, I, l, m, n, p,* and *t*. Review each letter name and sound. Then hold up letters at random and ask children to tell the letter name and sound.

Explain to children that you are going to show them how the sounds of a word can change when the letters in the word change. Say: **Use your Word Builder and Word Builder Cards to make new words with me. I will use the letters *p, e,* and *t* to make the word *pet*. Now you do the same. Blend the sounds with me: /p/ /e/ /t/, *pet*. If I take away the *e* and put *i* in its place, I have the word *pit*. Now you try it. Blend the sounds and say the word with me: /p/ /i/ /t/, *pit*.**

Build Words Have children continue with *pit* in their *Word Builder*:

Change the *p* to *l*. What word did you make? (*lit*)

Change the *l* to *h*. What word did you make? (*hit*)

Continue with the words *hat, ham, tam, tan,* and *den*. Then have children practice writing the words they built on their *Write-on/Wipe-off Boards*.

Distribute *Copying Master 41*. Have children trace the letters at the bottom of the page and cut them out. Help children identify the pictures. Then have children paste *a, e,* or *i* in the box to complete each picture name. (*pet, bed, rag, hen*)

242 Lesson 21

Day 1

RETEACH

High-Frequency Words

Distribute an index card *out* to children. Say the word and have children repeat it. Invite children to trace the word *out* on their card with a finger. Then distribute index cards for *my, here,* and *what.* Say each word, and have children repeat each word and hold up the correct card. Then hold up all the index cards in random order. Have children read the words aloud. If the word is *out*, have children clap. Repeat until children consistently recognize the word *out*.

High-Frequency Words	
here	my
out	what

RETEACH

Comprehension

Setting Remind children that a story's setting is where and when the story takes place. Then read this story aloud to them.

> **Jed wakes up and looks out his camper window at the campground. He sees the sun coming up over the trees. He hears birds chirping. He sees a tiny chipmunk carrying a piece of bread. As Jed gets dressed, he sees the lake sparkling in the sun. He sees his friend, Sam, coming from his family's camper. Jed runs outside to meet Sam. First, they go to the old tire swing hanging from the huge oak tree. They feel like they are flying in the clouds! Later, they play games on the paths that wind in the woods. They pretend they are explorers finding new lands. Finally, the families sit by a bright campfire in the dark summer night.**

Guide children to turn to page 122 in their *Practice Books*. Have them look at the pictures as you ask them to identify the setting of the story. Have them retell the story to one another, including the setting details.

RETEACH

Build Robust Vocabulary

Remind children of the Student-Friendly Explanations for *confer, mingle,* and *tidy*. Then discuss each word, using the following examples.

confer
What is something you might *confer* with your family about? Why?

mingle
Where are some places that people might *mingle*? Why?

tidy
Would you use a CD player or a dust rag to *tidy* your home? Why?

VOCABULARY
Student-Friendly Explanations

confer When you confer, you talk with others about what to do about something.

mingle When you mingle, you greet and talk with people who are gathered together.

tidy (v) To tidy a place means to make it neat and clean.

Grade K 243

LESSON 21

PHONEMIC AWARENESS
Phoneme Blending

PHONICS
Reteach Word Building

HIGH-FREQUENCY WORDS
Preteach who

COMPREHENSION
Preteach
Monitor Comprehension: Reread

BUILD ROBUST VOCABULARY
Reteach contrast, modify, compliment

Materials Needed:

Photo Cards   Word Builder and Word Builder Cards   Write-On/Wipe-Off Boards

Copying Master   Practice Book

Phonemic Awareness

Phoneme Blending Remind children that words are made of sounds and they can blend sounds to make words. Display *Photo Cards pig* and *pan*. Hold up *Photo Card pig*. Say: **Listen as I say these sounds: /p/ /i/ /g/. Now I will blend the sounds together to say the word: pig.** Have children repeat the sounds and the word with you. Then hold up *Photo Card pan* and repeat the process. Have children blend these sounds and say the words:

| /o/ /x/ (ox) | /i/ /n/ (in) | /t/ /e/ /n/ (ten) |
| /b/ /u/ /g/ (bug) | /s/ /e/ /t/ (set) | /m/ /a/ /p/ (map) |

RETEACH

Phonics

Discriminate Sounds Ask children: **What is the first sound in *it*?** (/i/) **What is the first sound in *at*?** (/a/) **How are the words the different?** (They have different beginning sounds.) **How are the words the same?** (They have the same end sound.) Continue with these words:

    bed, bad   **sit, pit**   **cat, rat**   **bet, beg**

 Model Word Building Distribute *Word Builders* and *Word Builder Cards e, g, h, l, n, o, p, s,* and *t*. Explain to children that when letters in words change, so do the sounds. Model word building and say: **Use your *Word Builder Cards* to make new words with me. I will use the letters *p, o,* and *t* to make the word *pot*. Now you do the same. Blend the sounds with me: /p/ /o/ /t/, *pot*. If I take away the *p* and put *g* in its place, I have the word *got*. Blend the sounds and say the word with me: /g/ /o/ /t/, *got*.**

Build Words Have children continue with *got* in their *Word Builder*:

Change the *g* to *l*. What word did you make? (*lot*)

Change the *o* to *e*. What word did you make? (*let*)

 Continue with the words *set, pet, pen, hen, ten,* and *ton*. Then have children practice writing the words they built on their *Write-on/Wipe-off Boards*.

Distribute *Copying Master 42* to review building words with short *e* and *o* with children. Help children name each picture and read the word choices below each picture. Then have children circle the word that names the picture and write the word. (Children should circle and write *pen, top, bed, men*)

244   Lesson 21

Day 2

PRETEACH

High-Frequency Words

 Give children the *out* index card from yesterday. Say the word and have children repeat it. Have children trace the word on their card with a finger. Display index cards for *my, here,* and *what*. Say each word, and have children repeat each word. Shuffle the cards, adding a card for *out,* then hold up each index card in random order. Have children read the words aloud. If the word is *out,* have children stomp twice. Repeat until children consistently recognize the word *out*. Distribute *Practice Book* page 123, and have children practice high-frequency words.

High-Frequency Words

| here | my |
| out | what |

PRETEACH

Comprehension

Reread Explain that when you read a story with many things happening, you can get confused. Remind children that if they reread parts of the story, they can keep better track of what is happening. Recall the story about Jed and his day at the campground from Day 1. Read the story and stop at appropriate points in the story to reread parts in order to clear up any confusion or to help children remember what happened. Copy the chart below on chart paper. Ask children to tell what they do not understand or remember, and what they learned after rereading. Write their responses under the correct heading.

| What I Don't Understand or Remember | |
| What I Found Out After Reading | |

RETEACH

Build Robust Vocabulary

Review the Student-Friendly Explanations for *contrast, modify,* and *compliment*. Then talk about each word, using the following questions.

contrast
Think about crayon and a pencil. How would you *contrast* them?

modify
If it starts to rain, how might you *modify* what you're wearing?

compliment
If you tell a friend, "You have a nice smile," are you giving your friend a *compliment*? Why or why not?

VOCABULARY

Student-Friendly Explanations

contrast When you contrast things, you tell how they are different.

modify To modify something means to change it a little.

compliment If you give a compliment, you tell someone that you like something about them.

Grade K   245

LESSON 21

DAY AT A GLANCE — Day 3

PHONEMIC AWARENESS
Phoneme Blending

PHONICS
Preteach Phonogram –ed

READING
Review Words With Phonogram -ed
Review High-Frequency Words

COMPREHENSION
Reteach Setting

BUILD ROBUST VOCABULARY
Reteach meander, sturdy, famished

WRITING
Reteach Writing Trait: Word Choice

Materials Needed:

Photo Cards | Phoneme Phone

Write-On/Wipe-Off Boards | Practice Book

Phonemic Awareness

  Phoneme Blending Display *Photo Card dog* and *cat*. Explain that you will blend sounds to say words. Hold up *Photo Card dog*. Say the verse, and have children blend sounds to say the word: **Say these sounds 1, 2, 3, Then blend the sounds you hear for me: /d/ /o/ /g/. What is the word?** (*dog*) Hold up *Photo Card cat*. Repeat the verse and have children blend sounds for the word /c/ /a/ /t/, *cat*.

Have children sit in a circle, and distribute the *Phoneme Phones*. Say the sounds /d/ /i/ /d/ and the word *did* into a phone, and model how to look at the position of your mouth. Then ask children to repeat the sounds and the word while they look at the position of their mouths in the mirror. Repeat with the following words:

/s/ /u/ /m/ (*sum*)   /b/ /a/ /t/ (*bat*)   /m/ /e/ /t/ (*met*)

Phoneme Identity: Final Remind children that they have listened for sounds in words. Now they will listen for the ending sounds in words. Say: **I will say two words: *tug, rig*. Say the words with me. The same sound is found in the word endings. The sound is /g/. What sound is the same in *tug* and *rig*?** (/g/) Have children repeat each pair of words, tell what sound is the same, and name the sound: *fed, tad* (ending; /d/); *not, hat* (ending; /t/).

PRETEACH

Phonics

 Identify Rhyming Words Remind children what rhyming words are. Say: **Listen to the words: *fed* and *led*. *Fed* and *led* both have /ed/, so they rhyme. What are the words?** (*fed, led*) **Do the words rhyme?** (*yes*) Continue with these word pairs: *kin, pin* (yes); *cap, rock* (no); *wed, Ted* (yes).

Read Words with -*ed* Write the word *red* on the board. Track the print as you read the word. Have children repeat after you. Then write the word *Ned*. Track the print as you read the word. Have children repeat after you. Ask how the words are the same. (They both have /ed/; they rhyme.) Say: **The words *red* and *Ned* are in the -*ed* word family because they both end in -*ed*.** Continue with the words *bed* and *Ed*.

Distribute *Write-on/Wipe-off Boards*. Write these words on the board: *tot, red, wed, lip, bed, led, hop*. Have children read the words and copy those words in the –*ed* family on their *Write-on/Wipe-off Boards*.

RETEACH

Reading

Read Words with Phonogram -ed Write the word *bed* on the board. Run a finger under each letter as you model how to blend the sounds. Say: /b/ /e/ /d/. **Let's say it together:** /b/ /e/ /d/, *bed*. Continue with the words *fed, led,* and *red*. Then point to the words at random and have children read them.

Review High-Frequency Words Distribute index cards for the high-frequency words *out* and *who* to children. As you say each word, have children repeat the word and hold up the correct card. Hold up each word card and have children read the word. Continue randomly holding up each card until children consistently read the words accurately.

Write these sentences on the board, and read them as you track the print. Then have children practice reading them.

> Who fed the cat?
> Who is in my bed?
> Who likes the red bed?

Day 3

RETEACH
Comprehension

  Setting Remind children that the setting of a story is where and when the story takes place. Tell children that they should pay attention to words and pictures to understand the setting. Have children listen as you read aloud the following story.

> Jen looked around her beroom and smiled. She thought it looked nice. Jen had worked all morning to clean her room. All of her story books were in order on the bookshelf. Her pink pencils and her bright blue notebook were stacked neatly on her desk. Her clothes were all folded and put away. Her doll with the red and gray dress was on the toy shelf. Jen's shoes were lined up in a row on her closet floor. Then her mom walked in with a special surprise for Jen. She had new pink and white striped sheets and blankets for Jen's bed! Jen and her mom agreed that her bedroom looked great!

Guide children to *Practice Book* page 124. Have them look at the pictures as you ask them to identify the setting of the story. Have them retell the story to one another, including the setting details.

RETEACH
Build Robust Vocabulary

Remind children of the Student-Friendly Explanations for *meander*, *sturdy*, and *famished*. Then discuss each word, asking children the following questions.

meander
If your friend was hurt, would you *meander* or run to get help? Tell why.

sturdy
Which plate is *sturdy*, a paper plate or a glass plate? Why?

famished
Would you feel *famished* after eating a big dinner? Why?

VOCABULARY
Student-Friendly Explanations

meander If you meander, you walk along slowly without a special place to go.

sturdy Something that is sturdy is strongly built or made.

famished If you are famished, you are very hungry.

248 Lesson 21

Day 3

RETEACH

Writing

Word Choice Remind children that when writing a description of a setting, it is important to choose words that give the reader a clear picture of what the place is like. Write the following sentence pair on the board. Read each sentence while tracking the print.

> The sand was warm.
> I was at the beach.

Ask: **What setting do these sentences describe?** (a beach) **Which sentence gives more ideas about the beach? Why?** (the first sentence mentions the sand and temperature.) Point out that the choice of words such as *warm* and *sand* give a clearer picture of the beach. Repeat with the following groups of sentences.

> The waves rolled in quietly.
> Tim could hear birds calling.
> Tim looked at the water.
> He looked at the birds.

Ask children to explain which group of sentences tells more about the setting and why: (The first sentence group; the noise of the waves and the sound of the birds.)

Grade K 249

LESSON 21

PHONEMIC AWARENESS
Phoneme Blending

PHONICS
Preteach Phonogram *-en*

READING
Review Words With Phonogram *-en*
Review High-Frequency Words

BUILD ROBUST VOCABULARY
Review *feast, soggy, sturdy, famished, unfortunate, treasure, compliment*

WRITING
Reteach Writing Form: Description of a Place

Materials Needed:

Write-On/   Practice
Wipe-Off   Book
Boards

Phonemic Awareness

Phoneme Blending Remind children that they blend sounds to say words. Have children blend sounds to say the word. Say: **Say these sounds 1, 2, 3, Then blend the sounds you hear for me: /p/ /e/ /t/. What is the word?** (*pet*) Repeat the verse for /b/ /u/ /n/, *bun*, /f/ /i/ /n/ (*fin*), /h/ /a/ /d/ (*had*), /d/ /o/ /t/ (*dot*), /b/ /e/ /d/ (*bed*).

Phoneme Categorization: Final Remind children that words are made of sounds. Have children should listen for the ending sound that is different in a group of words. Say: **I will say three words: *bet, bat, big*. Say the words with me. *Bet* and *bat* with /t/. *Big* has a different ending sound, /g/. What ending sound do you hear in *bet* and *bat*?** (/t/) **What ending sound do you hear in *big*?** (/g/) **Which word has a different ending sound?** (*big*) Continue with the words *ban, bin, box* (*box*); *pop, pat, pet* (*pop*); *wit, pass, fuss* (*wit*); *ham, lot, sum* (*lot*).

PRETEACH
Phonics

Identify Rhyming Words Remind children that two words with the same middle and ending sound are rhyming words. Say: **Listen to the words I say: *hen, pen*. *Hen* and *pen* both have /en/. Both words are in the *-en* family. What are the words?** (*hen, pen*) **Do the words rhyme?** (*yes*) Read the following word pairs and have children tell if they rhyme: *tip, dip* (*yes*); *ten, Jen* (*yes*); *Ken, red* (*no*); *pig, big* (*yes*).

Read Words with *-en* Write *hen* and *ten* on the board. Track the print as you read the words. Have children repeat after you. Ask how the two words are the same. (both have /en/; they rhyme.) Say: **Hen and *den* are in the *-en* family because they end in *-en*.** Continue with the words *Ken* and *ten*.

Distribute *Write-on/Wipe-off Boards*. Write these words on the board: *den, ten, kit, men, bet, Ken, rip*. Have children read the words and then copy those words in the *-en* family on their *Write-on/Wipe-off Boards*.

REVIEW
Reading

Words with Phonogram *-en* Write these phrases on chart paper. Track the print and read them together.

250   Lesson 21

Day 4

> go out to the pen
> a hen in the den
> who is ten
> Len is ten

Review High-Frequency Words Distribute the index cards for the high-frequency words *out* and *who*. Explain that you will play "Show and Tell." As you say each word, have children find the corresponding word card, show the word to you, and say the word. Repeat until each word has been identified correctly.

Have children turn to *Practice Book* pages 125-126. Help children cut and fold the book. Explain that they will read this book with their family at home.

REVIEW
Robust Vocabulary

Read the Student-Friendly Explanations for *feast, soggy, sturdy, famished, unfortunate, treasure,* and *compliment*. Determine children's understanding of the words by asking the following questions.

- When you are *famished*, do you want a feast or a nap? Tell why.
- Would you want dinner on a *soggy* plate or a *sturdy* plate? Tell why.
- Would it be *unfortunate* to be late for school or early for school? Why?
- What *treasure* might a dog like to have? Why?
- Would you be happy or sad if someone gave you a *compliment*? Why?

RETEACH
Writing

Description of a Place Remind children that a description is a group of sentences that tells what something is like. Discuss how including words that describe a place helps the reader to know what the place is like.

Tell children that together you will write a description of a fun place they know. Ask them to share words or phrases that describe this place. If necessary, prompt children with questions such as: *Is the place big or small? What is the first thing you see there? What sounds do you hear? Is there any smell?* Record their ideas on chart paper. Then use the children's ideas to write a description of this place. Invite them to write letters and words they know. Read the finished description to the children.

> The toy store has a big stuffed bear at the door.
> Children laugh and scream in the store.
> This store is bigger than a house.

VOCABULARY
Student-Friendly Explanations

feast If you are having a feast, you are eating a big meal with lots of different foods.

soggy Something that is soggy is so wet that it's squishy.

sturdy Something that is sturdy is strongly built or made.

famished If you are famished, you are very hungry.

unfortunate If you are unfortunate, you have bad luck.

treasure A treasure is something that is valuable to someone.

compliment If you give a compliment, you tell someone that you like something about them.

LESSON 21

PHONEMIC AWARENESS
Phoneme Blending

PHONICS
Preteach Consonant *Vv*

HIGH-FREQUENCY WORDS
Preteach *are*
Reteach *here, my, this, what*

BUILD ROBUST VOCABULARY
Preteach *protecting, volunteer, responsible*

Materials Needed:

Practice Book | Sound/Spelling Card *Vv*

Phonemic Awareness

Phoneme Blending Remind children that they can blend sounds to say words. Say: **Listen as I say these sounds: /f/ /u/ /n/. You repeat after me after I say the sounds again: /f/ /u/ /n/.** Have children repeat the sounds after you. Then say: **Now I will say the sounds again, blending the sounds: /ffuunn/. Now you blend the sounds.** Have children practice by blending the sounds. **We can now blend the sounds to say the word:** *fun*. **Say it with me:** *fun*.

Have children blend these sounds to say these words: /h/ /o/ /t/ (hot), /b/ /e/ /d/ (bed), /l/ /o/ /t/ (lot), /m/ /a/ /t/ (mat), /s/ /i/ /p/ (sip).

PRETEACH

Phonics

Sing "The Alphabet Song" Sing the Alphabet Song to children. Then sing the song again inviting children to join in. Have them stand up when they hear the letter that their name begins with. You may want to continue by having children raise their hands when they hear letters that they have recently learned about, such as *Ee*, *Ww*, or *Xx*.

 Consonant *Vv* Hold up the *Sound/Spelling Card Vv*. Explain that this is the consonant letter *Vv*. Say: **This is the letter *v*. Say the name with me.** (v) Point to the uppercase *V*. **This is the uppercase *V*.** Then point to the lowercase *v*. Say: **This is the lowercase *v*.**

Writing *V* and *v* Write *V* and *v* on the board and have children identify the letters. Say: **Watch as I write the letter *V* so that everyone can read it.** As you give the Letter Talk, trace the uppercase *V*. Do the same for the lowercase *v*.

Letter Talk for *V*	Letter Talk for *v*
1. Straight line down slant right.	1. Straight line down slant right.
2. Straight line up slant right.	2. Straight line up slant right.

Guided Practice Have children finger-write the uppercase *V* in the air as you repeat the Letter Talk. Have them do the same for lowercase *v*. Then have children turn to *Practice Book* page 127. Help children identify the letters *V* and *v*. Then have them trace the letters *V* and *v*.

Day 5

PRETEACH
High-Frequency Words

Tell children that they are going to be learning a new word. Write the high-frequency word *are* on the board. Point to and read the word. Then say the word in a sentence: **You *are* in kindergarten.** Write the word on an index card. Match the index card to the board and have children say it again with you.

Then write the previously-learned high-frequency words *here*, *my*, *this*, and *what* on index cards. Use these along with the new word *are* as flashcards. Show each card and have children identify the word. Continue until children are able to recognize the cards consistently.

PRETEACH
Build Robust Vocabulary

Tell children that they are going to be learning three new words. Read the Student-Friendly Explanations for *protecting*, *volunteer*, and *responsible*. Then discuss each word, using the following examples.

protecting
If a mother bear was *protecting* her cubs, would she keep them close to her or let them play far away? Why?

volunteer
Name a *volunteer* that helps in your class.

responsible
If your teacher asked you to be *responsible* for getting your homework home, would you put in your backpack or leave it on the table? Why?

High-Frequency Words

are	here
my	this
what	

VOCABULARY
Student-Friendly Explanations

protecting When you are protecting something, you are keeping it safe.

volunteer If you are a volunteer, you do work without getting paid.

responsible Someone who is responsible for something is expected to take care of it.

Grade K 253

LESSON 22

DAY AT A GLANCE
Day 1

PHONEMIC AWARENESS
Phoneme Blending

PHONICS
Preteach Relate Vv to /v/

HIGH-FREQUENCY WORDS
Reteach are, here, my, where

COMPREHENSION
Preteach Main Idea

BUILD ROBUST VOCABULARY
Reteach protecting, volunteer, responsible

Materials Needed:

Photo Cards | Sound/Spelling Card Vv | Word Builder and Word Builder Cards

Copying Master | Practice Book

High-Frequency Words

| are | my |
| here | where |

Phonemic Awareness

Phoneme Blending Remind children that they can blend individual sounds to say words. Say: **Listen as I say these sounds: /r/ /e/ /d/. Now I will blend the sounds to say the word: red.**

Display *Photo Cards* box, hat, sun. Ask children to listen as you say the individual sounds for each word: /b/ /o/ /x/; /h/ /a/ /t/; /s/ /u/ /n/. Have children point to the *Photo Card* that shows the picture of the word that has been blended.

PRETEACH

Phonics

Relate *Vv* to /v/ Say the words *vest* and *van* and have children repeat the words. Tell children that these words begin with the /v/ sound. Have children say /v/ several times.

 Connect Letter and Sound Display the *Sound/Spelling Card Vv*. Ask: **What is the name of this letter?** (v) **The letter *v* stands for the /v/ sound at the beginning of the word *vote*. Say /v/.** Have children repeat the sound several times.

 Discriminate /v/ Give each child *Word Builder Card v*. Say: **I'm going to say some words. If the word begins with /v/ hold up your card and say /v/. If the word does not begin with /v/, hold your card behind your back.** Say the words *vent*, *car*, *bike*, *valentine*, and *video*.

 Guided Practice Then have children turn to *Copying Master 43*. Help children identify the pictures. Have them trace the letter *Vv*. Then have them look at each picture and circle the letter that stands for the beginning sound of each picture name. (Children should circle *w* for *window*, *worm*; *v* for *volcano*, *vest*, *violin*.)

RETEACH

High-Frequency Words

 Make index cards for the words *are*, *here*, *where*, and *my*, and the punctuation symbols period and question mark. Say each word, and have children repeat each word. Show *Photo Card fish*. Ask children to say the picture name. Then use the word cards, the punctuation cards, and

254 Lesson 22

the *Photo Cards* to build the sentence frames shown below. Point to each word as you read the sentence. Ask children to read the sentence with you. Continue with other *Photo Card* combinations.

PRETEACH

Comprehension

Main Idea Explain to children that every story has a main idea. The main idea is what a story is mostly about. Then read this story aloud and discuss the main idea.

> Mr. Rodriguez is a police officer. He patrols our neighborhood. Officer Rodriguez comes to our school and talks about being safe. He explains that we should always wear a helmet when we are riding our bikes. We also need to look both ways before we cross the street. I want to be a police officer when I grow up, so I can help people to be safe too.

Guide children to turn to page 128 in their *Practice Books*. Have them look at the pictures and tell the main idea.

PRETEACH

Build Robust Vocabulary

Remind children of the explanations for *protecting*, *volunteer*, and *responsible*. Then discuss each word, using the following examples.

protecting and responsible
Haley is *protecting* her pet by bringing it inside during the bad weather. Tell how this is also being *responsible*.

volunteer
If I say something that a volunteer would do, say "A *volunteer* would do that." If not, don't say anything.
- take money for washing a car
- help a teacher in a classroom
- help a nurse in a hospital

VOCABULARY

Student-Friendly Explanations

protecting When you are protecting something, you are keeping it safe.

volunteer If you are a volunteer, you do work without getting paid.

responsible Someone who is responsible for something is expected to take care of it.

LESSON 22

PHONEMIC AWARENESS
Phoneme Blending

PHONICS
Preteach Consonant *Jj*

HIGH-FREQUENCY WORDS
Preteach they
Reteach come, down, go, where

COMPREHENSION
Reteach Generate Questions

BUILD ROBUST VOCABULARY
Preteach adore, melancholy, exquisite

Materials Needed:

Sound/Spelling Card *Jj* | Copying Master | Practice Book

Phonemic Awareness

Phoneme Blending Remind children that they have been blending individual sounds into words. Model again how to blend individual sounds into a word. Say: **Listen as I say the following sounds: /c/ /a/ /t/. Now I'll blend the sounds into the word: cat.**

Explain to children that they can also blend sounds to make word parts. Say: **The word *rowboat* has two word parts, *row* and *boat*. Listen as I say the following sounds: /r/ /ō/. When I blend the sounds together, I have *row*. This is the first part of the word.**

Have children blend the sounds to say the second word part: /b/ /ō/ /t/.

PRETEACH

Build Robust Vocabulary

Recite a Rhyme Write the nursery rhyme, "Jack and Jill" on chart paper. Track the words as you say the rhyme. Then have children join in when they feel comfortable. Invite volunteers to act like Jack and Jill as the class repeats the rhyme again.

 Consonant *Jj* Hold up the *Sound/Spelling Card Jj*. Explain that this is the consonant letter *Jj*. Say: **This is the letter *J*. Say the name with me.** Point to the uppercase *J*. **This is the uppercase *J*.** Then point to the lowercase *j*. Say: **This is the lowercase *j*.**

Writing *J* and *j* Write *J* and *j* on the board and have children identify the letters. Say: **Watch as I write the letter *J* so that everyone can read it.** As you give the Letter Talk, trace the uppercase *J*. Do the same for the lowercase *j*.

Letter Talk for *J*	Letter Talk for *j*
Straight line down and curve to the left.	1. Straight line down and curve to the left.
	2. Dot the top.

 Guided Practice Have children finger-write the uppercase *J* in the air as you repeat the Letter Talk. Have them do the same for lowercase *j*. Then help children with *Copying Master 44*. Have them identify the letters *J* and *j*. Then have them practice writing *J* and *j*.

256 Lesson 22

Day 2

PRETEACH

High-Frequency Words

Write the word *they* on the board. Point to the word and read it. Have children read the word with you. Say: **What are they doing?** Hold up an index card with the word *they* on it as you say the sentence. Then match the word card *they* to the word on the board. Repeat the word several times having children repeat it with you.

Then write the words *come, down, go,* and *where* on index cards. Have volunteers take turns picking a card and reading the word. Continue until all the words have been recognized several times.

 Have children turn to *Practice Book* page 129 to review high-frequency words and practice newly-learned words.

High-Frequency Words

come	they
down	where
go	

RETEACH

Comprehension

Generate Questions Remind children that asking questions when they read or listen to a story will help them understand the story better. Recall the story about the police officer, Mr. Rodriguez from Day 1. Reread the story and pause to ask questions. Write questions and answers on chart paper under the correct heading.

Question	Answer
Who is Mr. Rodriguez?	He is a police officer.
What does he talk about?	He talks about staying safe.

PRETEACH

Build Robust Vocabulary

Read the Student-Friendly Explanations for *adore, melancholy,* and *exquisite*. Then discuss each word, using the following examples.

adore
My sister adores her teddy bear. What is something you *adore*?

melancholy
If you were *melancholy*, would you most likely cry or laugh? Why?

exquisite
If I name something *exquisite*, say "That's exquisite!"
- a fancy vase
- a diamond necklace
- a trash can

VOCABULARY
Student-Friendly Explanations

adore To adore someone or something means to love that person or thing alot.

melancholy If you feel melancholy, you feel sad.

exquisite Something that is exquisite is very beautiful.

Grade K 257

LESSON 22

PHONEMIC AWARENESS
Phoneme Blending
Final Phoneme Identity

PHONICS
Preteach Relate *Jj* to /j/

HIGH-FREQUENCY WORDS
Reteach *are, they, a, at, and, the, want, where*

COMPREHENSION
Reteach Main Idea

BUILD ROBUST VOCABULARY
Reteach *adore, melancholy, exquisite*

WRITING
Reteach Writing Trait: Conventions

Materials Needed:

Phoneme Phone   Sound/Spelling Card *Jj*   Word Builder and Word Builder Cards

Photo Cards   Practice Book

Phonemic Awareness

Phoneme Blending   Remind children that they can blend individual sounds into words. Then model how to blend sounds into words. Say: **Listen carefully as I say the following sounds: /k/ /i/ /d/. Now blend the sounds into the word:** *kid*. Have children blend the following sounds into words: /v/ /e/ /s/ /t/ (vest), /j/ /a/ /m/ (jam), and /w/ /i/ /n/ (win).

Remind children that they can blend individual sounds to make syllables, or word parts. Say: **There are two word parts in the word** *upside*: *up* **and** *side*. **Listen carefully as I say the sounds in the first word part: /u/ /p/. Now blend the sounds:** *up*. **That is the first part of the word. Now listen to the sounds of the last part of the word: /s/ /ī/ /d/. Blend the sounds together into the word:** *side*. **When we put the parts together, the word is** *upside*. Repeat with these word parts:

/b/ /a/ /s/…/k/ /e/ /t/ (basket)   /h/ /a/ /p/…/p/ /ē/   (happy)

/t/ /e/ /n/…/n/ /i/ /s/ (tennis)

Final Phoneme Identity   Remind children that they have been listening to sounds in words. Now they should listen for the ending sound in words. Say: **I will say three words:** *pen, tan, win*. **Say the words with me. Which sound is the same?** (ending) **What is the sound?** (/n/) Have children identify the common final sound in the following groups of words:

pack, tock, click (/k/)   him, Sam, roam (/m/)

jig, fog, bag (/g/)   yet, bat, wet (/t/)

PRETEACH

Phonics

 Relate *Jj* to /j/   Say the words *jam* and *jack*, and have children repeat the words. Tell children that these words begin with the /j/ sound. Give each child a *Phoneme Phone* and encourage them to elongate the sound and look at their mouth position. Have children say /j/ several times.

Connect Letter and Sound   Display the *Sound/Spelling Card Jj*. Ask: **What is the name of this letter?** (*j*) **The letter *j* is at the beginning of the word** *joke*. **Say /j/.** Have children repeat the sound of the letter on the card several times.

Discriminate /j/   Give each child a *Word Builder Card j*. Say: **I'm going to say some words. If the word begins with /j/ hold up your card and say /j/. If the word does not begin with /j/, hold you card behind your back.** Say the words *jot, jail, hot, tree, jump,* and *jelly*.

258 Lesson 22

Day 3

RETEACH

High-Frequency Words

Distribute index cards with the words *they, at, the, where, and, want, a,* and *are* written on them. As you say each word, have children repeat the word and hold up the correct card. Show *Photo Card helicopter*. Ask children to say the picture name. Then use the word cards *they, are, at, the,* and *Photo Card helicopter* to build the first sentence frame shown below. Point to each word as you read the sentence. Ask children to read the sentence with you.

High-Frequency Words	
a	the
and	they
are	want
at	where

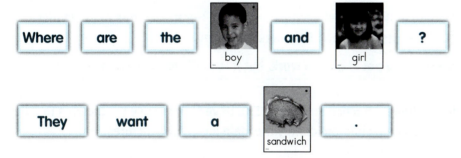

Then continue with the following sentences. Point to each word and have children read the sentences aloud.

Write the following sentence frame on the board: *They are at the ____ .* Have children copy and complete the sentence with a word or a picture.

Grade K 259

Day 3

RETEACH

Comprehension

  Main Idea Remind children that the main idea of a story is what the story is mostly about. Read the following story and talk about the main idea.

> **Jaela's New Puppy**
>
> On Jaela's birthday, she got the puppy she wanted for a long time. She was very nervous though. She wanted to give him the best care possible. Her mom took Jaela and the puppy to the veterinarian.
>
> "How do I take care of my puppy?" asked Jaela.
>
> "You must make sure your puppy is fed, clean, and gets plenty of exercise," said Dr. Oh.
>
> "I can do that!" Jaela felt much better about taking care of her new puppy.
>
> Now Jaela makes sure she feeds her puppy. Her mom helps her give him baths. They also take him for walks every day.
>
> "Caring for my pet is a lot of work, but it is fun!" Jaela exclaimed.

Guide children to *Practice Book* page 130. Have children use the pictures to tell a story. Then help children identify the main idea of the pictures.

RETEACH

Build Robust Vocabulary

Remind children of the Student-Friendly Explanations for *adore*, *melancholy*, and *exquisite*. Then discuss each word, using the following examples.

adore
If you *adore* chocolate, would you want to eat it or throw it away?

melancholy
If your friend is *melancholy*, what are some things you could do to help?

exquisite
If your mother bought an *exquisite* new necklace, would she protect it or let you play with it?

VOCABULARY
Student-Friendly Explanations

adore To adore someone or something means to love that person or thing a lot.

melancholy If you feel melancholy, you feel sad.

exquisite Something that is exquisite is very beautiful.

Day 3

RETEACH

Writing

Writing Trait: Conventions Remind children that quotation marks are used in dialogue, to show what people are saying. Point out an example of quotation marks around dialogue for children to see. Then write the following sentence on the board.

Read the sentence while tracking the print.

> "Caring for a pet is a lot of work, but it is fun!" exclaimed Jaela.

Ask: **Who is saying something?** (Jaela) **What is she saying?** (Caring for a pet is a lot of work, but it is fun.) **What type of punctuation is used around what she is saying?** (quotation marks) Ask a volunteer to circle the quotation marks. Point out that the quotation marks are used at the beginning and the end of what Jaela is saying. Write the following sentence on the board:

> "How do I take care of my puppy?" asked Jaela.

Ask a volunteer to circle the quotation marks around the dialogue. Discuss why quotation marks are used.

Grade K 261

LESSON 22

PHONEMIC AWARENESS
Phoneme Blending
Final Phoneme Categorization

PHONICS
Reteach Review /v/v, /j/j

READING
Review /v/v, /j/j
Review High-Frequency Words

BUILD ROBUST VOCABULARY
Review protecting, volunteer, responsible, adore, melancholy, exquisite

WRITING
Reteach Writing Form: Dialogue

Materials Needed:

Phoneme Phone | Sound/Spelling Cards Vv, Jj | Photo Cards

Practice Book

Phonemic Awareness

Phoneme Blending Remind children that they can blend individual sounds into words. Say: **Listen as I say these sounds: /j/ /a/ /m/. Now I'll blend the sounds into a word: jam.** Have children blend the following sounds into words: /v/ /a/ /n/ (van), /j/ /o/ /g/ (jog), /t/ /i/ /p/ (tip).

 Final Phoneme Categorization Remind children that words are made up of sounds. They have listened for sounds that are the same in each word. Now they should listen for the ending sound that is different in a group of words. Give each child a *Phoneme Phone* to help them. Say: **Listen as I say these three words: bat, hat, rim. Say the words with me. Which word has a different ending sound?** (rim) Have children repeat each word of the set into the *Phoneme Phone,* elongating the sounds and looking at their mouth position. Then have them name the word that has a different ending sound than the other two words:

big, sat, jog (sat)   win, Sam, him (win)   bet, men, cat (men)

RETEACH
Phonics

Connect Letters and Sounds Display *Sound/Spelling Card Vv.* Ask children what sound is at the beginning of the word *vine.* (/v/) Then have children tell you what letter stands for the /v/ sound. (v) Repeat with *Sound/Spelling Card Jj.*

Discriminate /v/ and /j/ Display *Photo Cards jacks* and *van.* Say the name of each item and have children repeat after you. Say: **What sound does jacks begin with?** (/j/) **What letter does /j/ stand for?** (j) Repeat with the *Photo Card van.*

Tell children that you are going to say some words. If the word begins with /v/ sound, then they should clap. If the word begins with the /j/ sound, then they should tap their feet. Say the following words: *joke, jelly, violin, vest, jump, vote, valentine, jar.*

Day 4

REVIEW
Reading

/v/v, /j/j Write the words *jet, Jan, Jed, van,* and *vet* on the board. Point to the words and have children read them.

Practice Book 131–132

High-Frequency Words Distribute a set of index cards for *are, they, out, who, we,* and *want* to each child. Organize children into pairs. Ask one partner to pick a card and read it. Then have the other partner find the matching card and read his or hers. Tell children to continue until they have read all of their words a few times through.

Have children turn to *Practice Book* pages 131–132. Help children cut and fold the book. Have children read the sentences to practice the skill.

High-Frequency Words

are	out
they	want
we	who

REVIEW
Robust Vocabulary

Remind children of the meanings of *protecting, volunteer, responsible, adore, melancholy,* and *exquisite.* Then determine children's understanding of the words by asking the following questions.

- If you are *protecting* your toys, what might you do?
- If you were going to *volunteer,* what would you like to do?
- What is something a *responsible* pet owner might do?
- Who is someone that you *adore*?
- When you are *melancholy,* what makes you feel better?
- Where could you find *exquisite* pieces of jewelry?

VOCABULARY
Student-Friendly Explanations

protecting When you are protecting something, you are keeping it safe.

volunteer If you are a volunteer, you do work without getting paid.

responsible Someone who is responsible for something is expected to take care of it.

adore To adore someone or something means to love that person or thing alot.

melancholy If you feel melancholy, you feel sad.

exquisite Something that is exquisite is very beautiful.

RETEACH
Writing

Writing Form: Dialogue Explain to children that dialogue is the words that a person or a character in a story is saying. Point out an example of dialogue in a familiar book or story.

Have children choose a favorite character from the story you chose. Tell children that together you will write an example of dialogue together. Ask them to suggest something the character might say. Record their ideas on chart paper. Then use children's ideas to write a sentence of dialogue. Invite them to add quotation marks and to write letters and words they know. Read the finished dialogue to the children.

> "I am not going back!" said Goldilocks.

Grade K 263

LESSON 22

DAY AT A GLANCE
Day 5

PHONEMIC AWARENESS
Phoneme Segmentation

PHONICS
Preteach Word Blending

HIGH-FREQUENCY WORDS
Preteach *she, like, one, up, you*

BUILD ROBUST VOCABULARY
Preteach *appreciate, grace, host*

Materials Needed:

Write-On/Wipe-Off Boards

Word Builder and Word Builder Cards

Practice Book

Photo Cards

Phonemic Awareness

Phoneme Segmentation Remind children that they have been blending sounds together to say a word. Now they will listen to a word and break it into its individual sounds. Give each child a *Write-On/Wipe-Off Board* and some markers. Have children find the side with the heart in the corner and three boxes. Say: **Listen as I say this word: *ham*. I will place a marker in a box for each sound. The sounds are /h/ /a/ /m/. There are three sounds. I have filled in three markers on my board.**

Have children place a marker in each box for the individual sounds in these words: *bit*, *up*, and *met*.

PRETEACH
Phonics

Sounds in a Word Tell children that you will blend sounds to say words. Say the following verse, and have children repeat after you. Say: **We're going on a Word Hunt. What's this word? /l/ /e/ /g/?** Together: *leg!* Continue with the words *red, bed,* and *get*. Then review the sounds you blended to make each word.

Teach/Model Display *Word Builder Cards m, e,* and *n*. Point to *m*. Ask: **What letter is this?** (m) **The letter *m* stands for the sound /mm/. What does *m* stand for?** (/mm/) Tell children that *m* can stand for the sound /m/, the sound at the beginning of *monkey*. Continue by reviewing the letters *e* and *n*.

Word Blending Place the *Word Builder Cards t, e, n* in the *Word Builder*. Point to *t* and say /t/. Have children name the letter and sound. Point to *e*. Say /eee/. Have children name the letter and sound. Slide the *e* next to *t*. Move your hand under the letters and blend the sounds: /teee/. Ask children to repeat after you. Point to *n*. Say /nn/. Slide the *n* next to *te*. Move your hand under the letters and blend the sounds /teenn/. Have children repeat after you. Then have children blend and read the word *ten* with you. Continue with the words *pen, pet, met,* and *net*.

 Have children turn to *Practice Book* page 133. Help children identify the pictures, trace the letter *e* in each word, and blend sounds to read the words.

Day 5

PRETEACH
High-Frequency Words

High-Frequency Words

like	one
she	up
you	

Tell children that they are going to be learning a new word. Write the high-frequency word *she* on the board. Point to and read the word. Then say the word in a sentence: **She is here.** Write the word on an index card. Match the index card to the board and have children say it again with you.

Then write the previously-learned high-frequency words *like*, *one*, *up*, and *you* on index cards. Say each word and have children repeat that word. Show the *Photo Card ring*. Then use the high-frequency word cards, the *Photo Card*, a card with the word *has*, and a period card to build the sentence frame shown below. Point to each word as you read the sentence. Then have children read the sentence with you.

| She | has | one | ring | . |

Replace *Photo Card ring* with *Photo Card pencil*. Point to each word as you read the sentence. Track each word again as children read the sentence aloud. Repeat with other *Photo Card* combinations.

PRETEACH
Build Robust Vocabulary

Tell children that they are going to be learning three new words. Go over the Student-Friendly Explanations of *appreciate*, *grace*, and *host*. Then discuss each word, using the following examples.

appreciate
I *appreciate* it if someone helps me clean the classroom. What kind of help do you appreciate?

grace
Who is more likely to move with *grace*, a ballerina or a robot? Tell why.

host
Would a *host* of a party be more likely to send the invitations or bring a present? Why?

VOCABULARY
Student-Friendly Explanations

appreciate When you appreciate something, you understand how good and special it is.

grace If you move with grace, your movements are smooth and lovely to watch.

host If you host a party or meeting, you run it.

Grade K

LESSON 23

PHONEMIC AWARENESS
Phoneme Segmentation

PHONICS
Preteach Word Building

HIGH-FREQUENCY WORDS
Reteach *she*, *he*

COMPREHENSION
Reteach Main Idea

BUILD ROBUST VOCABULARY
Reteach *appreciate*, *grace*, *host*

Materials Needed:

Practice Book   Copying Master   Write-On/Wipe-Off Boards

Word Builder and Word Builder Cards

Phonemic Awareness

Phoneme Segmentation Remind children that they can divide a word into individual sounds. Say: **Listen as I say this word: *leg*. I hear these sounds: /l/ /e/ /g/. There are three sounds in the word *leg*.**

Then say: *pet*. Ask: **How many sounds do you hear in *pet*?** (3) **What are the sounds?** (/p/ /e/ /t/)

PRETEACH

Phonics

Sounds in a Word Have children listen as you sing the following song to the tune of "Old MacDonald." Encourage them to echo each line after you.

What is a word for these three sounds? /d/ /e/ /n/ Den!

With a den, den here, and a den, den there.

Here a den, there a den, everywhere a den, den.

What is the word for these three sounds? /d/ /e/ /n/ Den!

Repeat using the words /h/ /e/ /n/ (hen), /s/ /e/ /t/ (set), and /w/ /e/ /t/ (wet).

Word Building Distribute *Word Builder* and *Word Builder Cards* *a, b, d, e, g, l, n, s,* and *t*. Review each letter name and sound. Explain to children that you will show them how a word changes when the letters in the word change. Say: **I will use the letters *b*, *e*, and *g* to make the word *beg*. Now you do the same. Blend the sounds with me: /b/-/e/-/g/, *beg*. If I take away the *e* and put *a* in its place, I have the word *bag*. Now you try it. Blend the sounds and say the word with me: /b/-/a/-/g/, *bag*.**

Build Words Have children continue with *bag* in their *Word Builder*.

Change *b* to *s*. What word did you make? (*sag*)

Change *g* to *d*. What word did you make? (*sad*)

 Guided Practice Continue with the words *sat*, *set*, and *net*. Have children practice writing the words they built on their *Write-on/Wipe-off Boards*. Distribute *Copying Master 45*. Have children trace the letters and cut them apart. Have children identify the pictures and paste *e* or *o* in the box to complete each picture name. (Paste *o* for *fox, top*; paste *e* for *jet, pet*.)

266 Lesson 23

Day 1

RETEACH
High-Frequency Words

Make index cards for the high-frequency words *she* and *he*. Say each word and have children repeat them. Then use the high-frequency word cards, an *is* word card, and a period card to build the sentence frames shown below. Point to each word as you read the sentence. Fill in the blank with a child's name. Continue by having children read the sentences and fill in other children's names.

| She | is | Tanna | . |

| He | is | | . |

High-Frequency Words
- he
- she

RETEACH
Comprehension

Main Idea Remind children that the main idea is what the story is mostly about. Tell children that often the title of the story gives a clue to the main idea. Then read this story aloud to them.

Alligators and Crocodiles

Do you know the difference between an alligator and a crocodile? Here are a few tips to help you figure out who is who. When an alligator's mouth is closed, you won't see any teeth. However, you can see the bottom jaw of the crocodile all the time. Alligators also have a wide, broad snout while crocodiles have a long, thin snout. One other tip is to look at their color. An alligator has a grayish black color. Crocodiles have a light tan color. Now you will have lots of information to tell these two similar animals apart!

Discuss the main idea of this story. Then guide children to turn to page 134 in their *Practice Books*. Have children look at the pictures and determine the main idea, or what the pictures are mostly about.

RETEACH
Build Robust Vocabulary

Go over the Student Friendly Explanations for *appreciate*, *grace*, and *host*. Then discuss each word, using the following examples.

appreciate and **host**
How will you tell a *host* that you *appreciate* all that he or she does?

grace
Would you say that a deer moves with *grace*? What about a frog? Explain.

VOCABULARY
Student-Friendly Explanations

appreciate When you appreciate something, you understand how good and special it is.

grace If you move with grace, your movements are smooth and lovely to watch.

host If you host a party or meeting, you run it.

Grade K 267

LESSON 23

PHONEMIC AWARENESS
Phoneme Segmentation

PHONICS
Reteach Word Building

HIGH-FREQUENCY WORDS
Preteach *good, she, come, down, they, want*

COMPREHENSION
Reteach Answer Questions

BUILD ROBUST VOCABULARY
Preteach *lush, marvelous, constantly*

Materials Needed:

Word Builder and Word Builder Cards | Write-On/Wipe-Off Boards | Copying Master

Practice Book

Phonemic Awareness

Phoneme Segmentation Remind children that they have been breaking words into their individual sounds. Model again how to break a word into its sounds. Say: **Listen as I say the following word: *beg*. I can hear the sounds /b/ /e/ /g/.**

Have children practice by breaking the following words into their individual sounds: *jet, bell, peg.*

RETEACH

Phonics

Discriminate Sounds Ask children to listen to these two words and tell how they are different. Say: **What is the beginning sound of *red*? (/r/) What is the beginning sound of *wed*? (/w/) How are the words *red* and *wed* different?** (They begin with different sounds; *Red* begins with /r/ and *wed* begins with /w/.) Then ask children to tell how *bed* and *led* are different.

Model Word Building Distribute *Word Builders* and *Word Builder Cards e, g, h, i, j, m, n, p,* and *t*. Remind children that when the letters in words change, so do the sounds. Have children following aloud as you model word building. Say: **Use your *Word Builder* and *Word Builder Cards* to make new words with me. I will use the letters *p*, *e*, and *n* to make the word *pen*. Now you do the same. Blend the sounds with me: /p/-/e/-/n/, *pen*. If I take away the *p* and put *t* in its place, I have the word *ten*. Now you try it. Blend the sounds and say the word with me: /t/-/e/-/n/, *ten*.**

Build Words Have children continue with *ten* in their *Word Builder*. Say:

Change the *e* to *i*. What word did you make? (tin)

Change the *n* to *p*. What word did you make? (tip)

  Guided Practice Continue with the words *hip, hem,* and *gem*. Then have children practice writing the words they built on their *Write-On/Wipe-Off Boards*. Distribute *Copying Master 46* to review building words with short *e* with children. Help children name each picture and read the word choices below each picture. Then children circle the word that names the picture. (Children should circle: *men, pen, hen,* and *ten.*)

268 Lesson 23

Day 2

PRETEACH
High-Frequency Words

Write the word *good* on the board. Point to the word and read it. Have children read the word with you. Say: **That is good.** Hold up an index card with the word *good* on it as you say the sentence. Repeat the word several times having children repeat it with you.

Write the words *come, down, she, they,* and *want* on index cards. Have children sit in a circle. Give each child one word card. Have them pass their cards around the circle until you tell them to stop. Ask: **Who has the word *good*?** The child with the word *good* shoud stand and read the word. Repeat with the rest of the words.

Have children turn to *Practice Book* page 135 to review high-frequency words and practice newly-learned words. Complete the page together.

High-Frequency Words

come	she
down	they
good	want

RETEACH
Comprehension

Answer Questions Remind children that asking and answering questions when they read will help them understand and enjoy what they read. Recall the story about the differences between alligators and crocodiles from Day 1. Reread the story and pause to ask and answer questions. Write the questions and their answers on the chart under the correct heading.

Questions	Answer
What shape snout does an alligator have?	Alligators have a wide, broad snout.

Guide children to listen for answers to those questions as you continue reading, and record them in the chart.

PRETEACH
Build Robust Vocabulary

Review Student-Friendly Explanations of *lush, marvelous,* and *constantly*. Then discuss each word, using the following examples.

lush
What would you see in a *lush* garden—growing vegetables or dead plants?

marvelous
If you had a *marvelous* time at a party, what might have happened there?

constantly
Justin *constantly* takes pictures. What do you like to do constantly?

VOCABULARY
Student-Friendly Explanations

lush A place that is lush is full of growing plants.

marvelous Something marvelous is terrific or wonderful.

constantly If you do something constantly, you do it all the time.

Grade K 269

LESSON 23

PHONEMIC AWARENESS
Phoneme Segmentation
Phoneme Identity Medial

PHONICS
Preteach Phonogram -et

HIGH-FREQUENCY WORDS
Reteach she, good, the, is, a

COMPREHENSION
Reteach Main Idea

BUILD ROBUST VOCABULARY
Reteach lush, marvelous, constantly

WRITING
Reteach Writing Trait: Ideas

Materials Needed:

Write-On/ Wipe-Off Boards   Photo Cards   Practice Book

Phonemic Awareness

Phoneme Segmentation Review with children that they have been breaking words into their individual sounds. Then model again how to break words into individual sounds. Say: **Listen carefully to the following word: hen. Now I will break the word into individual sounds: /h/ /e/ /n/. Now listen again as I say another word and break it into sounds: sun, /s/ /u/ /n/.** Have children break the following words into sounds: well (/w/ /e/ /l/), wet (/w/ /e/ /t/), gem (/j/ /e/ /m/), and get (/g/ /e/ /t/).

Phoneme Identity: Medial Tell children that they are now going to listen for the sound that is the same in a group of words. Say: **I will say three words: top, hot, log. Say the words with me. Which sound is the same?** (middle) **What is the sound?** (/o/) Say each of the following word pairs, elongating the middle sound and having children identify the common medial sound:

pet, well (/e/)   bin, pig (/i/)   cat, had (/a/)

Continue with these groups of words:

tan, hat, bag (/a/)   win, wig, tip (/i/)   red, bet, men (/e/)

PRETEACH

Phonics

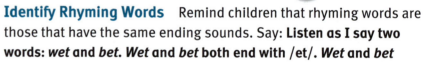

Identify Rhyming Words Remind children that rhyming words are those that have the same ending sounds. Say: **Listen as I say two words: wet and bet. Wet and bet both end with /et/. Wet and bet rhyme.** Continue with these word pairs, having children determine if the words have the same ending sounds: hen/hat; well/bell; nap/tap; set/jet; tick/tock.

Produce Rhymes Tell children that they are now going to think of words that rhyme. Say: **I want to think of a word that rhymes with set so I have to think of other words that end with /et/. Wet ends with /et/.** Continue by having children think of other words that rhyme with set and wet.

Phonogram -et Write the word *jet* on the board. Track the print as you read the word. Have children repeat after you. Then do the same with the word *met*. Ask how the two words are the same. (They both have /et/; they rhyme) Say: **The words jet and met are in the -et word family because they both end in -et.** Continue with the words *set*, *wet*, and *let*.

Distribute *Write-On/Wipe-Off Boards*. Write these words on the board: *get*, *bet*, *leg*, *ran*, *vet*. Have children read the words and copy those words in the -et word family on their boards.

270 Lesson 23

Day 3

RETEACH

High-Frequency Words

High-Frequency Words	
a	she
good	the
is	

Write the following high-frequency words on index cards: *she, is, a, good, the,* and the word *has*. Place them on the chalk ledge. As you say each word, have a volunteer point to the correct card. Then show *Photo Card cat*. Ask children to say the picture name. Then use the word cards *She, is, a, good, Photo Card cat*, and a period card, to build the first sentence frame shown below. Point to each word as you read the sentence. Ask children to read the sentence with you.

| She | is | a | good | [cat] | . |

Then continue with the following sentences. Point to each word and have children read the sentences aloud.

| The | [sandwich] | is | good | . |

| She | has | a | [hammer] | . |

Write the following sentence frame on the board: *She is a good ___.* Have children copy and complete the sentence frame with a word or a picture.

Grade K 271

Day 3

RETEACH
Comprehension

Main Idea Remind children that the main idea of a story is what the story is mostly about. Have children listen for the main idea as you read aloud the following story.

Practice Book 136

> **Making Lemonade**
>
> Lemonade is a drink that is easy and fun to make! First you need to get all of the ingredients: two lemons, sugar, and water. Ask an adult to help you cut the lemons in half. Then you need to squeeze them as hard as you can to get all the juice into your glass. Then add water to your cup. Fill your glass almost full with water. Last you add the sugar. Start with two teaspoons. Stir the lemon juice, water, and sugar together and taste. Does it need more lemon juice? Does it need more sugar? If so, add what you need. Then drink and enjoy!

Guide children to *Practice Book* page 136. Have children use the pictures to tell a story. Then help children determine the main idea based on the pictures.

RETEACH
Build Robust Vocabulary

Review the Student-Friendly Explanations for *lush*, *marvelous*, and *constantly*. Then discuss each word, using the following examples.

lush and **constantly**
Are gardeners that have *lush* gardens *constantly* taking care of them or leaving them alone? Why?

marvelous
What type of activities should you have at a party if you want it to be *marvelous?*

VOCABULARY
Student-Friendly Explanations

lush   A place that is lush is full of healthy, growing plants.

marvelous   Something marvelous is terrific or wonderful.

constantly   If you do something constantly, you do it all the time.

272 Lesson 23

RETEACH

Writing

Writing Trait: Ideas Remind children that it is a good idea to think of ideas about a topic before you begin to write a story. Ask children to think about the story about making lemonade that they read earlier. Ask: **The writer wrote or drew pictures of all of the steps to make lemonade before he or she wrote that story. What kinds of ideas do you think the writer had?** Record on chart paper what the writer's ideas may have been for the lemonade story. Guide children to offer ideas for phrases or pictures. Record these ideas in the form of a word web, with Making Lemonade as your center circle.

Then say: **Let's think of some ideas for our own story about making a sandwich. We can do just what the writer of the lemonade story did—we can draw and write ideas.**

On chart paper, begin a list of the ideas that children have for making a sandwich. Record children's ideas, inviting them to add letters or words they know. Encourage volunteers to draw pictures to illustrate each idea.

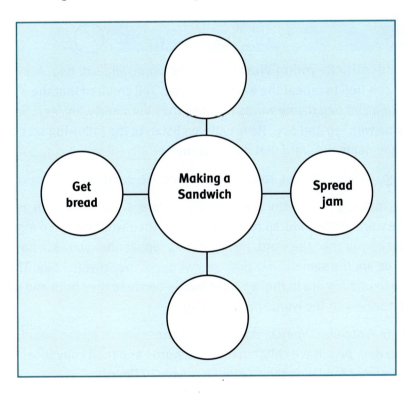

LESSON 23

PHONEMIC AWARENESS
Phoneme Segmentation
Phoneme Identity Medial

PHONICS
Preteach Phonogram *-eg*

READING
Review Phonogram *-eg*
Review High-Frequency Words

BUILD ROBUST VOCABULARY
Review appreciate, grace, host, lush, marvelous, constantly

WRITING
Reteach Writing Form: Story

Materials Needed:

Phoneme Phone   Write-On/Wipe-Off Boards   Practice Book

Phonemic Awareness

Phoneme Segmentation Remind children that they can break a word into its individual sounds. Say: **Listen as I say this word: *peg*. Now I'll break the word into its sounds: /p/ /e/ /g/.** Have children blend the following words into sounds: *leg* (/l/ /e/ /g/), *Meg* (/m/ /e/ /g/), *tell* (/t/ /e/ /l/).

Phoneme Identity: Medial Tell children that they can listen for the sound that is the same in a group of words. Give each child a *Phoneme Phone* to help them. Say: **Listen as I say these three words: *peg, leg, beg*. Say the words with me. Which sound is the same in all three words?** (the middle sound) **What sound is it?** (/e/) Have children repeat each word of the set elongating the sounds and looking at their mouth position. Then have children identify the medial sound of all the words in each group:

pack, sat, mad (/a/)   *win, tick, him* (/i/)   *bet, leg, well* (/e/)

RETEACH
Phonics

Identify Rhyming Words Say the words *leg, sat, beg*. Ask children to repeat the words after you. Tell children that the words *leg* and *beg* rhyme words because they both end with /eg/. *Sat* does not rhyme with *leg* and *beg*. Have children listen to the following sets of words and name the word that does not rhyme:

peg, Meg, wed (wed)   *cot, rod, lot* (rod)   *lick, let, bet* (lick)

Phonogram *-eg* Write the word *beg* on the board. Track the print as you read the word. Have children repeat after you. Then write the word *leg*. Track the print as you read the word. Have children repeat after you. Ask how the two words are the same. (They both end with *-eg*; they rhyme.) Say: **The words *beg* and *leg* are in the *-eg* word family because they both end with *-eg*.** Continue with the words *peg* and *Meg*.

Distribute *Write-On/Wipe-Off Boards*. Write these words on the board: *bet, beg, leg, dog, peg*. Have children read the words and then copy those words in the *-eg* word family on their *Write-On/Wipe-Off Boards*.

Day 4

REVIEW

Reading

 Phonogram -eg Write the words *peg* and *beg* on the board. Model blending the sounds of each word. Have children blend the sounds and read each word as you point to it.

Practice Book 137–138

High-Frequency Words Write the high-frequency words *she* and *good* on the board. Say: **Listen as I say a sentence with one of these words: *She is* [name of child].** Ask a volunteer to point to the high-frequency word you used in the sentence. Continue with a variety of sentences using *she* and *good*. Ask children to identify which word you used.

Have children turn to *Practice Book* pages 137–138. Have children read the story to practice the skills. Have children take it home to read with their families.

REVIEW

Robust Vocabulary

Tell children that they have been learning some interesting words this week. Remind children of the Student-Friendly Explanations of *appreciate, grace, host, lush, marvelous,* and *constantly.* Then determine children's understanding of the words by asking the following questions.

- If you *appreciate* a gift you just received, what should you do?
- Show how to move with *grace.*
- Is a *marvelous* party *host* likely to sit or walk around? Why?
- A rainforest is a *lush* place. Why?
- What does your mother or father *constantly* remind you to do?

RETEACH

Writing

Writing Form: Story Remind children that there are many types of stories. Every story needs a beginning, middle, and ending.

Tell children that they will write a story together about a character trying to make something. First decide on a character's name. Then talk with children about ideas to include in their story. Remind children that the story needs to be in a logical sequence. Use children's ideas to write the story. Invite them to write letters or words they know. Write a title and read the finished story to children.

Frank Makes Cookies

Frank loves cookies. He wanted to make his own cookies. He asked his mom for help. She showed him how to make chocolate-chip cookies. When Frank and his mom were done, he shared them with his friends. They were good!

High-Frequency Words

good

she

VOCABULARY

Student-Friendly Explanations

appreciate When you appreciate something, you understand how good and special it is.

grace If you move with grace, your movements are smooth and lovely to watch.

host If you host a party or meeting, you run it.

lush A place that is lush is full of healthy, growing plants.

marvelous Something marvelous is terrific or wonderful.

constantly If you do something constantly, you do it all the time.

Grade K 275

LESSON 23

DAY AT A GLANCE — Day 5

PHONEMIC AWARENESS
Phoneme Segmentation

PHONICS
Preteach Consonant *Yy*

HIGH-FREQUENCY WORDS
Reteach *are, they*
Review *the*

BUILD ROBUST VOCABULARY
Reteach *adore, appreciate, protecting*

Materials Needed:

Write-On/Wipe-Off Boards   Sound/Spelling Card *Yy*

Practice Book   Photo Cards

Phonemic Awareness

Phoneme Segmentation Remind children that they can break a word into its individual sounds. Give each child a *Write-On/Wipe-Off Board* and some markers. Have children find the side with the heart in the corner. There should be three boxes. Say: **Listen as I say this word: win. I will place a marker in a box for each sound. The sounds are /w/ /i/ /n/. There are three sounds. I have filled in three markers on my board.** Have children place a marker in each box for the individual sounds in these words: *fin*, *pan*, and *dock*.

PRETEACH

Phonics

Sing "The Alphabet Song" Sing "The Alphabet Song" to children. Then sing the song again, inviting children to raise their hands when they hear letters that they have learned about recently, such as *Ww*, *Vv*, or *Jj*.

Consonant *Yy* Hold up *Sound/Spelling Card Yy*. Explain that this is the consonant letter *Yy*. Say: **This is the letter Y. Say the name with me.** Point to the uppercase *Y*. Say: **This is the uppercase Y.** Then point to the lowercase *y*. Say: **This is the lowercase y.**

Writing *Y* and *y* Write *Y* and *y* on the board and have children identify the letters. Say: **Watch as I write the letter Y so that everyone can read it.** As you give the Letter Talk, trace the uppercase *Y*. Do the same for the lowercase *y*.

Letter Talk for *Y*	Letter Talk for *y*
1. Slant right down. 2. Slant left down. 3. Straight line down. 	1. Slant right down. 2. Slant left down below the other line.

Guided Practice Have children finger-write the uppercase *Y* in the air as you repeat the Letter Talk. Have them do the same for lowercase *y*. Then have children turn to *Practice Book* page 139. Help children identify and write the letter *Yy*.

Day 5

RETEACH

High-Frequency Words

 Tell children that they are going to be reading sentences with some high-frequency words. Write the high-frequency words *are* and *they* on the board. Point to and read the words. Have children say them again with you.

Then write the previously-learned high-frequency word *the* on an index card. Say each word and have chidren repeat that word. Show the *Photo Card house*. Then use the high-frequency word cards, the *Photo Card*, a card with the word *in*, and a question mark card to build the sentence frame shown below. Point to each word as you read the sentence. Then have children read the sentence with you.

| Are | they | in | the | house | ? |

Replace *Photo Card house* with *Photo Card helicopter*. Point to each word as you read the sentence. Track each word again as children read the sentence aloud. Repeat with other *Photo Card* combinations.

RETEACH

Build Robust Vocabulary

Review the Student-Friendly Explanations of *adore*, *appreciate*, and *protecting*. Then discuss each word, using the following examples.

adore
I *adore* a teddy bear that my mother gave me when I was young. What do you adore?

appreciate
I *appreciate* police officers who keep us safe. Which community helper do you appreciate?

protecting
I am *protecting* my puppy from other big dogs in the neighborhood. Who or what do you protect?

High-Frequency Words

| are | they |
| the | |

VOCABULARY
Student-Friendly Explanations

adore To adore someone or something means to love that person or thing a lot.

appreciate When you appreciate something, you understand how good and special it is.

protecting When you are protecting something, you are keeping it safe.

Grade K 277

LESSON 24

DAY 1

PHONEMIC AWARENESS
Phoneme Segmentation

PHONICS
Preteach Relate *Yy* to /y/

HIGH-FREQUENCY WORDS
Reteach are, they
Review my, the

COMPREHENSION
Reteach Characters

BUILD ROBUST VOCABULARY
Reteach volunteer, host, grace

Materials Needed:

Write-On/ Wipe-Off Boards | Sound/Spelling Card *Yy* | Word Builder and Word Builder Cards

Copying Master | Photo Cards | Practice Book

Phonemic Awareness

Phoneme Segmentation Remind children that they can break a word into individual sounds. Provide *Write-On/Wipe-Off Boards* for each child. Make sure that children are using the side of the board with the heart in the corner. Then say: **Listen as I say this word: *leg*. I hear these sounds: /l/ /e/ /g/. There are three sounds in the word *leg*. Let's put a marker in each box for all three sounds.**

Then say another word: *pet*. Ask: **How many sounds do you hear in *pet*?** (3) **Put a marker in the boxes for each sound you hear. What are the sounds?** (/p/ /e/ /t/)

Continue by asking children to put a marker in each box for the sounds in the following words: *jack*, *sun*, and *big*.

PRETEACH

Phonics

Start with the Sound Say the words *yarn* and *yogurt* and have children repeat the words. Tell children that these words begin with the /y/ sound. Have children say /y/ several times.

 Connect Letter and Sound Display the *Sound/Spelling Card Yy*. Ask: **What is the name of this letter?** (*y*) **The letter *y* starts at the beginning of the word *yam*. Say /y/.** Have children repeat the sound of the letter on the card several times.

 Discriminate /y/ Give each child a *Word Builder Card y*. Say: **I'm going to say some words. If the word begins with /y/ hold up your card and say /y/. If the word does not begin with /y/, hold your card behind your back.** Say the words: *yell*, *jump*, *yawn*, *yellow*, *yes*, *wad*, and *yesterday*.

 Guided Practice Distribute *Copying Master 47*. Have children trace each letter. Then have them circle the letter that stands for the beginning sound of each picture. (Children circle letter *y* in each box: *yo-yo*, *yarn*; children circle letter *j* in each box: *jet*; children circle letter *w* in each box: *web*, *wet*.)

278 Lesson 24

RETEACH

High-Frequency Words

Make index cards for the high-frequency words *are, they, my,* and *the*. Say each word and have children repeat. Then use the high-frequency word cards, a card with the word *in*, and a period card to build the sentence frame *They are in the _____*. Complete the sentence frame with *Photo Card igloo*. Point to each word as you read the sentence. Continue by having children to read the sentences and fill in other *Photo Card* combinations. Vary the activity by changing the sentence frame to *They are in my _____*.

High-Frequency Words	
are	the
my	they

RETEACH

Comprehension

Characters Remind children that the people or the animals in a story are called the characters. Then read this story aloud to them.

> It was the first day of ballet class and Mackenzie was nervous. She was wearing her new pink leotard and tights that she absolutely loved, but she could not help feeling shy. She stood quietly by the wall as she waited for class to begin.
>
> "Hi, I'm Sheena. Are you new?" said a girl beside her.
>
> "Yes," Mackenzie said quietly.
>
> "You can stand by me if you want. This is only my second class, so I'm pretty new too."
>
> Mackenzie took a place beside her new friend. She knew everything was going to be okay.

Talk about the characters in this story. Then guide children to turn to *Practice Book* page 140. Have children look at the pictures and identify the characters.

RETEACH

Build Robust Vocabulary

Remind children of the Student-Friendly Explanations of *volunteer, host,* and *grace*. Then discuss each word, using the following examples.

volunteer and **host**
If you *volunteer* to *host* a party, what type of party would you like to plan?

grace
A gymnast is an athlete that can move with *grace*. Name another type of athlete that can move with grace.

VOCABULARY

Student-Friendly Explanations

volunteer If you volunteer, you offer to help do work without getting paid.

host If you host a party or meeting, you run it.

grace If you move with grace, your movements are smooth and lovely to watch.

Grade K **279**

LESSON 24

PHONEMIC AWARENESS
Phoneme Segmentation

PHONICS
Preteach Consonant *Zz*

HIGH-FREQUENCY WORDS
Reteach *she, good*
Review *are, they, out, who*

COMPREHENSION
Reteach Monitor Comprehension: Make Inferences

BUILD ROBUST VOCABULARY
Reteach *responsible, constantly, melancholy*

Materials Needed:

Sound/Spelling Card *Zz*

Copying Master

Practice Book

Phonemic Awareness

Phoneme Segmentation Remind children that they have been breaking words into their individual sounds. Model again how to break a word into its sounds. Say: **Listen as I say the following word:** *hot*. **I can hear the sounds /h/ /o/ /t/.**

Have children practice by breaking the following words into their individual sounds: *mess, sod,* and *tuck.*

PRETEACH

Phonics

Sing "The Alphabet Song" Sing "The Alphabet Song" to children. Then sing the song again, inviting children to stand up when they hear letters that they have recently learned, such as *Yy, Xx,* or *Jj.*

 Consonant *Zz* Hold up the *Sound/Spelling Card Zz*. Explain that this is the consonant *Zz*. Say: **This is the letter *Zz*. Say the name with me.** Point to the uppercase *Z*. **This is the uppercase *Z*.** Then point to the lowercase *z*. Say: **This is the lowercase *z*.**

Writing *Z* and *z* Write *Z* and *z* on the board and have children identify the letters. Say: **Watch as I write the letter *Z* so that everyone can read it.** As you give the Letter Talk, trace the uppercase *Z*. Do the same for the lowercase *z*.

Letter Talk for *Z*	Letter Talk for *z*
1. Straight line across.	1. Straight line across.
2. Slant left and down.	2. Slant left and down.
3. Straight line across.	3. Straight line across.
Z	z

 Guided Practice Have children finger-write the uppercase *Z* in the air as you repeat the Letter Talk. Have them do the same for the lowercase *z*. Then help children with *Copying Master 48*. Have children circle each uppercase *Z* and underline each lowercase *z*. Then have them trace each letter and practice writing it on the line.

Day 2

RETEACH
High-Frequency Words

Practice Book 141 Review with children the high-frequency words *she* and *good*. Write them on the board. Point to each word and have children read it.

Write the words *she, good, are, they, out,* and *who* on index cards. Use these cards to play a game. Have children sit in a circle. Give each child one word card. At your signal, have them pass their cards around the circle until you tell them to stop. Ask: **Who has the word *she*?** The child with the word *she* should stand and read the word. Repeat with the rest of the words.

Have children turn to *Practice Book* page 141 to review high-frequency words and practice newly-learned words. Complete the page together.

High-Frequency Words

are	she
good	they
out	who

RETEACH
Comprehension

Monitor Comprehension: Make Inferences Remind children that sometimes authors will give clues to help readers understand characters or events in a story. Recall the story about Mackenzie and her ballet class from Day 1. Reread the story and pause to make inferences. Fill in the graphic organizer with information that the reader already knows, story clues, and then the inference.

What I Know +	Story Clues =	Inferences
Doing something with a friend makes it more fun.	Mackenzie met another girl in the class.	Mackenzie would not be shy anymore because she met a friend.

RETEACH
Build Robust Vocabulary

Remind children of the Student-Friendly Explanations of *responsible, constantly,* and *melancholy*. Then discuss each word, using the following examples.

responsible and **constantly**
If you were *responsible* for watching your puppy, would you watch him *constantly* or let him run away? Why?

melancholy
My friend was *melancholy* because she missed the school bus. When have you ever felt melancholy?

VOCABULARY
Student-Friendly Explanations

responsible Someone who is responsible for something is given the job of taking care of it.

constantly If you do something constantly, you do it all the time.

melancholy If you are melancholy, you are thinking about something that makes you sad.

Grade K 281

LESSON 24

PHONEMIC AWARENESS
Phoneme Segmentation
Phoneme Categorization: Medial

PHONICS
Preteach Relate Zz to /z/

HIGH-FREQUENCY WORDS
Reteach are, they, she, good
Review a, the, want

COMPREHENSION
Reteach Characters

BUILD ROBUST VOCABULARY
Reteach marvelous, exquisite, lush

WRITING
Reteach Writing Trait: Sentence Fluency

Materials Needed:

Phoneme Phone   Sound/Spelling Card Zz   Word Builders/ Word Builder Cards

Photo Cards   Practice Book

Phonemic Awareness

Phoneme Segmentation Review with children that they have been breaking words into their individual sounds. Then model again how to break words into individual sounds. Say: **Listen carefully to the following word: *cup*. I hear three sounds in the word *cup*, /c/ /u/ /p/.**

Give each child a *Phoneme Phone*. Model using the *Phoneme Phone* to look at your mouth as you elongate the word *cup*. Then, have children tell how many sounds they hear in the following words. Ask them to use the *Phoneme Phone* as they repeat the words after you and tell you the sounds they hear: *at* (2; /a/ /t/), *in* (2; /i/ /n/), *fed* (3; /f/ /e/ /d/), and *let* (3; /l/ /e/ /t/).

Phoneme Categorization: Medial Tell children that they are now going to listen to a set of words for the sound that is different. Say: **I will say three words: *cap, fan, mop*. *Cap* and *fan* have the same sound in the middle, /a/. *Mop* has a different sound in the middle, /o/. *Mop* has the different sound.** Have children identify the word with the different medial sound in the word sets below:

cut, nut, leg (*leg*)   bat, him, pig (*bat*)

dog, run, pot (*run*)   yet, pen, hot (*hot*)

Day 3

PRETEACH

Phonics

Relate Zz to /z/ Say the words *zebra* and *zoo* and have children repeat the words. Tell children that these words begin with the /z/ sound. Give each child a *Phoneme Phone*. Have them say the /z/ sound several times. Tell children to elongate the sound and look at their mouth position as they say /z/.

Connect Letter to Sound Display the *Sound/Spelling Card Zz*. Ask: **What is the name of this letter?** (z) **The letter z starts at the beginning of the word zipper. Say /z/.** Have children repeat the sound of the letter on the card several times.

Discriminate /z/ Give each child a *Word Builder Card z*. Say: **I'm going to say some words. If the word begins with /z/ hold up your card and say /z/. If the word does not begin with /z/, hold your card behind your back.** Say the words *zip, water, zebra, zoo, joke,* and *zag.*

RETEACH

High-Frequency Words

Write the following high-frequency words on index cards: *are, they, she, good, want,* and the word *is*. Place them on the chalk ledge. As you say each word, have a volunteer point to the correct card. Then show *Photo Card watermelon*. Ask children to say the picture name. Then use the words cards *They, want, a, good,* and *Photo Card watermelon,* and a period card to build the first sentence frame shown below. Point to each word as you read the sentence. Ask children to read the sentence with you.

Then continue with *Photo Cards dog, cat,* and *sandwich*. Point to each word and have children read the sentences aloud.

Write the following sentence frame on the board: *They want a good _____.* Have children copy and complete the sentence frame with a word or a picture.

High-Frequency Words	
a	the
are	they
good	want
she	

Grade K 283

Day 3

RETEACH
Comprehension

Characters Remind children that the people or animals that a story is about are called the characters. Have children listen for the names of the characters as you read aloud the following story.

> "Bam, bam, boom!" Dylan Dog was busy in his room making something. He wanted it to be a secret, so he closed his door while he worked. Amy Alligator soon came along.
>
> "Dylan, come out and play," she yelled from outside. All she could hear was "bam, bam, boom." Dylan was still working hard. He didn't even look up.
>
> Evan the Iguana came next. "Dylan, we need you for our game," he shouted. Evan could only hear "bam, bam, boom" too. Dylan really wanted to finish.
>
> Last, Regina Raccoon knocked lightly on his door. Dylan was now finished. He opened the door. He had a great big smile on his face. "Do you want to play?" Regina asked.
>
> Dylan showed her his surprise. "We can all play together now!" He excitedly ran out of his house to show all of his friends his new toy.

Talk about the characters in the story. Then guide children to *Practice Book* page 142. Have children use the pictures to tell a story. Then help children identify the characters based on the pictures.

Day 3

RETEACH
Build Robust Vocabulary

Remind children of the Student-Friendly Explanations of *marvelous, exquisite,* and *lush.* Then discuss each word, using the following examples.

marvelous
On my last trip, my family had a *marvelous* time. Talk about a marvelous time you have had with your family.

exquisite
At the museum, you can find many *exquisite* pieces on display. Have you ever seen anything exquisite? Describe it.

lush
The rainforest is a *lush* environment. Tell what you would see if you visited the rainforest.

RETEACH
Writing

Writing Trait: Sentence Fluency Remind children that it is a good idea to have different types of sentences in their writing. Explain that writing is speech written down. When people speak, they use both long and short sentences. When you write, you should have both long and short sentences too.

On chart paper, write the following sentences from the story: *Dylan Dog was busy in his room making something. He wanted it to be a secret, so he closed his door while he worked. Amy Alligator soon came along.* Invite volunteers to point out the long sentences and the short sentences.

VOCABULARY
Student-Friendly Explanations

marvelous Something marvelous is terrific or wonderful.

exquisite Something exquisite is very special and beautiful.

lush A place that is lush is full of healthy, growing plants.

Grade K **285**

LESSON 24

DAY AT A GLANCE Day 4

PHONEMIC AWARENESS
Phoneme Segmentation
Phoneme Categorization: Medial

PHONICS
Review Consonants /y/y, /z/z

READING
Review /y/y, /z/z
Review High-Frequency Words

BUILD ROBUST VOCABULARY
Review *adore, joyous, protecting, host, responsible, jolly, melancholy*

WRITING
Reteach Writing Form: Story

Materials Needed:

Sound/Spelling Cards Yy, Zz

Photo Cards

Word Builders/ Word Builder Cards

Practice Book

Phonemic Awareness

Phoneme Segmentation Remind children that they can break a word into its individual sounds. Say: **Listen as I say this word: kick. Now I'll break the word into its sounds: /k/ /i/ /k/.** Have children break the following words into sounds: *sad* (/s/ /a/ /d/), *cup* (/k/ /u/ /p/), *van* (/v/ /a/ /n/).

Phoneme Categorization: Medial Tell children that they can listen for the sound that is different in a set of words. Say: **Listen as I say these three words: peg, let, sap. Peg and let both have /e/ in the middle. Sap has /a/ in the middle. Sap has the different middle sound.** Have children identify the word with the different middle sound in each set of words:

    duck, sat, fun (*sat*)   win, tock, hop (*win*)   bet, leg, mad (*mad*)

RETEACH
Phonics

Review /y/y, /z/z Place the *Sound/Spelling Card Yy* on a chart stand. Ask children what sound is at the beginning of the word *yarn*. (/y/) Then have children tell you what letter stands for the /y/ sound. (*y*) Repeat with the *Sound/Spelling Card Zz*.

Discriminate /y/ and /z/ Place the *Photo Cards yarn* and *zipper* on the chalk ledge. Say the name of each item and have children repeat after you. Say: **What sound does yarn begin with?** (/y/) **What letter stands for the /y/ sound?** (*y*) Repeat with the *Photo Card zipper*.

Give children *Word Builder Cards y* and *z*. Tell children that you are going to say some words. If the word begins with a /y/ sound, then they should hold up their *y* card. If the word begins with a /z/ sound, then they should hold up their *z* card. Say the following words: *zebra, yarn, yellow, zip, zap, yesterday, zoo*, and *yes*.

286 Lesson 24

Day 4

REVIEW
Reading

Review /y/y, /z/z Write these words on chart paper. Track the print and read them together

 Practice Book 143–144

| zap | yip | yet |
| yam | zip | |

High-Frequency Words

| are | she |
| good | they |

Review High-Frequency Words Distribute to each child cards for *are*, *they*, *she* and *good*. Organize children into pairs. Ask one partner to pick a card and read it, then have the other partner find the matching card and read it. Tell children to continue until they have read all of their words a few times.

Have children turn to *Practice Book* pages 143–144. Help children cut and fold the book. Explain that they will read this book with their family at home.

REVIEW
Build Robust Vocabulary

Remind children of the Student-Friendly Explanations of *adore*, *joyous*, *protecting*, *host*, *responsible*, *jolly*, and *melancholy*. Then determine children's understanding of the words by asking the following questions.

- If you were *responsible* for *hosting* a party, how would you let everyone know about it?
- If you broke your favorite toy, would you feel *joyous* or *melancholy*?
- Who is someone that you *adore*?
- If you had to *protect* your backpack from the rain, what would you do?
- Name a *jolly* person in your class.

VOCABULARY
Student-Friendly Explanations

adore To adore someone or something means to love that person or thing a lot.

joyous When you feel joyous, you feel very, very happy.

protecting When you are protecting something, you are keeping it safe.

host If you host a party or meeting, you run it.

responsible Someone who is responsible for something is given the job of taking care of it.

jolly When you feel jolly, you feel cheerful and happy.

melancholy If you are melancholy, you are thinking about something that makes you sad.

RETEACH
Writing

Writing Form: Story Tell children that they are going to write a make-believe story together about a kindergarten class. Remind children that the story needs characters. The sentences should also show variety by including both long and short sentences.

Ask children to brainstorm ideas about a make-believe kindergarten class. Write their responses on the board. Then use children's ideas to write the story. Invite them to write letters or words they know. Then write a title to the story. Read the finished story to children.

Chester Goes to Kindergarten

Chester the worm was going to kindergarten today. He was scared and happy. When he got to school, he saw his friends Julia and Ken. He learned how to read and write. It was fun.

Grade K 287

LESSON 24

PHONEMIC AWARENESS
Phoneme Isolation

PHONICS
Preteach Short Vowel /u/u

HIGH-FREQUENCY WORDS
Preteach and
Review are, go, one, who

BUILD ROBUST VOCABULARY
Preteach hollow, scurry, watchful

Materials Needed:

Sound/Spelling Card Uu   Practice Book

Phonemic Awareness

Phoneme Isolation Remind children that words are made up of individual sounds. Tell them that they can listen carefully for each sound in a word. Say: **Listen as I say this word: *fun*. I hear /f/ at the beginning of the word *fun*. Now listen to another word: *hut*. I hear /h/ at the beginning of the word *hut*.**

Have children name the beginning sound of these words: *top, pick,* and *kit*.

Repeat the process for medial and final sounds in words. Have children name the sounds they hear in the middle of these words: *dock, pet,* and *fat*. Then have children name the sounds they hear at the end of these words: *cab, rig,* and *sad*.

PRETEACH

Phonics

Say a Rhyme Write the rhyme "Twinkle, Twinkle Little Star" on chart paper. Say the rhyme several times, inviting children to join in. Once children are familiar with the rhyme, have them point to letters that they have learned about recently, such as *Hh, Ww,* or *Yy*.

 Short Vowel /u/u Hold up *Sound/Spelling Card Uu*. Explain that this is the vowel *Uu*. Say: **This is the letter *U*. Say the name with me.** Point to the uppercase *U*. **This is the uppercase *U*.** Then point to the lowercase *u*. Say: **This is the lowercase *u*.**

Writing *U* and *u* Write *U* and *u* on the board and have children identify the letters. Say: **Watch as I write the letter *U* so that everyone can read it.** As you give the Letter Talk, trace the uppercase *U*. Do the same for the lowercase *u*.

Letter Talk for *U*	Letter Talk for *u*
1. Straight line down, curve right, and back up.	1. Straight line down, curve right, and back up.
	2. Straight line down.

Guided Practice Have children finger-write the uppercase *U* in the air as you repeat the Letter Talk. Have them do the same for lowercase *u*. Then have children turn to *Practice Book* page 145. Help children identify and write the letter *Uu*.

288 Lesson 24

Day 5

PRETEACH
High-Frequency Words

Write the high-frequency word *and* on the board. Point to and read the word *and*. Have children read the word with you. Write the word *and* on an index card. Match the word card *and* to the word on the board. Say the word and have children say it with you.

Then write the previously-learned high-frequency words *are, go, one,* and *who* on index cards. Say each word and have chidren repeat that word. Tell children that you are going to hold up the cards with the words on them. If the word is *and,* they should read the word and show a thumb up. If the card has another word, they should read the word and show a thumb down. Continue until children can consistently read the word *and*.

High-Frequency Words

and	are
go	one
who	

PRETEACH
Build Robust Vocabulary

Go over the Student-Friendly Explanations for *hollow, scurry,* and *watchful*. Then discuss each word, using the following examples.

hollow
Would small animals like to live in a *hollow* log? Tell why.

scurry
Name two animals that *scurry*. How do you know?

watchful
My dog is *watchful* over our home. Who is watchful in your family?

VOCABULARY
Student-Friendly Explanations

hollow Something that is hollow has an empty space inside.

scurry If you scurry, you move quickly with small steps.

watchful If you are watchful, you are watching someone or something in a careful, alert way.

Grade K **289**

LESSON 25

PHONEMIC AWARENESS
Phoneme Identity

PHONICS
Preteach Relate *Uu* to /u/

HIGH-FREQUENCY WORDS
Reteach *and*
Review *I, like*

COMPREHENSION
Reteach Details

BUILD ROBUST VOCABULARY
Reteach *hollow, scurry, watchful*

Materials Needed:

Sound/Spelling Card *Uu*   Word Builder and Word Builder Cards   Copying Master

Photo Cards   Practice Book

Phonemic Awareness

Phoneme Identity   Remind children that a word is made up of individual sounds. Then say: **Listen as I say three words: *cat*, *cup*, and *can*. These words all begin with the same sound. *Cat*, *cup*, and *can* begin with the /k/ sound.**

Repeat the process with the ending and middle sounds. Ask: **Listen as I say three words: *dad*, *sod*, *fed*. *Dad*, *sod*, and *fed* end with the /d/ sound. Let's try one more. Listen to these three words: *won*, *top*, *hot*. These words all have /o/ sound in the middle.** Continue by asking children to identify the sound that is the same in the following sets: Beginning: *bag, bat, bit* (/b/) ; Middle: *hit, pin, lid* (/i/); Ending: *pan, win, ton* (/n/)

PRETEACH

Phonics

Start with the Sounds   Say the words *up* and *under* and have children repeat the words. Tell children that these words begin with the /u/ sound. Have children say /u/ several times.

 Connect Letter and Sound   Display the *Sound/Spelling Card Uu*. Ask: **What is the name of this letter?** (*u*) **The letter *u* starts at the beginning of the word *up*. Say /u/.** Have children repeat the sound of the letter on the card several times.

Discriminate /u/   Distribute *Word Builder Card u*. Say: **I'm going to say some words. If the word begins with /u/ hold up your card and say /u/. If it does not, hold your card behind your back.** Say: *upstairs, umbrella, house, umpire, udder,* and *today*.

Tell children that /u/ can also be in the middle of a word, such as in *sun*. Use the same procedure for the medial position. Use the words: *fun, cup, dot, pup, hit,* and *yum*. Then have children discriminate the initial and medial sound. Use these words: *under, run, pun, us, undo,* and *cut*.

 Guided Practice   Distribute *Copying Master 49*. Have children trace each vowel. Then have them cut and paste the letter that stands for the middle sound of each picture. (*bed, cup, cut, pet*)

Day 1

RETEACH

High-Frequency Words

Make index cards for the High-Frequency Words *and, I* and *like*. Say each word and have children repeat. Then use the index cards, *Photo Cards fish* and *insects,* and a period card to build the sentence frame shown below. Point to each word as you read the sentence. Continue by having children write the sentence frame and fill in with pictures of two things that they like.

| I | like | fish | and | insects | . |

High-Frequency Words

and   I

like

RETEACH

Comprehension

Details Remind children that the small parts in the words and pictures that help a reader better understand a story are called details. Then read this story aloud to them.

> Did you know that the only country where you can find koalas is Australia? These cute marsupials eat only one thing, the leaves of certain eucalyptus trees. Eucalyptus trees can be found only in Australia. Therefore, koalas must live where they can survive.
>
> Besides eating eucalyptus leaves, koalas actually live in the trees. These slow-moving animals spend their time either eating leaves, or sleeping on the branches. Koalas can sleep up to 18 hours a day! Eucalyptus trees are essential to koalas.

Talk about the details of this story. Then guide children to turn to page 146 in their *Practice Books*. Have children look at the pictures and identify the details.

RETEACH

Build Robust Vocabulary

Remind children of the Student-Friendly Explanations of *hollow, scurry,* and *watchful*. Then discuss each word, using the following examples.

hollow and **scurry**
What are some reasons that a squirrel would *scurry* into a hollow log?

watchful
A mother bear is *watchful* over her cubs. What things might she do?

VOCABULARY
Student-Friendly Explanations

hollow Something that is hollow has an empty space inside.

scurry If you scurry, you move quickly with small steps.

watchful If you are watchful, you are watching someone or something in a careful, alert way.

Grade K   291

LESSON 25

DAY AT A GLANCE
Day 2

PHONEMIC AWARENESS
Phoneme Categorization

PHONICS
Preteach Blending /u/u, /g/g

HIGH-FREQUENCY WORDS
Preteach there
Review good, two, come, this

COMPREHENSION
Reteach Use Graphic Organizers

BUILD ROBUST VOCABULARY
Preteach cling, defend, ravenous

Materials Needed:

Word Builder and Word Builder Cards | Copying Master | Practice Book

Phonemic Awareness

Phoneme Categorization Remind children that they have been listening for the same sounds in words. Explain that now they will be listening for the sound that is different in a group of words. Say: **Listen to these three words: *cup, can, sat*. *Cup* and *can* begin with the /k/ sound. *Sat* begins with the /s/ sound. *Sat* has a different beginning sound than *cup* and *can*.** Have children practice by identifying the word with a different beginning sound: *big, fun*, and *fan*.

Repeat the procedure with the ending and medial sound. Say: **Now listen to these words: *cat, sit,* and *pan*. *Pan* has a different ending sound than *cat* and *sit*.** Have children practice by identifying the word with a different ending sound: *yak, set*, and *kick*.

Listen to these three words: *sack, hot, tan*. *Hot* has a different sound in the middle. Ask children to identify the word with the different medial sound: *tin, yum, pick*.

PRETEACH
Phonics

Blend Phonemes Say the following verse, encouraging children to join in by blending the phonemes into words. Say: **We're going on a word hunt! What's this word? /b/ /u/ /n/?** Together: **bun!** Continue using the following words: /s/ /u/ /n/ (sun), /b/ /u/ /g/ (bug), /y/ /a/ /m/ (yam). Then review the sounds you blended to make each word.

Blending /u/u and /g/g Place the *Word Builder Cards* u and g in the *Word Builder*. Point to *u*. Say /uu/. Have children repeat the name of the letter and sound. Point to *g*. Say /gg/. Have children repeat the name of the letter and the sound. Slide the *g* next to the *u*. Move your hand under the letters and blend the sounds: /uugg/. Have children repeat after you. Then have children blend and read the sounds /ug/ with you. Continue with the words *bug, tug,* and *mug*.

 Distribute *Copying Master 50* to children. Have them look at each picture and circle the word that best describes it. Then have them write the word on the line. (*rug, sun, nut, bug*)

Day 2

PRETEACH

High-Frequency Words

Practice Book 147 Write the word *there* on the board. Point to and read the word *there*. Have children read the word with you. Write the word *there* on an index card. Match the word card *there* to the word on the board. Say the word and have children say it with you.

Then write *good, two, come,* and *this* on index cards. Use these cards and the card *there* to practice identifying words. Say each word and have children repeat that word.

Have children turn to *Practice Book* page 147 to review High-Frequency Words and practice newly-learned words. Complete the page together.

High-Frequency Words

come	good
there	this
two	

RETEACH

Comprehension

 Use Graphic Organizers Remind children that we can use special drawings or charts to help us remember or understand a story better. Recall the story about koalas. Reread the story. Draw the following story web on the board and have children help you fill it in based on what they learned from the story.

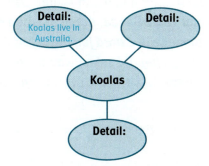

RETEACH

Build Robust Vocabulary

Read to children the Student-Friendly Explanations for *cling, defend,* and *ravenous.* Then discuss each word, using the following examples.

cling
If a frog *clings* to a tree, will it fall or stay on the tree? Tell why.

defend
I need to *defend* my toys from my baby brother. What type of things do you need to *defend*? Why?

ravenous
When you are *ravenous,* do you eat a meal or take a nap? Why?

VOCABULARY
Student-Friendly Explanations

cling When you cling to something, you hold on tight.

defend If you defend someone or something, you keep it safe or away from harm.

ravenous If you are ravenous, you are very hungry.

Grade K 293

LESSON 25

PHONEMIC AWARENESS
Phoneme Blending

PHONICS
Preteach Word Blending and Building

READING
Reteach *and, there*
Review *are, the, is, a, I, see*

COMPREHENSION
Reteach Details

BUILD ROBUST VOCABULARY
Reteach *cling, defend, ravenous*

WRITING
Reteach Writing Trait: Conventions

Materials Needed:

Phoneme Phone | Word Builder and Word Builder Cards | Write-On/Wipe-Off Boards

Photo Cards | Practice Book

Phonemic Awareness

Phoneme Blending Remind children that they have been listening for sounds. Tell them that they can blend individual sounds together to say words. Model how to blend sounds into words. Say: **Listen carefully to these sounds: /t/ /u/ /g/. I will blend these sounds together to say *tug*.**

Give each child a *Phoneme Phone*. Have children look at their mouth position as they blend the sounds to say the following words: /a/ /t/ (*at*), /s/ /i/ /t/ (*sit*), /c/ /o/ /t/ (*cot*), and /t/ /u/ /b/ (*tub*).

PRETEACH
Phonics

Model Word Blending Place the *Word Builder Cards* *b*, *u*, and *g* in the *Word Builder*. Point to *b*. Say: **/bb/**. Have children name the letter and sound. Point to *u*. Say: **/uu/**. Have children name the letter and sound. Slide the *u* next to *b*. Move your hand under the letters and blend the sounds: /bbuu/. Have children repeat after you. Point to *g*. Say: **/gg/**. Have children name the letter and sound. Slide the *g* next to *bu*. Move your hand under the letters and blend the sounds: /bbuugg/. Have children repeat after you. Say the word naturally, *bug*. Have children repeat.

Model Word Building Distribute *Word Builders* and *Word Builder Cards* *a, b, g, j, r, t,* and *u*. Review each letter name and sound. Say: **Now we are going to use your *Word Builder* and *Word Builder Cards* to make new words. I will use the letters *j, u,* and *g* to make the word *jug*. Now you do the same. Blend the sounds with me: /j/ /u/ /g/, *jug*. If I take away the *u* and put *i* its place, I have the word *jig*. Now you try it. Blend the sounds and say the word with me: /j/ /i/ /g/, *jig*.**

Build Words Have children continue with *jig* in their Word Builder:

- Change the *j* to *r*. What word did you make? (*rig*)
- Change the *g* to *b*. What word did you make? (*rib*)

 Continue with the words *rub, tub, tab.* Then have children practice writing the words they built on their *Write-on/Wipe-off Boards*.

294 Lesson 25

Day 3

RETEACH

High-Frequency Words

High-Frequency Words	
a	and
are	I
see	the
there	

Write the following *High-Frequency Words* on index cards: *There, are, the,* and *and*. Place them on the chalk ledge. As you say each word, have a volunteer point to the correct card. Then show *Photo Card boy* and *Photo Card girl*. Ask children to say the picture names. Then use the words cards, *Photo Cards,* and a period card to build the first sentence frame shown below. Point to each word as you read the sentence. Ask children to read the sentence with you.

Then continue with the following sentences. Point to each word and have children read the sentences aloud.

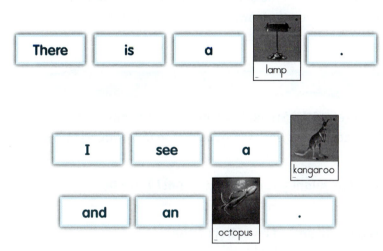

Write the following sentence frame on the board: *There are the ___ and ___.* Have children copy and complete the sentence frame with words or pictures.

Grade K **295**

Day 3

RETEACH
Comprehension

Practice Book 148

Details Remind children that details are the small parts of a story that an author uses to help a reader understand and enjoy a story. Details can be in both the words and the pictures. Have children listen for the details as you read aloud the following story.

> Have you ever seen the colors of a red-eyed tree frog? The tree frog has a bright green body with blue and yellow stripes on its sides, orange or red feet, a flash of blue on its thighs, and big red eyes. These bright colors help the frog to survive in the rainforest.
>
> The red-eyed tree frog sleeps during the day. Most times the bright green color helps to camouflauge it in the leaves. However, when a predator does see it and tries to catch it, the red-eyed tree frog wakes up and shows its bright red eyes. The big red eyes startle and confuse the predator. This gives the red-eyed tree frog a second to escape. So besides being beautiful, the red eyes of the red-eyed tree frog help it to stay away from danger!

Talk about the details in the story. Then guide children to *Practice Book* page 148. Have children add their own details to the picture.

RETEACH
Build Robust Vocabulary

Remind children of the Student-Friendly Explanations for *cling*, *defend*, and *ravenous*. Then discuss each word, using the following examples.

cling
On a windy day, might you *cling* to your hat? Tell why.

defend
How does a skunk *defend* itself from harm?

ravenous
If you were *ravenous*, would you go to the bedroom or to the kitchen? Tell why.

VOCABULARY
Student-Friendly Explanations

cling When you cling to something, you hold on tight.

defend If you defend someone or something, you keep it safe or away from harm.

ravenous If you are ravenous, you are very hungry.

296 Lesson 25

RETEACH

Writing

Writing Trait: Conventions Point out to children that when writing a letter, there are certain things they must make sure they use. There are always uppercase letters and commas used in the greeting and closing of the letter. Write the following letter on chart paper.

> Dear Mr. Toms,
> Thank you for visiting our class.
> We liked hearing about your job.
> From,
> Mrs. Kim's Class

Read the letter to children tracking the print. Point to the uppercase letters and commas in the greeting and in the closing. Ask volunteers to circle the uppercase letters and commas.

LESSON 25

PHONEMIC AWARENESS
Phoneme Segmentation

PHONICS
Reteach Short Vowel /u/*u*

READING
Review Short Vowel /u/
Review High-Frequency Words

BUILD ROBUST VOCABULARY
Review hollow, scurry, watchful, cling, defend, ravenous

WRITING
Reteach Writing Form: Friendly Letter

Materials Needed:

Word Builder and Word Builder Cards

Photo Cards

Write-On/Wipe-Off Boards

Practice Book pp. 149–150

Phonemic Awareness

Phoneme Segmentation Remind children that they can break a word into its individual sounds. Say: **Listen as I say this word: sub. Now I'll break the word into its sounds: /s/ /u/ /b/.** Have children break the following words into sounds: *bet* (/b/ /e/ /t/), *pup* (/p/ /u/ /p/), *sick* (/s/ /i/ /k/).

RETEACH
Phonics

Blend Sounds Write the word *fun* on the board. Model blending the sounds as you run a finger under each letter. Say: **Listen as I blend the sounds in this word: /ffuunn/. Say it with me: /f/ /u/ /n/,** *fun*.

 Next, give children *Word Builder Card u.* Randomly display one of the following *Photo Cards: cat, dog, hill, sun,* and *truck.* Have children name the picture and hold up the *Word Builder Card* if they hear the /u/ sound in the middle of the word. Fnally, follow the same procedure, but use spoken words. Say: **I am going to say some words. If you hear the /u/ sound in the middle of the word, hold up the *u* card and say /u/. If the word does not have the /u/ sound, hold the *u* card behind your back and say nothing.** Say the following words for children: *fun, fast, run, ruse, top, frog, mud, cup, sip, tap.*

REVIEW
Reading

 Short Vowel /u/*u* Write the following words on the board: *run, bug, rug,* and *tub.* Have children read each word by blending the sounds of the words.

Distribute *Write-on/Wipe-off Boards.* Ask children to write two of the words from the board on their board, and draw a picture to illustrate each word.

298 Lesson 25

Day 4

Review High-Frequency Words Organize children into pairs. Distribute two index cards to each pair. Have one partner write the word *and* on a card, and the other partner write the word *there* on a card. Then have children cut each card so they are individual letters. Have partners work together to put the words *and* and *there* back together.

Then have children turn to *Practice Book* pages 149–150. Have children read the story to practice the skills.

High-Frequency Words

and   there

REVIEW
Robust Vocabulary

Remind children of the Student-Friendly Explanations for *hollow, scurry, watchful, cling, defend,* and *ravenous*. Then determine children's understanding of the words by asking the following questions.

- **Would you describe a straw as *hollow* or *ravenous*? Tell why.**
- **If it were raining, would you *scurry* indoors or stand still? Why?**
- **Police officers *defend* our neighborhood by being *watchful*. Describe what they do.**
- **Name an animal that would *cling* to a tree. Show how they would do it.**
- **If you were *ravenous*, what would you do first?**

RETEACH
Writing

Writing Form: Friendly Letter Remind children that a letter is a writing form used by people often. Talk about reasons people write letters, such as to share news, to say thank you, or to invite people to parties.

Tell children that they are going to write a letter together to another class. Remind children that a letter has three parts: the greeting, the body, and the closing. Point out that the greeting and the closing always use uppercase letters and commas.

Ask children to brainstorm ideas about telling another kindergarten class about a project they made. Write their responses on the board. Then use children's ideas to write the letter. Invite them to write letters or words they know. Read the finished letter to children.

> Dear Mr. Anderson's Class,
>
> We made puppets in class today. It was fun. We used paper bags and markers. Your class should make puppets, too.
>
> From,
> Mrs. Menza's Class

VOCABULARY
Student-Friendly Explanations

hollow Something that is hollow has an empty space inside.

scurry If you scurry, you move quickly with small steps.

watchful If you are watchful, you are watching someone or something in a careful, alert way.

cling When you cling to something, you hold on tight.

defend If you defend someone or something, you keep it safe or away from harm.

ravenous If you are ravenous, you are very hungry.

Grade K **299**

LESSON 25

DAY AT A GLANCE
Day 5

PHONEMIC AWARENESS
Phoneme Deletion

PHONICS
Reteach Word Blending

HIGH-FREQUENCY WORDS
Preteach give

BUILD ROBUST VOCABULARY
Preteach lively, peek, arise

Materials Needed:

Word Builder and Word Builder Cards

Practice Book

Phonemic Awareness

Phoneme Deletion Tell children that they can say words without the beginning sound. Tell them to listen as you say a word and then say it again without the beginning sound. Say: **Jet. I can say *jet* without the /j/: *et*. Say it with me: *et*.** Work with children to take away the beginning sound from words. Say **man. What do we have if we say the word *man* without the /m/? *Man* without the /m/ is *an*. Now you say *man* without the /m/.**

Follow the same procedure using the following words. Ask children to say the words without the beginning sound.

Say *mug*. Now say *mug* without the /m/. (ug)

Say *hat*. Now say *hat* without the /h/. (at)

Say *ten*. Now say *ten* without the /t/. (en)

Say *top*. Now say *top* without the /t/. (op)

Say *cup*. Now say *cup* without the /k/. (up)

Say *fox*. Now say *fox* without the /f/. (ox)

Say *tin*. Now say *tin* without the /t/. (in)

Say *bad*. Now say *bad* without the /b/. (ad)

Say *bug*. Now say *bug* without the /b/. (ug)

Say *dock*. Now say *dock* without the /d/. (ock)

RETEACH

Phonics

 Word Blending Distribute Word Builders and word Builder Cards *a, b, c, e, g, i, j, m, n, p, t,* and *u* to children. Place the Word Builder Cards *u* and *p* in Word Builder. Point to *u*. Say /**u**/. Have children name the letter and sound. Point to *p*. Say /**p**/. Have children name the letter and sound. Slide the *u* next to *p*. Move your hand under the letters and blend the sounds: /**up**/. Have children repeat after you. Then add *c* and have children blend and read the word *cup* with you. Follow the same procedure to blend and read *bun, man, pet,* and *jig* with children.

Have children turn to *Practice Book* page 151. Help children identify the pictures. Have them trace the letter *u* in each word.

Day 5

PRETEACH

High-Frequency Words

Write the word *give* on the board. Read the word and have children repeat after you. Say: **Please give me a pencil.** Point to the word *give* as you say the sentence. Then write the word *give* on an index card. Match the card to the word on the board. Read the word again and have children repeat.

Display index cards for *give, good, here, like,* and *they*. Say one of the words and hold up a choice of two index cards, one of them correct. Have the children indicate which word is the one you said and repeat the word. Repeat the activity several times for each word.

PRETEACH

Build Robust Vocabulary

Tell children the Student-Friendly Explanations of *lively, peek,* and *arise*. Then discuss each word, using the following examples.

lively
Which animal is *lively*: a sleepy dog or a playful kitten? Why?

peek
Show how you would *peek* at a scary movie through your fingers.

arise
If you *arise* from a chair, do you sit down or get up?

High-Frequency Words

give	good
here	like
they	

VOCABULARY
Student-Friendly Explanations

lively Something that is lively is full of excitement or energy.

peek When you peek at something, you take a quick look at it without being seen.

arise When you arise, you get up from sitting or lying down.

Grade K 301

LESSON 26

DAY 1

PHONEMIC AWARENESS
Phoneme Deletion: Initial

PHONICS
Reteach Word Building

HIGH-FREQUENCY WORDS
Reteach give
Review I, you, this

COMPREHENSION
Reteach Details

BUILD ROBUST VOCABULARY
Reteach lively, peek, arise

Materials Needed:

Word Builder and Word Builder Cards | Write-On/Wipe-Off Boards | Copying Master

Photo Cards | Practice Book

Phonemic Awareness

Phoneme Deletion: Initial Remind children that they can say words without the beginning sound. Tell them to listen as you say a word and then say it again without the beginning sound. Say: **Listen while I say *let* without the /l/: *et*. Say it with me: *et*.** Work with children to take away the beginning sound from words: **Say *ham*. What do we have if we say the word *ham* without the /h/?** *Ham* without the /h/ is *am*. Now you say *ham* without the /h/.

Follow the same procedure using the following words:

Say *jack*. Now say *jack* without the /j/. (*ack*)

Say *head*. Now say *head* without the /h/. (*ead*)

Say *wish*. Now say *wish* without the /w/. (*ish*)

Say *ten*. Now say *ten* without the /t/. (*en*)

Say *pot*. Now say *pot* without the /p/. (*ot*)

RETEACH

Phonics

Word Building Distribute *Word Builders* and *Word Builder Cards* *h*, *u*, *t*, *n*, *b*, *s*, and *f*. Review each letter name and sound. Then hold up letters at random and ask children to tell the letter name and sound.

Explain to children that you are going to show them how a word can change when the letters in the word change. Say: **Use your *Word Builder* and *Word Builder Cards* to make new words with me. I will use the letters *h*, *u*, and *t* to make the word *hut*. Now you do the same. Blend the sounds with me: /h/-/u/-/t/, *hut*. If I take away the *h* and put *n* in its place, I have the word *nut*. Now you try it. Blend the sounds and say the word with me: /n/-/u/-/t/, *nut*.**

  Build Words Have children continue with *nut* in their *Word Builder*:

- Change the *n* to *b*. What word did you make? (*but*)
- Change the *t* to *n*. What word did you make? (*bun*)
- Change the *b* to *s*. What word did you make? (*sun*)

302 Lesson 26

Have children practice writing the words they built on their *Write-On/Wipe-Off Boards*.

Distribute *Copying Master page 51*. Have children trace and cut out the letters *o* and *u* at the bottom of the page. Help children identify the pictures. Children should paste the correct vowel in the box to complete the picture name, and then blend the sounds to read each picture name. *(box, cup, hut, top)*

High-Frequency Words

give	this
I	you

RETEACH

High-Frequency Words

 Display index cards for *I, give, you,* and *this*. Say each word, and have children repeat each word and hold up the correct card. Continue until children consistently choose and read the word give.

RETEACH

Comprehension

  Details Remind children that the details of a story are small parts in the words and pictures that help a reader understand the story. Then read this story aloud to them.

Jarrett and his dad wanted to wash the car. They got soap, the hose, a bucket, some rags, and some old towels. Then Jarrett sprayed the car with the hose. He was careful to soak every part of the car—even the wheels. Then Jarrett and his dad scrubbed the car with the old rags. Next, Jarrett rinsed all the soap off the car, and his dad dried it with the old towels. When they were finished, the car shone brightly in the sun.

Then guide children to turn to page 152 in their *Practice Books*. Have them look at each picture of something that happened in the story about Jarrett and his dad. Then have them describe details from the story using the three pictures.

RETEACH

Build Robust Vocabulary

Remind children of the Student-Friendly Explanations of *lively, peek,* and *arise*. Then discuss each word, using the following examples.

lively
If you wanted a party to be *lively*, should everyone read books or dance to loud music? Explain.

peek
When you *peek* at something, do you hear it, smell it, or see it?

arise
When you *arise* from your chair, do you stand up or sit down?

VOCABULARY

Student-Friendly Explanations

lively Something that is lively is full of excitement or energy.

peek When you peek at something, you take a quick look at it without being seen.

arise When you arise, you get up from sitting or lying down.

LESSON 26

PHONEMIC AWARENESS
Phoneme Deletion: Final

PHONICS
Reteach Word Building

HIGH-FREQUENCY WORDS
Preteach little
Review is, me, for, the

COMPREHENSION
Reteach Use Story Structure

BUILD ROBUST VOCABULARY
Preteach clever, boastful, quarrel

Materials Needed:

Word Builder and Word Builder Cards

Write-On/ Wipe-Off Boards

Copying Master

Photo Cards

Practice Book

Phonemic Awareness

Phoneme Deletion: Final   Remind children that they can say a word without the ending sound. Tell them to listen as you say a word and then say it again without the ending sound. Say: **Pen. I can say** *pen* **without the /n/:** *pe*. **Say it with me:** *pe*.

Work with children to take away the ending sound from words. Say: **hat. What do we have if we say the word** *hat* **without the /t/?** *Hat* **without the /t/ is** *ha*. **Now you say** *hat* **without the /t/.**

Ask children to take away the ending sounds of the following words.

Say *dog*. **Now say** *dog* **without the /g/.** (*do*)

Say *cup*. **Now say** *cup* **without the /p/.** (*cu*)

Say *pill*. **Now say** *pill* **without the /l/.** (*pi*)

Say *bad*. **Now say** *bad* **without the /d/.** (*ba*)

RETEACH

Phonics

Word Blending   Distribute *Word Builders* and *Word Builder Cards* *p, i, t, n, f, u, b,* and *s*. Review each letter name and sound. Then hold up letters at random and ask children to tell the letter name and sound.

Remind children that when letters in words change, so do the sounds, and that they can make new words by changing letters in words. Have children follow along with you as you model this process. Say: **I made the word** *pit* **with** *p, i,* **and** *t*. **Now if I take away the** *t* **and put** *n* **in its place, I have the word** *pin*. **Blend the sounds with me, /p/ /i/ /n/,** *pin*.

 Build Words   Have children continue with *pin* in their *Word Builder*:

- **Change the** *p* **to** *t*. **What word did you make?** (*tin*)
- **Change the** *t* **to** *f*. **What word did you make?** (*fin*)
- **Change the** *i* **to** *u*. **What word did you make?** (*fun*)

Have children practice writing the words they built on their *Write-On/Wipe-Off Boards*. Distribute *Copying Master 52* to review words with short *u* and *i* with children. Help children name each picture and read the word choices below each picture. Then have children circle the word that names the picture and write the word. (*bun, hut, pin, nut*)

Day 2

PRETEACH

High-Frequency Words

 Write the word *little* on the board. Read the word and have children repeat after you. Then write the word on an index card. Match the card to the word on the board. Read the word again and have children repeat. Display index cards for *the, little, is, for,* and *me*. Continue until children consistently recognize the word *little*.

Have children turn to *Practice Book* page 153 to review high-frequency words and practice newly learned words. Complete the page together.

REVIEW

Comprehension

Use Story Structure Remind children that sometimes the characters in a story have a problem that has to be figured out. Reread the story about Jarrett and his dad from Day 1. Tell children to think about what the problem is and how the characters figure it out. Then fill out a chart like the one below.

Characters: Jarrett, his dad

Problem: They want to wash the car.

Solution: They get together all the things they will need.

RETEACH

Build Robust Vocabulary

Tell children the Student-Friendly Explanations of *clever, boastful,* and *quarrel*. Then discuss each word, using the following examples.

clever
Do you think a monkey who can play the piano is *clever*? Why or why not?

boastful
What is something a *boastful* person could say about how he or she plays soccer?

quarrel
If you and I both want the last cookie on a plate, how could we avoid a *quarrel*?

High-Frequency Words

is	me
for	the
little	

VOCABULARY

Student-Friendly Explanations

clever Someone who is clever is smart and good at solving problems.

boastful If you are boastful, you talk about yourself with too much pride.

quarrel If you quarrel with someone, you argue or disagree about something.

Grade K 305

LESSON 26

PHONEMIC AWARENESS
Phoneme Deletion: Final
Phoneme Blending

PHONICS
Preteach Phonogram -un

HIGH-FREQUENCY WORDS
Reteach give, little
Review I, my, you

COMPREHENSION
Reteach Details

BUILD ROBUST VOCABULARY
Reteach clever, boastful, quarrel

WRITING
Reteach Writing Trait: Ideas

Materials Needed:

Word Builder and Word Builder Cards

Write-On/Wipe-Off Boards

Photo Cards

Practice Book

Phonemic Awareness

Phoneme Deletion: Final Remind children that they can say words without the ending sound. Tell them to listen as you say a word and then say it again without the ending sound. Say: **Jam. I can say** *jam* **without the /m/:** *ja.* **Say it with me:** *ja.*

Work with children to take away the ending sound from words: **Say** *sub.* **What do we have if we say the word** *sub* **without the /b/?** *Sub* **without the /b/ is** *su.* **Now you say** *sub* **without the /b/.**

Ask children to take away the ending sounds of the following words.

Say *hit.* **Now say** *hit* **without the /t/.** (hi)

Say *cap.* **Now say** *cap* **without the /p/.** (ca)

Say *jet.* **Now say** *jet* **without the /t/.** (je)

Say *big.* **Now say** *big* **without the /g/.** (bi)

Phoneme Blending Remind children that they can blend individual sounds to say words. Model an example from the words above. Say: **/j/ /a/ /m/. I will blend the sounds to say the word:** *jam.* Have children listen to the sounds of each of the following words and blend the sounds to say words: /h/ /a/ /d/ (had), /t/ /o/ /p/ (top), /l/ /e/ /d/ (led), /s/ /i/ /p/ (sip), and /p/ /u/ /n/ (pun).

PRETEACH

Phonics

Read Words with -un Write the word *bun* on chart paper. Track the print as children read the word. Then write the word *fun.* Again, track the print as children read the word. Ask children to read the two words and tell how the words are the same. (They both have /un/; they rhyme.) Explain that the words *bun* and *fun* are in the *-un* word family because they both end in *-un.* Continue by writing the words *sun* and *run* and having children read the words.

  Blend and Build Words Have children work with *Word Builders* and *Word Builder Cards b, f, n, r, s,* and *u.* Guide them in blending and building the words *sun, fun, run,* and *bun.* After children read each word, have them write it on their *Write-on/Wipe off Board.*

Day 3

RETEACH

High-Frequency Words

Display index cards for *give, little, I, my,* and *you.* As you say each word, have children repeat the word and hold up the correct card. Show *Photo Card egg.* Ask children to say the picture name. Then use the words cards, period card, and *Photo Card egg* to build the sentence frame shown below. Point to each word as you read the sentence. Ask children to read the sentence with you.

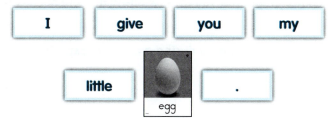

Then continue with the following Photo Cards. Point to each word and have children read the new sentences aloud: *truck, tiger, sandwich, pan, lamp,* and *box.*

Write the following sentence frame on the board: *Give me the little ____ .* Have children copy and complete the sentence with a word or a picture.

High-Frequency Words

give	my
I	you
little	

RETEACH

Comprehension

  Details Remind children that the details of a story are small parts in the words and pictures that help a reader understand the story. Have children listen as you read aloud the following story.

> The night was dark. The wind was blowing. The moon went behind a cloud. Darcy looked at the dark, old house. The shutters were falling off, and the roof had a hole in it. Dry tree branches clacked against the broken windows. Darcy walked slowly up to the door. Then Darcy held her breath and knocked on the door. After a long time, she heard footsteps in the house.

Guide children to *Practice Book* page 154. Discuss each picture and have children name details from the story.

Grade K 307

Day 3

VOCABULARY
Student-Friendly Explanations

clever Someone who is clever is smart and good at solving problems.

boastful If you are boastful, you talk about yourself with too much pride.

quarrel If you quarrel with someone, you argue or disagree about something.

RETEACH

Build Robust Vocabulary

Remind children of the Student-Friendly Explanations of *clever*, *boastful*, and *quarrel*. Then discuss each word, using the following examples.

clever
Would a *clever* dog have a hard time or an easy time learning to sit? Why?

boastful
What might a *boastful* person say after winning a game of checkers?

quarrel
Would people yell or talk politely during a *quarrel*? Explain.

RETEACH

Writing

Writing Trait: Ideas Remind children that thinking of different ideas before they begin writing will help them choose the best idea for their writing. Point out that people get ideas for writing in all kinds of ways. Some people make lists or draw pictures. Some people talk to their friends to get ideas. Then write this sentence on the board. Read it while tracking the print.

> The night was dark.

Ask children to suggest ideas they could write about based on the sentence. Ask: **What ideas come to your mind when you read this sentence?** List the children's ideas on the board.

LESSON 26

PHONEMIC AWARENESS
Phoneme Deletion

PHONICS
Preteach Phonogram -ut

READING
Review -un, -ut
Review High-Frequency Words

BUILD ROBUST VOCABULARY
Review lively, peek, arise, clever, boastful, quarrel

WRITING
Reteach Writing Form: Friendly Letter

Materials Needed:

Word Builder and Word Builder Cards

Write-On/ Wipe-Off Boards

Photo Cards

Practice Book

Phonemic Awareness

Phoneme Deletion Remind children that they can say words without the beginning or ending sounds. Use the following rhyme to have children say a word without the beginning (or ending) sound:

Listen to the word I say, and take the *beginning* (or *ending*) sound away.

Say *cut* without the /k/. (*ut*)   **Say *cut* without the /t/.** (*cu*)

Repeat the rhyme with these words:

Say *hen* without the /h/. (*en*)   **Say *hen* without the /n/.** (*he*)
Say *bug* without the /b/. (*ug*)   **Say *bug* without the /g/.** (*bu*)
Say *bat* without the /b/. (*at*)   **Say *bat* without the /t/.** (*ba*)
Say *mop* without the /m/. (*op*)   **Say *mop* without the /p/.** (*mo*)
Say *run* without the /r/. (*un*)   **Say *run* without the /n/.** (*ru*)
Say *bill* without the /b/. (*ill*)   **Say *bill* without the /l/.** (*bi*)
Say *hum* without the /h/. (*um*)   **Say *hum* without the /m/.** (*hu*)

PRETEACH

Phonics

 Word Blending Distribute to children *Word Builders* and *Word Builder Cards b, c, h, u,* and *t.* Place the Word Builder Cards *u* and *t* in Word Builder. Point to *u*; Say /u/. Have children name the letter and sound. Point to *t.* Say /t/. Have children name the letter and sound. Slide the *u* next to *t.* Move your hand under the letters and blend the sounds: /ut/. Have children repeat after you. Then add *c* and have children blend and read the word *cut* with you. Continue with the words *nut, hut,* and *but.*

Identify -*ut* Words Write the words *nut* and *hut* on the board. Blend the sounds and have children read the words. Ask them to tell how the words are alike. (They both end with -*ut*; they rhyme). Explain to children that these words are in the -*ut* word family. Continue by writing the words *cut* and *but* on the board. Discuss how the words *cut* and *but* are also in the -*ut* word family.

 Then have children listen as you say the words *nut, bed,* and *but.* As you say each word, have them write it on their *Write-on/Wipe-off Board* if it is in the -*ut* word family.

Day 4

RETEACH
Reading

Apply Phonics -un, -ut Write the words *cut, hut, but,* and *nut* on the board. Help children blend the sounds to read the words.

 Practice Book 155–156

Review High-Frequency Words Display index cards for *give* and *little*. Hold up each card and have children read them until they can identify them correctly each time.

Have children turn to *Practice Book* pages 155–156. Help children cut, fold, and read the book. Encourage them to read it with their family.

REVIEW
Robust Vocabulary

Remind children of the Student-Friendly Explanations for *lively, peek, arise, clever, boastful,* and *quarrel*. Then determine children's understanding of the words by asking the following questions.

- **If you *peek* into a *lively* party, what might you see? Explain.**
- **Do you have to be sitting down or lying down to *arise*? Why?**
- **Would a *clever* person try to stop a *quarrel*? Why or why not?**
- **Would someone be more likely to be *boastful* after getting a good grade or a bad grade on a test? Why?**

RETEACH
Writing

Writing Form: Friendly Letter Remind children the many reasons people write letters. Review the parts of a friendly letter. Then tell children that today they will write a letter to another kindergarten class in your school. Talk about things they could include in the body of the letter. Record their ideas on chart paper. Then use children's ideas to write a letter. Invite them to write letters and words they know. Read the finished letter to the children.

> Dear Mr. Dean's Class,
>
> We have fun in class. We like our teacher very much.
>
> Your friends,
> Ms. Adler's Class

High-Frequency Words

give   little

VOCABULARY
Student-Friendly Explanations

lively Something that is lively is full of excitement or energy.

peek When you peek at something, you take a quick look at it without being seen.

arise When you arise, you get up from sitting or lying down.

clever Someone who is clever is smart and good at solving problems.

boastful If you are boastful, you talk about yourself with too much pride.

quarrel If you quarrel with someone, you argue or disagree about something.

Grade K   311

LESSON 26

PHONEMIC AWARENESS
Phoneme Substitution

PHONICS
Preteach Consonant *Qq*

HIGH-FREQUENCY WORDS
Preteach *that*

BUILD ROBUST VOCABULARY
Review peek, watchful, lively, active

Materials Needed:

Sound/Spelling Card *Qq* | Practice Book | Photo Cards

Phonemic Awareness

Phoneme Substitution Tell children that they can change the sound they hear at the beginning of a word to make a new word. Say: **Listen as I say the word bug. I hear the sound /b/ at the beginning of the word. If I change the /b/ to /h/, I can make a new word. The new word is hug. Now, if I change the /h/ in hug to /r/, the new word is rug.**

Have children replace the initial phonemes in the word you say to make a new word. Say **sun. Now change the /s/ to /r/.** *(run)* Say **pot. Now change the /p/ to /h/.** *(hot)* Say **luck. Now change the /l/ to /d/.** *(duck)* Say **sat. Now change the /s/ to /c/.** *(cat)* Say **let. Now change the /b/ to /l/.** *(let)*

PRETEACH

Phonics

Consonant *Qq* Display Sound/Spelling Card *Qq*. Say: **The name of this letter is Q. Say the name with me.** Point to the uppercase *Q* and say: **This is the uppercase Q.** Point to the lowercase *q* and say: **This is the lowercase q.** Have children identify the letters *(Q, q)*.

Writing *Q* and *q* Write *Q* and *q* on the board and have children identify the letters. Say: **Watch as I write the letter Q.** As you give the Letter Talk, trace the uppercase and lowercase letters.

Letter Talk for *Q*	Letter Talk for *q*
1. Circle.	1. Circle.
2. Short slanted line.	2. Line straight down.
	3. Curve right.

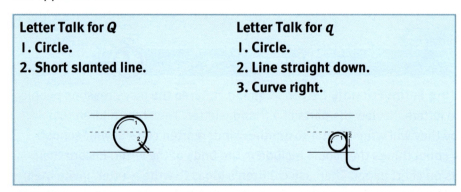

Guided Practice Have children finger-write the uppercase *Q* in the air as you repeat the Letter Talk. Have them do the same for the lowercase *q*. Then have children turn to *Practice Book* page 157. Have them practice identifying and writing *Qq*.

Day 5

PRETEACH
High-Frequency Words

 Write the following high-frequency words on index cards and distribute: *good, see, that, they,* and *want.* Say each word, and have the children repeat that word and hold up the correct card. Show *Photo Card apple.* Ask children to say the picture name. Then use the high-frequency word cards, the *Photo Card,* and a period card to build the sentence frame shown below. Point to each word as you read the sentence. Then have children read the sentence with you.

Repeat the activity with *Photo Cards milk, sandwich,* and *watermelon.*

REVIEW
Build Robust Vocabulary

Remind children of the Student-Friendly Explanations of *peek, watchful, lively,* and *active.* Then discuss each word, using the following examples.

peek
When you *peek* around a corner at something, what do you do? Show everyone.

watchful
Is a mother cat *watchful* when she's taking care of her kittens? Tell what she might do.

lively
I will name some things. Clap if the thing I name is *lively.* Tell why that thing is *lively.*
recess   a nap   a birthday party   a game of tag

active
If you had a friend who played video games all the time, how might you get him to become more *active* and *lively*?

High-Frequency Words

good	see
that	they
want	

VOCABULARY
Student-Friendly Explanations

peek When you peek at something, you take a quick look at it without being seen.

watchful If you are watchful, you are watching someone or something in a careful, alert way.

lively Something that is lively is full of excitement or energy.

active If you are active, you are doing something in a busy way.

Grade K   313

LESSON 27

PHONEMIC AWARENESS
Phoneme Substitution

PHONICS
Preteach Relate *Qq* to /kw/

HIGH-FREQUENCY WORDS
Reteach *that*

COMPREHENSION
Reteach Main Idea

BUILD ROBUST VOCABULARY
Review clever, boastful, famished, ravenous

Materials Needed:

Sound/Spelling Card *Qq* — Sounds of Letters CD — Word Builder and Word Builder Cards

Copying Master — Photo Cards — Practice Book

High-Frequency Words

see	that
they	

Phonemic Awareness

Phoneme Substitution Remind children that they can change the beginning sound of a word to make a new word. Say: **Sit. I can change the /s/ in *sit* to /f/. The new word is *fit*.**

Tell children they can also change the *ending* sound of a word to make a new word. Say: **Listen as I say a word: *pan*. I can change the /n/ in *pan* to /t/. The new word is *pat*.** Repeat using these words:

- Say *dip*. Change the /p/ to /g/. (*dig*)
- Say *man*. Change the /n/ to /d/. (*mad*)

PRETEACH

Phonics

  Relate *Qq* to /kw/ Display *Sound/Spelling Card Qq*. Ask: **What is the name of this letter? The letter *q* stands for /kw/, the sound at the beginning of *queen*. Say /kw/.** Have children repeat the sound as you touch the letter on the card several times. Use the *Sounds of Letters CD* to reinforce the /kw/ sound of *Qq*.

  Discriminate /kw/ Give children each a *Word Builder Card q*. Say: **If the word I say begins with /kw/, hold up your card and say /kw/. If the word does not begin with /kw/, hold your card behind your back.** Say the words *quick, queen, sick, question, answer, king,* and *quilt*. Now distribute *Copying Master 53*. Have children trace *Qq*. Then have them look at each picture and circle the letter that stands for the beginning sound of each picture name. (Children should circle *q* for *queen, question mark, quarter, quack, quilt*.)

RETEACH

High-Frequency Words

Distribute index cards for *that, they,* and *see*. Say each word, and have children repeat each word and hold up the correct card. Show *Photo Card pig*. Ask children to say the picture name. Then use the index cards, a period card, and the picture to build the sentence frame shown below. Point to each word as you read the sentence. Ask children to read the sentence with you.

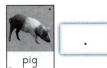

RETEACH
Comprehension

Main Idea Remind children that the main idea of a story is what it is mostly about. Then read this story aloud to them.

> Every animal lives someplace. Birds live in their nests. Badgers live in dens, and beavers build dams. Many animals, like owls and squirrels, live in holes in trees. Still other animals dig holes in the ground. Some of these animals are snakes, moles, and rabbits.

Guide children to turn to page 158 in their *Practice Books*. Have them look at the pictures as you read the story again. If the picture is *not* part of the main idea of the story, ask them to cross it out. Discuss their responses.

REVIEW
Build Robust Vocabulary

Remind children of the Student-Friendly Explanations of *clever, boastful, ravenous,* and *famished*. Then discuss each word, using the following examples.

clever
Would a *clever* person be helpful if you were trying to figure out a problem or if you were hungry? Explain why.

boastful
How would a *boastful* person act if she had just won a spelling contest?

ravenous and **famished**
If your dog was *ravenous* and *famished*, how could you help him?

VOCABULARY
Student-Friendly Explanations

clever Someone who is clever is smart and good at solving problems.

boastful If you are boastful, you talk about yourself with too much pride.

ravenous If you are ravenous, you are very hungry.

famished If you are famished, you are very hungry.

Day 1

Grade K 315

LESSON 27

PHONEMIC AWARENESS
Substitute Medial Sounds

PHONICS
Reteach Consonants /kw/q, /z/z

HIGH-FREQUENCY WORDS
Reteach have

COMPREHENSION
Preteach Monitor Comprehension: Reread

BUILD ROBUST VOCABULARY
Review cling, scurry, arise

Materials Needed:

Sound/Spelling Cards Qq, Zz   Phoneme Phone   Photo Cards

Copying Master   Practice Book

Phonemic Awareness

Substitute Medial Sounds Remind children that they can change the beginning or ending sounds in words to make new words. Tell them they can also change the middle sound of a word to make a new word. Say: **Listen as I say a word: wag. I can change the /a/ in wag to /i/. The new word is wig.**

Repeat the procedure, elongating the sounds in the words, and having children replace medial phonemes and say the new words.

Say: *fox*. I can change the /o/ in *fox* to /i/. The new word is *fix*.

Say: *hat*. I can change the /a/ in *hat* to /o/. The new word is *hot*.

Say: *sit*. I can change the /i/ in *sit* to /e/. The new word is *set*.

Say: *let*. I can change the /e/ in *let* to /o/. The new word is *lot*.

RETEACH

Phonics

 Reteach /kw/q and /z/z Show children the *Sound/Spelling Card Qq*. Ask: **What sound do you hear at the beginning of queen? What letter stands for /kw/ at the beginning of queen?** (Qq) Now display *Sound/Spelling Card Zz*. Ask: **What sound do you hear at the beginning of zipper? What letter stands for /z/ at the beginning of zipper?** (Zz) Model how to say the sounds /kw/ and /z/ into a *Phoneme Phone*. Have children do the same. Encourage them to look at their mouth position as they say the sounds.

 With both *Sound/Spelling Cards* on display, display *Photo Cards quarter* and *zebra*. Tell children that they are going to sort the cards by their beginning sounds. Have children say each picture name and tell which letter stands for the sound at the beginning of its name.

 Now distribute *Copying Master 54*. Have children trace *Qq*. Then have them look at each picture and write the letter that stands for the beginning sound of each picture name. (Children should write *q* for *quilt, question mark, quarter, quack, queen*.)

RETEACH
High-Frequency Words

Practice Book 159 Write the word *have* on the board. Point to and read *have*. Have children say it with you. Say: **I *have* a quarter.** Write the word *have* on an index card. Say *have*. Match the index card to the word on the board, say the word, and have children say it with you. Distribute index cards with the word *have* to each child. Have children point to the word and read it. Tell children that you will show them words, and when they see *have*, they should say the word and point to it on their card. Hold up index cards for *have, good, see,* and *that* until children consistently identify the word *have*.

Have children turn to *Practice Book* page 159 to review high-frequency words and practice newly learned words. Complete the page together.

High-Frequency Words

good	have
see	that

RETEACH
Comprehension

Monitor Comprehension: Reread Explain that a lot of things happen in a book. Say: **When I get confused, I can stop and reread the part that was confusing. That helps me to understand what happens.** Reread the story about animal homes from Day 1. While reading, stop at appropriate points in the story and model how to reread to clear up confusion or to help remember what happened.

REVIEW
Build Robust Vocabulary

Remind children of the Student-Friendly Explanations of *cling, scurry,* and *arise*. Then discuss each word, using the following examples.

cling
If it were a very windy day, would you want to *cling* to your hat? Why?

scurry
Which animal would be more likely to *scurry*, a mouse or a hippopotamus? Tell why.

arise
Would you be more likely to *arise* from your chair before or after eating dinner? Explain why.

VOCABULARY
Student-Friendly Explanations

cling When you cling to something, you hold on tight.

scurry If you scurry, you move quickly with small steps.

arise When you arise, you get up from sitting or lying down.

LESSON 27

DAY AT A GLANCE — Day 3

PHONEMIC AWARENESS
Substitute Initial and Final Sounds

PHONICS
Reteach Consonants /kw/q, /j/j

READING
Review /kw/q, /j/j
Review High-Frequency Words

COMPREHENSION
Reteach Main Idea

BUILD ROBUST VOCABULARY
Review hollow, defend, watchful, quarrel

WRITING
Reteach Writing Trait: Organization

Materials Needed:

Sound/Spelling Cards Qq, Jj

Photo Cards

Word Builders and Word Builder Cards

Practice Book

Phonemic Awareness

Substitute Initial and Final Sounds Remind children that they can change the sounds in a word to make a new word. Say: *Pat*. Say the word with me: *pat*. We can change the /p/ in *pad* to /h/. What is the new word? (*hat*) Now let's change the /t/ in *hat* to /m/. What is the new word? (*ham*) Use the following examples and ask children to say the new words:

Say *tuck*. Change the /t/ to /l/. (*luck*)

Say *men*. Change the /n/ to /t/. (*met*)

Say *sit*. Change the /s/ to /b/. (*bit*)

Phoneme Segmentation Remind children that they can break a word into its individual sounds. Say: *tub*. I hear the sounds /t/ /u/ /b/ in *tub*. Have children segment these words, clearly producing the beginning, medial, and final sounds.

bet (/b/ /e/ /t/)	**has** (/h/ /a/ /z/)	**sip** (/s/ /i/ /p/)
hot (/h/ /o/ /t/)	**lap** (/l/ /a/ /p/)	**dock** (/d/ /o/ /k/)

RETEACH

Phonics

Review Consonants /kw/q, /j/j Display the Sound/Spelling Card *Qq*. Ask: **What sound do you hear at the beginning of *quick*? What letter stands for the /kw/ sound at the beginning of *quick*?** Now display Sound/Spelling Card *Jj*. Ask: **What sound do you hear at the beginning of *jump*? What letter stands for /j/ at the beginning of *jump*?** (*j*)

With both Sound/Spelling Cards on display, display Photo Cards *quarter* and *jacks*. Have children sort the cards by their beginning sounds, first saying each picture name and then telling which letter stands for the sound at the beginning of its name.

Discriminate /kw/ and /j/ Give each child Word Builder Cards for *q* and *j*. Tell children to listen for the sound at the beginning of each word you say. If the word starts with /kw/, children should hold up letter card *q*. If the word starts with /j/, children should hold up letter card *j*. Say these words: *quilt, jet, jog, queen, jolly, question, jig,* and *queen*.

318 Lesson 27

Day 3

REVIEW

Reading

Review Consonants /kw/q, /j/j Write the words *quilt* and *jog* on the board. Point to the words, read them slowly, and have children repeat them after you.

Review High-Frequency Words Write the words *that* and *have* on the board. Read each word, and have children repeat after you. Point to the words randomly, having children say the word you point to each time until they identify it correctly consistently.

Then write the following sentence frame on the board: *Can I have that _____?* displaying the *Photo Card watch*. Point to each word and have children read the sentence aloud, adding the word pictured on the *Photo Card*. Repeat the activity with the other *Photo Cards*.

Grade K

Day 3

RETEACH
Comprehension

Main Idea Remind children that the main idea of a story is what it is mostly about. Have children listen for the main idea as you read aloud the following story. Pause during the story to ask children questions about what Haley saw.

Practice Book 160

> Haley and her dad went to the craft fair. There were many booths. Each booth had a different craft. At one booth, Haley saw cute cat toys filled with catnip. At the next booth, a craftsperson was selling purses and bags made from old blue jeans. Another booth had flower arrangements made with dried flowers, grains, and leaves. "There is so much neat stuff here," Haley said to her dad.

Guide children to *Practice Book* page 160. Have them look at the pictures as you read the story again. If the picture is *not* part of the main idea of the story, ask them to cross it out. After children have completed the page, ask them to state in their own words the main idea of the story above.

REVIEW
Build Robust Vocabulary

Read aloud the Student-Friendly Explanations for *hollow, defend, quarrel,* and *watchful*. Then discuss each word with children by asking the questions shown below.

hollow
Which would make a better home for a squirrel, a rock or a *hollow* tree? Why?

defend and **watchful**
A mother dog is very *watchful* over her puppies. Does that mean that she is always trying to defend her babies or run away from her babies?

quarrel
If you had a *quarrel* with a brother or sister, what might you be quarreling about?

VOCABULARY
Student-Friendly Explanations

hollow Something that is hollow has a space inside.

defend If you defend something, you keep it safe or away from harm.

quarrel If you quarrel with someone, you argue or disagree about something.

watchful If you are watchful, you are watching someone or something in a careful, alert way.

Day 3

RETEACH

Writing

Writing Trait: Organization Remind children that, when writing an invitation, it should include some kinds of information, but not other kinds. Write the following statements on the board. Read each line while tracking the print.

> Please come to my party.
> Where: At my house on 123 First Street
> When: 1:00 on Saturday May 17

Remind children that when writing an invitation, you need to write where and when the event takes place. This information should be on separate lines, one below the other.

Read the invitation on the board again. Ask children if it is organized in a way that is clear to the reader. Ask children if any of the statements are not about the party. Then ask whether any information should be organized or grouped differently.

Grade K 321

LESSON 27

PHONEMIC AWARENESS
Substitute Initial and Final Sounds

PHONICS
Review Consonants /kw/q, /j/j

READING
Review Consonants /kw/q, /j/j, /z/z
Review High-Frequency Words

BUILD ROBUST VOCABULARY
Review feast, squabble, peek, watchful, clever, boastful, ravenous, quarrel

WRITING
Reteach Writing Form: Invitation

Materials Needed:

Sound/Spelling Cards Qq, Jj, Zz | Phoneme Phone | Write-On/Wipe-Off Boards

Word Builders and Word Builder Cards | Practice Book

Phonemic Awareness

Substitute Initial and Final Sounds Remind children that they can change the sounds in a word to make a new word. Say: **duck. Say the word with me: duck. We can change the /d/ in duck to /l/. What is the new word?** (*luck*) **Say rip. Change the /r/ to /t/.** (*tip*) Use the following examples and ask children to say the new words: **Say peg. Change /p/ to /l/. What is the new word?** (*leg*) **Say den. Change /d/ to /h/. What is the new word?** (*hen*)

Phoneme Segmentation Remind children that they can break a word into individual sounds. Say: **sit. I hear the sounds /s/ /i/ /t/ in sit.** Have children repeat the phonemes in order. (/s/ /i/ /t/) Then have children segment the following words into individual sounds: *mad* (/m/ /a/ /d/); *man* (/m/ /a/ /n/); and *cub* (/c/ /u/ /b/).

REVIEW
Phonics

 Consonants /kw/q, /z/z, /j/j Display *Sound/Spelling Card Qq*. Ask: **What sound do you hear at the beginning of quiz? What letter stands for the /kw/ sound at the beginning of quiz?** Place *Sound/Spelling Card Jj* in the pocket chart. Ask: **What sound do you hear at the beginning of jacks? What letter stands for the /j/ sound at the beginning of jacks?** Display *Sound/Spelling Card Zz*. Ask: **What sound do you hear at the beginning of zip? What letter stands for the /z/ sound at the beginning of zip?**

 Distribute *Phoneme Phones* to children. Say each sound, and have children repeat the sound into their phones. As they repeat the sound, ask them to look at the position of their mouths in the mirror. Continue by having them repeat the words *quiz, jacks,* and *zip* after you. Have them pay attention to their mouth position in the mirror.

Name the Initial Sound Ask children to listen as you say the word *quiz*, emphasizing the initial sound. Ask: **Does quiz begin with /j/ or /kw/?** Repeat the procedure with the words *quick, queen, joke, jacks,* and *jam*.

 Discriminate /kw/ and /j/ Distribute *Write-on/Wipe-off Boards*. Display *Photo Cards quarter* and *jacks*. Tell children that they are going to sort the cards by their beginning sounds. Have children say each picture name and tell the letter that stands for the sound at the beginning of its name. Then have children write the letters *q* and *j* on their boards. Ask them to draw a picture that begins with each letter.

322 Lesson 27

REVIEW

Reading

Review Consonants /q/q, /j/j, /z/z Pass out *Word Builder Cards* q, z, and j. Have children hold up the letter that stands for the sound they hear at the beginning of these words: *quiet, jam, zebra, job, quite, quick*.

Review High-Frequency Words Display index cards with these high-frequency words written on them: *good, see, that, they, want,* and *have*. Read each word and point to it. Then ask children to use each word in a sentence.

Practice Book 162–163

Have children turn to *Practice Book* pages 161–162. Have children make the book and read the story.

REVIEW

Build Robust Vocabulary

Remind children of the Student-Friendly Explanations of *feast, squabble, peek, watchful, clever, boastful, ravenous,* and *quarrel*. Then determine children's understanding of the words by asking the following questions.

- **Would *ravenous* people be very interested in coming to a *feast*? Why?**
- **What are some things two friends might *quarrel* about?**
- **Do you like being around *boastful* people? Why or why not?**
- **Who is someone you think is *clever*? Why?**
- **Show how you might *peek* through your fingers.**
- **Would a good mother sheep be *watchful* over her lambs? Explain.**
- **Show with your fingers how two cats might *squabble* over milk.**

RETEACH

Writing

Writing Form: Invitation Show children several examples of invitations you have received. Talk about the purpose of invitations, such as asking a friend to play or come to a party. Tell children that together you will write an invitation for an event at their home. Discuss ideas with children for events they might want to write an invitation for, such as a play date or a birthday party. Write their ideas on chart paper.

Then use children's ideas to write an invitation, using the invitations on the charts as models. Remind children that when writing an invitation, we write where and when the event takes place on separate lines, one below the other. Invite them to write letters and words they know. Read the finished invitation to the children.

> Please come to my party.
> When: Saturday, 2:00
> Where: Marcie's house

VOCABULARY

Student-Friendly Explanations

feast A feast is a big meal with lots of different kinds of foods.

squabble If you squabble with someone, you argue about something that is not very important.

peek When you peek at something, you take a quick look at it without being seen.

watchful If you are watchful, you are watching someone or something in a careful, alert way.

clever Someone who is clever is smart and good at solving problems.

boastful If you are boastful, you talk about yourself with too much pride.

ravenous If you are ravenous, you are very hungry.

quarrel If you quarrel with someone, you argue or disagree about something.

LESSON 27

PHONEMIC AWARENESS
Syllable Blending

PHONICS
Reteach Word Blending

HIGH-FREQUENCY WORDS
Review we, have, a

BUILD ROBUST VOCABULARY
Preteach dare, gleaming, splendid

Materials Needed:

Photo Cards | Practice Book | Word Builder and Word Builder Cards

Phonemic Awareness

Syllable Blending Remind children that they have learned that words are made of parts. Words are like puzzles that can be taken apart and put back together again. The parts of a word are called syllables. Guide children to identify syllables in spoken words and to combine syllables to say words. Display the *Photo Card pencil*. Say: **Listen as I say a word: pencil. Pencil has two syllables: pen-cil. Tap your foot as you say each syllable. Now I'll put the two syllables together and say the word again: pencil.** Continue with these words that have a common second syllable:

jump-ing (*jumping*)   **runn-ing** (*running*)   **sleep-ing** (*sleeping*)

Say the following syllables. Have children tap a foot and count the syllables with you. Then have them combine the syllables to say the words.

el-bow (*elbow*)   **ig-loo** (*igloo*)   **quar-ter** (*quarter*)

sand-wich (*sandwich*)   **ti-ger** (*tiger*)   **ze-bra** (*zebra*)

RETEACH

Phonics

Blend Sounds Have children sit in a circle. Remind children that sounds can be blended to make words. Read the following verse, with children echoing you. Establish a rhythm and keep it going through the verse. Say: **We're going on a word hunt. What's this word? /r/ /u/ /g/ Together: rug!**

Say: **We blended /r/ /u/ /g/ to make the word rug. /r/ /u/ /g/. What word did we make?** (*rug*) Continue with the words /c/ /u/ /t (*cut*), /c/ /u/ /p/ (*cup*), /f/ /u/ /n/ (*fun*). Restate the sounds that were blended to make each word, and have children name the word that was made.

Word Blending Place the *Word Builder Cards* *u* and *s* in the *Word Builder*. Point to *u*. Say: **/uu/**. Have children name the letter and sound. Point to *s*. Say: **/ss/**. Have children name the letter and sound. Slide the *u* next to *s*. Move your hand under the letters and blend the sounds: **/uuss/**. Have children repeat after you. Then have children blend and read the word *us* with you. Continue with the words *bus, rub,* and *gum*.

Have children turn to *Practice Book* page 163. Help children identify the pictures. Guide them to trace the letter *u* in each word.

324 Lesson 27

Day 5

REVIEW
High-Frequency Words

Write the word *we* on the board and use it in a sentence, such as *We run*. Have children take turns using the word *we* in a sentence. Repeat with the word *have*.

Distribute index cards with high-frequency words *we, have,* and *a* written on them. Say each word, and have the children repeat that word and hold up the correct card. Then show the *Photo Card drum*. Ask children to say the picture name. Use the index cards, the *Photo Card,* and an index card with a period to build the sentence frame shown below. Point to each word as you read the sentence. Then have children read the sentence with you.

Replace *Photo Card drum* with *dog.* Point to each word as you read the sentence. Point to each word again as children read the sentence aloud. Repeat with other *Photo Cards*.

PRETEACH
Build Robust Vocabulary

Introduce the words *dare, gleaming,* and *splendid* by reading the Student-Friendly Explanations. Then discuss each word, using the following examples.

dare
Did anyone ever *dare* you to do something? What was it?

gleaming
Name something in your home that is *gleaming*.

splendid
If I told you that I had a *splendid* time on a vacation, would that mean that my vacation was wonderful or boring?

High-Frequency Words

a   have

we

VOCABULARY
Student-Friendly Explanations

dare If you dare someone, you try to get that person to do something that is scary or dangerous.

gleaming If something is gleaming, it is shiny and bright.

splendid Something splendid is wonderful and special.

Grade K **325**

LESSON 28

PHONEMIC AWARENESS
Syllable Segmentation

Phonics
Reteach Word Building

High-Frequency Words
Review *a, and, I, go, see, to, we*

Comprehension
Reteach Reality/Fantasy

Build Robust Vocabulary
Reteach *dare, gleaming, splendid*

Materials Needed:

Word Builder and Word Builder Cards | Write-On/Wipe-Off Boards | Copying Master

Photo Cards | Practice Book

Phonemic Awareness

Syllable Segmentation Remind children that words are like puzzles and that they can be taken apart and put back together again. Then model for children how to segment spoken words into syllables. Say: **Listen to this word: *elbow*. Listen as I break it into two parts, or syllables: *el-bow*. I will say the word again and clap for each part: *el-bow*.** Continue with the following words. Have children repeat each word after you and then name the syllables.

inside (in-side)   **insect** (in-sect)

rerun (re-run)   **return** (re-turn)

doctor (doc-tor)   **tractor** (trac-tor)

RETEACH

Phonics

Blend Words Distribute *Word Builder Cards b, e, d, r, u, g, m, h, l, g,* and *t.* Review each letter name and sound. Then hold up letters randomly and ask children to tell the letter name and sound.

Explain to children that you are going to show them how a word can change when the letters in the word change. Say: **Use your *Word Builder Cards* to make new words with me. I will use the letters *b, e,* and *d* to make the word *bed*. Now you do the same. Blend the sounds with me: /b/-/e/-/d/, *bed*. If I take away the *b* and put *r* in its place, I have the word *red*. Now you try it. Blend the sounds and say the word with me: /r/-/e/-/d/, *red*.**

  Build Words Have children build the word *bug* in their *Word Builder*:

Change the *b* to *r*. What word did you make?
(*rug*)

Change the *r* to *m*. What word did you make?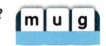
(*mug*)

Continue with the words *lug, leg,* and *let.* Then have children practice writing the words they built on their *Write-On/Wipe-Off Boards*. Distribute *Copying Master 55*. Guide children to trace the letter *e* and *u* at the bottom of the page and cut them out. Help children identify the pictures. Children should paste *e* or *u* in the box to complete each picture name. (*jet, sun, cut, bed*)

326 Lesson 28

Day 1

REVIEW
High-Frequency Words

Distribute index cards with the words *a, and, I, go, see, to,* and *we.* Say each word, and have children repeat each word and hold up the correct card. Write on the board the sentence frame *Dan and I see a _____.* Complete the sentence with *Photo Card fish.* Point to each word, and have children read the sentence aloud. Continue with other *Photo Card* combinations. Point to each word in the sentence, and have children read.

High-Frequency Words

a	see
and	to
I	we
go	

RETEACH
Comprehension

Reality/Fantasy Remind children that real stories are about things that can happen in real life. Make-believe stories are stories that can't happen. Then read this story aloud to them.

Kim was watching TV. Her cat Fluff walked over to her. Fluff jumped on Kim's lap and meowed loudly. "What do you want, Fluff?" asked Kim.

"Kim," said Fluff, "I want you to fix me a saucer of milk. Could you do that, please?"

Kim got up and walked into the kitchen. She poured some milk into a saucer and set in on the floor. Fluff lapped up the milk.

Guide children to turn to page 164 in their *Practice Books*. Have them look at each picture of something that happened in the story. If the event is one that could really happen, have children draw a circle around the picture. If not, have children draw an X through the picture. Have children explain their answers.

RETEACH
Build Robust Vocabulary

Read the Student-Friendly Explanations for *dare, gleaming,* and *splendid.* Then discuss each word, asking children the following questions.

dare
Would you be more likely to *dare* someone to take a nap or to go into a dark room? Why?

gleaming
After you wash your family's car, will it be dull or *gleaming*? Why?

splendid
If I name something that would look *splendid*, say "That's splendid." If not, don't say anything.

a rainbow   a pencil   a treasure chest   an eagle flying

VOCABULARY
Student-Friendly Explanations

dare If you dare someone, you try to get that person to do something that is scary or dangerous.

gleaming If something is gleaming, it is shiny and bright.

splendid Something splendid is wonderful and special.

Grade K 327

LESSON 28

PHONEMIC AWARENESS
Syllable Deletion

PHONICS
Reteach Word Building

HIGH-FREQUENCY WORDS
Review *I, give, you, that*

COMPREHENSION
Review Generate Questions

BUILD ROBUST VOCABULARY
Preteach *cautiously, festival, disaster*

Materials Needed:

Word Builder and Word Builder Cards | Write-On/Wipe-Off Boards | Copying Master

Photo Cards | Practice Book

Phonemic Awareness

Syllable Deletion Remind children that words are like puzzles and that they can be taken apart and put back together again. Model for children how to segment words. Say: **Listen to this word: order. I will break it into two parts, or syllables. or . . . der. I will say the syllables again: or . . . der. Tap your finger on the desk for each syllable. Now listen as I put the word back together again: order.**

Tell children that now that they can break words into syllables, they can say a word without one of its syllables. Say: **Listen to the word again: order. Now I will say the word *order* without the first syllable, *der*. Say it with me: *der*.**

Divide the group and say the word *sixteen*. Have one group say the first syllable: *six*. Have the other group say the second syllable: *teen*. Repeat several times. Continue with *rainbow, birthday,* and *snowman*.

Then say the following words and have the children say the word without the first syllable: *sandwich* (wich), *elbow* (bow), *cupcake* (cake)

RETEACH

Phonics

Model Word Building Distribute Word Builder Cards *c, u, t, n, h, a, m, p, l,* and *b*. Explain to children that when letters in words change, so do the sounds. Have the children following along as you model word building. Say: **I will use the letters *c, u,* and *t* to make the word *cut*. Now you do the same. Blend the sounds with me: /c/-/u/-/t/, *cut*. If I take away the *c* and put *n* in its place, I have the word *nut*. Now you try it. Blend the sounds and say the word with me: /n/-/u/-/t/, *nut*.**

Build Words Have children continue with *nut*. Say:

Change the *n* to *h*. What word did you make? (*hut*)

Change the *u* to *a*. What word did you make? (*hat*)

Change the *h* to *c*. What word did you make? (*cat*)

Continue building the words *cab, cub,* and *cup*. Then have children write the words they built on their *Write-On/Wipe-Off Boards*. Distribute *Copying Master 56* to review building words with short *u* and *a*. Help children name each picture and read the word choices below each picture. Then have children circle the word that names the picture and write the word. (*nut, cab, hut, bug*)

Day 2

REVIEW
High-Frequency Words

  Display index cards for *I, give, you,* and *that;* an index card with the word *will;* and an index card with a period. Build the sentence shown below. Point to each word and read the sentence. Ask volunteers to point to the words *give* and *that*. Complete the sentence with *Photo Card apple*. Have children read the sentence with you, as you point to each word.

| I | will | give | you | that | |

Continue with other *Photo Card* combinations. Have children turn to *Practice Book* page 165 to review high-frequency words and practice newly-learned words. Complete the page together.

High-Frequency Words

give	that
I	you

RETEACH
Comprehension

Generate Questions Explain that asking questions about a story while reading it helps you to understand and enjoy it. Reread the story from Day 1. Copy the Question/Answer chart shown below. Read the question in the first column. Then read the story again. Ask children to supply the answer. Have children suggest other questions and answers based on the Fluff story.

Question	Answer
What was Kim doing when Fluff jumped in her lap?	(Kim was watching TV.)

PRETEACH
Build Robust Vocabulary

Read the Student-Friendly Explanations for *cautiously, festival,* and *disaster.* Then ask children the following questions, and discuss children's responses.

cautiously
How might a mouse move it if were *cautiously* walking past a cat?

festival
Describe a *festival* you have been to or would like to go to.

disaster
What kind of *disaster* might happen while you are drying dishes?

VOCABULARY
Student-Friendly Explanations

cautiously When you do something cautiously, you are careful to stay away from danger.

festival A festival is a kind of celebration with different kinds of activities, foods, and decorations.

disaster A disaster is something terrible that happens suddenly.

Grade K 329

LESSON 28

PHONEMIC AWARENESS
Syllable Deletion

PHONICS
Preteach Phonogram -ug

HIGH-FREQUENCY WORDS
Review we, have, and

COMPREHENSION
Reteach Reality/Fantasy

BUILD ROBUST VOCABULARY
Reteach cautiously, festival, disaster

WRITING
Preteach Writing Trait: Word Choice

Materials Needed:

Write-On/Wipe-Off Boards

Photo Cards

Practice Book

Phonemic Awareness

Syllable Deletion Remind children that they have learned to break words into syllables. Review how to say a word without one of its syllables. Say: **Listen to this word: insect. I will break it into two syllables. in-sect. Now I will say the word insect without the second syllable, sect: in. Say it with me: in.**

Have children say each word without the first syllable.

Say *apple* **without the** *ap*. (ple)

Say *elbow* **without the** *el*. (bow)

Continue with the following words, having children say the word without second syllable.

Say *tiger* **without the** *ger*. (ti)

Say *pencil* **without the** *cil*. (pen)

PRETEACH
Phonics

Identify Rhyming Words Say the words *hug* and *bug*, and have children repeat them. Ask how the two words are the same. (They both have /ug/; they rhyme.) Tell children you are going to say pairs of words. If the words rhyme, children should raise their hands. If the words do not rhyme, children should do nothing. Use the following pairs of words.

| rug, tug | snug, hug | nod, plug |
| frog, rug | jug, bag | mug, dug |

Read Words with -ug Write the words *bug* and *tug* on the board. Track the print and have children read the two words. Point out that both words have /ug/; the words rhyme. Explain that the words *bug* and *tug* are in the *-ug* word family because they both end in *-ug*. Continue by writing the words *hug* and *dug* and having children read the words.

Distribute *Write-on/Wipe-off Boards*. Write these words on the board: *bug, sit, mug, bed, rug*. Have children read the words and copy those words in the *-ug* family on their *Write-on/Wipe-off Boards*.

330 Lesson 28

Day 3

RETEACH

High-Frequency Words

High-Frequency Words	
a	have
and	we

Distribute index cards for *we, have,* and *and* to children. As you say each word, have children repeat the word and hold up the correct card. Show *Photo Cards dog* and *cat*. Ask children to say the picture names. Then use index cards for *we, have,* and *and*, an index cards with *a*, a period index card, and *Photo Cards dog* and *cat* to build the first sentence frame shown below. Point to each word as you read the sentence. Ask children to read the sentence with you.

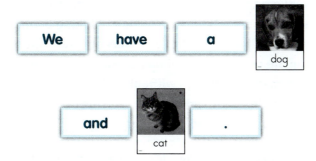

Then continue with the following sentences. Point to each word and have children read the sentences aloud.

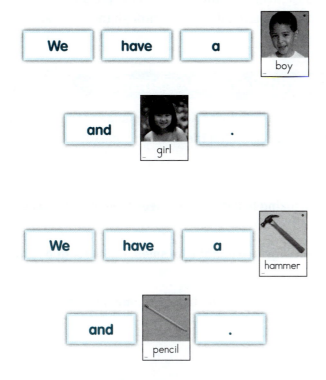

Read the sentences, and have children hold up the correct index card when they hear the high-frequency words *we, have,* and *and*.

Then write the following sentence frame on the board: *We have a _____ and a _____.* Have children copy and complete the sentence with words or pictures.

Grade K **331**

Day 3

RETEACH

Comprehension

Practice Book 166 **Reality/Fantasy** Remind children that some stories are real and some stories are make-believe. Tell them they will listen to a story. Ask children to think about which parts of the story are real and which are make-believe. Read aloud the following story.

> It was Will's birthday. He got lots of presents from his family and friends. From his aunt, he got a new hooded sweatshirt. His sister Amie gave him a CD. But the present he liked best was from his grandpa and grandma. It was a new pair of hiking boots. These were not ordinary hiking boots. They were special. Whenever Will put them on, he could hike right up the walls of his bedroom. He could hike across the ceiling—without falling down. He wore his new boots outside and hiked right up the side of his house to the roof. From the roof, he could see a long, long way.

Guide children to *Practice Book* page 166. Have them look at each picture of something that happened in the story. If the picture shows reality, have children draw a circle around the picture. If the picture shows fantasy, or make-believe, have children draw an X through the picture.

RETEACH

Build Robust Vocabulary

Remind children of the Student-Friendly Explanations for *cautiously*, *festival*, and *disaster*. Then ask children the following questions and discuss their responses.

cautiously
Does a person walking in a dark room need to walk *cautiously*? Why?

festival
What are some things you might see, smell, and hear at a *festival*?

disaster
What would you say to someone to warn someone of a weather *disaster*?

VOCABULARY
Student-Friendly Explanations

cautiously When you do something cautiously, you are careful to stay away from danger.

festival A festival is a kind of celebration with different kinds of activities, foods, and decorations.

disaster A disaster is something terrible that happens suddenly.

PRETEACH

Phonics

Writing Trait: Word Choice Remind children that when writing a thank-you note or other letter, it is important to choose words carefully. For example, the words used in a thank-you note should describe how you feel about what the person gave you or did for you.

Write the following sentences on the board and read them aloud.

> Thank you for the t-shirt.
>
> Thank you so much for the fantastic Pittsburgh Steelers t-shirt.

Ask: What are these sentences about? (Someone has gotten a t-shirt as a gift.) **How are the sentences different?** (The second one tells what kind of t-shirt it is, tells that the writer thinks the shirt is fantastic, and tells that he or she is really happy about it.) **Which sentence expresses more ideas about the person's feeling about the gift?** (the second one)

Repeat with the following pair of sentences.

> I love my new shirt and can't wait to wear it to school.
>
> I like the shirt.

Have children name other words or phrases that the writer could have used to describe how he or she felt. Say the following sentence and invite children complete it with a descriptive word: *I think my new shirt is _____!*

Grade K 333

LESSON 28

PHONEMIC AWARENESS
Onset/Rime Blending

PHONICS
Preteach Phonogram -up

READING
Review Phonogram -up
Review High-Frequency Words

BUILD ROBUST VOCABULARY
Review dare, gleaming, splendid, cautiously, festival, disaster

WRITING
Reteach Writing Form: Thank-You Note

Materials Needed:

Write-On/ Wipe-Off Boards

Practice Book pp. 167–168

Phonemic Awareness

Blend Onset/Rime Remind children that they have learned how to blend sounds to say words. Say: **Listen as I say a word in two parts. First I'll say /t/. Then I'll say op. Now I will blend the two parts to say a word: /t/-op, top. Let's do one together. Repeat after me: /m/-op, mop.**

Guide children to repeat the following onsets and rimes and blend them to make words.

/b/-ug (*bug*)	/b/-us (*bus*)	/b/-un (*bun*)
/w/-ig (*wig*)	/w/-ag (*wag*)	/w/-in (*win*)
/c/-ap (*cap*)	/n/-ap (*nap*)	/t/-ap (*tap*)
/p/-in (*pin*)	/f/-in (*fin*)	/t/-in (*tin*)

PRETEACH
Phonics

Identify Rhyming Words Say the words *pup, cup,* and *rug,* and have children repeat them. Point out that *pup* and *cup* rhyme because they both end with /up/. *Rug* does not rhyme with *pup* and *cup* because it ends with /ug/. Read the following pairs of words and have children tell you whether they rhyme:

up, pup	cup, rug
tug, bug	pup, pit
tug, tag	cup, up

Read Words with –up Write the word *up* on chart paper. Track the print as children read the word. Then write the words *cup* and *pup*. Again, track the print as children read the words. Point out that these words rhyme because they all end with /up/. Underline the *-up* in each word and point to it. Explain that the words *up, cup,* and *pup* are in the *-up* word family because they end in *-up*.

Distribute *Write-on/Wipe-off Boards*. Write these words on the board: *tug, up, cup, hog, sip, pup*. Read the words with children and have them copy those words in the *-up* family on their *Write-on/Wipe-off Boards*.

REVIEW
Reading

Write *up, pup,* and *cup* on chart paper. Read each word and have children repeat it. Then point to the words randomly and have children read the words.

Write these high-frequency words on chart paper: *see, give, that, we, have,* and *a*. Point to a word, say the word, and have volunteers use the word in a sentence. Review until several children compose sentences for each word.

Have children turn to *Practice Book* page 167–168. Help children make the book and read the story.

High-Frequency Words

a	see
give	that
have	we

REVIEW
Robust Vocabulary

Remind children of the Student-Friendly Explanations for *dare, gleaming, splendid, cautiously, festival,* and *disaster.* Then determine children's understanding of the words by asking the following questions.

- **What are some things people might do at a *festival*?**
- **Would someone be more likely to *dare* you to jump off a high diving board, or to help dry dishes?**
- **After a person washes a car, it is dull or is it *gleaming*? Explain.**
- **If a whole batch of cookies got burned in the oven, would that be *splendid* or would it be a *disaster*? Tell why.**
- **Would you walk *cautiously* through a dark room? Tell why or why not.**

VOCABULARY
Student-Friendly Explanations

dare If you dare someone, you try to get that person to do something that is scary or dangerous.

gleaming If something is gleaming, it is shiny and bright.

splendid Something splendid is wonderful and special.

cautiously When you do something cautiously, you are careful to stay away from danger.

festival A festival is a kind of celebration with different kinds of activities, foods, and decorations.

disaster A disaster is something terrible that happens suddenly.

RETEACH
Writing

Writing Form: Thank-You Note Remind children that we write thank-you notes to people who have done something nice for us. Remind children that when writing a thank-you note, it is important to choose words that describe how you feel about what the person did for you.

Together with children write a thank-you note based on the story about the hiking boots on page 332. Reread the story. Guide children to generate ideas for words or phrases. Record their ideas on chart paper. Then use their ideas to write a thank-you note from Will to his grandparents. Invite children to add letters and words they know. Read the finished note to children.

> Dear Grandma and Grandpa,
> Thank you for the magic hiking boots.
> I can walk right up walls!
> Love,
> Will

Grade K **335**

LESSON 28

PHONEMIC AWARENESS
Phoneme Isolation: Initial, Medial, Final

PHONICS
Review Short Vowel /a/*a*

HIGH-FREQUENCY WORDS
Review *you, look*

BUILD ROBUST VOCABULARY
Review *adventure, explore, tame (v)*

Materials Needed:

Word Builder and Word Builder Cards

Sounds of Letters CD

Practice Book

Photo Cards

Phonemic Awareness

Phoneme Isolation: Initial, Medial, Final Remind children that words are made up of sounds and that they can listen for the sounds in words. Tell them they will listen to the sound at the beginning of words. **Say: I am going to say a word:** *hat*. **I hear /h/ at the beginning. /hat/ Now listen as I say another word:** *gum*. **I hear /g/ at the beginning. /gum/** Have children name the sound they hear at the beginning of these words: *box, sun, dig*. Repeat the process for middle and final sounds. Have children name the sound they hear in the middle of these words: *jug, sip, men*. Have them name the sound they hear at the end of these words: *tap, pig, pen*.

REVIEW
Phonics

Blend Phonemes Play a game called "Say the Word" in which you say the sounds that are in a word and children say the word. Say: **I will say the sounds /c/ /a/ /t/. The word is** *cat*. **Let's do another one: /t/ /a/ /n/. The word is** *tan*. Continue, having children provide responses.

/r/ /a/ /p/ (rap)   /f/ /a/ /n/ (fan)   /n/ /a/ /p/ (nap)

/c/ /a/ /b/ (cab)   /p/ /a/ /d/ (pad)   /h/ /a/ /t/ (hat)

Short Vowel /a/*a* Place the *Word Builder Cards* p, a, and n in *Word Builder*. Point to *p*. Say /p/. Have children name the letter and sound. Point to *a*. Say /a/. Have children name the letter and sound. Point to *n*. Say /n/. Have children name the letter and sound. Slide the letters together. Move your hand under the letters and blend the sounds: /pan/. Have children repeat after you. Then have children blend and read the word *pan* with you.
Continue with the words *tap, pal,* and *bag*. Use the *Sounds of Letters CD* to build familiarity with the short *a*.

Have children turn to *Practice Book* page 169. Help children complete the activities.

Day 5

REVIEW
High-Frequency Words

Display index cards for *you, look, for,* and *the*. Say each word, and have the children repeat that word as you hold up each card. Then use the index cards and the period card to build the sentence frame shown below. Point to each word as you read the sentence. Reread it with children. Ask volunteers to point to the words *you, look, for,* and *the*. Place *Photo Card cat* to complete the sentence. Point to each word in the sentence, and have children read the sentence with you.

| You | look | for | the | cat | . |

Replace the *Photo Card cat* with *Photo Card hat*. Point to each word as children read the sentence to you. Repeat with *Photo Cards box, egg, lamp, pig,* and *drum*.

REVIEW
Build Robust Vocabulary

Read the Student-Friendly Explanations for *adventure, explore,* and *tame*. Then discuss each word, using the following examples.

adventure
What is your idea of an *adventure*? Describe it.

explore
Name a place that you would like to *explore*? Why?

tame
Do you think it would be easier to *tame* a snake or a dog? Why?

High-Frequency Words

look   you

VOCABULARY

Student-Friendly Explanations

adventure An adventure is something new you do that is exciting or dangerous.

explore When you explore, you go to a place you have never been before to see what it is like.

tame (v) When you tame an animal, you make it do what you want.

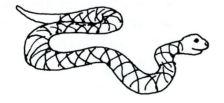

Grade K 337

LESSON 29

PHONEMIC AWARENESS
Phoneme Identity: Initial, Final

PHONICS
Review Short Vowel /e/e

HIGH-FREQUENCY WORDS
Review there, are

COMPREHENSION
Review Reality/Fantasy

BUILD ROBUST VOCABULARY
Review adventure, explore, tame (v)

Materials Needed:

Word Builder and Word Builder Cards

Write-On/ Wipe-Off Boards

Copying Master

Photo Cards

Practice Book

Phonemic Awareness

Phoneme Identity: Initial, Final Remind children that they have been listening for the sounds in words. Tell them you will say two words, and they will listen for the sounds that are the same in each of them. Say: **I will say two words: pet, pig. I hear /p/ at the beginning of each word. The sound at the beginning of each word is the same. Now listen as I say these two words: bad, red. I hear /d/ at the end of each word. The sound at the end of bad and red is the same.**

Follow the same procedure with the following word pairs. Have children tell which sound is the same. Then have them name the sound. *ten, toy* (/t/); *frog, leg* (/g/)

REVIEW
Phonics

Short Vowel /e/e Have children sit in a circle. As you read the following verse, have children echo you. Say: **We're going on a word hunt. What's this word? /p/ /e/ /n/** Together: **pen**! Continue for the word /r/ /e/ /d/. (red)

Now explain to children that a word can change when the letters in the word change. Say: **Use your Word Builder and Word Builder Cards to make new words with me. I will use the letters m, e, and t to make the word met. Now you do the same. Blend the sounds with me: /m/-/e/-/t/, met. If I take away the m and put g in its place, I have the word get. Now you try it. Blend the sounds and say the word with me: /g/-/e/-/t/ get.** Continue by saying:

- Change the *g* to *l*. What word did you make? (*let*)
- Change the *t* to *g*. What word did you make? (*leg*)

Have children practice writing the words they built on their *Write-On/Wipe-Off Boards*.

Distribute *Copying Master 57*. Have children trace the letters *Aa* and *Ee* and identify the pictures. Then have them write the letter for the middle sound. (*a* in the second and third boxes; *e* in the first and fourth boxes; *bed, cat, map, jet*.)

REVIEW

High-Frequency Words

 Display index cards for *there, are, and,* and *the.* Say each word, and have children repeat. Show Photo Cards *pig* and *fox.* Ask children to name the pictures. Then use index cards, the period card, and the pictures to build the sentence frame *There are the [Photo Card pig] and {Photo Card fox].* Point to each word as you read the sentence. Continue with other sentences.

High-Frequency Words	
are	there

REVIEW

Comprehension

 Reality/Fantasy Remind children that some stories are real because the things that happen could happen in real life. Some stories are fantasy because the things that happen are make-believe. Some stories contain elements of both reality and fantasy. Tell them to listen closely as you read this story aloud to them.

Sam was walking to school. He had his lunch in his backpack. It was his favorite—peanut butter and jelly. As he walked under a big tree, he heard a strange sound. It sounded like lips smacking. But they must have been very big lips because the sound was loud! Sam looked up and saw a face on the tree.

"Yum," said the tree. "I can smell your lunch, young man. I love peanut butter and jelly."

Sam climbed up the branches until he reached the tree's mouth. He stuffed in half of his sandwich. "Thank you very much," said the tree. "That was very tasty!"

Guide children to turn to page 170 in their *Practice Books.* Discuss the story. Then have them look at each picture. If the event is one that could not really happen, have students cross out the picture.

REVIEW

Build Robust Vocabulary

Remind children of the Student-Friendly Explanations for of *adventure, explore,* and *tame.* Then discuss each word, using the following examples.

adventure
Would it be an *adventure* for you to visit your bedroom or a jungle? Explain.

explore
Name a place you would like to *explore.* Why?

tame
What is something a *tame* seal at a zoo might do?

VOCABULARY
Student-Friendly Explanations

adventure An adventure is something new you do that is exciting or dangerous.

explore When you explore, you go to a place you have never been before to see what it is like.

tame (v) When you tame an animal, you make it do what you want.

LESSON 29

PHONEMIC AWARENESS
Phoneme Identity: Medial

PHONICS
Review Short Vowel /i/*i*

HIGH-FREQUENCY WORDS
Review *little, give*

COMPREHENSION
Preteach Answer Questions

BUILD ROBUST VOCABULARY
Review *amazed, completely, jolt(v)*

Materials Needed:

Write-On/ Wipe-Off Boards | Copying Master | Sounds of Letters CD

Photo Cards | Practice Book

Phonemic Awareness

Phoneme Identity: Medial Remind children that they have been listening for sounds in words. Tell them that they are going to tell which sound is the same in a pair of words. Say: **I will say two words: *hen, get*. I hear /e/ in the middle of each word. The sound in the middle of *hen* and *get* is the same.**

Follow the same procedure using the following sets of words. Have children repeat each set of words and name the sound that is the same in each set.

fox, not (/o/)   **mad, bat** (/a/)   **gum, bus** (/u/)

let, mess (/e/)   **sip, hit** (/i/)   **got, box** (/o/)

hum, nut (/u/)   **glad, pass** (/a/)   **thin, swim** (/i/)

REVIEW

Phonics

  Short Vowel /i/*i* Play a game called "Say the Word" in which you say the sounds that are in a word and children say the word. Say: **I will say the sounds in a word: /h/ /i/ /m/. The word is *him*. Let's do another one: /m/ /o/ /p/. The word is *mop*.** Continue, having children provide responses.

/m/ /a/ /n/ (man)   /b/ /o/ /x/ (box)   /l/ /i/ /t/ (lit)

/r/ /i/ /p/ (rip)   /p/ /e/ n/ (pen)   /b/ /u/ /g/ (bug)

Have children practice writing the words they say on their *Write-on/Wipe-off Boards*. Then on the board, write the words *man, box, lit, rip, pen,* and *bug*. Have children read the words, and write the words with short vowel *i* on their *Write-on/Wipe-off Boards*.

Distribute *Copying Master 58* to practice words with short *i* and *o* with children. Have children trace *Ii* and *Oo*. Help children to identify the pictures. Then have them write the letter of the sound that appears in the middle of the picture name. (Children write letter *i* in the first and third boxes, and letter *o* in the second and fourth boxes: *sit, top, pig, fox.*) Use the *Sounds of Letters CD* to build familiarity with short *i*.

Day 2

REVIEW
High-Frequency Words

  Write the high-frequency words *give, me, the,* and *little* on index cards. Use them and the period card to build this sentence frame:

Give me the little ____.

Point to each word as you read the sentence. Ask volunteers to point to the words *give* and *little*. Place *Photo Card nest* to complete the sentence. Have children read the sentence with you. Then replace *nest* with other *Photo Cards*.

Have children turn to *Practice Book* page 171 to review high-frequency words and practice newly-learned words. Complete the page together.

PRETEACH
Comprehension

Answer Questions Remind children that asking and answering questions about a story can help them understand and enjoy it better. Begin a chart like the one below by writing the question in the first column. Explain that as children listen again to the story from Day 1, they should try to answer this question. Reread the story about Sam.

Question	Answer
How does Sam feel about peanut butter and jelly sandwiches?	They are his favorite.

REVIEW
Build Robust Vocabulary

Remind children of the Student-Friendly Explanations for *amazed, completely,* and *jolt*. Then discuss each word, using the following examples.

amazed
I would be *amazed* if I heard a tree talking. What would amaze you?

completely
If you finished your dinner *completely*, would there be anything left on your plate? Why or why not?

jolt
Would it *jolt* you if you were riding down a smooth street in a big car, or if you were riding on a donkey?

High-Frequency Words

give   little

VOCABULARY
Student-Friendly Explanations

amazed If you are amazed, you are very surprised at something done or said.

completely Completely means totally or in every way.

jolt (v) To jolt means to move very suddenly.

Grade K **341**

LESSON 29

PHONEMIC AWARENESS
Phoneme Categorization: Initial, Final

PHONICS
Review Short Vowel /o/o

HIGH-FREQUENCY WORDS
Review you, there, are

COMPREHENSION
Review Reality/Fantasy

BUILD ROBUST VOCABULARY
Review amazed, completely, jolt (v)

WRITING
Reteach Writing Trait: Sentence Fluency

Materials Needed:

Phoneme Phone | Word Builder and Word Builder Cards | Write-On/Wipe-Off Boards

Practice Book

Phonemic Awareness

Phoneme Categorization: Initial, Final Remind children that words are made up of sounds and they can listen for the sounds in words. Tell them that now they will listen for the beginning sound that is different in a group of words. Segment the beginning sound in each set of words. Say: **/b/-ig, /s/-at, /s/-ip.** Then ask: **Which word has a different beginning sound? Big has a different beginning sound.** Repeat using the word groups *hammer, hat, girl; pig, egg, elbow;* and *drum, tree, tiger*. Then repeat the process for ending sounds using the following word groups: *pan, man, hat; fix, hill, box; hill, fall, sun; mess, bus, boat*.

Have children sit in a circle. Distribute the *Phoneme Phones*. Say the words *pet* and *pan*. Ask children to repeat the words while looking at the position of their mouths in the mirror. Ask: **Do *pet* and *pan* have the same beginning sound?** (yes) **What is the sound?** (/p/) Repeat with these word pairs:

pet, net   dig, dirt   sun, bun   wind, watch   neat, new

Now repeat the same procedure for ending sounds using these word pairs:

lamb, lap   clock, pick   big, dog   house, face   pin, fan

REVIEW

Phonics

 Short Vowel /o/o Have children sit in a circle. As you read the following verse, have children echo you. Say: **We're going on a word hunt. What's this word? /t/ /o/ /p/** Together: *top*! Continue for the words /h/ /o/ /g/ (hog), /b/ /o/ /x/ (box).

Now explain that a word can change when the letters in the word change. Say: **Use your *Word Builder* and *Word Builder Cards* to make new words with me. I will use the letters *l, o,* and *g* to make the word *log*. Now you do the same. Blend the sounds with me: /l/-/o/-/g/, *log*. If I take away the *g* and put *t* in its place, I have the word *lot*. Now you try it. Blend the sounds and say the word with me: /l/-/o/-/t/ *lot*.** Continue by saying:

- **Change the *l* to *h*. What word did you make?** (hot)
- **Change the *t* to *p*. What word did you make?** (hop)

Have children write the words they built on their *Write-On/Wipe-Off Boards*.

Day 3

REVIEW

High-Frequency Words

Prepare index cards for *you, are,* and *there* along with a question mark and comma. Build the sentence frame *Are you there, ____?* Read the sentence frame. As you say each word, have children repeat the word. Point to each word as you read the sentence. Ask children to read the sentence with you. Then point to a student, fill in his or her name, and reread the completed sentence. Have the child answer, *"Yes, I am here."* Write the new sentence on the board, having all the students read along with you. Repeat with as many names as time permits.

High-Frequency Words

are   you

there

Grade K 343

Day 3

VOCABULARY
Student-Friendly Explanations

amazed If you are amazed, you are very surprised at something done or said.

completely Completely means totally or in every way.

jolt (v) To jolt means to move very suddenly.

REVIEW
Comprehensive

 Reality/Fantasy Remind children that some stories are real because the things that happen could happen in real life. Some stories are fantasy because the things that happen are make-believe. Have children listen as you read aloud the following story.

> Maria went shopping with her dad. They needed to buy a bush for the back yard. Maria also needed some new shoes. First they went to the garden store. Her dad picked out a bush. When they got in the car, Maria's dad said, "Now we can go home."
>
> "But Dad," said Maria, "what about my shoes?"
>
> Maria's dad smiled. He said, "Just wait."
>
> When they got home, Maria and her dad planted the new bush. Then Maria watered the bush. Suddenly, a new pair of shoes grew between the leaves on the bush. Maria tried them on. "They're perfect, Dad," she said. "I like this shoe bush."

Guide children to turn to page 172 in their *Practice Books*. Have children decide whether each picture shows something that could really happen. If the event could not really happen, have students cross out the picture.

REVIEW
Build Robust Vocabulary

Remind children of the Student-Friendly Explanations for *amazed*, *completely*, and *jolt*. Then discuss each word, using the following examples.

amazed
Would you be *amazed* to see a cat sleeping in the sun or a cat playing the guitar? Why?

completely
If a refrigerator was *completely* full, would there be any room left for a milk bottle? Why?

jolt (v)
Which could you *jolt*: a full glass of water or a school bus? Explain.

344 Lesson 29

Day 3

RETEACH

Writing

Writing Trait: Sentence Fluency Remind children that writing is speech written down. Point out that when we speak, we use long and short sentences, and writing can have both kinds, too. Tell students you are going to read the story about Maria and the shoe bush again. This time, when they hear a sentence they think is a short one, have them say "Short." When they hear a sentence they think is a long one, have them say, "Long." (Responses will vary, although, in general, sentences with dependent clauses, compound subjects or predicates, or direct quotations may be considered long by the children.) If necessary, reread sentences about which opinion differs and ask students to explain their judgments.

Grade K 345

LESSON 29

DAY AT A GLANCE
Day 4

PHONEMIC AWARENESS
Phoneme Categorization: Medial

PHONICS
Review Short Vowel /u/*u*

READING
Review Short Vowel /u/*u*
Review High-Frequency Words

BUILD ROBUST VOCABULARY
Review *adventure, explore, tame (v), amazed, completely, jolt (v)*

WRITING
Reteach Writing Form: Personal Narrative

Materials Needed:

Write-On/Wipe-Off Boards

Sounds of Letters CD

Practice Book 173–174

Phonemic Awareness

Phoneme Categorization: Medial Tell children to listen carefully as you say two words: *bug, run.* Say: **Bug and run have the same middle sound: /u/. What is the middle sound?** (/u/).

Then ask children to name the middle sound in each word in a three-word set and the word with a different middle sound. Say: ***Rug.* Say *rug*. What is the middle sound in *rug*?** (/u/) ***Red.* Say *red*. What is the middle sound in *red*?** (/e/) ***Rest.* Say *rest*. What is the middle sound in *rest*?** (/e/) ***Rug, red, rest.* Say *rug, rest, red*. Which word has a different middle sound than the other two?** (rug)

Continue in the same way with these sets of words.

<u>tell</u>, hot, box	lift, <u>fat</u>, fix
push, pull, <u>pot</u>	mess, <u>much</u>, men
<u>pit</u>, pet, hen	hum, truck, <u>hat</u>
<u>bed</u>, bad, bat	nip, <u>bump</u>, fin

REVIEW

Phonics

Short Vowel /u/*u* Write the word *tub* on the board. Read the word. Then erase the *b*, write *g* and say: **Change *b* to *g*. What word did you make?** (tug)

Continue the procedure by saying:

- **Change *t* to *b*. What word did you make?** (bug)
- **Change *b* to *h*. What word did you make?** (hug)
- **Change *h* to *m*. What word did you make?** (mug)
- **Change *m* to *t*. What word did you make?** (tug)

Now distribute *Write-on/Wipe-off Boards.* Write the following incomplete words on the board: m__g, c__b, h__t, f__n, h__m. Have children copy the incomplete words on their boards and write the letter *u* to complete each word. Ask them to read the words to a partner. Use the *Sounds of Letters CD* to build familiarity with short *u*.

Day 4

> **REVIEW**
> ## Reading

 Short Vowel /u/u Write these words on the board: *fun* and *pup*. Read each word and have children repeat them. Continue with the words *dug, sum,* and *cut*.

High-Frequency Words Write these high-frequency words on chart paper: *look, little, give, me, at,* and *the*. Slowly read these sentences: *Look at the little pig. Look at the pen.* Have volunteers point to each high-frequency word as they hear it read.

Have children turn to *Practice Book* pages 173–174. Have children make the book and read the story with their family.

> **REVIEW**
> ## Build Robust Vocabulary

Remind children of the Student-Friendly Explanations for *adventure, explore, tame, amazed, completely,* and *jolt*. Then determine children's understanding of the words by asking them the following questions.

- If you *tame* animals, do you work at a zoo or an office? Why?
- If you *jolt* someone carrying a big tray of plates, what might happen?
- If a kitchen is *completely* clean, what might it look like?
- Describe an *adventure* you might want to go on.
- Would you be *amazed* to see a rabbit riding a bicycle? Why or why not?
- What things might you see if you went to *explore* a cave?

> **RETEACH**
> ## Writing

Writing Form: Personal Narrative Remind children that a personal narrative is a story about something that really happened to the writer and that the story events are told in the order in which they happened.

Tell children that together you will write a personal narrative about what your class does in a typical day. Have children name ideas. Record their ideas on chart paper. Then use children's ideas to write a personal narrative. Invite volunteers to add letters or words they know. Read the finished narrative to the children. Track the print on the chart paper as you read.

> We listened to a story.
> We had a snack.
> We took a nap on our rug.

Discuss the importance of telling the events in the order in which they happened.

High-Frequency Words

give	little
look	

VOCABULARY
Student-Friendly Explanations

adventure An adventure is something new you do that is exciting or dangerous.

explore When you explore, you go to a place you have never been before to see what it is like.

tame (v) When you tame an animal, you make it do what you want.

amazed If you are amazed, you are very surprised at something done or said.

completely Completely means totally or in every way.

jolt (v) To jolt means to move very suddenly.

Grade K 347

LESSON 29

PHONEMIC AWARENESS
Phoneme Blending

PHONICS
Review Word Blending and Building

HIGH-FREQUENCY WORDS
Review *where, the, is*

BUILD ROBUST VOCABULARY
Review *dare, adventure, explore*

Materials Needed:

Word Builder and Word Builder Cards | Practice Book | Photo Cards

Phonemic Awareness

Phoneme Blending Remind children that they can blend individual sounds to say words. Model for children how to blend sounds to say a word. Say: **Listen as I say these sounds: /s/ /i/ /t/. I will say the sounds again, blending the sounds: /ssiit/. Now I will blend the sounds to say the word: *sit*.** Have children blend these sounds and say the word: **/b/ /a/ /d/.** (*bad*) Then continue the activity with these words:

/k/ /i/ /s/ (*kiss*)	/r/ /u/ /n/ (*run*)	/f/ /o/ /ks/ (*fox*)
/t/ /e/ /n/ (*ten*)	/b/ /a/ /t/ (*bat*)	/s/ /i/ /t/ (*sit*)
/h/ /u/ /m/ (*hum*)	/h/ /o/ /p/ (*hop*)	/b/ /e/ /t/ (*bet*)

REVIEW

Phonics

Word Blending and Building Say: **Listen to the sounds I say: /m/ /a/ /n/. The word is *man*. Now you try one: /w/ /i/ /g/. What is the word?** (*wig*) Say the following words, and have children name the word:

| /p/ /e/ /t/ (*pet*) | /t/ /o/ /p/ (*top*) | /t/ /u/ /b/ (*tub*) |

  Distribute *Word Builders Cards p, i, g, n, t, h,* and *s* to children. Display the cards *p, i,* and *g* with spaces between the letters. Have children do the same. Say the sounds, one at a time. Slide the letters together and blend the sounds. Have children do the same. Say the word *pig* and have children repeat it. Continue the procedure by saying:

- Change *g* to *n*. What word did you make?
- Change *p* to *t*. What word did you make?
- Change *n* to *p*. What word did you make?
- Change *t* to *h*. What word did you make?

Have children turn to *Practice Book* page 175. Help children identify the pictures. Have them trace the middle vowel in each word and say each word.

Day 5

REVIEW

High-Frequency Words

 Display index cards for high-frequency words *where, the,* and *is*. Say each word, and have the children repeat that word as you hold up each card. Hold up the index card *where* and read it to children. Emphasize the word *where* as you say: **Where is it?** Then pass the card to a child, having him or her use the word *where* in a sentence. Continue with the rest of the group.

Then use the index cards and a card with a question mark to build the sentence frame shown below. Point to each word as you read the sentence. Reread it with children. Ask volunteers to point to the words *where, is,* and *the*. Place *Photo Card rabbit* to complete the sentence. Point to each word in the sentence, and have children read the sentence with you.

Replace the *Photo Card rabbit* with *Photo Card zebra*. Point to each word as children read the sentence to you. Repeat with Photo Cards *ant, fish, otter,* and *frog*.

High-Frequency Words

is	where
the	

REVIEW

Build Robust Vocabulary

Read aloud the Student-Friendly Explanations for *dare, adventure,* and *explore*. Then discuss each word, asking children the following questions.

dare

Did you ever *dare* a friend to do something? What was it?

adventure

Would you be more likely to go on an *adventure* in your bedroom or in the woods? Why?

explore

Would you be more likely to *explore* a forest or your family's kitchen? Why?

VOCABULARY

Student-Friendly Explanations

dare (v) If you dare someone to do something, you try to get that person to do something that is scary or dangerous.

adventure An adventure is something new you do that is exciting or dangerous.

explore When you explore, you go to a place you have never been before to see what it is like.

Grade K **349**

LESSON 30

PHONEMIC AWARENESS
Phoneme Segmentation

PHONICS
Review Word Blending and Building

HIGH-FREQUENCY WORDS
Review *go, like, look, see, the, they, to, we,* and

COMPREHENSION
Review Draw Conclusions

BUILD ROBUST VOCABULARY
Review: *splendid, gleaming, amazed*

Materials Needed:

Word Builder and Word Builder Cards | Copying Master | Practice Book

Phonemic Awareness

Phoneme Segmentation Assign each of three children one sound in the word *rat*. Have the first child stand and say /r/, the second child stand and say /a/, and the third child stand and say /t/. Count the children standing. Say: **Rat has three sounds.** Repeat with *fin, jet, mug, top, map, big, red,* and *fun*.

REVIEW
Phonics

Blend Words Practice blending two-letter words with children. Write these words on the board: *it, at, in, up*. Have children blend and read the words. Then write these three-letter words on the board, having children blend and read them: *fit, sat, pin, cup*.

Display the *Word Builder Cards* for *d, o, t, h, i,* and *x* and review the letter names and sounds. Hold up letters at random and ask children to tell the letter name and sound. Then distribute the *Word Builder Cards* to children. Explain to children that you are going to show them how a word can change when the letters in the word change. Say: **Use your *Word Builder Cards* to make new words with me. I will use the letters *i* and *t* to make the word *it*. Now you do the same. Blend the sounds with me: /i/-/t/,** *it*. **If I add an *h*, I have the word *hit*. Blend the sounds and say the word with me: /h/-/i/-/t/,** *hit*.

Word Blending and Building Have children build the word *dot* and continue to build new words:

- Change the *d* to *h*. What word did you make? (*hot*)
- Change the *o* to *i*. What word did you make? (*hit*)
- Change the *t* to *p*. What word did you make? (*hip*)

Distribute *Copying Master 59*. Have children trace the letters at the bottom of the page and cut them out. Help children identify the pictures. Then children paste *a, e, i,* or *u* in the box to complete each picture name. (Children should form the words *pin, rag, bed, nut*.)

Day 1

REVIEW

High-Frequency Words

Create and display index cards for *go, like, look, see, the, they, to, we,* and *and*. Say each word, and have children repeat each word. Then use the index cards and a period card to build the first sentence frame shown below. Point to each word as you read the sentence. Ask children to supply the name of a place they like to visit (zoo, mall, circus, pool, etc.). Record their responses, and have them read the sentence with you. Elicit several different responses. Then continue with the second sentence.

High-Frequency Words

and	the
go	they
like	to
look	we
see	

REVIEW

Comprehension

Draw Conclusions   Remind children that the author sometimes puts clues in a story to help readers understand things he or she doesn't say. Read aloud this story.

> Today was a special day. It was Mark's dad's birthday. Mark waited on the front door stoop until he saw his dad walking up the street. Mark had been waiting for this day for a long time. When his dad reached their front door, Mark stood up quickly. "Don't go in the living room, Dad," he cried. "Whatever you do, don't go in the living room!"

Guide children to turn to page 176 in their *Practice Books*. Have them use the pictures to draw conclusions about why Mark didn't want his father to go into the living room and what Mark may have prepared for his dad's birthday.

REVIEW

Build Robust Vocabulary

Remind children of the Student-Friendly Explanations for *splendid, gleaming,* and *amazed*. Then discuss each word, asking children the following questions.

splendid

What might happen on a vacation that was *splendid*?

gleaming

Are your teeth *gleaming* after you go to the dentist? Explain.

amazed

Would you be *amazed* to see a space ship or a pickup truck? Why?

VOCABULARY
Student-Friendly Explanations

splendid Something that is splendid is wonderful and special.

gleaming If something is gleaming, it is shiny and bright.

amazed If you are amazed, you are very surprised at something said or done.

Grade K **351**

LESSON 30

PHONEMIC AWARENESS
Phoneme Deletion

PHONICS
Review Word Blending and Building

HIGH-FREQUENCY WORDS
Review *a, she, have, can, I*

COMPREHENSION
Review Make Inferences

BUILD ROBUST VOCABULARY
Review *festival, completely, tame*

Materials Needed:

Word Builder and Word Builder Cards

Copying Master

Photo Cards

Practice Book

Phonemic Awareness

Phoneme Deletion Remind children that they can say words without the beginning or ending sound. Tell children to listen as you say a word and as you say it again without the beginning sound. Say: **Box.** I can say *box* without the /b/: *ox.* Say it with me: *ox.* Repeat with the word *nest.* Say this word without the *ending* sound: **Bud.** I can say *bud* without the /d/ *bu.* Say it with me: *bu.*

Follow the same procedure using the examples below. Ask children to say each word without the beginning or ending sound.

Fog. Say *fog* without the /f/. (/og/)

Wish. Say *wish* without the /w/. (/ish/)

Hum. Say *hum* without the /m/. (/hu/)

Pen. Say *pen* without the /n/. (/pe/)

REVIEW
Phonics

 Word Blending Place the *Word Builder Cards b, a,* and *t* in the Word Builder. Point to each letter in turn, say the letter sound, and have children name the letter and sound. Slide the letters together. Move your hand under the letters and blend the sounds: /bat/. Have children repeat after you. Then have children blend and read the word *bat* with you. Continue with the words *red, fin, pop,* and *nut.*

Word Blending and Building Distribute *Word Builders Cards s, u, n, t, a,,* and *g.* Have the children following along as you model word building. Say: **I will use the letters s, u, and n to make the word sun. Now you do the same. Blend the sounds with me: /s/-/u/-/n/, sun. If I take away the n and put b in its place, I have the word sub. Now you try it. Blend the sounds and say the word with me: /s/-/u/-/b/, sub.** Have children continue with *sub* in their *Word Builder:*

- Change the *s* to *t.* What word did you make? (*tub*)
- Change the *u* to *a.* What word did you make? (*tab*)

Distribute *Copying Master 60* to review building words. Help children name each picture and read the word choices below each picture. Then children circle the word that names the picture and write the word. (Children should circle and write the words *lip, map, hen,* and *nut.*)

Day 2

REVIEW
High-Frequency Words

Create and display high-frequency index cards for *a, have, she, can,* and *I*. Say each word, and have the children repeat that word as you hold up each card. Then use the index cards, *Photo Card ring,* and a period card to build the sentence frame. Point to each word in the sentence, and have children read the sentence with you.

| She | can | have | a | ring | . |

Repeat with *Photo Cards lamp, quarter, hammer,* and *drum*.

Have children turn to *Practice Book* page 177 to review high-frequency words and practice newly learned words. Complete the page together.

High-Frequency Words

a	I
can	she
have	

REVIEW
Comprehension

Make Inferences Remind children that authors sometimes give clues to help readers understand things about a story. Reread the story about Mark and his dad from Day 1 and model for children how to make an inference.

Copy the following chart onto chart paper. Guide children to offer ideas about the story, and add them to the chart.

What I Know	Story Clues	Inference
It's hard to sit still when you're excited.	Mark jumps up when he sees his dad.	Mark must be very excited.

REVIEW
Build Robust Vocabulary

Remind children of the Student-Friendly Explanations for *festival, completely,* and *tame*. Then discuss each word, using the following examples.

festival
Would people probably be happy or sad at a *festival*? Why?

completely
What might a *completely* busy person look like? Describe him or her.

tame
Do you think it would be easier to *tame* a dog or a fly? Explain.

VOCABULARY
Student-Friendly Explanations

festival A festival is a kind of celebration with different kinds of activities, foods, and decorations.

completely Completely means totally or in every way.

tame (v) When you tame an animal, you make it do what you want.

Grade K 353

LESSON 30

PHONEMIC AWARENESS
Phoneme Substitution: Initial, Final

PHONICS
Review Word Blending and Building

READING
Review Read Words
Review High-Frequency Words

COMPREHENSION
Review Draw Conclusions

BUILD ROBUST VOCABULARY
Review cautiously, disaster, jolt

WRITING
Review Writing Trait: Voice

Materials Needed:

Write-On/Wipe-Off Boards   Photo Cards   Practice Book

Phonemic Awareness

Phoneme Substitution: Initial, Final Tell children that they can change the beginning sound in a word to say a new word. Say: **Listen as I say a word: *jet*. Say the word with me: *jet*. What word will we have if we change the /j/ in *jet* to /w/?** *Wet*. **The new word is *wet*. Say it with me: *wet*.** Now ask children to change the beginning sound in the word *hug*. Say: **Hug. What word will we have if we change the /h/ in *hug* to /m/?** (mug)

Follow the same procedure with the following words.

Say *hat*. Change the /h/ in *hat* to /s/. (sat)

Say *fed*. Change the /f/ in *fed* to /b/. (bed)

Say *hit*. Change the /h/ in *hit* to /l/. (lit)

Say *top*. Change the /t/ in *top* to /p/. (pop)

Say *jam*. Change the /j/ in *jam* to /h/. (ham)

Follow the same procedure to review changing the ending sound in a word. Change the word pairs below:

man to mat   peg to pen   fish to fix   hut to hum

REVIEW

Phonics

 Word Blending and Building Have children sit in a circle. As you read the following verse, have children echo you. Establish a rhythm and keep it going throughout the verse.

We're going on a word hunt.

What's this word?

/f/ /o/ /x/

Together: fox!

Continue for the following words:

/b/ /a/ /d/ (bad)   /b/ /e/ /t/ (bet)   /n/ /e/ /m/ (him)

/c/ /u/ /t/ (cut)   /j/ /a/ /m/ (jam)   /f/ /e/ /d/ (fed)

/b/ /i/ /t/ (bit)   /h/ /u/ /m/ (hum)

Write each word on the board. Then have children copy them on their *Write-On/Wipe-Off Boards*.

354 Lesson 30

Day 3

REVIEW
Reading

Read Words Write the words *cap, mop, him,* and *bug* on chart paper. Have children read them in the order that you listed them until they can do so fluently. Then point to each word randomly, and have children read the words.

Review High-Frequency Words Display index cards for *here, look, want, what, do, you, I,* and *the* to children. As you say each word, have children repeat the word and hold up the correct card. Show *Photo Card umbrella*. Ask children to say the picture name. Then use the words cards, question mark and period cards, and *Photo Card umbrella* to build the first sentence frame shown below. Point to each word as you read the sentence. Ask children to read the sentence with you.

| Look | here | , | ____ |

| What | do | you | want | ? |

| I | want | the | [umbrella] | . |

Have volunteer pairs repeat the dialogue, adding the name of the second child in the blank. Repeat the activity using different pairs of children and the words *apple, dog, hammer, insects, jacks, pencil,* and *watch.*

Conclude by writing the following sentence frame on the board: *I want the ____ .* Have children copy and complete the sentence with a word or a picture and read their sentence to the group.

High-Frequency Words

do	the
here	want
I	what
look	you

Grade K 355

Day 3

REVIEW

Comprehension

Practice Book 178

Draw Conclusions Remind children that the author of a story sometimes puts clues in a story to help readers understand things he or she doesn't say. Read aloud the following story. Ask children to think about why Lily decided not to jump off the diving board.

> All the kids were at the swimming pool. They were playing games like tag and keep-away in the shallow end. Lily was one of the best at tag. She could also throw the ball the farthest of all the kids. She was having a fantastic time. Lily loved the swimming pool. Then her friend Mikayla said they should all go jump off the diving board.
>
> Lily looked at the diving board. It seemed so high. Then she said, "Umm, you guys go ahead. I'm tired from the keep-away game. Oh, and I also stubbed my toe. I think I'll stay in the shallow end."
>
> Mikayla and the rest of the kids agreed. They decided that having a snack would be more fun anyway. No one jumped off the diving board.

Guide children to *Practice Book* page 178. Have children use the pictures to draw a conclusion about why Lily and her friends decided not to jump off the diving board.

REVIEW

Build Robust Vocabulary

Remind children of the Student-Friendly Explanations for the words *cautiously*, *disaster*, and *jolt*. Then discuss each word, asking children the following questions.

cautiously
Which thing would you do *cautiously*: cross a busy street or turn on the TV? Why?

disaster
Is a flood an example of a *disaster*? Why or why not?

jolt
If you *jolt* your arm while carrying a full glass of juice, what might happen?

VOCABULARY

Student-Friendly Explanations

cautiously When you do something cautiously, you are careful to stay away from danger.

disaster A disaster is something terrible that happens suddenly.

jolt (v) If you jolt something, you shake it or move it with hard force.

REVIEW

Writing

Writing Trait: Voice Remind children that when writing a personal narrative we use our own words to tell a story about ourselves. Using words such as *I, my,* or *we* in the story helps the reader know that the story is about us. Write *I, my,* and *we* on the board. Read each word with children. Then read the following story to children. Ask them to raise their hands whenever they hear *I, my,* or *we* in the story.

My name is Lily. I love the swimming pool. I meet my friends there. We play games like keep-away and tag. We have fun. My friend Mikayla comes too. When we get tired, we have snacks. And then we go back to playing games.

Ask: **Who is this story about?** (a girl named Lily) **Who wrote this story? How do you know?** (Lily wrote it because she says *I*; that means the story is about the person who wrote it) **Who does the writer mean when she says *I*?** (Lily means herself) **When she says *we*?** (Lily and her friends)

Ask children to use the words *I, my,* and *we* in sentences. Record their responses on chart paper. Have volunteers underline *I, my,* or *we* in each sentence.

> I went to the zoo.
> Carlos is my friend.
> We play in the sandbox.

Day 3

Grade K

LESSON 30

DAY AT A GLANCE
Day 4

PHONEMIC AWARENESS
Phoneme Substitution: Medial

PHONICS
Review Word Blending and Building

READING
Review Word Blending and Building
Review High-Frequency Words

BUILD ROBUST VOCABULARY
Review festival, tame, splendid, cautiously, gleaming, explore

WRITING
Review Writing Form: Personal Narrative

Materials Needed:

Write-On/Wipe-Off Boards

Practice Book

High-Frequency Words

is	where
the	

Phonemic Awareness

Phoneme Substitution: Medial Remind children that they can change a sound in a word to make a new word. Tell them they will now change the middle sound in a word to make a new word. Say: **Listen as I say a word: hot. Say the word with me: hot. What word will we have if we change the /o/ in hot to /i/?** Hit. **The new word is hit. Say it with me: hit.** Ask children to change the middle sound in the word rug. Say: **Rug. What word will we have if we change the /u/ in rug to /a/?** Rag. **The new word is rag.**

Assign each of four children the sounds /d/, /o/, /i/, and /g/. Have the children with the sounds /d/, /o/, /g/ stand in a row and say the sounds in sequence to produce the word dog. Then have the "/o/" child step aside and let the "/i/" child stand in. Have children say their sounds again, and then say the new word dig. Have children repeat the kinetic procedure with the following words: cat/cut, pot/pet, hum/him, and pan/pen.

REVIEW
Phonics

 Word Blending and Building Play a game called "Say the Word" in which you say the sounds that are in a word and children say the word. Say: **Listen as I say the sounds /l/ /e/ /t/. The word is let. Let's do another one: /m/ /u/ /g/. The word is mug.** Continue, having children provide responses, with these words:

/h/ /i/ /p/ (hip)   /p/ /a/ /t/ (pat)

Distribute Write-on/Wipe-off Boards. Write these words on the board: met, mug, hip, pat, not, and gum. Have children read the words. Then read the words, in random order, and have children copy each word on their Write-on/Wipe-off Boards.

REVIEW
Reading

 Word Blending and Building Write the words cat, hen, pig, fox, and but on chart paper. Point to the words randomly and have children read the words until they read them fluently.

High-Frequency Words Display index cards for the high-frequency words and, here, my, and out to children. As you say each word, have a child point to the word and read it. Then have another child use the word in a sentence.

Have children turn to Practice Book pages 179–180. Help children make the book. Read the story with them, and encourage them to read it at home.

REVIEW

Robust Vocabulary

Remind children of the Student-Friendly Explanations for *festival, tame, splendid, cautiously, gleaming,* and *explore.* Determine their understanding by asking the following questions.

- **How you would walk if you were walking *cautiously*? Show an example.**
- **What kind of things might a *tame* elephant do?**
- **Which do you think is *splendid*: a warm sunny day, or a cold rainy day? Why?**
- **Describe a *festival* you would like to go to. What might you do there?**
- **What might you see if you were going to *explore* a jungle?**
- **Describe something in your home that is *gleaming*.**

REVIEW

Writing

Personal Narrative Remind children that they recently heard a story about a group of children at a swimming pool, a popular place in the summertime. Tell children that together you will write a personal narrative about fun things to do in the summer. Remind children that a personal narrative is a story that tells about something that has really happened to the writer. Writers of personal narratives use words like *I, me, we,* and *our* to show that the narrative is about what happened to them.

Ask children to name things they like to do in the summertime. Record their ideas on chart paper. Then use children's ideas to write a personal narrative from an individual writer's point of view, using first person pronouns. Invite children to write letters and words they know. Read the finished personal narrative to the children.

> I like to swim.
> We go to the park
> I wash my dog.

Ask volunteers to point to the words that show this is a personal narrative. *(I, we, my)*

Then have children copy the sentence frame *I like to _____* onto a piece of paper and complete the sentence with a word or picture.

VOCABULARY

Student-Friendly Explanations

festival A festival is a kind of celebration with different kinds of activities, foods, and decorations.

tame (v) When you tame a wild animal, you make it do what you want.

splendid Something that is splendid is wonderful and special.

cautiously When you do something cautiously, you are careful to stay away from danger.

gleaming If something is gleaming, it is shiny and bright.

explore When you explore, you go to a place you have never been before to see what it is like.

Grade K

LESSON 30

DAY AT A GLANCE

Day 5

PHONEMIC AWARENESS
Phoneme Substitution: Initial, Medial, Final

PHONICS
Review Word Blending and Building

HIGH-FREQUENCY WORDS
Review *is, here, my, out*

BUILD ROBUST VOCABULARY
Review *dare, adventure, amazed, completely, disaster, jolt*

WRITING
Review Personal Narrative

Materials Needed:

Word Builder and Word Builder Cards

Photo Cards

High-Frequency Words

here	my
is	out

Phonemic Awareness

Phoneme Substitution: Initial, Medial, Final Remind children that they can change the sounds in a word to say a new word. Say: **Listen as I say a word:** *wish*. **Say the word with me:** *wish*. **What sound do you hear at the beginning of** *wish*? /w/ **What word will we have if we change the /w/ in** *wish* **to /f/?** *Fish*. **The new word is** *fish*. **Say it with me:** *fish*. Now ask children to change the middle sound in the word *fix*. Say: **Listen as I say a word:** *fix*. **Say the word with me:** *fix*. **What sound do you hear in the middle of** *fix*? /i/ **What word will we have if we change the /i/ in** *fix* **to /o/?** *Fox*. **The new word is** *fox*. **Say it with me:** *fox*. Finally, do the same for an ending phoneme with the words *ham* and *hat*.

REVIEW

Phonics

Word Blending and Building Distribute *Word Builders* and *Word Builder Cards s, u, n, f, i, t, h, o,* and *g* to children. Have children build the word *sun* in their *Word Builder* along with you. Read the word and then write it on the board. Continue the procedure by saying:

- Change *s* to *f*. What word did you make? (*fun*)
- Change *u* to *i*. What word did you make? (*fin*)

REVIEW

High-Frequency Words

Display index cards for *here, my, out,* and *is*. Say each word, and have the children repeat that word as you hold up each card. Then use the index cards, *Photo Card ring,* and the period card to build the sentence frame shown below. Point to each word as you read the sentence. Reread it with children. Ask volunteers to point to the words *my, is, out,* and *here*.

| My | ring | is | out | here | . |

Replace the *Photo Card ring* with *Photo Card pencil*. Point to each word as children read the sentence to you. Repeat with *Photo Cards hammer, drum, watch,* and *yarn*.

Day 5

REVIEW

Robust Vocabulary

Tell children that they have been learning some interesting words. Remind children of the Student-Friendly Explanations of *dare, adventure, amazed, completely, disaster,* and *jolt.* Then determine children's understanding of the words by asking the following questions.

- If you are *completely* finished with your work, do you have a little work left to do, or no work left to do?
- Could you *jolt* a refrigerator? Explain why or why not.
- If you wanted to *dare* somebody to jump off a high diving board, what could you say?
- If something bad happened slowly, could it be a *disaster*? Explain.
- Name somebody in a book or movie who went on an *adventure.*
- Would you be *amazed* if it snowed tomorrow? Why or why not?

REVIEW

Writing

Writing Form: Personal Narrative Remind children that they just wrote a personal narrative about what they like to do in the summer. Remind them that a personal narrative is a story that tells about something that has really happened to the writer. Writers of personal narratives use words like *I, me, we,* and *our* to show that the narrative is about what happened to them.

Ask them to name things they like to do in the winter. Record their ideas on chart paper. Then use children's ideas to write a personal narrative from an individual writer's point of view, using first person pronouns. Invite them to write letters and words they know. Read the finished personal narrative to the children.

VOCABULARY

Student-Friendly Explanations

dare (v) If you dare someone to do something, you ask to them to do something that takes courage.

adventure An adventure is something new you do that is exciting or dangerous.

amazed If you are amazed, you are very surprised.

completely Completely means totally or in every way.

disaster A disaster is something terrible that happens suddenly.

jolt (v) To jolt means to make something move very suddenly.